# Retelling Stories,
# Framing Culture

CHILDREN'S LITERATURE AND CULTURE
VOLUME 5
GARLAND REFERENCE LIBRARY OF THE HUMANITIES
VOLUME 1975

# Children's Literature and Culture

Jack Zipes, *General Editor*

# Retelling Stories, Framing Culture

## Traditional Story and Metanarratives in Children's Literature

John Stephens
Robyn McCallum

Garland Publishing, Inc.
A member of the Taylor & Francis Group
New York and London
1998

**Library of Congress Cataloging-in-Publication Data**

Stephens, John, 1944–
    Retelling stories, framing culture : traditional story and metanarratives
in children's literature / John Stephens, Robyn McCallum.
        p.    cm. — (Garland reference library of the humanities ; v. 1975.
Children's literature and culture ; v. 5. )
    Includes bibliographical references and index.
    ISBN 0-8153-1298-9 (alk. paper)
    1. Children's literature—History and criticism.    I. McCallum, Robyn.
II. Title.   III. Series: Garland reference library of the humanities ; v. 1975.
IV. Series: Garland reference library of the humanities. Children's literature
and culture ; v. 5.
PN1009.A1S83   1998
809'.89282—dc21                                                    97–38561
                                                                          CIP

Cover illustration depicting Merlin as leader of the British by Richard Hook/
Linden Artists, in John Matthews and Bob Stewart, *Legends of King Arthur and
His Warriors* (1987). Reprinted by permission of Richard Hook/Linden Artists.

Printed on acid-free, 250-year-life paper
Manufactured in the United States of America

# CONTENTS

# GENERAL EDITOR'S FOREWORD

Dedicated to furthering original research in children's literature and culture, the Children's Literature and Culture series will include monographs on individual authors and illustrators, historical examinations of different periods, literary analyses of genres, and comparative studies on literature and the mass media. The series is international in scope and is intended to encourage innovative research in children's literature with a focus on interdisciplinary methodology.

Children's literature and culture are understood in the broadest sense of the term *children* to encompass the period of childhood up through late adolescence. Owing to the fact that the notion of childhood has changed so much since the origination of children's literature, this Garland series is particularly concerned with transformations in children's culture and how they have affected the representation and socialization of children. While the emphasis of the series is on children's literature, all types of studies that deal with children's radio, film, television, and art will be included in an endeavor to grasp the aesthetics and values of children's culture. Not only have there been momentous changes in children's culture in the last fifty years, but there have been radical shifts in the scholarship that deals with these changes. In this regard, the goal of the Children's Literature and Culture series is to enhance research in this field and, at the same time, point to new directions that bring together the best scholarly work throughout the world.

Jack Zipes

# Preface

*The key to the treasure is the treasure.*
                    —John Barth, *Chimera*

In the chapters which follow, we advance and explore a general theory dealing with the processes through which traditional, or already known, stories are retold for young readers. While some areas of retold story, such as fairy tale, have been extensively discussed, and other areas have been occasionally illuminated by individual studies, no one has yet undertaken to examine common elements which shape retellings across a variety of story categories. We have found ourselves drawn to the task on the one hand by the volume and persistence of retold stories as part of the domain of children's literature, and on the other hand by several tantalizing questions which arise from the processes of retelling what purports to be the same story. In what sense can two narratives be the same if they are so organized that there are differences in the manner of telling, or in the point of view adopted, or in the atmosphere evoked, or in the apparent attitudes towards the participants and their experiences, or in the potential moral impact on audiences? Obviously enough, two versions of a story involving the *same* characters, settings, and events can differ substantially in their implications or significances. What seems to us to be the crux of the difference is that any particular retelling may purport to transmit elements of a culture's formative traditions and even its sustaining beliefs and assumptions, but what it always discloses is some aspect of the attitudes and ideologies pertaining at the cultural moment in which that retelling is produced.

Such an observation seems quite self-evident. A less certain step is to attempt to identify a common impulse or, better, informing metanarrative which molds seemingly and actually diverse processes. Is it possible to discern one or more shared metanarratives lying behind retellings of the Bible and *Beowulf*, or of *The Arabian Nights* and *Treasure Island*? And do attempts to engage from a moral perspective with issues of race, gender or class which inhere in traditional story share a more or less common outlook? Our argument here is that diverse genres and social issues imbricated in already existing stories are always dealt with in relation to or in dialogue with an overarching cultural and moral perspective, or assumed bundle of values, which we will refer to as the Western metaethic. We explain the concept at length in chapter 1, where, in summary, we argue that over and above any tendencies towards the conserving of culture, which may be endemic to children's literature, retellings of traditional story are especially apt not just to preserve culture but to reproduce conservative outcomes because of their shared assumptions about the functions of story and about what constitutes significant human experiences. In other words, if outcomes of other kinds are to be achieved, a reteller has to struggle with and overcome material which is always to some extent intractable because of its combination of strong, familiar story shapes with already legitimized values and ideas about the world.

In attempting to formulate and expound a metanarrative for retellings, we inevitably asked ourselves if we were only seeking a version of the illusory "key to all mythologies" rendered notorious by the deluded figure of Casaubon in George Eliot's *Middlemarch*. Joseph Campbell might seem to have already produced just such a key in the middle of the twentieth century, inspired by Jung, and there are several places in our discussion where we will need to point to his influence on subsequent retellers of story. It has not been our purpose here to reconfigure Campbell, however. Rather, we have found it salutary to remember that, in the end, a powerful interpretive stance may lack the delicacy to account for a range of text types in their contexts of cultural production and reception. Our theory, then, is a model which we have necessarily modified from chapter to chapter in a dialogue between its broad principles and the varieties of conformity and resistance that emerged in our focused examples. Like the seekers in many a quest, we have not always known where our paths lay, what resources would be called upon, or what awaited us at the end. There were some maps to follow, but we found that if we left a particular path to travel by another route the place was not the same when we arrived. The sparkling baubles in Aladdin's cave often turned out to be no more than sparkling baubles.

It has been with such considerations in mind that we have evolved our own metanarrative in an attempt to define some principles underlying the ways whereby the retelling of stories produces cultural significations. We have found that not every door we opened has yielded up the anticipated treasure, and the moment of opening is always a moment of hesitation at the threshold. The expected Aladdin's Cave on the other side could turn out to be Bluebeard's forbidden room, and the difference might depend upon which key is used to unlock the door. For example, incorporating some of the interpretive possibilities offered by Campbell's *The Hero with a Thousand Faces* will enable readings very different from those enabled by *The Feminist Companion to Mythology* (1992). The former is an inspirational reminder that it is legitimate to quest for an opening onto what is both transcendent and yet deeply human; the latter is a timely warning that essential substance may be missing from a powerful interpretive key, that the "deeply human" might turn out to be deduced from a base that is narrow and exclusive.

What we think remains fundamentally important in all this is the insight from Barth's *Chimera* we have used as our epigraph: "The key to the treasure is the treasure." In approaching that large body of texts which comprises the domain of retold stories, an essential component of reading is awareness that the process of retelling is always implicated in processes of cultural formation, of recycling frames used to make sense of culture. Thus, insofar as we argue that the discourse which shapes the cultural implications of a retelling is more significant than what is retold, we reaffirm the centrality of the key.

# Retelling Stories, Framing Culture

# 1 PRE-TEXTS, METANARRATIVES, AND THE WESTERN METAETHIC

*As the cauldron bubbled, an eldritch voice shrieked: "When shall we three meet again?"*

*There was a pause.*

*Finally another voice said, in far more ordinary tones: "Well, I can do next Tuesday."*

—Terry Pratchett, *Wyrd Sisters*

When compared with general literature, the literature produced for children contains a much larger proportion of retold stories. In part this is because some domains of retellings, especially folk and fairy tale, have long been considered more appropriate to child culture than to adult culture, but this relegation is not entirely because such materials might seem ingenuous and accessible to children. Rather, retold stories have important cultural functions. Under the guise of offering children access to strange and exciting worlds removed from everyday experiences, they serve to initiate children into aspects of a social heritage, transmitting many of a culture's central values and assumptions and a body of shared allusions and experiences. The existential concerns of a society find concrete images and symbolic forms in traditional stories of many kinds, offering a cultural inheritance subject to social conditioning and modification through the interaction of various retellings. Although the notional significance of a story is thus potentially infinitely intertextual, subject to every retelling and every significance that has ever accrued to it, it is also arguable that the processes of retelling are overwhelmingly subject to a limited number of conservative metanarratives— that is, the implicit and usually invisible ideologies, systems, and assumptions which operate globally in a society to order knowledge and experience. The major narrative domains which involve retold stories all, in the main, have the function of maintaining conformity to socially determined and approved patterns of behavior, which they do by offering positive role models, proscribing undesirable behavior, and affirming the culture's ideologies, systems, and institutions.

The ideological effect of a retold text is generated from a three-way relationship between the already-given story, the metanarrative(s) which constitute its top-down framing, and its bottom-up discoursal processes. Obviously enough, to be a retelling a text must exist in relationship to some kind of source, which we will refer to as the "pre-text," though it is perhaps only a minority of cases in which this source is fixable as a single work by an identifiable author. Even when this is so, few retellings are simple replications, even when they appear to reproduce the story and point of view of the source. In such cases, the purpose is generally cultural reproduction, in the sense of transmitting desired knowledge about society and the self, modes of learning, and forms of authority. The most overt example we will discuss in this study is the plays of Shakespeare (see chapter 9). But that example shows two things: because retellings do not, and cannot, also reproduce the discoursal mode of the source, they cannot *replicate* its significances, and always impose their own cultural presuppositions in the process of retelling; and second, even the most revered cultural icon can be subjected to mocking or antagonistic retellings. The resulting version is then not so much a retelling as a *re-version,* a narrative which has taken apart its pre-texts and reassembled them as a version which is a new textual and ideological configuration.

Reversions are frequent in a second common circumstance of retelling, when narratives emerge within a network of story versions for which there is no identifiable "first telling" or else the latest version is based on intermediate forms. A familiar fairy tale such as *Cinderella* may derive from Perrault's version, or the Disney film, or British pantomime tradition, but is more apt to borrow freely from amongst these and from versions of them circulating orally. Even where there is a strong pre-text such as Perrault, retellers are most likely to use intermediate versions—to produce a retelling of a retelling. Similarly, Robert Leeson's (1994) retelling of selected "Robin Hood" stories is unusual in its story area because it is based mainly on the oldest extant source for much of the legend, *A Gest of Robyn Hode,* which probably dates from the early fifteenth century (Dobson and Taylor, 1989, p. 74). Leeson's expressed motive in seeking pre-texts without the accretions of the last hundred years is to allow the legend's innate "message" to speak for itself: that is, "that truth, justice and courtesy should be defended, if need be *against* the law" (p. 96). Even this retelling, however, is influenced by motifs that entered with Howard Pyle's *The Merry Adventures of Robin Hood* (1883), and a famous episode such as the contest for the silver arrow

(Leeson, pp. 72–77) departs from the stated pre-text in story detail, structure, and character motivation. In other words, the "message" of the story has to be reproduced by substantial intervention. At another extreme lies Tony Robinson's spoof of this story as "Robert the Incredible Chicken" in his television series *Maid Marian and her Merry Men* (1988–89). Robinson can and does assume that his audience is familiar with some specific details—especially that Robin goes to the contest in disguise—which were introduced by Pyle but have long been generally considered intrinsic to the story and disseminated throughout retellings.[1] The assumption enables the effects of incongruity to be heightened as the production drastically transforms the mode and tenor of the story by drawing on pantomime, ironic farce, and feminist reversal (Knight, 1994, p. 241).

A still looser form of pre-textual context is genre. Here a particular narrative has its relationships not so much with a recognizable story but with a range of generic features.[2] In including such narratives, we are aware that we push the notion of retold story or reversion to its limit, and many readers will prefer to consider these narratives as standing in intertextual relationships to genres (as expounded in, say, Northrop Frye's *Anatomy of Criticism*). We do, however, see some point in including them here as part of a distinguishable cline beginning with replication and moving away towards more diffuse or merely allusive reversions. We argue, for example, that a moral story consciously mapped onto a Bible story is in effect a reversion; that *The Lion King* is a reversion of the pattern of a hero's life, rather than a generically identifiable narrative; that certain modern novels about female heroes are reversions which invert that pattern; and that a motif invented after but not based on *The Arabian Nights*—the "setting the genie free" motif—generates multiple reversions (as well as being exported back into reversions of the *Aladdin* story). To a great extent, such reversions are constituted by motifs; by narrative structures isomorphic with those visible in generic pre-texts; and/or by a shared habitus—that is, a conjunction of physical and social spaces where sociality is organized by social distances and hierarchies, and where a system of schemata (that is, social codes) organizes action and practice, and thought and perception (see Bourdieu, 1986, chapter 3; 1990, chapter 8). Feudal castles and the tents of desert tribes in Tamora Pierce's *Song of the Lioness* sword-and-sorcery tetralogy are clear examples of such a functioning of habitus.

## METANARRATIVE AND METAETHIC

The pre-texts for a retelling, then, are known, or already given, "stories," however precisely or indeterminately evoked. The principal domains in children's literature include biblical literature and related religious stories; myths; hero stories; medieval and quasi-medieval romance; stories about Robin Hood, which constitute a large and distinctive domain; folktales and fairy tales; oriental stories, usually linked with *The Arabian Nights;* and modern classics. Two central aspects about such traditional materials are that they come with predetermined horizons of expectation and with their values and ideas about the world already legitimized. In other words, they are always already shaped by some kind of metanarrative, and their status makes them a good site on which to impose metanarratives expressing social values and attitudes prevailing in the time and place of the retelling. As we said above, a metanarrative is a global or totalizing cultural narrative schema which orders and explains knowledge and experience. A simple illustration is offered by Leeson's summary of the message of Robin Hood stories which we cited earlier. The statement that "truth, justice and courtesy should be defended, if need be *against* the law" is presented as if it expresses self-evident propositions. It only does this, however, because it is enabled to do so by evolved cultural assumptions which furnish the statement's metanarratives: in all stories, in Western cultures at least, where truth and justice are an issue, the metanarrative which informs and shapes the outcomes of particular stories furnishes the assumption that they will—or morally should—prevail. Moreover, truth and justice are transcendent significations which occupy positions in a moral and intellectual hierarchy above attempts to codify them specifically as law; truth and justice are absolute values, whereas law is contingent and relative. An interesting place is then occupied in this larger schema by "courtesy," since its interlinking with the other terms offers the presumption that it, too, is the outworking of a metanarrative; people whose behavior is prompted and guided by intersubjective relationships, by consideration for others, and by self-modesty, represent an exemplary ideal in culture. Key words which have been used to express such a concept, apart from *courtesy* itself,[3] are *civility* and *piety* (that is, in the old *Oxford English Dictionary* definition as "faithfulness to the duties naturally owed to parents and relatives, superiors, etc.; dutifulness"). Leeson's statement, then, comes charged with an enormous weight of culturally determined beliefs and assumptions which not only function as ideological presuppositions but also have a presence as narrative forms. When a particular exemplification replicates the metanarratival shape, the outcome is socially and emotionally satisfying and confirms the metanarrative; if the shape is not replicated, the outcome is recognized as "tragic." In other words, metanarratives both supply the structure for individual narratives and the criteria for perception and appreciation by which sense is made of that structure. This is why ideas about the social world can seem self-evident.

Our argument throughout this book is that the retelling of traditional stories for young audiences takes place within the frame of such meta-narratives. They do not function randomly, however, but as a large inter-locked set, which implies the existence of a less readily definable meta-metanarrative, so to speak, operating at a still more abstract level. This is what determines that a particular narration has value because it offers a patterned and shapely narrative structure, expresses significant and univer-sal human experiences, interlinks "truth" and cultural heritage, and rests moral judgments within an ethical dimension. We are going to refer to this as the "Western metaethic," which is not a pretty phrase but is definitely preferable to meta-metanarrative. We think it is important to remember that this metaethic has been evolved within European-based or derived cultures; so, "Western" always has the effect of a reminder that, despite any implicit or overt assumptions to the contrary, the metaethic expresses a culture-specific idea of transcendence and not a universal. Because of this, there are some domains of retold story we have deliberately excluded from our dis-cussions because the metaethic will always be imposed from outside, and we have decided that such retellings lie outside the scope of our present en-quiry. One such domain is narratives which appropriate the beliefs and sto-ries of indigenous peoples within the post-colonial societies of North America, Australia, New Zealand, and so on. We think such retellings are of a drastically different order, even when not extremely insensitive to the metanarratives of another culture, and would really require a book in them-selves (see the discussion of some of the problems in Nodelman, 1996, pp. 264–267). Second, stories retold from other cultures involve not just ques-tions of trampling on religious beliefs in quest of some vague intercultural understanding, important as this consideration may be, but also involve mis-apprehension and misapplication of metanarratives, as will happen with sto-ries borrowed from, say, Chinese cultures. Regardless of whether or not retellers are equipped with appropriate cultural knowledge, such as the metanarratives generated by Confucianism or by the centrality of the family in a Chinese habitus, it is practically certain that the majority of audiences will have little alternative but to misread by contextualizing such stories within the Western metaethic, even if, as Nodelman suggests, audiences are provided with some of the distinctive qualities and conventions of these stories (p. 267). Because metanarratives are invisible and self-evident and Western audiences assume their metaethic is naturally universal, it is very difficult to resist West-ernizing a story at the stages both of production and reception.

The Western metaethic is perhaps no more clearly evident than in notions about canons. For some time now theorists of mainstream literature have been actively engaged in defining the literary canon—"a body of texts larger than the sum of its members, a grand cultural narrative" (Gorak, 1991, p. 259)—in order to dismantle it. Gorak's "grand cultural narrative" points in the same direction as our "metaethic," and the postmodern world is skeptical of metanarratives, as everybody knows—everybody, that is, except most of the people who retell traditional stories for children. Theorists and practitioners of children's literature are generally still quite active in the construction of a canon of children's literary texts, an enterprise that can be seen quite clearly in the Children's Literature Association's publication of the *Touchstones* volumes (1985–87). These volumes, subtitled "Reflections on the Best in Children's Literature," seek to identify those "classic" texts, or "touchstones," written for children: "book[s] beside which we may place other children's books in order to make judgments about their excellence" (Nodelman, 1985, p. 2). Canonization does have a pragmatic function, in that it enables definition of the parameters of children's literature as a genre, what that genre consists of, what matters in it, and "what needs to be discussed and studied and understood" (Nodelman, p. 6). Such an enterprise is only ostensibly informed by notions of literary excellence, however. Instead it is largely driven by ideologies—ideologies which inform the decisions made by the culture about "what matters" in children's literature, including decisions as to the criterion of literary merit. As Nodelman contends, a list of "classic texts," such as the *Touchstones* volumes provide, is not prescriptive in so far as it simply "describes communal values" (p. 11), but, to continue Nodelman's line of argument, it is precisely those values, or ideologies, which implicitly prescribe the parameters of the literature. As Nodelman suggests, these values can be discussed, explored, explained, and disagreed with, and thus the *Touchstones* enterprise seeks to "open a dialogue," to show that "far from being sacrosanct and unquestionable, [the 'classic' texts] do indeed offer much to think about, much to disagree about" (p. 11). The practice of retelling and rewriting classics for children is part of this dialogue. Reversions disclose the ideologies and metanarratives driving those classic texts because they both legitimize and open to question their "classic" pretexts. They affirm the status of such classic texts, while at the same time entering into a dialogue and calling into question the ideologies informing both the texts and, by implication, the ideological basis of the canonical enterprise. So while what we are arguing here about the retelling of traditional stories may seem intellectually and culturally oppressive, there are always possibilities for resistance, contestation, and change. This occurs on two fronts: by the introduction of new or rival metanarratives, which effectively dispute the grounding metaethic, and in actual textual processes, the bottom-up production of narrative discourses.

The relationships between a retelling and its pre-text(s) are, in the main, dominated by metanarratives which are androcentric, ethnocentric, and class-centric, so the purposes of inducting audiences into the social, ethical, and aesthetic values of the producing culture are colored by those particular alignments. Any retelling is oriented towards those metanarratives and their informing metaethic in stances which are usually legitimizing, but may develop interrogative positions. The pre-text is always bearer of some historically inscribed ideological significances, but does not invariably fix ideological significance. Rather, it functions as a site on which metanarratival and textual processes interact, either to reproduce or contest significance. Because both of these are subject to change between one historical moment and another, any particular retelling becomes, at least potentially, a new negotiation between the already given and the new. When new metanarratives are acutely incompatible with the older metanarratives that have shaped a given story, the outcome can be a moment of cultural crisis. For example, the modern women's movement, and feminist social and critical analysis in particular, has produced a bundle of metanarratives so incompatible with the metanarratives which have informed many traditional stories in the past that if feminist metanarratives become socially dominant—and hence implicit and invisible—many traditional stories will be rendered unreadable and beyond recuperation.

A domain where we see this already happening is classical mythology, where inherent metanarratives are more persistent than in any other domain of retellings. It is not hard to argue that the metanarratives which informed classical mythology until well into the modern era were grounded in social assumptions which were masculinist, misogynistic, socially elitist, imperialistic, and often militaristic and violent. Thus Barbara G. Walker's *Feminist Fairy Tales* (1996), a collection of New Age, goddess-focused feminist stories and reversions, quite systematically addresses and overthrows these assumptions in most traditional story types we are concerned with here. Walker's collection does not, however, attempt to rework any of the better-known classical myths, and where she does deal with classical motifs she reshapes them into a female-centered archetype by blending them with other mythological systems. The effect is to represent classical mythology as a derivative and redundant corruption of the archetype. Read from a more traditional perspective, the reversals of roles and the transformations of ideology and outcomes in these stories seem very heavy-handed, though that does have the useful function of highlighting how an equivalent heavy-handedness has become invisible in the widely known myths.

In general, adults whose retellings reproduce stories from classical mythology, or who write about these retellings, are still apt to assert those metanarratives developed historically within education systems and a hegemonic social class; that is, that classical myths (among other functions) embody "timeless and universal" significances and are an indispensable part of Western cultural heritage, that they are metaphorical expressions of spiritual insights, and that they address archetypal aspects of the human psyche. If, in the face of such assumptions, myth is read from a feminist and/or cultural materialist position—that is, from an ideological stance which begins in rejecting the basis of the positions outlined—then myth may well be unrecuperable as part of children's experience of culture. As far as children's texts go, it remains a domain from which a substantial body of feminist rewriting is significantly absent. We will return to this issue in more detail in chapter 3.

## RETELLINGS AND REGISTER

As we suggested above, metanarratives can be subject to modification, as well as reproduction, within actual textual processes. A key component of these processes is the *register* which a reteller selects as the ground for her or his discourse. As the narrative genres and informing metanarratives of traditional stories are produced textually, authors select from amongst three registers, which we will refer to as *hieratic, epic* (for want of a better term), and *demotic.* Any particular domain of retold story may be characterized by a predominant preference amongst the three registers. Categorization is not necessarily fixed or stable, because texts from different domains share many structures and features, but it is nevertheless useful in pointing to some domain-specific qualities. We are using *register* here in the common sense of a variety of language defined according to situation of use. Linguistic choices constituting a register are determined by three elements. First, by *field,* or the subject matter or situation which grounds the story: examples are creation-myth; an encounter between a mortal and a divinity; a hero's battle with an evil adversary; an encounter with a magic-worker; a quest in folktale; and so on. Second, by *tenor,* or the relationships between participants in situations: examples are social hierarchies; gender relationships; conversational exchanges between the hero of a story and another participant, such as a god, a dragon, a wizard, a victim-in-distress, and the like. Third, by *modality,* or the interpersonal function of register which expresses relationships between textual "voices" and audience: in particular, varieties of omniscient ("third-person") narration (expository, factual, or didactic mode, emotive mode, and so on); and zero, limited, or extensive character focalization (and which may involve single or multiple characters).

Hieratic register is apt to be figurative, especially metaphorical or allegorical, and implicitly grounded in transcendent significances which are usually too abstract to be articulated in children's literature. It proceeds by representation of concrete events and incidents, and will often directly assert some aspects in which these are temporal expressions of a transcendent and eternal order "above." Its usual domain is thus religious or mythological narratives, exemplified in our study by biblical narrative and classical mythology, and from there it is extended into modern fantasy literatures.

Epic register is exemplary, grounded in more mundane or material significances, normally set within firmly hierarchical social institutions, and therefore apt to affirm social order conservatively. Its language choices will move between everyday discourse and less usual forms, such as archaisms, or forms of overwording (that is, signifiers whose meaning is in excess of contextual requirements, or which are clearly "elevated"), and descriptive terms which are apt to occur as doublets or in clusters. The following exchange illustrates some aspects of this discourse: "'Have you heard tell of Sir Tristram of Lyonesse?' 'Yea, noble Arthur, and him have I seen full often'" (Green, 1953, p. 133). This is not particularly complex linguistically, but no part of it is untouched by archaic vocabulary ("heard tell of; yea; *full* often") or archaic syntax ("Yea, noble Arthur; him have I seen"). The characteristic domains of epic register are heroic legend, saga, and romance, but beyond those domains it can be drawn on variously by both fantastic and realistic literatures. Reading epic register is an acquired skill, however, even if it is not particularly difficult for an able reader to acquire it; therefore the register tends to mark a discourse as high culture or minority property. As Bourdieu commented in a different context, "the possessors of a sophisticated mastery of language are more likely to be seen in a museum than those who don't have this mastery" (1990, p. 133).

Finally, demotic register, also grounded in the mundane, is apt to be metonymic and event-focused; lexical and syntactic choices are, broadly, taken from everyday discourse, though sustained dialect is a demotic form. Most retellings, in fact, have a demotic base on which hieratic and/or epic registers are raised, but in some domains demotic is the staple. It tends, however, to occur mainly in folktale and reversions of modern classics, and is of course the staple of nontraditional realist fiction, biography, and some forms of historical fiction.

The choice (and mixing) amongst hieratic, epic, and demotic registers may function normatively, but can also be used to destabilize norms; likewise, focalization (that is, origin of perception and perspective within the narrative) can be employed for either purpose, especially in determining the question of whose interests are addressed and served. So to examine how or if textual processes intervene in the production of metanarratives, the following questions might be asked: Who takes effective action? Whose actions deliver a social benefit? Who is linguistically privileged? Who focalizes? Who operates socially within intersubjective relations? and Who expresses judgments? The implications can be seen virtually at a glance in a novel such as Pratchett's *Wyrd Sisters,* a reversion of Shakespeare's *Macbeth* in which the answer to all of these questions is "the three witches."

Many retellings do not reproduce the register or register-mix of the pre-text, and the most common direction of change is toward an authoritative narrative voice aligned with a culturally ascendent language. In other words, the texts speak from a cultural center and sometimes efface elements which might be potentially disruptive. Such an effect is evident in quite diverse texts, and we will briefly illustrate it here in Arthurian romance and folktale. Linda Yeatman's "The Knight of the Kitchen" (1991, pp. 88–97) is an abbreviated retelling of the first half of Malory's "The Tale of Sir Gareth."[4] The pre-text is substantially Malory's invention, though constructed from common romance motifs: the quest; the hero as a "fair unknown" who proves to be of noble birth; the damsel in need of rescue; and the incremental series of adventures of increasing difficulty through which the hero proves himself. In form it coincides with what is perhaps the most common romance metanarrative, the hero's quest for self-definition and identity, which is achieved against the odds, and which is expressed narratively by the metonymy of a desirable marriage. The register of Malory's story shifts between epic and demotic, often doing so to achieve comic effects. This is especially evident in the conversational exchanges between Gareth and his reluctant guide, Linnet, who continually flings abuse at him and is met with studied, ironic politeness, as here:

> [Linnet]: Lat be, . . . thou bawdy kychyn knave! Sle hym nat.
> [Gareth]: Damesell, . . . your charge is to me a plesure, and at youre commaundement his lyff shall be saved. (p. 306: note that the *thou/you* contrast is at this time a strong marker of social orientation; it alone indicates Linnet's contempt)

Much of Malory's writing in this story is very funny indeed, but its broad comic element is not reproduced in the reversion. Instead, Yeatman narrows the range of registers, presumably on the assumption that narratives derived from medieval romance are a mode of high seriousness, but also reflecting how in children's literature epic register is both exemplary and apt to affirm hierarchical social order. Thus the above exchange becomes:

> "No, stop, you kitchen knave. Spare this man's life," Linnet called out. So Gareth stopped his sword in mid air, and said to the knight in green. . . .

That is, the strong contrast in register between Malory's speakers has been smoothed over by rendering Linnet's command in more polite language and replacing Gareth's reply with a narrated epic cliché.

Second, the English folktale "Tom Tit Tot" (Briggs, 1970, pp. 535–539), a variant of the "Rumpelstiltskin" tale type, was first published in the *Ipswich Journal* 15 (1878), the contributor, Mrs. Thomas, "having heard it as a girl from her old West Suffolk nurse" (cited in Crossley-Holland, 1987, p. 370). Like so many folktales it thus enters recorded folk literature simultaneously authenticated as demotic discourse and mediated through literary collecting. It is valued for its local Suffolk flavor (Crossley-Holland, ibid.; Carter, 1991, p. 238). In the "original" demotic text there is little differentiation between the language of narrator and of characters, with the narrative language containing many nonstandard idioms and forms, both grammatical and syntactic. The version of this tale most usually printed is that of Jacobs's *English Fairy Tales*, in which the Suffolk dialect was reduced. In his reversion of Thomas in *British Folk Tales*, Crossley-Holland seeks to preserve the local flavor in the dialogue, where he makes few changes to his pre-text, but reworks the narrative components so they conform more both to standard English and to literary narrative. The Thomas text begins as follows:

> Well, once upon a time there was a woman, and she baked five pies. And when they come out of the oven, they were that overbaked the crust were too hard to eat. So she says to her darter:
> "Maw'r ['girl; daughter']," says she, "put you them there pies on the shelf an' leave 'em there a little, an' they'll come agin." She meant, you know, the crust 'ud get soft.
> But the gal she says to herself, "Well, if they'll come agin, I'll ate 'em now." And she set to work and ate 'em all, first and last. (Briggs, p. 535)

This narrative is event-focused, moving straight into the story without offering any information about the characters or setting, and offering little motivation for incidents. It is up to the audience to infer from the wordplay that the girl is not clever, and from her actions that she is prone to gluttony, details which will prove central to the unfolding situation. In contrast, Crossley-Holland begins in this way:

> There was once a little old village where a woman lived with her giddy daughter. The daughter was just sixteen, and sweet as honey-suckle.
>
> One fine morning, the woman made five meat pies and put them in the oven. But then a neighbor called round and they were soon so busy with snippets of gossip that the woman completely forgot about the pies. By the time she took them out of the oven, their crusts were almost as hard as the bark of her old oak tree.
>
> "Daughter," she said, "you put them there pies in the larder."
>
> "My! I'm that hungry," said the girl.
>
> "Leave them there and they'll come again."
>
> "Come again?"
>
> "You know," said the woman. And she hurried out into the warm wind and her waiting neighbor.
>
> "Well!" said the girl. "If they'll come again, I'll eat these now." And so she went back to the larder and picked up the pies and ate them all, first and last. (p. 47)

In the shift from (at least putative) oral to literary folktale, Crossley-Holland has almost doubled the length of this sequence (164 words compared to 95) by introducing spatio-temporal settings and descriptive epithets ("giddy daughter," "meat pies"), and a causal explanation for the hardness of the pie crusts. An audience must now make the simple inference that the pies would be difficult to eat and the much more complex inference that the girl has misunderstood the meaning of "come again." The reshaping of the narrative to mark the girl as giddy and nubile and the mother as domestically negligent foregrounds the tale's underlying folktale schema, the subjecting of a beautiful female character to an unperformable test of her domestic competence. This happens, though, by allowing the comedy of the opening to be carried by the stock antifeminist joke about women's gossip rather than by the "come again" wordplay.

In general, Crossley-Holland's retelling is beautifully crafted and a delight to read. It does not introduce drastic changes, and follows the Thomas version quite closely after the opening movement. But, as with the Jacobs version, the strategy of differentiating the language of narrative and dialogue has substantial implications. It means that a center-periphery perspective is constructed whereby the folktale characters and their world, viewed from the normative center of standard English and literary narrative, become peripheral, other, representatives of an exotic culture mediated to readers through the "standard" narrative components.

## METANARRATIVES AND IDEOLOGY

We argued above that metanarratives determine interpretive strategies as well as strategies for text production. In this regard, it is essential to recognize that children's literature has been, and remains, a crucial repository of humanist ideology. While the humanist tradition pervades, and indeed grounds, children's literature in general, it manifests itself most apparently in those kinds of text which are, in some sense, a reversion of a known story. Further, to a great extent children's literature attempts in this way to cultivate ethical and cultural values which would function as a replacement for or surrogate of older forms of socially inscribed transcendent meaning, especially religion. The extent to which this is embraced by retellers of traditional stories is reflected in the almost immeasurable influence exerted over the field by the writings of Joseph Campbell, especially his *The Hero with a Thousand Faces*. The appeal of Campbell is not just because his account of myth points toward a universal story spanning epochs, places, and cultures, but because it is a thoroughly transcendent vision consistently expressed in a hieratic register. For example, in *The Power of Myth* this is how he defines the "one great story":

> We have come forth from the one ground of being as manifestations in the field of time. The field of time is a kind of shadow play over a timeless ground. And you play the game in the shadow field, you enact your side of the polarity with all your might. But you know that your enemy, for example, is simply the other side of what you would see as yourself if you could see from the position of the middle. (1988, pp. 54–55)

The paradoxes and the metaphoricity evoke large metanarratives dealing with temporality, binarisms of good and evil, the struggle between conflicting impulses within the human psyche, the value of transcending selfhood to achieve a visionary state, the subordination of sociality to individual heroic striving, and so on. And apart from anything it actually says, the language itself is excited and inspirational, the traces of archaic expression implying timeless and arcane wisdom. In actual practice, retellings for young readers don't reproduce these effects, but merely operate under their assumptions, looking for strategies to direct readers from story to its significance. A primary model is still found in biblical literature, in that the forms that can be seen in place in biblical reversions and their spin-offs are replicated in other contexts which make use of traditional literature.

As an example of how a retold story produces an ideological effect, though not in this case humanistic, we will examine a brief retelling of a Bible story. As Northrop Frye points out (1982, p. 7), hieratic language such as that of the Bible is "the culturally ascendant language, a language that, at the time or later, is accorded a special authority by its society." Beyond language itself, of course, Bible narratives long occupied a comparable status, functioning, implicitly if not explicitly, as normative models both for narrative structures and outcomes and for moral and ethical structures and outcomes. Such a status is still claimed for biblical reversions, as when McLean (1990, p. 6) introduces her collection by asserting that "The Bible has been called 'the greatest book in the world'. It certainly is, for its stories are more stirring and dramatic than any tale ever conceived by a storyteller." This rather simple-minded assertion of the primacy of truth over fiction (implicit in the opposition between "story" and "tale"), on the basis that true stories are innately "more stirring and dramatic" than invented ones, evades the question of signification. The greatness, at this prefatory moment, lies in the narrative power of the stories rather than in their exemplary possibilities or in any claim for spiritual or moral insight or edification, though the unstated significance is presumably the raison d'être of the volume. A key assumption about retold stories is that they are invested with the equivalent of *truth* as implied here; that is, their capacity to be retold over centuries suggests their unique value as stories in themselves, but also implies that they continue because they are bearers of transcendent meanings. But Bible story is also unique in that it operates under the further premise that its narrative outcomes derive from an irrefutable divine authority. Further, modern Bible retellings also often serve the same purpose of conserving cultural and literary tradition we mentioned earlier in relation to myth.

The reversion we have chosen to comment on is "Naaman's Little Maid," from David Kyles's *Classic Bible Stories for Children* (1987, pp. 117–120). The episode, from 2 *Kings* 5, is a miracle story which is part of the saga of Elisha but, as the titling indicates, a minor character, an enslaved Israeli child, has been moved into a frame position. In 2 *Kings* 5:3 her role is to say to her mistress, "Would God my lord [Naaman] were with the prophet that is in Samaria! for he would recover him of his leprosy." At this point the biblical account says that someone reported her words to Naaman and his King sent him with a letter to the King of Israel, ordering him to cure Naaman. The cure is effected when Elisha instructs Naaman to bathe seven times in the River Jordan, and Naaman thus comes to recognize the preeminence of the Hebrew God. Kyles expands this account by inferring absent details: for example, why Naaman's wife didn't pass on the information, and how the King learned of it. Subsequently, he explains that when Naaman sought advance forgiveness because his bond to his king would compel him to acknowledge his king's god, Elisha's response—"Go in peace"—was not a sanctioning of such an action; rather, "He probably would have been better pleased if Naaman had shown more courage in the matter of following the only true God" (p. 120). Finally, Kyles omits the last third of the episode (verses 20–27), which tells of the sin of Gehazi, Naaman's servant, in seeking to profit from Naaman's healing and his own contracting of leprosy as punishment. Instead, he reintroduces the "nameless" little maid, commenting, "Her story has thrilled boys and girls in all ages since, and all over the world: how, instead of moaning about her sad lot, she looked upon herself as a missionary, carrying the message of the true faith to a foreign land" (p. 120). This conclusion is part of the process whereby the whole story has been more or less implicitly transformed by the imposition of a Christian evangelical schema. Two crucial components of this schema are that the weak and marginalized are instrumental in converting the powerful, and that proselytizing in foreign lands is, of course, an unchallengeable institution (the schema precludes the possibility that it might actually be a form of cultural imperialism). The assertion of a boundless temporal and spatial vista in which her story "has thrilled boys and girls" implicates the audience with that schema, building in the desired emotional and religious responses: to be "thrilled," and to bear witness to "the message of the true faith" wherever one happens to be. In 2 *Kings* 5:3 the intention of the girl's utterance is uninterpreted; it becomes meaningful in the reversion because the evangelical schema offers particular default values which imbue it with meaning. It is only when interpreted that the girl's story might even be noticed, let alone responded to as "thrilling." Finally, the schema underlines the transcendent significance of the dramatic, but unexplicated, details of the narrative: the affirmation of divine providence and power; the miraculous healing; the bathing in the Jordan as a type of baptism. In terms of the schema that is operating here, the problem of Naaman's dual worship must be addressed because it deviates from the implicit assumption that physical healing should unequivocally figure spiritual healing.

"Naaman's Little Maid" is a very obvious example of how a retelling can be filtered through a common metanarrative, right down to the use of demotic register for the language of comment and instruction. What happens in this telling is, nevertheless, paradigmatic of how metanarratives operate in other domains of retold stories. In Bible story we expect it. Of the substantial body of secondary literature dealing with reversions in children's literature, only that relating to fairy tale can be said to be self-consciously grounded in an awareness that neither literary representations nor critical perspectives are objective and value-free. When values are identified in children's books, and when they are commended, they are usually presented as *natural* human values which reflect the world as it is. On the contrary, retellers and their commentators are both engaged in producing interpretations of the world, and, in some cases, in attempts to change it by changing the consciousness of readers and their attitudes toward pre-existing narratives and concepts. The crucial strategy which interprets narrated experience for readers is the representation or construction of subjectivity. What is seldom acknowledged—because it is natural, an invisible assumption of the metaethic which gives significance to works of children's literature and informs most of the literature about them—is that the values, attitudes, and conceptualization of individual subjectivity which inform the literature are firmly grounded in the Western humanist tradition.

## HUMANISM AS THE GROUND OF THE WESTERN METAETHIC

The concepts comprising the metaethic on which the production and reception of children's literature seem to depend clearly originate in a humanist/historicist paradigm. Literary humanism promotes tradition and the conserving of culture; imagination and its cultivation; separation of literary texts from other forms of human activity (politics, for example, or ideology), while valuing altruistically intersubjective social and personal relationships; and the organic unity of texts shaped towards teleological outcomes. The interpretive metanarrative which underlies this bundle of ideas is widely naturalized in interpretive discourses and hence generally unarticulated. For example, in 1968 Penelope Lively, author of many children's books, published a trenchant assault on C.S. Lewis's "Narnia" series. This was an attack by a humanist novelist on a body of texts she considered to be anti-humanist, though the attack was not couched in those terms. Lively's criticisms were based on two arguments: that in writing his didactic Christian apologia Lewis condescended to children, writing at them rather than for them, and that his moral—depending on a "theology of a world in which Good and Evil are locked in an eternal struggle which can only be resolved by violence" (1968, p. 128)—was "distasteful and alarming" (p. 127). In other words, Lewis offends against two liberal humanist tenets: the first textual (the outcome is imposed on the narrative process, rather than being an organic outgrowth); and the second intellectual (the texts are determinist and authoritarian, and Lewis offends against humanist principles through his espousal of violence, his theological reductionism, his approval of hierarchy and caste systems, his implicit racism, and his religious intolerance).

Further, humanism's two most important and constant characteristics are first, that it focuses on human beings and starts from human experience—all beliefs, values, and knowledge are derived by human minds from human experience; and second, that individual human beings have a value themselves, grounded in the power to communicate, and in the power to observe themselves, to speculate, imagine, and reason. These powers enable freedom of choice and will, innovation, and the possibility of improving the self and the human lot. Two things necessary for this are individual freedom and cultivation of a young person's humanness. This complex of ideas drives Lively's textual objections to Lewis, in that the child characters are "never more than cardboard figures" and display neither convincing child language nor any possibilities of character development (p. 127); and their adventures lack urgency because subordinated to the interventions of Aslan and the presentation of the Christian message behind the stories. A humanist expectation is that awareness needs to be evoked through a rounded development of personality and of a character's abilities and talents, derived by human minds from human experience, a possibility not open to Lewis's characters. Further, the characters' lack of agency or focalization contributes to a failure to construct an interrelation of parts and whole which might lead to a narratively convincing teleology.

A revealing contrast to Lively's discussion of Lewis is Peter Abbs's discussion of Lively, significantly titled "Penelope Lively, Children's Fiction and the Failure of Adult Culture" (1975). No overt reference is made to humanist thought in this paper, which proves to be a good illustration of how in such critical discourse the interpretive metanarratives have become naturalized and invisible. In setting a humanist conception of culture against what he sees as the disorder and shallowness of postmodern society, Abbs gives overt expression to a position which widely pervades the discourse of and about children's literature. Thus in the one camp stands humanistic children's literature, which, offering an "alert and imaginative response to our age" (p. 119), presents transcendent truths, images of integration and transformation, and teleological structures; and in the other camp, the "diseases" of impoverished mass culture (actually postmodernism): pop art, mass-produced shapes and rhythms, unstructured sensation, and a failure of ethics or values. What Abbs seems to be expressing is despair at how postmodern discourses—with their fixation on surface detail, resistance to depth, and metafictive absorption in textuality for its own sake—apparently preclude the possibility of a humanist representation of reality with a capacity simultaneously to express and transcend contemporary culture. Lively's children's fiction certainly offers powerful ammunition to this argument, excelling as it does through her concern for the relationship between past and present and in her consummate skill in using a sense of historical continuity to map the growth of a character's individual subjectivity. *The Driftway*, for example, constructed as a framed set of retold stories, illustrates this exquisitely.

A humanist educational program proposed by Bullock (1985, pp. 186–187) focused on the themes of conscience, conflicts of loyalty, rebellion and authority, the ambivalence of feelings, the search for identity, the power of art and myth, and passions and compassion. Moreover, as might conventionally be expected in a humanist stance, Bullock sees value not just in any results such a program might produce, but in the activity itself, "engaging the imagination and the emotions in the penetration of other people's worlds and ideas . . . fostering the emotional, subjective side of human nature" (p. 187). This complex of themes, aspirations, and values, which is such a precise description of the dominant processes in retelling stories, is also the ground on which oppositional contemporary thinkers have sought to assail and overthrow humanism's cultural hegemony.

The controversies about the sway of humanism over intellectual life and artistic production in the twentieth century are too large and complex to explore here, but we do want just to glance at some aspects which are of special interest to the production of retold stories for child readers. The focal issues of contention are the necessarily abstract notions of the self and the related concept of the subject. Since neither selfhood nor subjectivity is a demonstrable entity or state, they always remain a hypothesis about being, but once hypothesized occupy a central position in the humanist tradition. The humanist subject pivots on the further notion of "agency," which Paul Smith defines as "a form of subjectivity where, by virtue of the contradictions and disturbances in and among subject-positions, the possibility (indeed, the actuality) of resistance to ideological pressure is allowed for (even though that resistance too must be produced in an ideological context)" (1988, p. xxxv). Thus, although it is posited on the notion of a self which is essential, the subject which manifests itself implies a multiplicity of being. This is an important issue because humanist ideology is often rightly accused of falsely or naively constructing a unified subject as a romantic unitary self capable of action outside ideological systems, and such a notion of the self pervades children's literature. At the other extreme, characteristically associated with the thought of Althusser, is the conceptualization of the subject as an inscribed function of discursive and institutional structures and, incapable of agency, thereby inserted into social formations. Neither of these extremes had retained much intellectual currency by the 1990s, but only the former has ever been widely exhibited in stories retold for children—and, it should be added, usually quite anachronistically. We now seem to be in a climate in which the "death of the subject," a possibility widely proposed in the 1970s and 1980s, is becoming constituted as a particular historical moment, with something like Smith's account of subjectivity-as-agency emerging as the present orthodoxy. Agnes Heller's description of the subject as "the idiosyncracy of the interpretation of human world-experience and self-experience under the condition of modernity" (1992, p. 283) precisely fits the discovery of agency in Lively's *The Driftway,* and would seem to be good news for mainstream children's literature. It would be a pity, though, if current intellectual developments enabled a foreclosure on any challenge to the continuation of the status quo before it has been substantially exposed to such a challenge.[5]

The modernist view of being, presenting an image of human experience produced without any universal referent or uncontestable code of values, proposed that consciousness was fragmentary, experience ambiguous, and truth relative, and that human lives and social relationships were driven by nonrational impulses. This view of existence has generally proved anathema to children's literature, its scant appearances virtually being confined to young adult literature. The result of this situation is that no attempt has been made to interrogate the basis of retellings, or their underlying assumptions about transhistorical meaning, the existence of "truth," or the efficacy of role models. Hence important questions are not asked—questions about how we are to produce and consume literary reversions—since the representation of significant heroic figures as role models, allegories, or precursors is a common point at which metanarratival significances are expressed in children's literature.

The literary and cultural formations re-presented in retold stories are often apparent bearers of clear attitudes to such things as power (political, social, and personal), hierarchy, gender, class, and race. If the function of a canon is to construct, preserve, and perpetuate particular forms of cultural knowledge, then in their assumptions and reassertions of canonicity retold stories are deeply implicated in this process. The effect of a canon is to mediate the ways ideas are transformed as they pass from one historical-ideological situation to another, in a myriad number of transformations. An analysis of the process would thus need to consider not just the represented content of a text, which may be transmitted virtually unchanged, but also the modes of representation and then, crucially, any critiques of that representation or others like it. Texts enter (or leave) a canon by means of the discourse which surrounds them; in effect, Lively's paper sought to displace Lewis from a central position in the canon, whereas Abbs's presented a case for Lively's admission. This suggests an institutionalized process which interlocks content, mode, and critique, and in part this is so, though its processes are probably not quite that well-contained. It is possible to argue, however, that while the Lewis-Lively opposition appears to represent a state of healthy difference and debate, that opposition functions within a very narrow and elitist cultural band. It offers a small example of how over time a hierarchy of ideas is modified, but a harsher view would be that what is really at stake is whether the "tradition" to be disseminated through childhood reading, libraries, and educative systems is to be grounded in conservative Christianity or liberal humanism. For someone who subscribes to neither, but prefers to argue that literary canons function to uphold ideological, national, gender, and class hegemonies, the effect would be the same. In such a context, the retelling of old stories requires careful scrutiny. In all of the domains of reversion we are concerned with here there is a high probability that replication of an old content and mode of representation may result in the further replication of, for example, old masculinist and antifeminist metanarratives. At the same time, retold stories have the potential to disclose how old stories suppress the invisible, the untold, and the unspoken. Such a potential will be realized through changing the modes of representation as well as, and more than, changing the content: by careful attention to point of view; by focalization strategies, since agency cannot be manifested by characters who do not focalize; and by textual self-reflexiveness or other strategies which remind readers not only of how they read the text but of how they read the world.

In the chapters which follow we have pursued these questions by focusing in each on a particular domain.[6] Readers will, no doubt, readily point to missing examples, other possibilities, the absence of their own favorite texts. It has not been our purpose to be encyclopedic; we are more interested in what we perceive as symptoms of a long sustained trend within Western cultures, and have pursued this even at the risk of seeming sometimes capricious in our choice of illustrative texts and the paths we have followed. We have occasionally made same observations about influences and innovations, but our argument rarely depends on priority; that something appears and reflects or affects culture is more important than whether one reteller or another was first to do it. Thus it is probably true to say that in 1982 the "setting the genie free" motif was first interpolated into the *Aladdin* story, by Geraldine McCaughrean, but it wouldn't really matter if she weren't the first to do this. What does matter is how widespread the motif became within ten or twelve years, during one of the Western world's most materialistic decades.

## NOTES

1. For much of the audience, the most likely pre-text would be the slightly earlier television version, *Robin of Sherwood* (1984).

2. Throughout this book we have followed Mary Gerhart's use of *genric* instead of the more usual *generic*. We accept her argument that *genric* emphasizes "the functions of the concept of genre in interpretation," whereas *generic* "has come to connote aspects such as non-specificity and common variety" (1992, p. 228, n. 7).

3. *Courtesy* is especially semantically charged when associated with a "medieval" text, in that it is a preeminent value in medieval romances. A bundle of linked terms equivalent to those we give here can be found, for example, attributed to the ideal knight in *Sir Gawain and the Green Knight*, lines 652–654, where *cortaysye* is joined by *fraunchyse* 'generosity,' *felawschyp* 'love of fellow men,' *clannes* 'purity, chastity,' and *pité* 'compassionateness.'

Leeson's metanarrative also coincides in interesting ways with the humanist/realist metanarrative articulated by the narrator of George Eliot's *Adam Bede:*

> There are few prophets in the world; few sublimely beautiful women; few heroes. I can't afford to give all my love and reverence to such rarities: I want a great deal of those feelings for my everyday fellowmen, especially for the few in the foreground of the great multitude, whose faces I know, whose hands I touch, for whom I have to make way with kindly courtesy.
> (Harmondsworth: Penguin Books, 1980, pp. 224–225)

4. See Eugene Vinaver, ed. *The Works of Sir Thomas Malory* (1967, Vol. I, pp. 293–363). Yeatman's reversion covers the material on pages 293–326. The second half of Malory's narrative, which Yeatman summarizes in four lines, deals with events leading up to the marriage of Gareth and Lyonesse. It is misleading, however, to suggest that Yeatman's relation to Malory is unmediated: an examination of the language and the processes of inclusion and omission in Roger Lancelyn Green's version (1953, pp. 117–131) suggests that this has also served as a pre-text, though there are also some substantial differences. We will say more about the pervasive influence of Green in chapter 5, below.

5. Once again, the notable exception is the critical discourse centering on fairy tale, where writers have been able to demonstrate the extent to which ideas and individual actions are both socially produced.

6. Chapters 1, 3, and 5 were evolved collaboratively; chapters 2 and 9 were primarily written by Robyn McCallum, and chapters 4, 6, 7, and 8 by John Stephens.

# Authority, Wisdom, and Cultural Heritage

## Biblical Literature as Pre-Text

*"The children have much to learn," continued Noah, "if they are still to inherit the Earth."*

—Pippa Unwin and Kate Petty, *Wake Up, Mr. Noah!*

We begin our discussion of the patterns and frames which shape the retelling of familiar material with biblical literature and narratives with biblical pre-texts because they most clearly show how narratives about social behavior are framed by structures of authority. These structures are initially validated by assumptions about divine authority, and then remain as frames when biblical story is secularized within more humanistic discourses. More generally, such frames and the models of authority they sustain are carried over into retellings of other kinds of traditional story, so that these particular conceptualizations of authority then inform most humanistic discourses and social practices, and have an actual or potential impact on the writing and reading of retold stories of all kinds. We are arguing, therefore, that the relationship between Bible story and stories from other sources is substantially closer than is often thought, because Bible story is the bearer of an interpretive tradition which informs all acts of interpretation involving traditional stories. To put this more bluntly, the ground on which traditional narratives are retold or contested is always the Western metaethic.

The attraction of Bible story derives from the presence of at least two of four main aspects: engaging and shapely narrative, transmission of cultural heritage, moral exemplum, and religious lesson (see Phy, 1985, p. 165; Potter, 1986/87, p. 192). Only the fourth is generally absent from retellings of other kinds of traditional story, and because its explicit presence is apt to be suppressed in biblical narratives aimed at a wide audience (nondenominational or secular), their cultural uniqueness as narratives becomes a matter of identifiable content rather than of discourse or of world-view. The interpretive practice we are identifying, and how it extends to the production and reception of other areas of storying, is revealingly demonstrated in Potter's eloquent, Christian-humanist advocacy of Bible story. She begins by arguing that, because many adults have been in childhood shaped as readers by the King James Bible, they "find in the great literary classics dimensions of space and feeling doubly those of their own souls, dimensions known by cultural orientation as well as by the intimations of imagination" (p. 186).

This argument is in substance much the same as arguments advocating retellings of classical and (by association) other mythologies, as we will show in chapter 3. Like those arguments, Potter's is grounded in a notion of a specific kind of cultural capital, evident in the privileging of "the great literary classics" and the imagination, the vague grandiloquent language, the high cultural (rather than religious) use of "souls," and the calculated reminiscence of Wordsworth (the paper goes on to list or cite a further eighteen classics of literature or art). Accordingly, Potter distinguishes and commends the first three kinds of value listed above, but substitutes an imprecise "sublime" for the fourth, the "religious lesson." The idea of the sublime, as deployed here, is derived from Eric Auerbach's account of the *figura* in biblical or religious narrative: "a *figura* is a participant which simultaneously has a primary literal or historical presence and discloses a symbolic significance, a fulfilled truth" (Auerbach, 1959, p. 71). The concept has two useful functions in modern Bible retellings, though neither can really be attributed to Auerbach: it enables the kind of fuzziness of signification taken up by Potter; and it offers a source of significant meaning which is an effective variation to the typological practices which, as Phy points out (p. 168), have increasingly weakened during the twentieth century. Figural reading is a form of typology, but does not reduce a participant to a mere prefiguration or a mere allegory of an attribute, virtue, or moral perspective. Rather, it delineates that participant's situation within the larger moral or spiritual order of the world. Various forms of typology still flourish, as our discussions of Kyles in chapter 1 and of Beer, below, indicate. Potter identifies explicitly typological techniques in Helga Aichinger's *The Shepherd,* and her own commendation of the capacity of biblical literature to represent nature "as a hieroglyphic of usable truth" (p. 191) has obvious typological implications.

Auerbach's overall intellectual position was not, of course, Christian, but humanist, and, as Paul Bové has argued, the role he saw for scholars was "mythographical preservation in hope of having 'an effect'" (1986, p. 179), a project to conserve the humanity that had developed over time and within culture and consciousness in order to create future possibilities. This is also Potter's project. The main focus of her reading of biblical retellings can be summarized in some of her own phrases: "artistic identity," "grace of language," "cultural history," "moral responsibility," and "sublime truths." This complex of literary, moral, and indeterminately transcendent concepts is symptomatic of the production and reception of those biblical retellings which don't display an explicit didactic intent. We have illustrated it from Potter's discussion because she does it in such a detailed and paradigmatic way, and because her use of Auerbach is very illuminating. The same complex is also evident in less elaborated accounts of biblical retellings, as for example in Ingraham's (1990) brief survey, which, beginning from the breathtaking premise that the Bible "holds an unshakeable place of primacy in world literature" (p. 300), specifies that retellings "should be *inspirational* and affirmative, awakening or strengthening a sense of good in the world, of role and purpose, of the universality and perpetuity of human values. They should be literary and instructive, presenting the richness of biblical language and fostering the understanding of so much of literature, art and culture which has been influenced by the Bible." As a signifying concept, the "universality of human values" tends to drift between transcendent morality and cultural heritage, collapsing together key components of the Western metaethic.

Northrop Frye has made the historical point that as Christian theology gained cultural ascendancy, thought began to take on a deductive shape in which everything followed from the perfection of God, because of the need for irrefutable premises (1983, p. 10). In modern narratives for children, the equivalent of irrefutable premises is divine authority as represented in Bible stories and mediated by authoritative adults. Thus authority and decision-making are concentrated in one source, "God," and thence in whatever institutions or people that can claim to have divine authority invested in them. At its most basic level, this representation of authority conceals that its basis and the tenets which uphold it and which it upholds are socially conditioned and culturally inherited.

Authority is constituted by establishing boundaries, so that rules, prohibitions, and so on, presuming that those boundaries are natural and universal, teach that moral and social normality is defined by refusal to transgress them. The existence of the boundaries themselves is placed beyond question, with the consequence that processes of judgment are already foreclosed; boundaries may thus structure the relationships of selves to world, but they militate against any questioning of whether those boundaries themselves are desirable or undesirable. Resistant readings therefore need to cultivate disruptive or subversive narrative strategies. We will shortly examine this process at work in the best-known biblical complex of boundary and transgression, the myth of the Fall. Before doing that, however, we will consider a particularly palpable example, the re-presentation of the Jonah story in V. Gilbert Beers's *With Sails to the Wind* (1977, pp. 6–11).

*With Sails to the Wind* is one of a series of retold Bible stories with a common formation: a Bible story and a modern story are paired, with each followed by a set of questions. The questions following the Bible story are headed "What do you think?", and those following the contemporary story are headed "Let's talk about this"—that is, both sets of questions are presented as if they introduce a process of open-ended deliberation. On the contrary, however, both introduce a closed process designed to instill definite modes of behavior, and in doing this presuppose a particular narrative structure and way of reading it. Thus each heading is immediately followed by a subheading, "What this story teaches." The story of Jonah teaches a particular relationship between God and "His people": that obedience is expected. The segment then poses two sets of questions: one is designed to elicit the salient points of the story (here only told up to the point at which Jonah was regurgitated by the fish) and explicate its significance; the second asks the audience to apply that significance to their own lives. In this case it asks, "When God asks you to do something which you may not want to do, should you try to hide?" The relationship between subordinate clause and main clause in this question very obviously, to an outsider, enables the largest part of its teaching to be merely assumed—that "God asks you," and that this is knowable and recognizable. How this actually works only becomes fully clear with the contemporary story, which tells of a small girl who ran away to avoid her domestic chores and was caught in a storm. When she returns home, without being missed, her father happens to read her the Jonah story, "about a man who tried to run away from God and got into trouble in a storm" (p. 11). The discussion segment then explains that "we are happier when we obey God, and those He puts over us, than when we try to run away from what they expect," and the following questions explicate the analogies between the two stories, ending with another application to the lives of the audience and an exhortation to cheerful obedience of those "put over us." The manifestly social intentions of this text are generally characteristic of rewritings of Bible stories for children, as Bottigheimer (1996) has demonstrated.

Beers's stories seem very heavy-handed, though the total structure, with its four interlocked parts, is quite complex. At the same time, the process discloses, layer by layer, how Biblical reversions sustain a discourse which purports to be an all-embracing interpretive metanarrative. First, they establish a process for understanding Bible narratives as always already exemplifying a particular structure of authority and obligation between God and the individual, a hierarchical and moral relationship which is then shown to apply in the same way to the reader. Second, Bible narratives, together with the reader subject position constructed by the inscribed mode of interpretation, then constitute a process and a religious and moral frame for reading all other narratives.

Such an interpretive metanarrative presupposes two premises as irrefutable: that divine-human relationships are always structured in that particular moral hierarchy; and that human experience in history is shaped by realities which are timeless, permanent, and essential. The second premise becomes meaningful only insofar as it depends on the first, but the hierarchy is not immutable. Potter contends that one of the Bible's major themes is that "the moral responsibility of the individual can be fully exercised only in its supernatural dimensions" (p. 191), but such a phrasing already opens the possibility for a humanist restructuring of the metaethic. As Bottigheimer's (1996) analysis of pre-twentieth century Bible story shows, this restructuring has been happening over a couple of centuries. Writers such as Lively and Garfield, whom we will discuss toward the end of the chapter, illustrate how a humanist project emerges by reaffirming the second premise and moving it to the primary position, while simultaneously substituting human intersubjective responsibility for the first premise. Thus, religious and humanist interpretive projects do not merely operate as rival cultural forces, but the latter engages with the former in an attempt to wrest one of its key premises onto a different ground, now using it to conserve cultural knowledge and experience as a basis for moral meaning and growth towards enlightenment.

## Types of Biblical Reversions

Biblical narratives for children demonstrate a wide range of registers, literary, genric, and narrative styles, and organizational styles. While the Bible, in its various versions and translations, is usually written in a hieratic register, retellings of Bible narrative utilize all three of the registers outlined in chapter 1, hieratic, epic, and demotic, and these different modes are put to quite different purposes in traditional religious, literary, and secular retellings and reversions.

Dickinson's (1989) reflections about how his collection, *City of Gold,* was conceived have implications for the writing of retellings in general. Dickinson has claimed that he was initially reluctant to do this collection for two related reasons. First, there is the matter of what he calls "voice." He had assumed "that there were only two possible voices in which to tell

Bible stories: low style and high style" (p. 78). "Low style" in Dickinson's definition is "as-told-to-children, bland, simple, homogenized," whereas "high style" is "all sound, words lovingly deployed, language as it was never spoken and was written only for the purpose of translating Homer and retelling Bible stories" (p. 78). These two voices correspond roughly with what we have been referring to as demotic and hieratic register. In defining these two registers as "voices" Dickinson highlights the implications that register has for narrative technique and narratorial situation. Demotic and hieratic registers are characterized by a predisposition for particular modes of narration—hieratic registers tend to coincide with third person omniscient, while demotic register is more suited to the first person. Furthermore, although these registers and concomitant narrative modes presuppose specific and different types of relations between the audience and the text, both situate readers in disempowered interpretive positions when used to retell Bible story in the manner described by Dickinson.

Second, Dickinson perceives a problem in the dominant cultural attitude toward Bible stories. They are often seen as having a historical basis, and entertainment is not usually perceived to be their primary function. Dickinson suggests that Bible story needs instead "to be written or spoken in the voice of someone who is trying to tell you something important, to instruct or persuade or explain" (p. 79), thus intrinsically tying narrative voice and register to situation and purpose. His solution to what he sees as the problem of "voice" is to construct a narrative frame for each of the stories he retells which elaborates the social and historical setting in which the story might have been retold. The socio-historical context in which a story is told, the purpose for which it is told, and the specific relation between audience and storyteller, readers and texts, are factors which determine the register and narrative techniques. In a society in which Christian humanism is still a pervasive—albeit implicit—ideology, readers approach Bible stories with a reverence for authority different from what informs their approaches to most other kinds of literature, and Dickinson's strategies make this attitude visible.

Bach and Exum's comments on the functions of gap-filling in both retelling and reading in their introduction to *Moses' Ark* (1989) also implicitly acknowledge the influence of dominant cultural attitudes on approaches to biblical material. As they suggest, just as readers "fill gaps by supplying [their] own selection of details when [they] read stories," retellers of Bible story also fill gaps by providing story details. Some gaps can be filled through our common experience of the world—for example the noise that the animals on the ark might have made—and Bach and Exum also fill in details about the everyday life and language of the ancient Israelites by drawing on "scholarly findings" of historians, archaeologists, and language specialists for their retellings (p. 3). However, any kind of gap-filling process is going to be ideologically driven insofar as it draws on, and thereby instantiates and validates, interpretive schemata associated with specific kinds of cultural knowledge. In acknowledging their sources, commenting on individual stories, and disclosing their reasons for selecting stories and for making alterations to the conventional story form, Bach and Exum do potentially offer their readers empowered subject positions. However, at the same time, the specific interpretive schemata that they use—namely schemata associated with historical research and writing—are structured by and sustain the same interpretive metanarrative that Dickinson sees as dominating cultural constructions of the Bible, that is the Bible as history. *Moses' Ark* and *Miriam's Well* are both excellent collections of Bible story and, as we will show later in this chapter, they certainly make a substantial contribution toward undermining dominant cultural interpretations of the Bible, but they do so from within a pervasive humanist metanarrative wherein the Bible is perceived as history and as either implicitly or explicitly offering some kind of instruction to readers.

Dickinson's comments and his collection of self-reflexive retellings in turn reflect on other retellings of Bible story, especially the assumptions about audience and the purpose underlying the retelling. As he suggests, a primary assumption about Bible stories is that they are instructive and that reading is followed by reflection and exegesis. Thus the structure and discursive mode of Beers's *With Sails to the Wind,* discussed above, is informed by the assumption that stories have a message for their readers which connects the content and theme of any story and the child reader's life. This connection is made explicit by the combination of a traditional story and a modern story which replicates the theme and basic "story" content of the older story, and by the use of a demotic register for both stories. The strategies used by Beers, whereby traditional retellings and contemporary reversions are presented consecutively, are of interest not only in the way that they aim to focus reader attention on the thematic and ideological implications of the narrative (rather than the "story"), but also in the way that they make these kinds of reading strategies explicit in order to inculcate them. The structure of the retellings— wherein the contemporary story constructs a modern context for the older story—assumes that meaning transcends the social and historical context.

The assumption that the meaning of a particular story can be transmitted unchanged in a different narrative form is one that informs many retellings of Bible story for children, both traditional and literary. As we have suggested in chapter 1, any retelling is going to be influenced by the context in which it is retold and by changes to the content, narrative voice, and discourse. However, a common effect of the discursive strategies of both traditional and literary retellings is that the potential significance of a story is restricted to a specific interpretive metanarrative. A function of the structure and discourse of stories in Beers's collection is to limit the play of meaning and to limit the potential for meaningful dialogue between retellings and their pre-texts. The use of demotic discourse for both traditional and contemporary versions of stories is especially instrumental in limiting this potential. A concomitant effect is to narrow the possible interpretations of stories down to a literal and single interpretation and to impose a hierarchical relation between readers and texts which reflects and reinforces the explicit moral and social message of many of the stories, that is, obedience to an authoritative adult, text, or God. In contrast, the combination of epic and hieratic discourses in de la Mare's more literary retellings (1921; repr. 1961) allows a play of meaning, thereby opening texts to metaphoric and allegorical readings, as opposed to purely literal readings. However, the "fuzziness" of signification in de la Mare's literary retellings is nonetheless contained within a Christian typological metanarrative which limits the range of signification by assuming that meaning transcends the social, historical, and narrative context. For example, a typological reading would see the Crucifixion (and hence salvation) as prefigured in the story of the Fall: the Crucifixion redeems the Fall; and the Tree of Life represents salvation—literally, in that it conventionally provided the wood for the cross, and metaphorically, in that it prefigures the Eucharist. De la Mare refers directly to Christ in his retelling of the Fall (p. 35), but a typological reading is also immanent in the associations evoked by de la Mare to describe the two trees in the Garden of Eden: "And midway on the green of the mountain slope there was a Tree, the Tree of Knowledge of Good and Evil, while above it, but well-nigh invisible in the light that dwelt upon it, there was another Tree, and that on the heights beyond" (p. 30). "Light" is clearly functioning metaphorically here to imply the conventional connection between Christ and the Tree of Life—for example, "In him was life; and the life was the light of men" (*John* 1:4)— and the passage exploits the semantic range of spatial terms ("midway, above, heights beyond") in order to evoke a (literal and metaphoric) transcendence which can only be read typologically.

## THREE CATEGORIES OF BIBLICAL RETELLING

Biblical narratives for children fall into three broad categories: traditional religious retellings and reversions; literary retellings and reversions; and secular humanist retellings and reversions. Traditional religious retellings of Bible story almost always seek to instruct child readers and are situated within and instrumental in sustaining conventional Judaeo-Christian interpretive metanarratives. The aim to teach a religious lesson is more or less explicit in these narratives, and the relation between implied readers and the text is usually clearly defined. Where, as in the example discussed earlier, traditional religious retellings are combined with contemporary reversions, this instructive purpose prevails. The contemporary reversions are shaped so as to exemplify and explicate the religious moral of the traditional story. Narratives usually follow the basic structure of the biblical story, and the vocabulary tends to be limited (and repetitive) and the syntax simple, so that the range of signification available to readers is narrowed. There are two main types of religious retelling which may be distinguished by register, discoursal mode, and narrative technique. Works of the first type are largely based on modern translations of the Bible and are characterized by biblical quotation, and hence a dominance of hieratic discoursal modes, and third person narration, with minimal character focalization—for example Kyles's *Classic Bible Stories for Children* (1987). Works of the second type are characterized by demotic register, signaled by the use of contemporary idiomatic discourse, and by more varied narrative techniques such as character focalization and/ or indirect modes of discourse representation for speech and thought.

Literary retellings of the Bible also retain the contemporary biblical context and usually remain quite close to the basic story structure of the biblical pre-text. They differ from traditional retellings in the use of more varied discourses, especially epic registers associated with romantic genres; in greater variation of narrative tone and technique; and in the absence or suppression of an explicit religious lesson. Framing strategies are also common in literary retellings, where the frame narrative recontextualizes a familiar story, and there is more play with language and hence an increase in the semantic range of texts. Secular humanist retellings and reversions frequently resituate the story in another, usually modern, context, or "retell" the story either as a kind of sequel to the pre-text or as another version of the pre-text. For this reason the distinction between a retelling and a reversion can become quite blurred. These types of retellings are often quite overtly intertextual and self-consciously playful. The biblical pre-text will frequently be directly quoted or referred to—thus these types of narratives tend to be characterized by the self-conscious combination of hieratic, epic, and demotic registers. To explore the different kinds of retelling, we will begin with the ideological functions of traditional and literary retellings of the Fall myth. We will then consider retellings of stories about women and representations of women, especially Bach and Exum's collection of Bible stories about Old Testament women, *Miriam's Well*. Finally we will examine modern secular reversions of the Creation, the Fall, and the Flood.

As we suggested in chapter 1, where a retelling or reversion replicates the content and mode of representation of its pre-text, it is also apt to replicate a pre-existing metanarrative. Masculinist and antifeminist metanarratives dominate Judaeo-Christian interpretive traditions, and traditional retellings of Bible stories for children reflect, and frequently accentuate, this dominance. A key strategy for undermining such metanarratives within the biblical tradition is to retell the "same" story from another point of view, a point of view that has previously been suppressed or silenced. The primary narrative mode used in the Bible is third person omniscient narration, with first person narration occurring in prophetic books, such as *Ezekiel, Ezra,* and *Nehemiah*, and in the lyrics, such as the *Psalms*. Most contemporary retellings and reversions use at least some third person focalized narration, a strategy which encourages reader alignment and is hence aimed at making the content and ideology of the story more accessible to a child reader. In the case of fairly straight "translations" of Bible story, such narrative strategies have as a primary underlying motivation the initiation of the child reader into a social and religious heritage. In other more radical secular humanist and feminist retellings, such narrative strategies can disclose how old stories suppress the invisible and the unspoken, and the disclosure may then undermine traditional Christian and patriarchal interpretations of biblical material.

The processes of selection, organization, and framing of stories and packaging of texts, especially collections, is important in shaping and reshaping the ideologies of the stories, and hence in the (re)construction of interpretive metanarratives. The extent to which selection and organization affect the way individual stories are read and interpreted becomes more obvious when a collection deviates from conventional selection criteria. A collection such as *Miriam's Well* (Bach and Exum, 1991), comprising twenty-one stories in which female characters have primary narrative functions, reads quite differently from a more conventional collection such as Kyles's, in which females tend to be secondary (and often silent or unnamed). Two quite different metanarratives emerge from the macrodiscoursal patterning and effects of these collections. The particular stories selected for retelling indicate assumptions about the audience and about the importance of the material itself. A canon of Bible stories for children is formed by the most commonly retold stories, such as the Fall, the Flood, Jonah and the Whale, and the Nativity. In collections, stories are almost always organized chronologically, so that the organization replicates the overall structure of the Bible and implies a sense of historicity which, like the Bible itself, is patrilineal. Framing strategies used for collections and for individual stories also have an important ideological function. A common strategy is to embed stories within a narrational frame, wherein the retold story is a story told to an audience. Bach and Exum use this strategy for retelling the story of Judith in *Miriam's Well,* in which the story is told in retrospect by a much older Judith to an audience of young Israelite men and women. The books of the Old Testament have a long oral tradition, as many Biblical scholars have suggested, and this framing technique constructs a historical and narrative context for the story. Dickinson also uses this strategy throughout *City of Gold.*

The packaging of texts—the inclusion of paratextual information such as introductions, footnotes, and other textual details—is also instrumental in the construction of interpretive paradigms for stories. The inclusion of historical and anecdotal material can lend historical authenticity to stories—for example, McLean's *Old Testament Bible Stories* includes information about roses, spices, and animals of the Bible, Jewish festivals and customs, and so on. The more scholarly collections by Bach and Exum (1989; 1991) provide an interesting contrast to McLean's more conventional collection for children. As we commented earlier, Bach and Exum include explanatory footnotes, notes about sources and translation, and an introduction setting out their criteria for selection and retelling. They claim that to their knowledge *Moses' Ark* is the "only collection of Bible stories based on the original language, informed by the fruits of biblical scholarship, and written especially for children" (p. 2).

Collections which introduce the stories as "literature," such as Baldwin's *Old Stories of the East* (1895) or De la Mare's *Stories from the Bible* (1961), or which declare their contents "myth," such as Green's *The Tale of Ancient Israel* (1969) or Bailey et al.'s *Gods and Men* (1981)—a collection in which Old Testament stories are retold alongside stories from Polynesia, Australia, Egypt, North America, and so on—may potentially be read differently from collections which explicitly interpret stories as moral or historical lessons. However, the ideological implications of texts are determined by the interaction between the macrodiscoursal framing of stories and the microdiscoursal patterning of individual stories. For example, the title of Baldwin's collection and of individual stories in it—"The Garden of Delight," or "The Great Chief"—and references to the stories as "Hebrew Scriptures" initially defamiliarize familiar Bible stories. Most changes to the discursive structuring of individual stories are nevertheless superficial. They defamiliarize the biblical stories, but only in minor ways, and at the same time ascribe quite conventionalized meanings to them. Many commentators and retellers have clearly perceived a need to champion Bible story, explicitly claiming for it the status of "literature." Baldwin asserts that Bible story should have the same status as "classical myth" and "literature." De la Mare asserts the inherent value of biblical literature, describing it as a kind of receptacle of human nature: it contains "all that man is or feels or . . . thinks . . . loves or fears or delights in, grieves for, desires and aspires to" (p. 9). He laments that the Bible is no longer read as widely as it once was, as do Frye (1983) and Chambers (1984). For De la Mare this means a loss of the somewhat vague qualities of "wisdom, divination, truth, candor, simplicity, directness,"—that is, the Bible is of inherent value in itself as literature. For Frye and Chambers the Bible is also of value for reading other literature and understanding culture more generally. Thus defining and valorizing the Bible as "literature" positions Bible story culturally and ideologically; the Bible is to be read not simply for religious instruction, but as part of a process of initiation into and education within a cultural heritage. Chambers, for example, writes of a "truth" which is "the inescapable relationship that exists between our ways of thought, our means of speech, and our cultural assumptions and the focusing reality given to them all by the great Bible code that enlivens and informs them still" (p. 247). Green may describe his collection of Old Testament stories as "myths," but his argument that myths express some kind of abstract "truth" about humanity's experience and understanding of the world replicates the constitution of Bible story as "literature." Furthermore, Green claims that "the myths of Ancient Israel are of all myths those that come nearest to the truth" (p. xiv), implicitly suggesting that these myths, especially the story of the Creation (p. xii), are in a sense the seminal or originary myths lying behind all other myths.

## THE FALL

As we suggested earlier, the myth of the Fall is probably the best known biblical complex of boundary and transgression. It involves a breach of interdiction and conforms to a common story structure wherein characters transgress boundaries by performing a prohibited action and thereby bring about radical change. The same story structure is common in folktale and in classical myth, as in the stories of Pandora and Prometheus which we will discuss in chapter 3. In the myth of the Fall the boundaries that constitute divine authority structure the relationships of selves to the world, of selves to each other, and selves to the divine being. By eating from the Tree of Knowledge Adam and Eve transgress these boundaries and bring about a change in these relations.

The basic story structure of the Fall myth, built around a sequence of interdiction, temptation, transgression, consequence, and punishment, is as follows: Adam and Eve are placed in the Garden of Eden, where they are allowed to eat from any tree or plant with the exception of the Tree of Knowledge. Eve is tempted by the serpent and eats fruit from the Tree. She then offers fruit to Adam, who in turn also eats. This transgression is followed first by God's gender-specific curses on Adam and Eve (and the serpent), and by punishment, whereby Adam and Eve are driven out of the garden. Within Judaeo-Christian interpretive traditions, the myth of the Fall has had two primary ideological functions. First, it constructs an authority paradigm, that is a paradigm for a hierarchical relation between individuals and God (Brenner, 1992, pp. 48–49). In retellings for children this also functions as a paradigmatic structure for teaching filial obedience, as the relationship of Adam and Eve to God is analogous with the relationship of a child to its parents and other adults. Second, the Fall sets up a gender paradigm, that is a paradigm which structures the social roles and relationships between men and women and the physical relations of men and women to the world. This paradigm entails schemata for the construction and representation of male and female sexuality, though the extent to which these schemata are explicit in retellings for children varies across individual retellings and reversions. Retellings of the Fall often open either "in the beginning" with the story of the Creation or with the creation of Eve; both types of opening set up the relationship of Eve and Adam, often prefiguring the Fall through this relationship.

Retellings of Bible story for children engage with and sustain either or both of these paradigms. The authority paradigm tends to dominate traditional religious retellings which explicitly seek to teach a religious lesson. However, the implications of the Fall story for male-female relationships will often be more or less implicit in these retellings. In more literary and secular retellings the idea that the Fall implies a gender paradigm is more dominant, and the implications of the story for female sexuality tend to be more explicit.

The basic story structure is usually retained in traditional religious and literary retellings and reversions, but ideological variations arise through the treatment of the main story components, the characterization, and the narrative techniques and registers used. Each of the story components offers multiple alternative interpretive possibilities in which either or both of the authority and gender paradigms are constructed, and cumulatively, the specific encoding of components functions in the construction of interpretive paradigms. Possible encodings for each of the story components may be summarized as follows (encodings labeled by small roman numerals are optional, but when more than one is present one or another will be foregrounded):

1. Interdiction
   a. reasons are not given for the prohibition, and therefore God's authority is represented as arbitrary and unmotivated.
   b. reasons are given for the prohibition which correspond with the consequences/punishment of transgression.
2. Temptation
   a. the temptation constitutes an appeal to (i) Eve's physical appetite; (ii) her envy of God; (iii) her physical sensual (and sexual) appetite; (iv) her intellect.
   b. the tempter (serpent) is represented as (i) Satan (external to Eve); (ii) an externalization of Eve's own desire (internal to Eve).
3. Transgression
   a. the act of transgression is represented as (i) an act of disobedience; (ii) the sin of greed; (iii) the sin of envy; (iv) a sensual or sexual act.
   b. Eve: transgression is usually motivated by greed, envy, sensual or sexual desire, and her "temptation of Adam" is usually more or less implicitly sexual.
   c. Adam: transgression is usually motivated by foolishness, and/or the (sexual) temptation constituted by Eve (as temptress).
4. Consequence of transgression
   a. knowledge of good and evil, and/or awareness of nakedness. In retellings where the knowledge of good and evil is actually specified, it is usually depicted more or less explicitly as sexual knowledge—implicit in the inclusion of Adam and Eve's awareness of their nakedness. Two exceptions to this are Bach and Exum (1989) and Dickinson (1980).
   b. representation of characters as changed in some way.
   c. representation of a changed Garden.
   d. the curses/punishments pronounced by God. In many retellings there is little distinction made between the consequences of and the punishment for eating the fruit, so "knowledge of good and evil" is not specified.
5. Punishment
   a. Three curses are pronounced by God on Eve, Adam, and the serpent. These are frequently abbreviated and one or more will often be omitted.

b. Adam and Eve are driven from/leave the Garden (i) as punishment; (ii) so they don't eat of the Tree of Life; (iii) as a consequence of their actions.

The two ideological paradigms that structure the Fall myth emerge most clearly in the treatment of the temptation, transgression, consequence, and punishment components.

Ideological variations also arise through the narrative and registers used. Like most Bible narratives, the Biblical version of the Fall in *Genesis* is narrated as third person omniscient in a hieratic register. In retellings for children, if the narrative is focalized it is usually Eve who does so, though some narratives also construct the serpent as focalizer; Adam rarely, if ever, focalizes. Biblical language—if it is used at all—tends to be used more for dialogue, where it functions as quoted hieratic register, than for narrative. The traditional religious retellings that we have examined, such as Lindvall (1991) and Beers (1976), tend to use a high proportion of demotic register for both dialogue and narrative—that, is contemporary idiomatic language. This strategy aims at making the content accessible to a young audience and in making the links between the biblical text and readers' lives explicit. More literary retellings, such as De la Mare and Baldwin, combine hieratic register for character dialogue with epic register for the narrative discourse.

## THE AUTHORITY PARADIGM

Representations of the Fall as constructing a paradigm for hierarchical relationships between individuals and God predominate in traditional religious retellings where the temptation constitutes an appeal to Eve's envy or greed, and transgression is depicted as an act of disobedience. In most versions Adam and Eve are simply told not to eat from the Tree of Knowledge, so God's authority is represented as arbitrary and unmotivated. In Beers's retelling, "Don't Eat That!" (1976, pp. 14–17), the moral function of the story is given emphasis by the title and by the repetition of the prohibition at least four times throughout what is a relatively short retelling. The discourse used for both narration and dialogue constructs the relationship of Adam and Eve to God according to a hierarchical schema for child/parent relationships. God's interdiction is couched in the discourse of a stereotypic parental prohibition—the fruit "would not be good for" them—and the language with which Adam and Eve try to shift the blame when questioned by God is stereotypically childlike (p. 16). The moral of the story, that disobedience leads to punishment, is given emphasis by the ending, in which Adam and

Eve are "sorry" (stated twice) that they had not obeyed God (p. 17), and by the questions that follow. By presupposing only one answer, the questions make the moral of the story quite explicit—that Adam and Eve are punished for their greed and disobedience.

"Don't Eat That!" is followed by a contemporary reversion, "Mrs. Fry's Pies," in which Bobo attempts to steal a blueberry pie from a neighbor. There is no overt textual interdiction here, but the story conventions and the disapproval of the other children instantiate a cultural schema whereby stealing is interdicted. Further, the isomorphism between the stories (taking the fruit and attempting to steal the pie) limits the transgressive action to stealing because of greed. The reversion and the questions that follow also implicitly assert a figural reading of the Fall: Bobo's punishment (he doesn't get any pie at all) is the negative correlative for the other children's reward (they receive a second pie to share), but Bobo (and readers) can attain forgiveness and salvation through repentance. The second pie, served topped with ice cream, metonymically signifies the other tree in the Garden, the Tree of Life.

While it is still a traditional religious retelling, Lindvall's version of the Fall reshapes the ideological implications of the story by omitting God's curses (1985, pp. 16–19). The narrative moves directly from Eve and Adam about to eat the fruit to a depiction of them working hard in another garden, now of thorns and thistles. The effect of these omissions is to shift the responsibility for action entirely away from God and to stress the human characters' moral responsibilities. Adam and Eve's fate is the consequence of their actions, rather than punishment for their disobedience. Theologically, the retelling implies a Christian Protestant interpretation of the story, but ideologically it also preempts humanist transformations of the story which substitute hierarchical human-divine relationships with human intersubjective responsibility. Similarly, in *The Curse of Cain,* Southall's (1968) novelistic version of the first nine books of *Genesis,* neither God nor the serpent is represented directly. Eve's dialogue with the serpent is recounted retrospectively by Eve to Adam, who does not believe that the serpent can speak, and Adam's dialogues with God are recounted by Adam to Eve, with whom God has not spoken. Thus the focus of the narrative is more on human thought and action than on supernatural interdiction and intervention, but the gender paradigm is also implicit here too in that the first strategy suggests an identification between Eve and the serpent—and hence between women and temptation—and the second implies that there are different schemata for how men and women relate to God.

In his more literary retelling of the Fall, Dickinson (1980) uses framing strategies to contextualize his narrator's telling of the story within a hierarchical paradigm wherein the story reflects the cultural situation of the act of narration. It is told by a Hebrew in exile, servant to a Babylonian nobleman, at an open-air feast. Thus the narrator draws analogies between the Garden of Eden and the nobleman's garden and between the hierarchical social relations between Adam and God and between a slave and the nobleman in both gardens.

## THE GENDER PARADIGM

Traditional retellings usually follow the Judaeo-Christian tradition which stresses Eve's initiating role in the Fall. Retellings by Beers and Lindvall both focus primarily on Eve's temptation and transgression. The narratives of both texts omit Adam's eating of the fruit, although this story detail must be inferred by readers as occurring within a temporal gap in the narrative for the narratives to cohere. Beers's text uses character-focalized narration and indirect discourse to represent Eve's thoughts, feelings, and motivations for action. Her point of view is, however, mostly trivialized, as in "She had never heard of good and evil before. It sounded like fun to know more about that" (p. 15). These narrative techniques also locate the source of temptation within Eve. While the serpent is represented in the text, Eve is already looking at the fruit before the serpent speaks and her temptation is represented as a struggle between (physical) desire—"she wanted to eat the fruit more than anything else in the garden"—and conscience—"she felt bad doing it, for God had told her not to." Thus it is Eve's own desire that tempts her rather than the serpent. These features implicitly construct Eve as the initiator of the Fall and hence as having primary responsibility. Baldwin's retelling also uses focalized narration to locate the source of temptation within Eve— though here it is the serpent who focalizes, "he knew that she wanted to taste it" (1895, p. 10).

The illustration for Lindvall's retelling, "Adam and Eve Disobey God" (1985, pp. 16–17), uses pictorial strategies to construct Eve as the primary instigator, depicting her in the foreground gazing at the fruit. In the written text, however, the narratee is directed to focalize, as in "See that fruit in Eve's hand" (p. 16). The narrative uses direct address to a narratee and present tense narration to situate the narratee (and the implied reader) in Eve's position at precisely the moment just prior to her sin: "Now she will eat [the fruit]." Again, though the text makes it clear that Adam also eats the fruit, the focus is entirely on Eve and the present moment of narration. In both of these traditional religious retellings Eve's role and responsibility for events is implicitly given emphasis. Underlying this emphasis are conventional Christian interpretations of the story, which see it as constructing a paradigm for male-female relations and as entailing schemata for the construction and representation of male and female sexuality. However, both texts displace the sexual dimension of Eve's desire, encoding her temptation instead as motivated by physical appetite. It is, of course, not unusual in children's texts for concupiscence to be expressed as greed for food rather than as sexual appetite.

Literary retellings of the Fall, such as de la Mare's "The Fall from Grace" (1961), stress the sexual dimension of Eve's desire and her "fall from grace," though this is mostly implicit in the discursive and narrative strategies used by de la Mare. He follows Milton's *Paradise Lost* in constructing the serpent as a primary focalizer in the temptation scene. His elevated literary register is also resonant of Milton, as is the characterization of Eve, as when, for example, she is described admiring her reflection in the water. It is more usual in retellings for Eve to focalize the temptation scene, so that readers are aligned with her while it is played out. Instead, Eve is here depicted almost entirely as she is seen by the serpent. Further, the relationship between Eve and the serpent is represented as implicitly sexual through these focalization strategies. Both are described in visual terms which stress their physicality and sensuality and which suggest sexual undertones in their body language: Eve "sat sleeking her hair" while the serpent is "rippling" and "rimpling" his scales (p. 28). This mutual preening, combined with literary echoes of Milton's characterization of Eve in *Paradise Lost,* implies that Eve's fall is predetermined by her sexuality. The actual dialogue in this episode is quite close to the biblical text, but there are additions to the serpent's speech, in particular his flattery of Eve and the sexual overtones of his language, as in "for even though thou share it not with me, thou hast thine own secret wisdom" (p. 28).

Eve's transgression is also depicted as implicitly sexual. Her eating of the fruit, and its effects, is described in terms evocative of sexual orgasm and postcoital lassitude: "She tasted and did eat, and shuddering at its potency that coursed her veins, she stayed without motion and as if asleep. With her long gentle hand she drew back her hair that lay heavy as gold upon her shoulders, and supple as the serpent himself languished in her own beauty" (p. 31). Hence the knowledge of good and evil is equated with sexual awakening and Eve's consciousness of her own sexuality. The description of the tree itself, with its branches "burdened" with "ripening and ripe" fruit, is also replete with sexual connotations. The tree is described in terms of its effect on Eve, "ravishing her eyes" and making "her heart pine within her" (p. 31), but because the narrative at this point is focalized by Eve it is suggested that the description is a projection of her own desire. Again, the effect of these techniques is to attribute moral responsibility for the Fall to Eve and to imply the sexual nature of that fall.

There are two other main variations unique to de la Mare's version: normally, the Tree of Knowledge is readily accessible to Eve, and she is conventionally depicted as eating the fruit on an impulse. Here, Eve and the serpent make a long and symbolic journey through rugged terrain to reach the tree. This journey is narrated from Eve's point of view, and there is an emphasis on its strangeness and difficulty as they trek through weird and hidden parts of the garden. The elevated emotive register used to narrate the journey forges a genric link with romance and gothic conventions, as in "and in silence they continued on their way going up now through the secret places of the Garden, and hidden in a shade so deep no star of night could pierce it, or the moon shine in" (pp. 29–30). The combination of terms such as "silence," "secret places," and "hidden in a shade" is typical of the discourse of gothic fiction, and here the semantic scope of the language evokes a vague sense of foreboding and impending doom which is compounded by the echo of *Macbeth,* I, iv, 51–52 ("Stars, hide your fires! Let not light see my black and deep desires"). Symbolically, Eve's journey conveys the momentousness of her decision to eat the fruit and the extent of her subsequent fall. However, it is also an inversion of conventional images of the arduous way to salvation, images familiar to de la Mare's young readers because they structure religious narratives such as *Pilgrim's Progress,* from which they are borrowed, into more secular texts. Thus Eve's journey to damnation, which takes her almost to the Tree of Life, typologically prefigures the way to salvation.

## FEMALE INTELLECT AND REVERSIONS OF MASCULINIST METANARRATIVES

Traditional Judaeo-Christian interpretations of the Fall, especially fundamentalist Christian readings, have stressed the ideological function of the story in circumscribing conventional social roles and relationships for men and women. Key story elements used to support such arguments are the creation of Eve from Adam (*Genesis* 2:18–24); Eve's role in initiating the Fall, wherein she is conventionally characterized as weak, susceptible to temptations of a sensual nature, and/or the temptress of Adam; and the gender-specific curses pronounced by God, in which it is decreed that women are to bear children and be subservient to their husbands (*Genesis* 3:16). Needless to say, interpretations of the Bible which see it as proscribing and endorsing a gender differentiation in which women take an inferior place and a subservient role to men are problematic for contemporary humanists and feminists. Attempts to undermine or subvert these assumptions in retellings and reversions for children are fraught with difficulties, however, because the basic story components carry with them a tradition of cultural interpretation. In replicating the content of the story, there is always a risk of replicating the metanarratives that the micro-discoursal patterning of the story conventionally implies. An alternative is to omit or reformulate these story features and thereby evade traditional masculinist metanarratives. Three retellings which seek to do this are Hutton's picture book version, *Adam and Eve,* Bach and Exum's retelling in *Moses' Ark,* and Dickinson's retelling in *City of Gold.*

Hutton's version of the Fall is particularly interesting because the text and pictures construct a dialogue between traditional masculinist interpretations of Eve which represent her in the role of temptress and hence stress her sexuality, and less traditional interpretations which seek to minimize culturally constructed gender differences. Hutton's strategy is to omit from the verbal text those elements which conventionally ascribe assumptions about male and female roles and relationships, namely Eve's status as a "helpmeet" for Adam (*Genesis* 2:18), Adam's comments about Eve—"This at last is bone of my bones and flesh of my flesh; she shall be called Woman, because she was taken out of Man. Therefore a man leaves his father and his mother and cleaves to his wife, and they become one flesh" (*Genesis* 2:23–24), and the last two phrases of God's curse on Eve—"yet your desire shall be for your husband, and he shall rule over you" (*Genesis* 3:16). The verbal text is otherwise virtually straight biblical quotation (*RSV*). But while the verbal text successfully evades masculinist interpretations of Eve, assumptions underlying these interpretations are quite overtly reinscribed in the pictorial text where visual representations of Eve stress the sensuality of the female body and the sexual connotations of her association with the serpent. The temptation scene, for example, depicts Eve from behind, her head bowed and her arms in a position of supplication, facing the serpent whose body is entwined around her legs (see Plate 1). This same image of Eve is repeated in the scene in which God confronts Adam and Eve after they have eaten the fruit. Again Eve is facing God (who is in the position occupied by the serpent in the previous scene), again she is seen from behind, her head bowed and arms in position of supplication (in contrast, Adam's head is raised to face God), and the serpent is positioned behind and to the right of Eve, its body crossing over and entwining the shadow of her legs. In other illustrations of Eve, the play of light and dark on her body stresses her physical sensuality in contrast to Adam.

In this way, the visual and verbal texts of Hutton's retelling produce a clash of ideologies, which is reflected by a corresponding clash between the discourses of pictures and text. As virtual straight quotation the written text functions as authoritative (hieratic) discourse. The pictorial technique, however, is more unconventional for the subject matter. The watercolor illustrations are impressionistic in style and depict pastoral scenes, whereas biblical illustrations for children are usually in a realist style, and hence "serious" in tone, though Hutton does conform to conventions in depicting the

*Plate 1. Eve and the Serpent. Reprinted with the permission of Margaret K. McElderry Books, an imprint of Simon & Schuster Children's Publishing Division, from* Adam and Eve, *written and illustrated by Warwick Hutton. Copyright ©1987 by Warwick Hutton.*

garden as lush, exotic, and ambivalently idyllic. The presence of the serpent in many pictures, often almost obscured in a corner, preempts the Fall. Thematically, Hutton's *Adam and Eve* is a text about the human condition, and his pictorial techniques—the treatment of light and shade, composition, and viewpoint—stress the human drama of the story, ascribing it with heroic and romantic significance. The use of distal viewpoints accentuates the contrast between human figures and the immense landscape that surrounds them—conventional pictorial techniques for conveying fatalism and existential angst. Combined with the emotive use of light and dark, these conventions thereby convey a sense of the powerlessness of human beings in relation to (inhuman) nature or an omnipotent God—Hutton's representation throughout of God as a glowing white space heightens this sense of the unknowable God.

The versions of the Fall by Bach and Exum (1989) and Dickinson (1980) use similar strategies to undermine conventional masculinist interpretations of the story. It is conventional for retellings to distinguish between the motivations of Eve and Adam through an opposition between the sensual and the intellectual. For example, Hutton's portrait-style illustrations for this same scene reproduce a cliché by depicting a wide-eyed Eve sensually devouring the fruit while Adam contemplates the fruit he holds, his eyes narrowed in thought. By contrast, in both these versions the temptation constitutes an appeal primarily to Eve's intellect rather than to her physical appetite, sexual, or sensual nature. In Bach and Exum's version, while Eve does have the primary narrative function—she is the primary focalizer and she initiates the action, by entering into dialogue with the serpent and by taking the fruit from the tree and giving it to Adam—both Adam and Eve are present in the temptation scene and both "look up at the tree" (p. 12). The nature of Eve's temptation in this version is sensual (she appreciates the beauty of the tree and the smell and sight of the fruit appeals to her senses) but also intellectual: she considers the serpent's arguments and her actions are motivated by intellectual desire, the desire for wisdom and knowledge. In contrast, Adam is depicted as simply looking at the fruit "without curiosity" (p. 13); his actions lack either physical or intellectual motivation. By these strategies, Bach and Exum dismantle the conventional gendered opposition between the sensual and the rational.

In Dickinson's retelling the sensual aspect of Eve's desire is simply omitted and Eve's desire for knowledge is couched in language which is both ambiguous and intertextual. When she comes across the serpent gazing at its reflection on the surface of a stream and asks what it is studying, it replies, "I am considering why I am as I am" (p. 15). The reply echoes both the biblical description of God (*Exodus* 3:14 "I am that I am") and the first premise of Descartes's theory of knowledge (*cogito ergo sum*), and it implies that the knowledge that Eve (and the serpent) seek is specifically self-knowledge, or consciousness. This idea is continued in the changes that occur in the garden after both Eve and Adam have eaten the fruit, as the animals begin to behave according to their "nature" the lion stalks and kills the lamb. It is not so much that the garden changes as a result of their action (that is, by eating of the tree they bring death into the world), but that the world appears differently as a result of a change in their perception of it. That they now see "with the eyes of knowledge" (p. 15) implies that what was seen before was seen with ignorance and was hence an idyllic illusion. Therefore, their acquired knowledge not only changes the way they see the world, but that world also changes as a result of the change in the way it is seen. Dickinson is also thereby humanizing the myth of the Fall in that Adam's and Eve's fall and expulsion into a world of contingency is represented as the consequence of their acquisition of knowledge rather than a punishment for disobedience. Thus, like Hutton, Dickinson is using the story to make a statement about the human condition—specifically, about human frailty in an uncertain and contingent world.

These two collections by Bach and Exum and Dickinson are also contextualized historically. Dickinson does this by constructing a narrative frame for each story that reflects the social and cultural situation in which stories might have been retold. By contextualizing the stories in *Moses' Ark* historically and linguistically, Bach and Exum again undermine conventional masculinist interpretations of the Fall story. As they note, the Hebrew word *'adam,* from which the proper name Adam is derived, can refer to a man, but it most often is used as a collective term for humanity, and it is not clear in the original Hebrew texts whether the first human created is male or simply a human being in the generic sense (pp. 15–16). Thus, in their retelling the sex of the first human is not specified until the creation of the second, and neither human being is actually named—they are simply referred to as "the man" and "the woman." A second aspect of terminology they comment on is their use of the word "side" instead of the more conventional translation, "rib," to describe the creation of woman from man. They see the term as being "intentionally ambiguous" and the possible interpretation they give for the text's meaning—that "when the side of the human is taken away to form the woman, what remains after divine surgery is a man" (p. 16)— again undercuts conventional interpretations which see the formation of woman as a subtractive process, whereby the end result, "woman," is less than "man."[1] Finally, Bach and Exum also comment on the historical and social context of the story. They explicitly deny the conventional moral interpretations of the story which see the curses pronounced on the man and the woman as a "justification for the subordination of woman to man" (p. 16). Instead, they see these curses as reflecting the social and cultural context in which the story was told and written. By historicizing the story in this way, they refuse the implication that the content of the story transcends its context or is socially prescriptive in its intent.

## BIBLE STORIES ABOUT WOMEN

The ideological power of selecting and commenting on biblical material in specific ways can be seen in the companion volume to *Moses' Ark, Miriam's Well,* a collection of stories about women in the Bible. The introduction to the collection opens with the assertion that "most of the Bible's stories center on men" and "women, if they appear at all, are minor characters," sometimes becoming "the focus of attention for a brief moment in a man's story," or appearing "on the scene only to disappear from the story after they have served their purposes" (p. xiii). In retelling these women's stories, Bach and Exum aim to "give the women a voice where the Bible often relegates them to silence and to tell the stories from their point of view" (p. xiv). Some of these stories are also given a coherent sense of story structure where it is lacking—mostly through the construction of a narrative voice—and gaps in the biblical accounts are filled by details about customs and social, economic, and political conditions supplied by Rabbinic materials and historical research or gleaned from other parts of the Bible itself. The concluding chapter of this collection comprises seven short stories told from the point of view of biblical women who are either not named in the Bible, are not the primary focus of a narrative, and/or are traditionally disparaged as foolish or wicked, and hence have prompted some well-known antifeminist sentiment—for example, Delilah, Job's wife, Lot's wife, and Jezebel. Bach and Exum have selected stories which "show the range and variety of roles open to women in biblical times" (p. xv). They have deliberately omitted stories in which there is violence committed against women, choosing instead to retell stories in which women are portrayed in "positive roles," as "leaders, not victims" (p. xviii). However, they do also include the story of possibly one of the most maligned women in biblical history, Jezebel, whose story we will return to shortly.

Moses's sister Miriam lends her name to the title of the collection and, as Bach and Exum note, she "has no story in the sense of a narrative that focuses on her." Instead, Bach and Exum have "woven" her story from scattered fragments in *Exodus* and *Numbers,* using a fictive narrator, Dinah, to give the story continuity (p. xiv). This metaphor of weaving together a continuous narrative out of scraps of stories informs the overall structure of the collection as a coherent narrative of biblical women woven out of fragments. All of the stories in *Miriam's Well* are from the Old Testament, and like other collections of this kind the material is for the most part presented chronologically, though chronology is disrupted in the last chapter, "A Mosaic for Miriam." However, the narrative focus for each of the stories is primarily female, and stories are narrated either in the voice of or from the viewpoint of the female characters. As we suggested earlier, any reading of Bible story is going to be informed by dominant cultural attitudes and ideologies at least to some extent. Patrilineal chronologies form a key component of the interpretive schemata that are brought to Bible story. One effect of *Miriam's Well* is to construct an alternative female chronology, which in turn implies an alternative feminist metanarrative implicitly read against the more familiar male chronology and metanarrative. The characters listed on the contents page of *Miriam's Well* are Sarah, Hagar, Rebekah, Leah and Rachel, Miriam, Eluma and Hannah, Naomi and Ruth, Michal, Abigail, the Wise Women of Tekoa, and Abel, Esther, and Judith. Such a list evokes in its absence a (patrilineal) list of male counterparts, the corresponding male names (Abraham, Isaac, Jacob and Esau, Moses, Samson, Samuel, and David) which dominate the contents pages of more conventional collections such as Kyles's *Classic Bible Stories*. These male characters do appear in *Miriam's Well,* but, because the stories are told from the viewpoint of the women concerned, male characters are positioned in the narrative in secondary positions—Jacob, for example, is "Rebekah's son." Thus they occupy similar positions to many women in Bible stories, whose position is defined as the spouse or child of another. In this way, the collection foregrounds the way that male characters and masculine concerns typically dominate traditional Bible story collections.

Of the stories told in *Miriam's Well* only those of Naomi and Ruth, Esther, and Judith[2] are usually told as stories specifically about women from their point of view, though, interestingly, these three stories are excluded from Kyles's collection. However, where these stories are retold for children in conventional collections, they are frequently subsumed within a metanarrative which is either masculinist, Christian, or traditional humanist—very few compilers or adapters have seen these stories as specifically about women or about issues that concern women. The story of Ruth and Naomi, for example, is often subsumed to a Christian or humanist metanarrative which sees it as a story about human friendship and loyalty—as opposed to a more specific loyalty between women—and the need for cross-cultural exchange and trust. In a religious retelling by Pewtress (1943) the story is subsumed within a metanarrative structured around the Protestant work ethic.[3] Many of the story details are omitted, including the journey to Bethel and Ruth's famous statement of loyalty to Naomi, "Where you go, I shall go." Instead Ruth's loyalty is exemplified by her capacity for hard work whereby she provides food for Naomi and herself, and for which she is ultimately rewarded with marriage to Boaz in an ending which omits Boaz's obligation to Naomi and Ruth. The moral of the story is spelled out in the prayer that follows it, which opens, "Please, God, bless all the people who work so hard that we may have food to eat" (p. 30). Another retelling, by Asimov (1972), assumes that both the original text and retelling will have a primary and common didactic intent, namely to guard against racism and suspicion of foreigners. He includes extensive interpretive commentary which stresses the didactic function of the story, and closes with a plea to modern readers to "look at each person closely, as an individual with his own virtues and faults, and judge him for that and not for anything else" (pp. 101–102). The reversion to the masculine pronoun is indicative of the way that the story has been subsumed into a universalizing humanist metanarrative. In contrast, Bach and Exum's retelling is situated within a metanarrative which is feminist in focus and which constructs meaning as contingent, and hence produced within a particular cultural context, rather than universal. In their commentary on their retelling of the book of Ruth they stress that this is a story about issues specific to women of that time: it is a "story of one woman's courage and loyalty to another in a time when a woman's well-being depended on having a husband and sons to care for her" (1991, p. 78).

*Miriam's Well* is not merely some kind of young woman's companion to the Bible. Ideologically, a primary effect of the collection is to undermine stereotyped constructions of women in retellings and interpretations of biblical stories and to implicitly critique patriarchal social structures by focusing on the implications that these social structures have had for women. The content of the stories is not substantially different from traditional retellings, though there are some divergences because the pre-texts are Hebrew sources rather than English translations. However, the selection of stories specifically about women has implications for the content and thematic concerns of the collection as a whole which run counterpoint to other more traditional masculinist collections. Many of the stories center on particularly female subject matter, especially the need imposed by society on women to marry and bear children—as in the stories of Sarah, Leah and Rachel, Eluma and Hannah—and they depict women in brave, defiant, and often altruistic roles—for example, Rebekah, Miriam, Michal, Esther, and Judith. Other stories juxtapose wise women with foolish men—Abigail and Nabal, Judith and Holofernes, for example. By telling their stories from the point of view of the women the narrative undermines conventional biblical interpretations of them.

Perhaps the most remarkable retelling in this collection is the story of Jezebel. As with Miriam, Jezebel does not really have a story in the Bible in the sense of a coherent narrative that focuses on her, but appears merely as a player in the stories of Ahab, Elijah, and Elisha. Biblical interpretation, however, has emphasized her role in introducing the worship of foreign gods (Ba'al and Asherah) in Judah,[4] her killing of Israelite prophets and support of the prophets of Ba'al and Asherah, and her role in the death of Naboth. Although episodes in Elijah's story are frequently retold for children,[5] Jezebel usually either does not appear or is only mentioned in passing. However, where she is mentioned or given a role in the narrative she is always portrayed as wicked and her foreignness is emphasized, though her rather gruesome fate is often omitted. Kyles's *Classic Bible Stories*, for example, includes Jezebel in retelling the story of Elijah, but the narrative is shaped around Elijah and closes with Elisha taking the place of Elijah (2 *Kings* 2), thereby omitting Jezebel's role in the death of Naboth and her own death. Kyles follows the biblical account of Elijah (1 *Kings* 17–2 *Kings* 2) fairly closely, but stresses Jezebel's wickedness and her role in encouraging the cult of Ba'al.

Bach and Exum's collection is unique in that Jezebel's story is retold from her point of view, is told sympathetically, and she provides the primary narrative focus. The narrative stresses the extent to which Jezebel has been culturally displaced and is alienated within Israelite society. She is depicted in the opening of the narrative "longing for a view of the sea" while staring out of her window "at the rolling hills of this strange land whose culture was so different from her own" (p. 151), and she introduces the prophets of Ba'al as one of many actions aimed at easing her "longing for her own country" (p. 152). She has also brought with her objects from her homeland as well as such Phoenician skills as techniques for dying cloth purple. She is represented as an educated woman who spends her time studying the books of laws of the land of Judah, and is thus contrasted with her husband, Ahab, who prefers "holding feasts to holding discussions" (p. 152). In this way, Jezebel's actions are represented as motivated by loneliness, alienation, and boredom rather than by a wicked intent, and furthermore her story illustrates a process of cultural exchange between husband and wife: Jezebel reads of the Hebrew God and in exchange teaches her husband about her own God. This exchange is implicitly unequal in that she studies and teaches, and hence she appears better educated than her husband, and perhaps Israelite society seems less civilized than her own. Her actions in plotting the death of Naboth are also depicted sympathetically as something that she does for her husband. Bach and Exum's retelling also emphasizes the child-parent associations implicit in the relation between Jezebel and Ahab through the use of demotic register for Jezebel's dialogue, as in "Some fine king you are! Get out of bed and eat your dinner" (p. 154).

## MODERN RETELLINGS AND REVERSIONS OF BIBLE STORY

Modern secular retellings and reversions of Bible story for children vary in how closely they are linked to their pre-text. A common strategy is to resituate a familiar Bible story in another, usually modern, historical context, and to thereby retell the story within an alternative metanarrative. This strategy is often used to retell the story of the Flood either as another version of the biblical story, as Harris (1968) does, or as a kind of modern sequel to the pre-text, a second flood—for example, Burnford (1973), Lively (1978), or Mayne (1990). The Flood story has apocalyptic associations and contemporary retellings frequently link these with current ecological disaster metanarratives. Another strategy is the construction of bricolage texts which utilize story motifs borrowed from a biblical pre-text, but combined in innovative ways. Such texts are not strictly speaking "retellings," or even "reversions," though they are genrically and thematically linked with their pre-texts. In this section we will look first at secular reversions of the Flood, and then at three bricolage texts: Lively's *The Voyage of QV66*, Garfield's *The Pleasure Garden*, and Dickinson's *Eva*.

As many commentators have pointed out, the Flood myth is one of the oldest and most common stories across a range of distant cultures and countries. Harrison and Stuart-Clark (1983) compile a number of these versions in *Noah's Ark*, a collection of flood stories for children. The narratorial situation in which Dickinson's retelling is placed in *City of Gold* draws attention to the multiplicity of flood stories and the intertextuality and instability of any one version, when the Hebrew narrator mentions that he might borrow some details from the earlier Babylonian version, *The Epic of Gilgamesh*. However, the biblical story of Noah is the most commonly retold version, and it is the most commonly retold Old Testament story for children, with an extensive corpus of religious retellings ranging from picture books to novels. We will only deal with this corpus in a cursory fashion here, as we wish to concentrate instead on secular reversions of the Flood story which position it within the context of ecological disaster. It is necessary, though, to look briefly at the conventional ideological functions of the story within a religious paradigm in order to see how the story is translated and transformed ideologically within a secular paradigm.

The myth of the Flood has accrued some resilient associations especially through its elaboration within Christian typologies. In traditional Christian retellings of the biblical Flood, the story usually has a double typological significance, developed from the images of "washing clean" and beginning a new life, in which it prefigures, first, Christian baptism and hence salvation, and second, the Christian Apocalypse. Noah has been conventionally interpreted as a type of Christ, "emerging from the ark/sarcophagus that floated on a watery grave just as Christ left the tomb" (Piehl, 1989, p. 41) and the Flood itself has apocalyptic associations (flood now, fire next). Noah's unquestioning obedience and faith in God is conventionally depicted as exemplary Christian behavior. The covenant of God symbolized by the olive branch, the dove, and the rainbow conventionally prefigures Christ's promise of salvation. Christian typological readings of these kinds are activated in traditional retellings for children through the associative connotations of the discourses used. For example repeated references to "washing the world clean," "cleansing," the "newness" of the world after the Flood, and emphasis on God's covenant in Kyles (1987), Pewtress (1943), and McLean (1990) ascribe to the Flood a metaphoric function that prefigures Christian baptism and salvation. The presence of a Christian metanarrative is signaled quite overtly in, for example, French's *Rise, Shine* (1989), where in the penultimate illustration, depicting people of diverse races approaching the gates of Heaven, is a reprise of the animals entering the Ark. Now, however, the scene interrogates the traditional typological link in order to reject an Old Testament ideology in which God's actions are motivated by considerations of race and culture, and the text reinforces this: "Tell St. Peter, 'Don't be so choosy.'"

Many of these retellings are often rather vague about what exactly the world is to be cleansed of and omit references to the fate of the people left behind, thereby eliding the apocalyptic associations of the story. Instead they focus on the consequences of the Flood and the covenant for the key characters, Noah and his family. In this way, these retellings imply a New Testament concept of a God of forgiveness, as opposed to the Old Testament God of retribution and punishment. However, God's action in causing the Flood implies an Old Testament concept of God as retributive and punitive, and the Flood itself also has associations with the Apocalypse and the Day of Judgment. Beers's retelling, for example, closes with Noah and his family still on the ark, and the effect of this curtailment, leaving out the rainbow and God's covenant, is to omit the conventional association with forgiveness and salvation. In this way, God's "promise" to Noah is the Flood itself, and the story thereby evades conventional Hebrew interpretations of the story and limits Christian interpretations so that the Flood simply prefigures the apocalypse. In this version the association between the Flood and the apocalypse is implicitly evoked by references to the people left outside the ark, whereas, by comparison, it is made quite explicit in de la Mare's literary retelling through references to the "day of judgement" (p. 45), the "trumpeting wind" (p. 49), "strange lamentations, as if from bodily wanderers" (p. 47), and the representation of the post-Flood world as a new Eden (p. 56).

In secular versions of the Flood, this double typological significance is subsumed into narratives of ecological disaster. The motif of the ark has a long and varied literary history, and more recently has been used in a range of popular culture texts for children and teenagers, such as various *Dr. Who* series, Adams's *The Hitch Hiker's Guide to the Galaxy*, and Elton's film *Stark*. The narrative structure of the Flood myth follows a causal pattern: human wickedness leads to the destruction of the earth (instigated by God); human obedience and faith leads to salvation and redemption of the earth and the human species. In terms of character and action, the key narrative function in the Flood myth is God. Noah is the exemplum of obedience and faith and his actions are entirely determined by God. Reversions of the myth secularize it by substituting some other story component for the character-function conventionally occupied by God, which thereby recasts the story within a secular and, usually, humanistic paradigm. By taking God out of the scheme of things, events in the Flood story are ascribed with human cause and consequence. In an ironic inversion of the Flood myth in *The Hitch Hiker's Guide*, the function of God is performed by the dominant classes in society, who fabricate an impending apocalypse in order to rid society of whole categories of people who are neither creative nor productive—hairdressers, telephone sanitizers, public relations executives, and so on, otherwise described as "useless bloody loonies" (p. 272). They are loaded onto a spaceship, known as the "B-Ark," and launched into space. In ecological reversions of the story either nature or humanity itself is substituted for the character-function conventionally occupied by God—either way humanity is depicted as the cause of its own destruction.

Burnford's *Mr. Noah and the Second Flood* (1973), Unwin and Petty's *Wake Up, Mr. Noah!* (1990), Wildsmith's *Professor Noah's Spaceship* (1980), and Burningham's *Oi! Get Off Our Train* (1989) are all modern sequels to the biblical flood story set within the context of contemporary ecological disaster—the modern version of the Apocalypse. In each of these texts the

Flood story is a pre-text which constructs an implied reader position dependent upon recognizing the prior text lying behind the modern story. In *Mr. Noah and the Second Flood* the original Noah's great-great-many-times-grandson, Noah, and his family are farmers living on a high mountain. They are depicted according to the 1970s ideal of subsistence living; they have no modern machinery and live entirely off the land. Their only contact with the outside world is through the bank manager who comes once a year. Noah builds a second ark to save the animals and his family when a second flood, caused by the melting of the icecaps due to global warming, is imminent. The rest of the human race has built its own ark—a rocket base from which to colonize the Moon now that Earth is no longer able to sustain life. In this scheme, named (ironically) "Operation Noah," no animals will be taken, only humans. While the role of God in causing the first flood is assumed, the second flood is entirely the consequence of human activity—in causing pollution, over-population, and so on—rather than a punishment for "wickedness," as in the biblical version. Thus, towards the close of the novel, the narrative takes an unusual turn when Noah decides to discontinue the human species on earth by closing the ark door on his sons and daughters-in-law. This close is fairly pessimistic about the possibility of redeeming the human race and hence the possibility of salvation, though the Moon does appear in the sky "for all the world like another Ark" (p. 94).

In *Wake Up, Mr. Noah!*, Noah is still living in the ark, which is halfway up a mountain and has become a house. The narrative opens with the arrival of an oil-spattered seabird who tells Noah of the pollution in the world while Noah cleans the oil from his feathers. Parrot and Dove set out on a journey around the world to see how other animals are faring and they send the various animals they find back to Noah. As in *Mr. Noah and the Second Flood*, human actions have caused the present situation—thoughtlessness, pollution, poaching, deforestation, and so on. Insofar as human beings are responsible for the earth's destruction, God is completely absent from the story. In God's absence, however, Noah takes on the function of God in trying to save the animals—though the close of the narrative makes it clear that saving the animals is collaborative and can't be achieved by one person. Unwin and Petty's ecological sequel differs crucially from that of Burnford and from its biblical pre-text, in that there is no second flood and no apocalypse. Instead, the narrative has an open ending which disrupts the teleology of the biblical narrative structure and diverts the didactic intent of conventional biblical versions. Initially Noah starts to build another ark. However, as the Elephant and the Gorilla point out, a floating ark isn't much use to them in Africa, especially as there is no suggestion of a second flood.

An underlying implication here is that in the absence of a flood the ark would simply function as a kind of zoo in which to preserve the animal species outside of their natural habitat. Instead, Noah builds an Ark Park—a school in which children can learn how to "save the animals" in their own countries and hence avert the apocalyptic implications of the Flood story. In this way the narrative structure implicitly asserts the inadequacy of end-determined apocalyptic fictions which presuppose the possibility of a new world after the end, an assertion which is implicit in Noah's comment, "The children have much to learn . . . if they are still to inherit the earth" (pp. 25–26), and it firmly places responsibility for action with the human species, rather than any supernatural intervention.

The relationship of Burningham's *Oi! Get Off Our Train* to the Flood myth is more oblique than these other texts. The ark is now a train which travels across the world picking up endangered animals. Ideologically, Burningham's position is similar to that of Unwin and Petty in that the narrative has an open ending and there is no second flood and no God. Unwin and Petty's proposition that the future of many animal species lies in the education of children is taken further, however, by placing a young boy in the position of Noah, now a train driver.

The last group of texts that we will discuss in this chapter are what we have termed bricolage texts. These are not strictly speaking retellings nor reversions but are constructed intertextually from a range of generically linked story motifs and discursive elements; for example, Lively's *The Voyage of QV66* (1978), Mayne's *The Farm That Ran Out of Names* (1990), Hughes's *Tales of the Early World* (1988), and Garfield's *The Pleasure Garden* (1976). Mayne and Hughes offer illuminating examples of how their pre-textual materials can be turned to comic use. In essence, all of these bricolage texts are secular humanistic reversions; they retell stories which are intertextually linked with biblical pre-texts, but which, like the ecological reversions of the Flood we have just been discussing, resituate this biblical material within humanistic metanarratives. In doing so, texts construct a position from which to interrogate the ideologies of religious metanarratives. However, this is not simply a process of substituting one metanarrative for another. Instead it might be understood as a process of supplementation where each metanarrative is discreet and coherent—that is, it has an exchange value—but at the same time neither operates in isolation from the other. In other words, meaning is produced via a dialogic exchange between two ideological positions. It is a process that operates at the level of signification to simultaneously acknowledge and interrogate (and so reject) religious meanings. As we suggested in chapter 1, where a retelling or reversion replicates the content and mode of representation of its pre-text, there is a likelihood that old metanarratives will be replicated. In the case of these secular bricolage texts, simple replications are avoided through the substitution of humanistic metanarratives for religious metanarratives, but at the same time the operation of these humanistic metanarratives depends on the presence of religious metanarratives as a trace which must be both affirmed and rejected at the level of signification.

An examination of *The Voyage of QV66* and *The Pleasure Garden* illustrates something of the range of textual strategies employed in such bricolage texts to construct their dialogue between religious and humanistic meanings. Their strategies hark back to the discursive strategies of traditional and literary retellings of Bible story for children that we outlined in the introduction to this chapter. As we suggested, a common effect of the discursive strategies of retellings is that the potential significance of a story is limited within a specific interpretive metanarrative. Traditional retellings do this by limiting the play of meaning, and, hence, the possible interpretations of stories. Literary retellings can have the same effect by allowing a play of meaning which opens texts to metaphoric and allegorical readings, which are nonetheless contained within a Christian typological metanarrative. The intertexts of Lively's and Garfield's novels are also handled in this way, though the effect in both is to displace and thereby call into question the religious metanarrative and posit an alternative (humanistic) metanarrative.

In *The Voyage of QV66* intertextual discourses are incorporated as the nonsignifying signs of a Christian biblical tradition. The novel is a modern reversion of the Flood myth, in which England has been covered by water, all humans have disappeared, and the land is inhabited by wandering groups of animals. One such group finds a boat and journeys to London on a quest for the identity of one of their number, a monkey called Stanley. Motifs borrowed from the Flood myth and other biblical texts include the flood itself; the boat which unlike Noah's ark has no "Noah" and does have a tiller; the rainbow (p. 43); and numerous references to biblical texts, such as the Fall (p. 62), which occur primarily in the speech of Offa, a pigeon who, having been reared in Lichfield Cathedral, has read and quotes the Bible. However, the potential significance of these familiar and recognizable biblical motifs is limited, and they do not construct a coherent pattern of significance. Furthermore, while the Flood story lies behind Lively's text, the key narrative functions of the Flood myth are omitted or elided. As we were arguing earlier, in some reversions of the Flood God is omitted from the story, but the plot function that God performs within the narrative is filled by some other causal component—either the earth, nature, or humanity itself. In Lively's

reversion God and Noah are absent both as characters and as plot functions—hence, conventional moral ideologies ascribed to the myth are also
omitted. The teleology of the narrative structure is determined, not by the
flood itself, but by Stanley's quest for identity. Initially this quest takes the
form of a search for another like himself, but the novel closes with Stanley's
realization that his sense of a selfhood is constructed intersubjectively in relation to the other animals on the boat who are different from himself. In
this way, the narrative substitutes a humanistic quest for intersubjectivity for
the conventional religious metanarrative.

In contrast, the discursive strategies of *The Pleasure Garden* are closer
to those of the literary retellings we discussed earlier. As in de la Mare's
retellings, the discourse works primarily through producing an excess of signification which opens the text to metaphoric and allegorical readings. Biblical motifs abound in the setting and the discourse of the novel. The Mul-
berry Pleasure Garden is run by Mrs. Bray and Dr. Dormann, who employ
a team of street urchins to eavesdrop on patrons who are then selectively
blackmailed. The discourse of the novel is thick with religious symbolism
and metaphor and there are numerous allusions to the Garden of Eden and
the Fall—for example, "the revellers go out of the pleasure garden, out into
the black garden of pain" (p. 10). As in Lively's novel, these biblical motifs
do not construct a coherent pattern of religious significance, but their effect differs because, as in the example just quoted, they often seem weighted
with an excess of significances (see Hunt, 1980, pp. 235–237); the novel lacks
a thematic center if read simply as a Christian allegory. Instead, religious
images and themes are subsumed to Garfield's more complex humanistic
thematic concerns. He uses biblical language and images to evoke the simplified notions of good and evil associated with Eden and the Fall in order
to glance at the moral chaos that potentially underlies human existence, and
the precariousness of the social structures developed to maintain some sense
of moral purpose.

A novel which goes further still than *The Voyage of QV66* or *The
Pleasure Garden,* while drawing on the same biblical intertexts, is Dickinson's
*Eva* (1988b). *Eva* is in part a reversion of the *Genesis* story, which is signaled by the title and by references to an "Adam and Eve" cartoon that the
main character watches, and it is also genrically an example of post-disas-
ter apocalyptic fiction, a genre which has intertextual associations with biblical apocalyptic literature. However, as in Lively's novel, the semantic range
of these intertexts is limited by the narrative context in which they are incorporated. Human society in *Eva* is depicted as completely devoid of a sense
of spirituality and human beings are emotionally and socially isolated. Fur-

thermore, the novel's intertexts have in common teleological narrative structures which are at odds with the narrative structure of the novel, in which human civilization is depicted as simply winding down as the final outworking of evolutionary process. Humans are no longer fit to survive, and evolutionary development must begin again with another branch of the ape family. In this way, the conventional moral and mythic functions of the religious metanarratives underlying the intertexts are radically discounted.

As we have been arguing, biblical literature has enormous implications for the processes of retelling stories. It ranges from discourses which assume that meaning is predetermined and immanent, and the task of retelling is simply one of mediating authority-based significances, to discourses which construct biblical pre-texts as sites of contestation on which to argue out the grounds of human existence. In particular, the challenge has been thrown out by feminist and humanist conceptions of subjectivity and being-in-the-world, and they have often demonstrated shared objectives. In the next chapter we will examine classical mythology, where mainstream-mediating discourses have followed procedures similar to those in evidence for biblical literature. The responses of feminism and humanism, however, are now sharply divergent.

## NOTES

1. Bach and Exum's interpretation is reminiscent of Lillie Devereux Blake's interpretation of the naming of Woman in *The Woman's Bible* (Stanton, 1895; 1985): "'She shall be called Woman,' in the ancient form of the word Womb-man. She was man and more than man because of her maternity" (1985, p. 22).

2. The book of Judith is not included in either the Jewish or Protestant Bibles and is seldom retold for children.

3. Bottigheimer's (1993) study of eighteenth and nineteenth century children's Bibles has shown that the work ethic dominated exemplary Bible tales for children from about 1850 onward.

4. Jezebel has conventionally been credited with attempting to introduce her own Phoenician religion and the worship of the Tyrian Ba'al and his consort Asherah in Israel, though as Frymer-Kensky (1992) and Brenner (1992) have pointed out, the cult of Asherah (as mother goddess and consort of the Hebrew deity YHWH) is not Phoenician in origin (Frymer-Kensky, 1992, p. 157) and appears to have flourished as late as the sixth century B.C.E. without major opposition from the official monotheistic cult of YHWH (Brenner, 1992, p. 53).

5. Collections for children usually retell the stories of Elijah being fed by the ravens or of his encounter with the widow of Zarephath.

# 3   CLASSICAL MYTHOLOGY

## THE MYSTERY UNDERLYING EVERYDAY THINGS?

*Next to those old Romances, which were written in the Christian middle age, there are no fairy tales like these old Greek ones, for beauty, and wisdom, and truth, and for making children love noble deeds, and trust in God to help them through.*

—Charles Kingsley
Preface to *The Heroes* (1855)

*The Harpies were female demons inducted into the Powers of Darkness after the collapse of classical mythology.*

—Roger Zelazny and Robert Sheckly
*Bring Me the Head of Prince Charming* (1991)

A century after Kingsley addressed the children who were to read *The Heroes*— the boys who would learn to read Greek, and the girls who wouldn't— Robert Graves lamented in *The Greek Myths* (originally published in 1955) that the place of the classics in education had declined so far that "an educated person" was no longer expected to recognize references to classical mythology. Instead, "current knowledge of these myths is mostly derived from such fairy-story versions as Kingsley's *Heroes* and Hawthorne's *Tanglewood Tales*" (1960, p. 11). For Graves, then, myth had been stripped of significance and relegated to children's literature along with fairy/folk story, even though "English literature of the sixteenth to the nineteenth centuries cannot . . . be properly understood except in the light of Greek mythology," and "it is difficult to overestimate [the value of Greek myth] in the study of early European history, religion, and sociology."

Nearly half a century further on again, with educational systems seeming to make diminishing space for any of those aspects of precontemporary culture which Graves argued were illuminated by Greek myth, and with young readers able to choose from a vast and various selection of literary kinds, it would seem hardly surprising if classical myth had virtually disappeared even from children's literature. It hasn't, however, and though it clearly survives as a lesser genre, new retellings consistently appear. The interesting question for children's literature is not why the status of classical myth has declined, but why it has survived at all. A primary reason it does so, as with all the kinds of retold story we are considering in this book, is because of the power of story and the attraction many young readers feel towards strange alterities. Adults who produce the retellings, however, generally further assume that myths also perform important literary and social functions. As with Bible stories, a myth functions as a story with tangible links to a larger system or pattern of narratives, and this relational network guarantees that the specific story has a significance over and above mere story outcome: its meaning is determined by its relationship to a presumed whole. In other words, any particular example is always already interpretable as a moral fable or allegory whose significance is shaped by a powerful, sometimes indefinable, emotional supplement and by its articulation within culture. Parallels with biblical literature need to be handled carefully, because they exist partly by coincidence and partly because many Greek and Hebrew myths have a common origin (see Kirk, 1970), but parallels are reinforced in the retelling, whether by cultural or authorial practice, as the Judaeo/Christian tradition informs and reframes the classical. (In children's literature this is a one-way traffic, incidentally.) These literary and "constructed" links are what interest us here. Myths thus offer children privileged patterns of thinking, believing, and behaving which explain or suggest ways in which the self might relate to the surrounding world. The interrelationship of retold stories within a frame is a crucial part of this effect, and we will see in subsequent chapters that retellers of stories characteristically desire unifying frames. Of course such a frame on a simple level makes a volume feel unified and coherent, but its implications for the significance of stories is more powerful still.

For adults who retell stories from classical mythology, or who write about these retellings, a myth may have five kinds of significance, in addition to the pragmatic classroom function of filling gaps in children's literary knowledge. First, a myth is invested with value as *story* itself. That is, as a narrative which audiences may recognize as similar to other such narratives because it is patterned by archetypal situations and characterizations, a story transmits its latent value as a particular outworking of perennial human desires and destinies. The structural pattern itself signifies without needing to be interpreted, because the meaning lies in the repeatability and the deeply laid similarity amongst otherwise apparently diverse stories. All of the types of traditional story we examine in this book are liable to be subjected to such a story-only focus. Underlying it is a cultural assumption which could be explained according to a variety of theories—Jungian archetypes, Proppian morphologies, or Frye's mythic structuralism, for example—but few retellers engaged in reproducing story would go on to articulate it in such terms. Frye's suggestion that all literature is the "story of the loss and regaining of identity" (1964, p. 55) is attractive to the criticism of children's literature (because it is an obviously recurrent theme), and a very large number of the stories we discuss in subsequent chapters are readily reducible to that pattern (King Arthur; Ragnell, "the Loathly Lady"; Robin Hood; Marwen of *The Dragon's Tapestry;* Simba of *The Lion King;* the characters of *A Midsummer's Night's Dream;* and so on). We will not proceed in this direction, however, because we think that such reductiveness ultimately says too little about either the signifying potential of the narratives or the motives of the retellers.

In the discourse about classical myth, the latent value of story is apt to be expressed in the cliché that myths embody putatively timeless and universal significances, and this in turn is combined with the second significance (again a cliché) commonly attributed to classical myth, namely that it forms part of "our" cultural heritage. Thus in the foreword to his *Myths of the Greeks and Romans,* Grant argues that one of the values of classical myth is for understanding people in the past, as well as for understanding Western art, literature, and ways of thinking (1962, p. xvii). Similarly, in Roger Lancelyn Green's author's note appended to his contemporary retelling for "younger readers" (1958), Green adduces both a larger narrative system and the notion of cultural capital. On the one hand, he was attempting to "tell the tale of the Heroic Age as that single whole which the Greeks believed it to be," and to this end the stories are subsumed to a linear narrative pattern. On the other hand, the value and purpose he attached to the retelling of classical myth is explicit: "Their stories are a part of the world's heritage, they are part of the background of our literature, our speech, of our very thoughts. We cannot come to them too early, nor are we ever likely to outgrow them as we pass from such simple re-tellings as this to the Greek authors themselves. . . ." (pp. 200–201). In the different world pertaining at the end of the twentieth century, such a position can hardly be conceded without acknowledging that it is deeply problematic. Certainly, the underpinning assumptions about cultural capital have largely disappeared, but quite modern retellings still often lack any apparent awareness that the corollary production of subjective wholeness attributed to the influence of classical mythology is radically flawed by the individualism, imperialism, masculinism, and misogyny which pervade that mythology. In particular, classical mythology, as with biblical literature, is endemically produced by and for an androcentric community (Exum, 1993, p. 11). As a quite recent example, we point to Anthony Horowitz's *The Kingfisher Book of Myths and Legends* (1985), in which the ubiquitous presence of a contemporary demotic idiom only serves to foreground the replication of archaic social and political values.

The remaining attributed significances seem less obviously problematic. The third is that because myths are linked with religious urges and aspirations they express spiritual insights in oblique narrative form. Fourth, as narrativized expressions of impulses within the human unconscious they distill psychic truth. And fifth, subsuming elements of the first three into a modern configuration, myths facilitate intercultural communication by bringing out the similarities between various world cultures, and hence affirm the common humanity of the world's peoples. Importantly, the last three of these offer intersections amongst mythologies drawn from diverse cultures and hence imply a frame so comprehensive that individual mythic systems appear to be only so many reflections of a common impulse. Classical mythology might therefore seem to lose its pre-eminence and become one amongst many.

A book of myths published in the late twentieth century is thus less likely to be yet another volume devoted to classical myths than a thematically organized international anthology (e.g., Bailey et al., 1981; Pilling, 1993; Philip, 1995). Often, however, the internationalism is largely an adjunct as classical myths function as nodes of significance within a larger web of eurocentric relationships. This is perhaps inevitable because the target audience belongs mainly or wholly to European or European-derived societies, and because the function of transmitting cultural heritage always remains a residual, if not a central, concern, but it does constitute a problem insofar as the tendency of such collections is to privilege similarity over difference. A still more powerful explanation is found in the generation of actual or implicit framing structures, because, we suggest, the informing model is derived from Greek mythology and shaped by the Western metaethic. The predominance of Greek mythology is not simply a consequence of intellectual tradition, but lies in the nature of that system. As Kirk says,

> No other mythology known to us—developed or primitive, ancient or modern—is marked by quite the same complexity and systematic quality as the Greek, by the same prominence of non-legendary heroes, and by a similar preponderance of folktale themes. (1973, pp. 205–206)

In some collections the Greek-derived frame is clearly assumed, as for example in Horowitz (1985), where sixteen of the thirty-five myths included are Greek: in this collection no other culture is allocated more than three places, and the division of the index included at the back of the volume into "Greek characters" and "non-Greek characters" asserts an obvious hierarchy.

The implicit centrality of Greek myth in other collections is a factor of numbers, space, and range: in Pilling's *Realms of Gold* only three of the fourteen myths included are Greek, but the other eleven are drawn from eleven different cultures. The three Greek myths, moreover, also reflect the range alluded to by Kirk: "Persephone" concerns fertility and death; "How Perseus Killed the Gorgon" is a hero/demi-god story; and "The Golden Touch" (the well-known Midas story) is folkloristic. A similar effect of proportion and range is found in Philip's *The Illustrated Book of Myths,* a much larger collection (sixty-seven stories from over thirty source cultures). The fourteen classical myths are only about twenty percent of the whole, but this is still twice as many as the next largest source group (Germanic, mainly Norse). In addition, European myths are simply given more space (between them, Greek and Norse myths occupy forty-five percent of actual narrative space; five Native American myths occupy nine pages, but seven Norse myths occupy twenty-five pages). The organization of *The Illustrated Book of Myths* into six sections conforms with Graeco-Christian eschatology, though there are no Bible stories included,[1] and the first Greek myth (the story of Prometheus) appears as the nineteenth story. The opening sections ("Creation Myths" and "Beginnings") and the closing section ("Visions of the End") are an obvious eschatological frame, while the three central sections ("Fertility and Cultivation"; "Gods and Mortals"; "Gods and Animals") incorporate legendary tales, variously heroic, folkloristic, and etiological. In themselves, Philip's retellings are bare, story-focused, and self-referential, and rarely suggest overt cultural, thematic, or moral significances. Examples such as "The Fall of Icarus" (pp. 112–113), in which Icarus's destruction is morally foreshadowed in his narcissistic vanity and idleness, are exceptions. The impression that the retellings reproduce the "facts" of the myths is reinforced by the page layouts, which follow a layout typical of information books. Wide margins contain ancillary information, such as photographs of places, people, artefacts, and objects, and boxed summaries and glosses. Mistry's illustrations also have a strong factual aspect: each may include several incidents from the story, and participants are identified by a label and pointer. The illustrations spill across the pages, breaking up the text and frequently extending into or even dominating the marginal spaces. Although the book is strongly reminiscent of information book genre, these other components are nevertheless paratextual, in that they are "a fundamentally heterono-mous, auxiliary, discourse devoted to the service of something else which constitutes its right of existence, namely the text" (Genette, 1991, p. 269). In some kinds of retellings of traditional stories, and most particularly of myths, the most forceful pointers towards significance may be the paratextual elements, especially introductions and afterwords. This clearly applies to *The Illustrated Book of Myths,* where cultural, thematic, or moral significances are implied by Philip's general introduction and the framing structure as well as by the paratextual components already discussed. For example, that the story of Persephone (pp. 82–83) is an allegorical, etiological myth explain-ing the four seasons might seem largely self-evident, but is firmly established by the running header "Fertility and Cultivation" and two paratextual ref-erences linking Persephone's departure and return with winter and summer. The other category of retold story most apt to use such strategies is Bible story (see, for example, McLean and Hodges, *Old Testament Bible Stories* [1990]), where paratextual elements may be used to supply spatial and cul-tural contexts for remote and strange narratives.

We remarked above that myths are thought of as expressing timeless and universal significances, and international collections accentuate this by their implication that the stories exist atemporally. So while *The Illustrated Book of Myths* includes photographs of particular places and objects and even people (Voodoo dancers [p. 117]; a man dressed up as a "Viking trader" [p. 121]), and the illustrations localize stories iconically by clichés of dress,[2] ornamentation, artefact, and landscape, the implication that the myths are timeless and independent has a homogenizing effect. They mean much the same things in much the same ways. The illustrations promote this effect also, because despite the abundance of local allusions the representational style is consistently Western and the same palette and layout strategies are used throughout. Philip is conscious of the homogenizing process, and his concern is with the emerging pattern. He asserts that "Myths are the dreams of mankind. Like dreams, they are at once utterly strange and hauntingly familiar" (p. 9), that their proper reception is analogous to the reception of poetry (p. 10), and that "their wisdom, their inner meaning and mystery" is accessed as narrative form. In essence, through his introductory comments, framing structure, and paratextual elements, he claims for myth all of the functions we identified above.

Before we pass on from this brief discussion of international collec-tions to consider in more detail a couple of classical myths and their impli-cations, we want to return to the point mentioned earlier that such collec-tions are eurocentric. As a supplement to his retellings, Philip includes a short

"Who's Who in Mythology" in which he provides charts outlining the Greek and Norse pantheons. After Greek, the Norse system is the most elaborate and apparently consistent of Western mythologies, thanks largely to the antiquarian work of Snorri Sturluson in thirteenth-century Iceland (indeed, one of the most frequently retold Norse stories, "Thor in the Land of Giants" [Philip, pp. 118–124], seems to be largely, if not entirely, Snorri's own invention). Together, myths from the traditions of Germanic and Celtic peoples make up a further twenty percent of Philip's collection. The literary status bestowed upon Celtic and Scandinavian literatures during the nineteenth century as a by-product of the efforts of eighteenth-century antiquarians to stimulate historical and linguistic interest in medieval texts (Taylor and Brewer, 1983, p. 16) still reverberates in late twentieth-century post-Tolkien fantasy and other forms of modern medievalism. As well, the mythologies of Western and Northern Europe have secured a place, especially in children's culture, as aspects of an English-speaking cultural heritage. In part this is concomitant with the previous point, though it is more likely to have been represented as a consequence of English history during the first millenium of the Christian era. That is, because English people were the product of successive invasions that had taken place by the end of the eleventh century— by Celts, Romans, Anglo-Saxons, Danes, and Normans—they can be thought of as inhabiting a culture which incorporates, if only as traces, the beliefs and stories of those invading peoples. Beyond explaining the meaning which underlies the names of the week from Tuesday through Friday, though, the force of the argument is probably more ideological than actual. Experience here replicates Graves's experience with educated readers and classical myth: those with any knowledge of these "local" mythologies tend to have acquired it as children's literature or, nowadays, from various kinds of reversions from children's television. For example, the story of Ragnarok, the apocalypse described in the Old Icelandic *Voluspa* ("The Shamaness's Prophecy"), may be found in Crossley-Holland's selection of Norse myths *Axe-Age, Wolf-Age* (1985) or in Philip's international collection (1995), but in the early 1990s many young people would know it because it was used both in Richard Carpenter's *Robin of Sherwood: The Time of the Wolf* (television series and novelization, 1988) and in the Dr. Who stories *The Greatest Show in the Galaxy* (1988; script: Stephen Wyatt) and *The Curse of Fenric* (1989; script: Ian Briggs). These stories, however, impart mythological knowledge as bricolage. It functions self-referentially up to a point, but never alludes to a coherent mythological context. Rather, it is subsumed into the larger narratives of the series which have appropriated it.[3] The coincidental accidence of the almost simultaneous appropriations then happens to suggest an effect of transcendence, inasmuch as it implies not just a common cultural motif but also a metanarrative confirming the value and importance of indomitable struggle against evil, entropy, and loss. All in all, it is a random dissemination of information, characteristic of the situation whereby (as the second epigraph to this chapter self-reflexively reminds readers) any motifs from nonrealistic genres are up for grabs for subsuming into late twentieth-century fantastic pastiche. More characteristic of the state of knowledge would be our own classroom experience in which only a small minority of readers were able to grasp the bases of Diana Wynne Jones's *Eight Days of Luke* (1975) in Scandinavian mythology, and for the rest it remained largely meaningless when explained.

Myths are retold in contrasting ways, then. They can be self-referential, somewhat exotic stories, appearing to be of the same formulaic kind as modern fantasy action stories, or they can be retold within a frame which seeks to express or evoke their capacity to be, as Egan expresses it, "powerful abstract concepts structured in concrete content" (1989, p. 283). By displacing experience into the exotic—in practice the archetypal—the second kind implies that everyday life does not consist merely of insignificant unique moments, but is informed by some element of deeper mystery. *This* moment is like *that* moment, *in illo tempore*, in mythic time. What individuals experience in daily life is part of a cline of experience which culminates in transcendent human qualities. In effect, and no doubt at times in intention, the second kind of retelling opposes the first in a clash of cultural metanarratives, though this may be more evident in acts of interpretation than in actual retellings. The extreme position sees the telling and teaching of myths, especially classical, as an aspect of cultural conservation central to the production of children as subjects which are both unified and possess social integrity. This is to ascribe to classical myth a function earlier ages ascribed to the classics as a whole. Especially where young people are concerned, the purpose is to invoke a metaethic to stand against the perceived self-absorption and fracturing of identity attributable to late twentieth-century (post)modernism, materialism, and cultural relativism: see, for example, Jones (1985) and our discussion of Abbs (1975) in chapter 1. Jones envisages the cultural threat as coming primarily from a "sapping of religious belief and religious values," leading to a destruction of the individuality of young people and of "their integrity as persons" (1985, p. 27). The argument, a kind of Arnoldian suspicion of mass culture, is not new, of course, but in the context of myth retellings it finds a particularly influential formulation in Joseph Campbell's dictum that, in a community afflicted with the "slough of pride, fear, rationalized avarice, and sanctified misunderstanding. . . . It is not society that is to guide and save the creative hero, but precisely the reverse" (1968, p. 391). The effect of such pressures on retellings is apparent in, for example, retellings of the Icarus myth. These illustrate the range in retellings of one myth from a simple moral story on the theme of "pride goes before a fall" to complex engagements with sociality.

## THE ICARUS MYTH

A striking aspect of the story of Icarus is that, in retellings for children, it tends to overshadow the story of Daedalus, Icarus's much greater father. This is perhaps for three reasons: Daedalus is not a hero, and as a creative genius with demeaning, even criminal, tendencies, is morally too complex; humans have long been fascinated with flight and its ambivalent symbolic significances, that is, of achievement and hubris; and Ovid's retelling in *Metamorphoses* 8: 183–235 is succinct and quotable and lends itself to illustration. Further, the moral implications of Breughel's painting, *The Fall of Icarus,* which illustrates Ovid's version, reinforce the interpretive potential of the story by posing the question, does a unique, heroic achievement have any significant impact on everyday life?

In his version of the Daedalus story, Ovid had only implied the narrative, causal, and moral links between the birth of the Minotaur, the building of the labyrinth, the story of Theseus and Ariadne (where the assistance rendered by Daedalus is unmentioned), and the flight of Daedalus and Icarus. Ovid does, however, thematize the capacity for creativity and art to produce outcomes which transcend utility or morality. Thus the winding passages of the labyrinth are so subtly deceptive (*fallacia*) that Daedalus himself can scarcely find his way back to the entrance ("vix ipse reverti / ad limen potuit," ll. 167–168), and at the death of Icarus he comes to curse his creative skills ("devovitque suas artes," l. 234). This intellectually and morally complex idea tends to drop out of retellings which follow Ovid, such as Snelling (1987) or Oldfield (1988), in which Icarus is responsible for his own death. Such retellings draw instead on the implications of Daedalus's warning to Icarus to travel a middle path ("medio . . . limite curras," l. 203). In Snelling, Daedalus's need to escape Crete is prompted by King Minos's envy of his talent, and Icarus's death comes about because his response to "the lightness, the freedom, the power" of flight (p. 35), emphasized by a shift in perspective to an earthbound shepherd who looks up and identifies the two winged figures as gods (from Ovid, l. 220: "credidit esse deos"), is to forget the warning and his limitations: "The thrill of flying went completely to his head. He could not resist going higher . . . and higher . . . and still higher" (p. 36). In Oldfield, the terms of the interdiction are changed slightly—

"remember, come as quickly as you can and do not fly too high" (1988, p. 50). The effect is that the interdiction is breached in two ways: Icarus flies too slowly, as he begins to enjoy flight, and then flies too high (attempting to locate his father). So although the conventional connection with pride is made explicit (in "How graceful I am"), its metaphoric association with flying too high is only implied.

Other retellings are more explicitly moral in their purpose. Philip, for example, in deriving his story from Graves's synthesized account (1960, pp. 311–313) resubordinates the story of Icarus to that of his father, and frames the story so that there seems to be an implied causal relationship between their behavior and characters and the death of Icarus. On the other hand, the retelling apparently reflects a contradiction between the uses of myth as universal significance and as cultural heritage, so that it seems to disclose an urge to disregard its own moral implications. Thus the first half, unusually for retellings, relates how Daedalus, "overcome with jealousy" because of the talents of his young nephew Talos, "lured the boy to the top of the temple of Athena and then pushed him to his death" (1995, p. 12). Icarus is introduced as "a vain boy with none of Talos's quickness," and when he and Daedalus are imprisoned by Minos, he "spent his days preening himself and thinking idle thoughts." Through this selection of detail and pejorative language the comparatively reticent account of Icarus's flight and death which follows is given an attitudinally moral introduction. Graves had suggested that the myths of Talos and Icarus are variants of a myth dealing with the sacrifice of the solar king's surrogate (1960, p. 316), but no such significance is implied here, despite Philip's innovation in introducing a contrast between the two boys. Instead, the relationship must be read as structural, the element of similarity indicating a causal link. Philip reproduces the Ovidian warning, now coupled with an irony—"Keep a middle course. With these wings, we shall escape" (1995, p. 113)—and attributes Icarus's failure to observe the warning to innocuous sensations, to his "feeling young and carefree, and enjoying the buffeting of the wind." But instead of describing his fall, the narrative at this point is switched to Daedalus's perspective, and the order of events follows Graves, rather than Ovid. Thus Daedalus misses Icarus, calls for him, sees feathers floating on the waves "and a few faint ripples spread from the spot where Icarus had fallen to his doom." Only then, to conclude the story, comes the explanation that Icarus had flown too close to the sun, "and the wax binding his wings had melted like butter." Unless the point of this shift of perspective and reordering of details is to focus attention on Daedalus and to imply that he is being punished, despite the absence of the kind of judgmental language found in the first of the half of the story, the retelling must seem quirky and unbalanced, strongly moral in the first half and merely descriptive in the second. However, the oddness of the version may be explained more simply as a consequence of following Graves's account but trying to inject a moral perspective in place of fanciful solar myths.

A much more explicitly moral retelling is found in *Wings* (1991), text by Jane Yolen with illustrations by Dennis Nolan, where the peritext includes a summary of the story and an assertion that in all classical versions "it is the Greek passion for punishing *hubris*—pride—that remains at the core of the tale." Yolen's is a comprehensive version, the narrative proper beginning with the death of Talos, taking in the slaying of the Minotaur (though not Theseus's subsequent betrayal of Ariadne), and extending to the death of Minos after he had pursued Daedalus to Sicily. It is also a highly patterned version, in which, for example, the death of Talos prefigures that of Icarus, labyrinths recur as both actual and metaphoric articulations of the corruptibility of knowledge, the participants marked by evil are cross-linked, and there are numerous verbal and narrative parallels. In his self-absorption, pride in his own achievements, and disregard for the consequences of his actions, Yolen's Daedalus seems to demonstrate the "sapping of religious belief and religious values" proposed by Jones (1985) as a source of contemporary cultural crisis. But *Wings* functions more like an interactive picture book than most retellings of classical myth, and Nolan's pictures are more interpretive than illustrative or informational. The moral teleology articulated by the narrative patterning and by the choric references to the gods which close each page of text is confirmed and modified by the illustrations, especially in the pervasive presence of the gods in cloud formations. The verbal and visual references to the gods function in dialogue with the narrative to construct an ironic reading position, in that their more authoritative and omniscient perspective imposes a metanarrative grounded in universal principles of justice against which the participants in the story act and fail. But they also affirm that justice is not simply imposed transcendentally. Nolan, in depicting Icarus as a child barely past infancy, effaces any responsibility of Icarus for his own fate, but also at the moment of his fall depicts the gods reacting with grief. The final full-page illustration is a long shot of Daedalus skimming a huge sea swell against a murky sky in which, for the first time, the gods have no presence.

Nolan's pictures remind audiences that "the gods" are metaphorical projections of human thought and emotion, and so qualify the more rigidly moral formulation of the justice metanarrative in Yolen's text. Thus the illustration for the book's opening summary characterization of Daedalus includes anthropomorphic gods—meditating, weighing, considering—but no human participants. Elements of the verbal text constitute part of a frame, and are later repeated to link Daedalus morally with Minos and the Minotaur:

> But Daedalus never understood the labyrinth of his own heart. He was clever but he was not always kind. He was full of pride but he did not give others praise. He was a maker—but he was a taker, too. The gods always punish such a man. (p. 5)

> [Daedalus] built a labyrinth for the king with countless corridors and winding ways. He devised such cunning passages that only he knew the secret pathway to its heart—he and the Minotaur who lived there. *Yet the gods marked the secret way as well.* (p. 12)

And the narrative concludes, with the gods having (been) withdrawn from the illustration:

> Minos was clever but he was not kind. He had a heart scabbed over with old remembered wounds. The gods always punish such a man. (p. 34)

Such explicit evaluations work to shape reader point of view in accordance with a particular metanarrative. In contrast, Nolan constructs comparable relationships within single picture frames. The clearest example is page 15 (Plate 2), which depicts Daedalus's happy family life on Crete. The picture is constructed on the basis of two diagonal vectors, intersecting in the figure of an infant Icarus. One vector runs from the bottom left-hand corner to the top, from Daedalus through Icarus, elevated in Daedalus's arms, to an infant god in the sky; the second runs from the mother's upturned profile in the lower right foreground through Icarus. The god is thus both apart from the family triangle formed in the lower half of the picture and a projection of its focal joy. In such ways, Nolan uses the gods to suggest that value lies in intersubjective responsibility rather than in the pursuit of personal desires.

The Icarus myth, as with many others, has been used more allusively in children's literature. The pursuit of ambition regardless of the consequences is the theme of a picture book which uses the myth inexplicitly, Chris Van Allsburg's *The Wreck of the Zephyr* (1983). The Icarus myth is identifiable here insofar as the book is an account of the abuse of the power of flight, with a consequent punishment of the hubris involved, and because, in the pictures depicting yachts in flight, Van Allsburg has made use of a palette much the same as used by Breughel for *The Fall of Icarus*. Events take place in an insular and somewhat archaic world, however. In contrast, one of the more overt uses of classical mythology in an interrogative relationship with postmodern culture is to be found in Paul Zindel's use of the Icarus myth in *Harry and Hortense at Hormone High* (1984). In this novel

Plate 2. Daedalus and Icarus. *Illustration from* Wings *by Jane Yolen, copyright* ©1991 *by Dennis Nolan, reprinted by permission of Harcourt Brace & Company.*

Jason Rohr, a teenage schizophrenic who thinks that he is the reincarnation of Icarus, arrives at Hormone High and begins posting up notices, distributing pamphlets, and so on, with messages of impending doom. For example, after he has befriended Harry (the narrator) and Hortense, he defines the root of the problem: "Today the deity of selfishness stalks our lands again. All anyone cares about is ME ME ME! No one cares what happens to anyone except himself!" (p. 32). Although Jason is clearly mentally unstable and his characteristic tone is that of a hysterical evangelism, his view of the world accords with the picture of decadence and moral chaos which Harry's introduction to the story paints of Hormone High (the "pseudonym" itself indicates a world driven entirely by desire). In his sane insanity, Jason encapsulates a solution to and an exemplum of moral disorder. Hortense, aspiring amateur psychiatrist, diagnoses his behavior as an externalization of his own loss and despair (his father had murdered his mother), and she explains that he has appropriated the Icarus story in order to construct a voice and subject position for himself. That is, if Jason hadn't read the Icarus myth then "he might have had no identity and been trapped into some terrible darkness and silence of his mind—so alone and speechless, nothing from the outside world could ever have touched him . . ." (p. 149). Zindel is here ascribing to myth the kind of power attributed to it by Joseph Campbell, and Hortense's formulation is a version of Campbell's position: "It has always been the prime function of mythology and rite to supply the symbols that carry the human spirit forward, in counteraction to those other constant human fantasies that tend to tie it back" (1968, p. 11).

Zindel has, in fact, transformed the significance of the Icarus myth by mapping it precisely on to Joseph Campbell's paradigm for the heroic life. This mapping enables an interface between hieratic myth and the demotic narrative of school experience as metonymic of postmodern existence. Although Campbell is not specifically cited, the pattern of the hero's life—"the paths heroes have to take" (p. 86)—pieced together out of Harry's interpretation of events and Jason's oracular utterances follows Campbell and uses his language. Thus Harry frequently adduces the Call to Adventure (p. 60, etc.; Campbell, 1968, pp. 49–58);[4] and he bundles together the "fight against the dragon forces," "supernatural aid," and the "gift" from the "little old crone or withered man" which serves to "help the hero get to where he's got to go" (p. 86). Jason links his own experiences to a sojourn in the desert, that is, an exile in the wilderness, whence visions come (p. 107). He sees himself as the demigod "who can help people find the god in themselves" (p. 49), who can help tap "the archetypal forces . . . inside all of us" (p. 131). Most significantly, Jason's quasi-evangelistic inveighing against a materialist culture in which nobody believes in anything, where there are "problems of freedom and individuality" (p. 32), and where young people no longer have faith in "their country and schools" (p. 32) recalls Campbell's description of modern society as "a secular state, in hard and unremitting competition for material supremacy and resources," where "every last vestige of the ancient human heritage of ritual, morality, and art is in full decay" (1968, pp. 387–388).

At the end of the novel, trying to make sense of Jason's death, Harry reaches a solution by puzzling through the missing "boon," which he defines as "something the hero wins and brings back so the rest of the world can be better . . . some kind of elixir for society or somebody . . . something that makes the whole sacrifice worthwhile" (p. 148),[5] and realizing that this boon was the "call to adventure" experienced by Hortense and himself: "Because of him we, too, had risen from ancient magic and we would go forth with amulets against all dragon forces. Hortense and I would always hear the Call to Adventure and *we would go!*" (p. 150). The meaning of the Icarian flight has thus been rendered metaphoric: Jason's flight and death has meaning to the extent that it enables the other two main characters to ascribe meaning to their own lives, in other words to aspire. For this meaning to emerge, the Icarus story has had to undergo quite drastic reinterpretation. The result, though, accords with other rereadings of texts of the past in order to establish a sense of identity and to emphasize the significance and validity of an individual's present experience of and response to the world. Zindel's rereading is comparable with, for example, Campbell's reading of the meaning of the Minotaur's labyrinth: on entering the labyrinth, it is found that "the heroes of all time have gone before us; the labyrinth is thoroughly known; we have only to follow the thread of the hero-path. And where we had thought to find an abomination, we shall find a god; where we had thought to slay another, we shall slay ourselves; where we had thought to travel outward, we shall come to the center of our own existence; where we had thought to be alone, we shall be with all the world" (1968, p. 25).

*Harry and Hortense at Hormone High* is one way of putting an argument for the production of subjects who escape the snare of solipsism. In contemporary Western societies the broad, albeit far from universal, desire to inculcate a sense of justice with regard to issues of ethnicity, gender, and class needs to be grounded in an ethic which will balance altruism against egotism, justice against self-interest, and even enable justice to prevail. It needs to inculcate an acceptance of both common and different desires amongst individuals differentiated by sex, ethnicity, cultural situation, and the accidents of socio-economic background. In the prevailing humanistic view, the relationships between the self and others in classical myths pivots on what can be described as a conflict between *piety* and *impiety,* where *piety* (corresponding to its source in the Latin *pietas*) entails the condition of showing respect and duty towards "the gods" and society, and respect and compassion towards one's fellow human beings.[6] How does a society establish grounds for saying that altruism is preferable to egotism or that the wielding of power or hegemony should be subject to moral constraints? The desire to assert that such grounds exist underpins the identification of "inextinguishable, universal truths" that "still impinge . . . upon the mind and feelings, and illuminate aspects of our human condition" (Grant, 1962, p. xviii). A formulation such as "our human condition" overtotalizes, however, and the ways in which various cultures attempt to deal with existential questions are multifarious. But, as Gombrich has pointed out, "no style of life is conceivable in which the tension between the urge for [personal] satisfaction and the pressures of cultural demands fails to find expression" (1987, p. 694). It is within this tension that actions can be categorized as examples of *piety* or *impiety.* Everyday situations and decisions become relatable (as they are endemically in Christian thought, of course) to a wider context, a "cosmic" narrative. In his argument about the teaching of history, Egan proposes that a "cosmological context" enables history to be taught "as the great stories of human struggles for freedom against oppression, for security against danger, for knowledge against ignorance, and so on" (1989, p. 290). The argument here assumes a priori the value of the privileged terms, and we think this generally happens in the retelling of myths. There are good reasons to ask further questions about the nature of such concepts as "freedom" and "knowledge," because they are really culturally specific rather than universal. Moreover, the tendency to focus attention on the actions of great mythological heroes rather than on eschatological and existential issues is apt to preclude the production of a social or civic humanist self.[7] In these contexts, piety cannot achieve its full capacity.

## PERPETUATING ANTIFEMINISM: RETELLING PANDORA

Few classical myths have offered more scope for exploring existential issues as contexts for the struggle of freedom against oppression and of knowledge against ignorance than the story of Prometheus. Moreover, perhaps no other classical myth demonstrates such a disparity of significances produced by the horizons of reading shaped by cultural metanarratives. Modern retellings are formed in a context which looks two ways. On the one hand authors look back to multiple classical sources in order to construct a narrative: the preeminent example is Green (1958), though even he does not simply reproduce classical ideology. Others draw rather on previous modern retellings, especially Graves, all of which to some degree have been shaped or touched by Romantic Prometheanism (and even Green is susceptible). Bloom points out that

> The Prometheus of the ancients had been for the most part a spiritually reprehensible figure, though frequently a sympathetic one, in terms both of his dramatic situation and in his close alliance with mankind against the gods. But this alliance had been ruinous for man in most versions of the myth, and the Titan's benevolence toward humanity was hardly sufficient recompense for the alienation of man from heaven that he had brought about. (1994, pp. 213–214)

Romantic interpretations of Prometheus emphasize the duality apparent in the figure, and here the significances attributed to the conflictual relationship between Prometheus and Zeus pivot on the linked values of individualism and creativity. More specifically, retellings are shaped by the Romantic conception of Prometheus whereby he became "a symbol of protest against traditional religion and morality, against any limitation to human endeavor, against prejudice and the abuses of political power" (Mayerson, 1971, p. 46), and in which he is used to assert that it is better to be damned for choosing one's own path than to be saved by obeying God's will (see Booth, 1992, p. 95). Such a position is to be seen even in Snelling's simple retelling (1987), where some motifs are extracted from Graves and reshaped into a creation myth in which human beings are the material focus of Prometheus's rebellion against Zeus and the older culture-hero is undergoing transformation into a civic humanist hero. Snelling's Prometheus teaches humans "how to build houses and make clothes, how to cure themselves when they were ill, how to add and subtract, how to grow crops and keep cattle," and the gift of fire then enables them to make "iron and bronze . . . machines and many other wonderful things," knowledges which are practical versions of the more generally expressed knowledges which, according to Graves, Prometheus learned from Athene and passed on to humankind: "architecture, astronomy, mathematics, navigation, medicine, metallurgy, and other useful arts" (I.144). By omitting any reference to Pandora, Snelling makes Prometheus the vicarious bearer of Zeus's revenge. The conclusion leaves him "chained to a great rock on the edge of the world" and shifts focus to human beings and the consequences of fire—the development of civilization. To reorganize the Graves material in this way reflects Romantic Prometheanism in its insistence that creativity and civilization are achieved against the odds. Thus the power relationship between Prometheus and Zeus is always represented as unequal, whether through speech representation (only Zeus's speech is represented directly), through narrative description, such as "Prometheus begged," "Zeus had Prometheus chained," or through reader alignment with Prometheus by emphasizing his cleverness or by narrator intrusion (for example, "Poor Prometheus!").

Pandora's absence from this version is significant. In a sense, the Prometheus myth is a discourse rather than a known story because the various motifs it consists of are put together in various ways. But the inconsistently reproduced bundle of motifs which comprise this story mark it as very problematic, especially insofar as Pandora's role functions to make Prometheus less guilty and more sympathetic. As Jane Ellen Harrison long ago pointed out, key elements had been invented by Hesiod as part of a process whereby pre-Hellenic goddesses were reduced to subordinate roles within a patrifocal pantheon (Harrison, 1903; Spretnak, 1978; Sidwell, 1981). The most notable of Hesiod's innovations was to redefine Pandora as the instrument through which Zeus finally thwarted Prometheus's labors on behalf of humankind. To do this, Hesiod transformed Pandora from a hypostasis of bountiful Mother Earth to the origin of all evils and diseases. Despite occasional reminders that this Hesiodic version is, as Graves puts it, "not a genuine myth, but an antifeminist fable" (1960, § 39, 8), it nevertheless remains the only version commonly retold. We will here consider a range of retellings, beginning with some simplified examples which divorce the story from the context of the struggle between Zeus and Prometheus, and then looking at the more complex meanings produced when Pandora becomes part of the story of Prometheus. Before we do that, however, we want to look a little more at the endemic misogyny of classical myths.

Feminist thinkers have been especially suspicious of the subjectivity aligned with classical myth, because the subject so produced is not only an artefact of "high" culture but is gendered male. Classical myth is predominantly masculinist and antifeminist. As Ostriker points out, myth has been the domain of "the conquering gods and heroes, the deities of pure thought and spirituality so superior to Mother Nature; . . . the sexually wicked Venus, Circe, Pandora, Helen, Medea, Eve, and the virtuously passive Iphigenia, Alcestis, Mary, Cinderella" (1985, p. 316). A feminist re-visioning of classical myths begins, according to Ostriker, with "the challenge to and correction of gender stereotypes embodied in myth," though this is more than a matter of remaking the myths themselves. Retellings must confront the social and literary conventions which sustain the myths (p. 318). In a studied interrogation of the kinds of significance attributed to classical mythology that we identified at the beginning of this chapter, Huse has redirected this argument towards retellings of classical myth for children, arguing that knowledge of the misogynistic representations of women in myth "is essential not only to an understanding of literature, but also to all other branches of our culture" (1987, p. 65). Purkiss, however, is more skeptical about the possibilities for success here, and argues that much more is needed in retellings than a change of narrative focus, the conversion of a negative representation into a positive one, or a realignment of reader subject-position (1992, pp. 441–442, 444). The meanings of a story are bound up with its history in culture and literature, and "old" versions cannot merely be excised. Purkiss goes further than most in questioning whether classical myth can be recuperated at all. Ostriker argues that myths have a double signification: on the one hand, they are a province of high culture, transmitted by "religious, literary, and educational authority"; on the other hand, they are the terrain of the psyche, "the stuff of dream life, forbidden desire, inexplicable motivation" (p. 317). Her argument is an attempt to rethink and reconfigure commonly held conceptions of myth, an attempt to change the meaning of the structure. But Purkiss, arguing from a cultural materialist perspective, rejects Ostriker's second significance, and argues that myths are culturally specific and produce meanings rather than reflect them. She favors abandoning any notion of myth as expressing a "buried truth of culture."

The intransigence of "the structure" is apparent in the story of Pandora, which is retained by most retellings of the Prometheus myth for young readers, and in these retellings she invariably functions as the instrument of Zeus's revenge on humankind. The articulation of her role within the Prometheus narrative predetermines that a patrifocal metanarrative will be instantiated, because it already informs the metanarratives which structure the retellings. Structurally, Pandora's jar (or box, etc.) parallels and offsets Prometheus's gift of fire, so that the male gift of knowledge, education, and culture which the fire signifies is marred by the evils introduced by female solipsism. As long as this structural relationship pertains the story will always be a myth of origins which assigns the female the role of essential origin of evil. This may be expressed as simple, knee-jerk misogyny, as in Green's Hesiodic replication—"Meanwhile [Zeus] was busy on a surer punishment for Man: he was making the first Woman" (1955, p. 37); or it may be the human flaw which hinders Promethean striving, as in Garfield and Blishen—"Even as in Pandora the passions of the gods opposed each other, so they would in men. All aspiration would be lamed, all achievement warped as man eternally fought within himself a battle that could be neither lost nor won" (1970, p. 82). The gendered language, especially in the latter example, carries the (not so) implicit misogyny.

Another possibility has been to separate the Hesiodic Pandora story from its function within the Prometheus narrative, but the result is to accentuate the misogyny or, at the very least, to reduce the story to a moral fable about curiosity. An extreme example can be found in Rosemary Wells's *Max and Ruby's First Greek Myth: Pandora's Box* (1993), a picture book for a preschool audience in which a stripped-back "Pandora" is presented as a lesson about "sneaking and peeking." The function of myth to convey everyday morality is evoked by this book's explicit structure: when Ruby finds Max has disobeyed her and "sneaked into her room to see what was in her jewelry box," she reads him a story about "a little girl named Pandora" who breaks a promise not to open her mother's magic jewelry box. When she does so, out swarm bees, ants, and weevils; left inside the box is a little green spider which spins a large web and so captures and eats the escaped insects. The spider then extracts a fresh promise from Pandora, that she "will never snoop again." When Pandora's mother returns, she rewards Pandora for being "a good bunny" by taking her to the cinema, for which they dress up using jewelry from the box: Pandora wears a necklace of golden insects, and her mother an emerald brooch shaped like a spider.

The final twist has quite a dramatic effect: the jewelry box is "magic," but the correspondence between actual and specific insects and the jewelry, mediated by the promise made to the spider, seems to suggest that the literal insects are in fact projections of Pandora's guilt—the implication is that whatever the box contains will change its significance if illicit use is made of it. Whether or not this subtler point is recognized, the book carries a clear message about obedience and proper child behavior. Further, what seems particularly striking is that by telling the story as a discrete entity and with a child protagonist, Wells now communicates a model of behavior far removed from the theme which has informed retellings of the Prometheus story since the Romantic period. Prometheus might function, as Thomas Bullfinch put it in *The Age of Fable* (1855), as "the symbol of magnanimous endurance of unmerited suffering, and strength of will resisting oppression," but Pandora's role allowed no space for constructive transgression to put beside Prometheus's grand acts of disobedience, and so it is hardly surprising to see it reduced to a vehicle for a simple moral lesson.

The representation of Pandora as a naughty child probably originated in Hawthorne's *A Wonder Book* (1851) where, in "The Paradise of Children," the Pandora story is retold under the influence of Milton's *Paradise Lost* as a version of the Judaeo-Christian Fall (an effect enhanced by the omission of the Prometheus myth as context). The analogy between Pandora and Eve is an ancient *topos,* but had been given force in English tradition by Milton's description of the marriage of the world's first couple:

> The genial angel to our sire
> Brought her in naked beauty more adorned,
> More lovely than Pandora, whom the gods
> Endowed with all their gifts, and O too like
> In sad event, when to the unwiser son
> Of Japhet brought by Hermes, she ensnared
> Mankind with her fair looks. (*Paradise Lost,* IV.712–718)

Although Hawthorne's Epimetheus, like Milton's Adam, eventually becomes complicit in Pandora's disobedience, the two are sharply distinguished by gendered behavior. Intrusive narratorial comments and the representations of Epimetheus and Pandora as focalizing characters firmly align the implied reader with a broadly antifeminist narratorial position. Speech reporting tags alone would have this effect: for example, "exclaimed, pouting her lip"; "cried Pandora, pettishly"; "answered our pettish little Pandora"; "said Pandora, looking sideways." In addition, her nagging is said to be "babble" and she is constantly described as "naughty." In contrast, Epimetheus is said to be "a very good-tempered child," until he too succumbs to temptation and lets slip the opportunity to prevent Pandora from opening the box. As in Milton, the consequence of the Fall reverberates throughout the physical world, bringing temporality and death; and as in Christian interpretations of the Fall as fortunate (because enabling redemption), Hawthorne's loss of Paradise has its positive spiritual dimension:

> Hope spiritualizes the earth; Hope makes it always new; and, even in the earth's best and brightest aspect, Hope shows it to be only the shadow of an infinite bliss hereafter! (p. 124)

In pivoting on the notion of a fallen, post-Edenic, imperfect world which is a mere shadow of the eternal, Hawthorne's "Pandora" has entirely assimilated the antifeminist fable to a Christian eschatology. The conjunction of two such powerfully patrifocal elements has shaped almost all subsequent retellings, though there has been at least one attempt to produce a re-vision of the myth by relocating it within a prepatriarchal goddess tradition. In her *Lost Goddesses of Early Greece* (1978), Charlene Spretnak grounds her reimagining of female figures in the argument that classical Greek mythology is the imposition of an invading, patrifocal culture, that the classical myths contain implicit political references which represent an interplay of matriarchal and patriarchal politics, and that the patriarchal myths contain revisions and inversions of the goddess religions. She further suggests that a culturally determined bias among many Victorian and contemporary scholars prevented them from accepting the evidence that deity was originally perceived as female in most areas of the world. An important aspect of this argument, bearing on the assumption that myths distill psychic truth from the human unconscious, is that Jungian appropriations of Greek goddess mythology, in search of archetypes of a female psyche, generally fail to distinguish between classical and pre-Hellenic myths. The archetypes evoked thus tend to be patriarchal revisionist portraits of goddesses, and hence patriarchal constructions of femininity are naturalized as archetypes. This process, we suggest, is perpetuated and exacerbated by the efforts of retellers to enfold individual myths within systematic narrative structures.

Spretnak's imaginative reconstruction of the portraits of eleven pre-Hellenic goddesses offers a series of enabling fictions, expressions of "nurturing integration, growth, and a sense of our embeddedness in nature" (1978, p. 38). According to Frymer-Kensky (1992, p. 1), the Goddess of modern neopaganism is "earth-centered, immanent and immediate . . . [and] serves as a refuge from, and counterbalance to, what many consider the remote and punitive god of Western religions," and it is this goddess which Spretnak, following Harrison, perceives in Pandora. Hesiod transformed an earth-born goddess into a human woman fashioned by Zeus, and thereby her name—meaning "giver of all gifts"—became ironic, an aspect of her innate deceptiveness. In its selection of details, Spretnak's representation of Pandora implies that classical mythography has transferred her positive attributes to Prometheus. Thus she is here represented as the creator of humankind, and her subsequent gifts include agriculture, handcrafts, and art. Most importantly, she is the giver of fire—the crucial element in the Prometheus myth—and hence of knowledge and wisdom. Finally, her outpouring of gifts includes key constituents of sociality, (re)appropriated from Prometheus and his transformation from culture-hero to civic humanist hero in Romantic Prometheanism: justice with mercy, caring and communal bonds, courage, strength, endurance, loving kindness for all beings, and the seeds of peace (1978, pp. 56–57).

Such a reworking of the tradition, and especially the attempt to formulate a hieratic feminist narrative, has been taken up again in a couple of the stories in Walker's more recent *Feminist Fairy Tales*. It is a reed against the stream, however. A comparison with the retelling in Horowitz's popular anthology (1985) indicates that the patrifocal metanarrative is firmly entrenched. Horowitz, throughout his collection, strives for a discoursal mode which is demotic, witty, and parodic, and part of this discourse is an endemic antifeminism. To access the demotic language of contemporary popular culture does not necessarily introduce perspectives that differ from the cultural assumptions expressed in a hieratic discourse. On the contrary, it may either imply the existence of a universal truth because it has transcended the specificity of culture, or it imports gendered attitudes already replicated in popular culture. In this particular example, the story's misogyny is exacerbated by an unusual narrative move whereby the Prometheus myth is subordinated to the story of "Pandora's Box": the title in effect frames the Prometheus story, and shifts focus to the consequences of Prometheus's actions, and to Pandora. Thus Prometheus is disposed of by the middle of the retelling, the rest dealing with Pandora. In all retellings the narrative structure implies a teleology, and the simple linear relation whereby Pandora's story follows Prometheus's (as also in Green's version) results in a strongly gendered outcome. The interwoven, polyphonic narrative structure striven for by Garfield and Blishen makes possible another teleology, even if with limited success.

All of the characters in Horowitz's version are treated comically. Zeus is short-tempered and somewhat obtuse, and Prometheus is represented both as a doting parent (in relation to humans), and as a trickster figure (in relation to Zeus), hence parodying and trivializing the hieratic significances attributed to Prometheus in texts like Green and McLeish (1981). Hence their conflict is represented as a kind of game, and the description of humans as pets and as "little pink creatures" (p. 82) reduces them to pawns in this game. They are not, however, mocked by gender-based satire as Pandora is. She has now become the *eternal feminine*—sexual, childish, shallow, stupid, and petulant, and destined "to cause more trouble to mankind than any woman before or any woman since" (p. 85). Once again, the quasi-generic term *mankind* does refer only to males. The following conversational exchange about the "box" encapsulates the representation:

> "I bet you keep all sorts of super things in that big, black box of yours," she would say in her syrupy voice. "Why don't you let your little Pandy look inside?"
>
> "It is not for you, my dear," Epimetheus would reply. (p. 85)

The extent to which a reader instantiates the metanarrative implied by genric association without noticing the negative implications of that metanarrative or of the encoding discourse is, it seems, well illustrated by a brief article in *Books for Keeps* (1993) praising Horowitz's collection and its aptitude for classroom use, especially for "plugging the classical gap." In this article, Bennett recognizes the unusual style—it is "droll" and "savour[s] of the oral tradition"—and offers this as a reason for the book's success as a classroom text. A further reason postulated is that the tales "deal with very basic, real and identifiable human emotions and traits, and their original function was to explain what often seems inexplicable." The pupils' response can thus, perhaps, be explained because "the magic of these tales, when told well, is that they strike resonant chords in that part of us which is about what it is to be human" (1993, p. 20). Bennett has, of course, resorted to the standard significances of universality, temporal transcendence, and psychic insight attributed to myth, and his doing so is testimony to the force of the underpinning cultural metanarrative which enables a book to be extolled for features which, if viewed from a perspective genuinely and more comprehensively human, serve to sustain a narrow, patrifocal, and mysogynistic construction of "what it is to be human."

As a final comment on this collection, we should point out that a book which so egregiously discloses some major flaws in the metanarrative can apparently do so independent of authorial intentions. That is the nature of the Western metaethic. *The Kingfisher Book of Myths and Legends* is sexist because the discourse of humor is often grounded in sexist social assumptions. Yet the huge, comically incongruous list of eighty evils emanating from the opened box at the end of the story begins by rewriting the list from Graves ("Old age, hard work, sickness, vice, anger") and goes on to include the sequence "taxation, inflation, pollution, unemployment, fascism, racism, *sexism,* terrorism, communism, nepotism, cubism, patriotism . . . etc." (p. 87; our emphasis). As a ridiculous jumble of commonly recognized social ills and idiosyncratic dislikes, the discourse lacks seriousness, and ultimately it seems impossible to speculate as to whether Horowitz does see "sexism" as one of the things "that make life difficult" (p. 87) or has any awareness of the sexism that pervades his own discourse. But then, as we have been arguing, the metanarratives of classical mythology are inherently sexist anyway.

The various issues we have been discussing in this chapter come to a head in the intellectually ambitious and narratively complex, but controversial, retelling of myths in *The God Beneath the Sea* (1970) by Leon Garfield and Edward Blishen (with illustrations by Charles Keeping). Like Green before them, Garfield and Blishen strove to relate the myths within a coherent and continuous narrative, and hence worked with the presumption that a particular story has its significance in relation to an implicit whole, a metanarrative. In their afterword to *The God Beneath the Sea,* they express the components of this metanarrative in the familiar terms of humanist classicism, but now tempered by Romantic Prometheanism. Thus they cite: "the nature of human destiny"; "the quality and force of human passion"; an inherent and inextinguishable intention in the tales "if not to explain life, then to provide a pattern that would act as a vast imaginative alternative to an explanation"; the strength and persistence of the elements as opposed to the frailty and brevity of human existence; and "that paradox that lies in our power to imagine, and almost at times to become part of, forces both purer and infinitely more lasting than ourselves" (1970, pp. 165–166). The Promethean tempering of the retelling is apparent not just in the section dealing directly with Prometheus but in the prominent and framing role allotted to outcasts, especially in the use of the story of Hephaestus as primary frame narrative as well as in various embedded and intertwined narratives. Thus, for example, the fire stolen by Prometheus is taken not from the chariot of Helios, as in most versions of the story, but from the forge of Hephaestus (p. 75),[8] who in turn is employed by Zeus to make Pandora. The only meeting of Hephaestus and Prometheus, "the two great outcasts" (p. 75), occurs when Prometheus steals fire while Hephaestus is making a clasp for Aphrodite's girdle, and the clasp is given the shape of a hand holding a torch, representing Hephaestus's "own fierce love for Aphrodite—and Prometheus's aching love for mankind" (p. 75). The crucial thematic link between the two is that they are outcast *creators,* giving form to shapeless substances through the power of imagination and mimesis or by seeking the form inherent in the substance itself (as in the description of the making of Pandora on page 77).

Garfield and Blishen's story of Prometheus is more immediately framed by references to the Fates, whereby creation and death are set in parallel. Prometheus, whose name means the "foreknowledge" he is gifted with, is thus placed in the forefront of the conflict between elemental processes and the frailty of human existence. When the first of his creations dies, he whispers, "What can you do against the gods and the Fates with the fragile, pitiful life I've given you?" (p. 69). In other words, how can humanity fulfil its moral and cultural potential in the face of finitude and death? In this regard, the Promethean hero is unlike legendary heroes such as Theseus, who undertook the adventure of the Minotaur largely for the glory of the deed, and all his subsequent behavior—abandoning Ariadne, carelessly causing his father's death—reflects the self-centeredness of the typical hero. In contrast, Garfield and Blishen's Prometheus reflects aspects of two types of civic humanist hero: the rebel/revolutionary, willing to sacrifice himself for the cause, prepared to go on defiantly even though the cause seems in vain, and the person who places the well-being of others ahead of self (that is, the unheroic hero). After he has given his creatures the gift of fire, enabling them to exploit that creative spark to evolve from nature to culture, ignorance to knowledge, for the rest of the volume (and also for most of the sequel, *The Golden Shadow*) he remains a chained and suffering observer. And so, for example, his suffering is exacerbated when Demeter ravages the earth in grief for lost Persephone (pp. 129–130) in an episode which once more highlights the vulnerability of humans to elemental forces and causes Prometheus more pain than the vulture's beak. The links and cross-references are too numerous (and self-evident) to be listed here; it is enough to point out how extensively Garfield and Blishen have developed the image of the creative artist in conflict with the hegemonic forces of Olympus or, in effect, with the self-perpetuating power of the official "State." By incorporating the more modern significance imposed on the Prometheus myth in this way, they have thereby varied the metaethic, though by doing so they have heightened the stress on the civic humanist hero as individualist.

This retelling, then, illustrates how meaning can accrue to a myth, so that material derived from an earlier period is appropriated as a means by which a "new" ideology legitimizes itself. In the representation of Pandora, however, the inherent androcentrism of the Hesiodic source cannot be entirely done away with, even though the episode is more narratively complex than in most other retellings and to some extent self-consciously deconstructs the inherited Hesiodic position. The authors are careful to abandon the Hesiodic notion of Pandora as the *first* woman and instead represent her as an embodiment of contrary human and social formations evolved in the development from nature to culture. The creation of Pandora thus problematizes the question of whether human subjectivity, and specifically female subjectivity, is innate or culturally produced. Having been made from clay stolen from Prometheus, but without "the divine substance of Chaos from which all things had been created" which Prometheus had added for his creatures (p. 68), Pandora "had neither passions nor qualities" (p. 77). The authors here reverse the process whereby gods are projections of human sociality, attributes, and aspirations, depicting the gods interpellating Pandora into subject positions which not only oppose one another but constitute the contradictory elements of an androcentric discourse of femininity. For example, Pandora's sexuality is palpably androcentric in construction, especially in its impossible mix of desirable traits and its regulation of female sexuality:

Next great Apollo gave her sweet and tempting grace of movement—
such as he himself delighted in; but straightway his moon-sister
Artemis gave her defensive quickness, modesty and virginity.

Glorious Demeter shook her head. Never quite in sympathy with
Artemis, she blessed the woman with a richly fertile womb—and the
knowledge of it. (pp. 78–79)

Female eroticism is seen entirely from a male point of view, as "sweet and
tempting," and is clearly separated from procreation. We would like to think
that there is a narrative perspective here which self-consciously disrupts the
narrative and cultural codes responsible for the standard representations of
Pandora, though it is more probably just a deconstructive potentiality produced by the text's complexity. On the one hand, the focus of irony in the
chapter title, "An Ordinary Woman," is not clear—in origin and appearance
Pandora is manifestly extraordinary, but might seem quite ordinary as a
metonym for a patriarchal discourse of femininity; on the other hand, the
retelling cannot set aside the story demand that Pandora be a shallow-minded
sex object, capable of befuddling Epimetheus with desire and unleashing the
evils in the box. Thus the final gift Pandora receives is a *loan* from Aphrodite
of the girdle made for her by Hephaestus, "the girdle that kindled desire"
(p. 79).

Also coming into play here is the evolution of the Western metaethic
from biblical literature, in that the temptation of Epimetheus in the orchard
echoes the Fall in the Garden of Eden, especially that tradition in which the
Fall is prompted by sexuality and woman is seductive and therefore dangerous. There is a general isomorphism between the scene played out by
Epimetheus, Pandora, Hermes, and Prometheus and the configuration of
Adam, Eve, serpent, and divine interdiction, and the similarity is evoked by
more direct links: Hermes laying his apple-tipped staff against Pandora's
breast (p. 80), or Epimetheus and Pandora retreating from the orchard, hands
clasped, in an echo of the closing lines of *Paradise Lost* (p. 82). Such a connection makes it difficult indeed to interpret the episode in a way other than
that determined by the tradition.

The myth of Prometheus has the potential to raise several basic existential questions: Where do I come from? Why am I here? Why does evil
exist? Is the universe just? Why must I die? Yet the answers to those questions will always be muddled, less than satisfactory, as long as the answers
are imbricated with assumptions such as that which sees female sexual
agency as a source of disaster, so that Pandora's role imputes to woman the
negation of Prometheus's aspirations for humankind. It is not surprising to

find this gendered parable reproduced in Green's retelling of the story as a cultural artefact, or in Horowitz's further reduction of cultural artefact to a light amusement, because neither interrogates the story's ground. It is also not surprising to find it surviving recalcitrantly in *The God Beneath the Sea*, despite the conscious effort there to construct symbolic or transcendent meanings which offer fresh interpretations of the relationship between universals and specific social formations, because the shape and outcome of the story finally offer very little room to move.

The large differences in the meanings and functions attributed to myths constitute a major challenge for children's literature, because it is potentially, if not yet actually, a critical area of conflict amongst desires and impulses within the children's literature community. That is, the urge to maintain traditional knowledge and a sense of the past, and to foster understanding of the modes of signification used in texts of the past, conflicts with the desire to reconstruct cultural formations, especially with regard to gender. So far, though, classical myth has been the area of retellings least engaged by feminist writers and critics, so it remains to be seen how incompatible the various desires might be. In principle, as *The God Beneath the Sea* suggests, it should be possible to effect a deconstructive retelling which simultaneously reconstructs a myth's gender representations, though, as we will have cause to argue about other genres in subsequent chapters, the success rate in children's literature has not been very remarkable.

Even with issues of gender representation remaining largely unaddressed, myth is the most ideologically charged area of retold stories because of the complex of significances which may be evoked. Classical myth is especially fraught because of the "cultural heritage" issue. For most of the modern era, and hence for most of the history of children's literature, classical mythology has held a privileged position. Like biblical literature, its grounding discourse was hieratic, and if it did not directly speak of transcendent mysteries, it always seemed to hint at them by producing a complex of literary, moral, and indeterminately transcendent concepts. There is a domain of intellectual slippage here, which is already evident in the easy way Kingsley passed, in the passage cited as epigraph to this chapter, from "fairy story" to the transcendent abstractions "beauty, and wisdom, and truth" on his way to exemplary moral outcome ("making children love noble deeds"). The slippage might serve as a reminder that the classics in general were given a central role in the evolution of postmedieval humanism, and Kingsley may be attempting to transfer classical myth away from a secular humanist domain and back into the ambit of Christian practice. The distance is not great if myth is thought of as "the stuff of dream life" or "buried truth." When Philip's introduction refers to the "wisdom, inner meaning and mystery" of myths, it recalls that secular humanist thinking still sacralizes aspects of intellectual and emotional being.

We pointed out in chapter 2 that one way to retell Bible story, especially in the freer intertextualities of fiction and in retellings which don't display an explicit didactic intent, is to replace notions of the divine with a more secularized vision of transcendence. Conversely, classical myth is a principal genre of retellings and readings which shares its metaethic with the telling and reading of Bible story. Thus Ingraham's prescription that Bible story tellings "should be *inspirational* and affirmative, awakening or strengthening a sense of good in the world, of role and purpose, of the universality and perpetuity of human values" (1990, p. 300; emphasis in original) coincides with a general view of the functions of classical mythology. It also applies to retellings in most other genres, but has some areas of special affinity with Bible story. Both are grounded in a self-consciousness that what is represented is not merely story but a process of signification whose reading demands that distinctions be made between surfaces and depths and between material and transcendent meanings. Both assert or imply that narrated events occur in relation with numinous or mysterious forces, and their understanding will assist readers to make sense of being and existence, of what their places are in the world. Both address moral issues in relation to transcendent ethical meanings, and hence purport to offer guidance in everyday life. Both affirm that goodness and beauty are innate to the organic world and hence are "natural" objects of aspiration for human beings. Finally, both are inclined to frame stories around particular individuals whose representation drifts between exemplary individuality and the civic humanist hero.

NOTES

1. There are identified Bible analogues, however. "Myths of a great flood, such as the one Noah survived in the Bible, are found worldwide—here, in the Sumerian [specifically Akkadian] story of Gilgamesh and the Serbian tale entitled The Great Flood" (p. 41). These are not independent fabrications, however, as seems to be implied. The Serbian story derives from the biblical Flood, which in turn derives from the Akkadian myth. The assumed knowledge here that "Noah" and "the Bible" constitute the node of reference and are familiar to the audience addressed indicates the writer's cultural metanarrative. The volume's concluding stories, the Norse *Ragnarok* and the Zoroastrian apocalypse, are analogues for the Christian apocalypse (and again, though less certainly, the former is influenced by Christian myth and the latter probably influenced Semitic beliefs underlying Christianity). The Grail myth, retold on pages 89–91, is of course a post-biblical Christian myth.

2. We can't forebear from pointing out the erroneous, hoary old chestnut whereby Vikings are endowed with horned helmets (pp. 121–122).

3. The fanzine *Dark Circus* 5(1991): 9–10 illustrates the process of reception

very well. The authors, Paul Fitzgibbons and Kate Orman, summarize the *Voluspa* material (now from a medieval retelling in Snorri Sturluson's *Edda*), match quotations from Snorri and the Dr. Who scripts, and at some points draw attention to isomorphic relationships. The clearest example is their explanation of how Ragnarok is reflected in *The Greatest Show:* "By the end of the battle, every living thing will be destroyed—except two mortals who will survive and repopulate the earth. Now, when the Circus is destroyed, Kingpin starts up a new circus. Mags and Kingpin, the two new acts" (p. 9).

4. Campbell begins this section with a retelling of "The Frog Prince," which Harry also retells, though with a different outcome, and frequently recalls (p. 18, etc.).

5. Campbell speaks of the hero returning "to confront society with his ego-shattering, life-redeeming elixir" (1968, p. 216).

6. A practical limitation on the concept in classical societies (though not confined to classical societies) is that "fellow human beings" was a restricted category, excluding people of another race, nationality, class, sex, religious affiliation, and so on, as not fully human.

7. The "social self" and "the civic humanist" self are delineated by Booth (1992) and Eagleton (1992).

8. The motif originates in Plato's *Protagoras*. It is also used in McLeish's syncretic version.

# 4 DISTINCTION, INDIVIDUALITY, SOCIALITY

## PATTERNS FOR A HEROIC LIFE

*Success . . . is a utilization of self and not, as warriors would have us believe, the ability to triumph over another.*

—Louise Lawrence, *The Warriors of Taan*

*A hero's character is quietly woven from the threads of a hundred honest actions, a thousand selfless deeds.*

—Marine Bates, *The Dragon's Tapestry*

Since the early nineteenth century the literature and history of medieval Europe have been a fertile source for stories to be retold and for literary themes and motifs. The interest in this period shows no signs of abating by the end of the twentieth century—on the contrary, it seems to be flourishing more than ever, especially in oblique transformations in various kinds of contemporary fantasy literature. This chapter examines representations of heroes and heroic behavior in stories whose sources lie, in some sense, in the Old English epic *Beowulf.* We will consider several modern retellings of *Beowulf* in relation to concepts of the pattern of a heroic career, and will make some comparisons with a modern formulation of this pattern in the children's film *The Lion King* (1994). Finally, we will look at two female-authored fantastic novels which interrogate the conventionally male orientation of heroic story and its patriarchally gendered ideologies, and hence revalue notions of the heroic, contributing towards the evolution of a contemporary female hero paradigm.[1] Heroic literature involves an intertextuality which in its focused content is quite different from what we have been looking at previously, though the intertextual functions have much in common. Its texts are inspired by that world which was for a long time referred to as "The Dark Ages," the early medieval period between the collapse of late classical culture and the universal hegemony of Christian culture over Europe with the

High Middle Ages—say, the twelfth century forward. In Western Europe, at least, there appears to have been a shift in sensibility discernible from about the beginning of the twelfth century, a shift perhaps most evident in the rise of Franciscan affective piety, the shift in representations of the crucified Christ from heroic to "pathetic," the intensification of the cult of the Virgin, and changes in the literary presentation of women as Romance paradigms replaced Heroic.[2] This watershed separates the material to be discussed in this chapter from the Arthurian material to be discussed in chapter 5, and points towards different answers to key questions: What lies behind the modern fascination with medieval stories, themes, and culture? Do texts focus on different medieval periods and/or societies in order to express different modern metanarratives and hence values?

This earlier period is commonly referred to as the "heroic age," a designation derived largely from the major concerns of what the modern period has reconstructed as its normal social structures and its major literature. As far as English literary history is concerned, the really important text is *Beowulf,* the first English "epic." But, as we have been finding generally, the "story" of *Beowulf* is a different story with each retelling, as the traditions of literary production re-produce it with each retelling, making new texts out of the old, and generating new ways of reading, writing, and contextualizing old texts. Retellings sometimes also handle the large episodic structure of *Beowulf* by telling only part of the story, especially the fight with Grendel, and hence reframing the material as an uncomplicated heroic triumph. Such selections are characteristic of anthologies rather than of separate editions. As we've argued several times already, the use of "old" material is never merely aesthetic, and with this particular kind of material it is also not merely historic—it is, once more, largely ideological. Any apparently subjective response to a text, or a version of it, is already preconditioned by the cultural values which furnish the context for both the telling and the reading. Put another way, the history of the transformations of a text is the history of the socially oriented metanarratives which shape the uses to which it is put and hence the appropriations made of it.

## Beowulf and Cultural Capital

A story such as *Beowulf,* like the stories of the destruction of Celtic Britain, of the indomitable but doomed Norse gods, and of fearless Vikings, is considered to be of interest for several interrelated reasons. A simple reason is that the retelling of exciting stories from the past may stimulate an interest in history. Thus Brad Turner's introduction to his version for younger readers, *Beowulf's Downfall,* identifies the poem as "probably the oldest-known work of English literature" and goes on to suggest that it offers "a window through which we can see the distant past. It shows us Scandinavia as it was in the sixth century—the midnight of the Dark Ages" (1992, p. 5). The ambiguous slippage of "oldest-known" towards "oldest" and the intensification of darkness combine to suggest that the deepest past offers a frisson of excitement. The metanarrative implicit in Turner's argument emerges more clearly from the more complex arguments evoked by Robert Nye in a brief note to his retelling of *Beowulf*.[3] Nye explains why interest in this poem should extend beyond the domain of scholars: "*Beowulf* is the longest surviving poem in Old English, an epic recording the great deeds of its warrior hero" (1994, p. 87). To this he adds that the poem might have existed in oral form for centuries before being written down at the end of the tenth century, and that he has retold the story in the hope that its meaning will be still alive for children, for whom myth has "a peculiar importance." These comments pick up how, for English writers and their audience, cultural conservation and nationalism combine to give *Beowulf* a unique status.

First, the poem has innate status because it is ancient, and although it is not as old as the epics of Greece and Rome, its transmission within oral tradition gives it powerful status as the expression of a people's ideals and aspirations. Nye's use of "record" further imparts actuality and validity to that process. Such a view has pertained for at least a century, as evidenced by Ker's version of the argument in *Epic and Romance* (1896): "whatever its faults may be, [*Beowulf*] holds a position by itself, and a place of some honor, as the one extant poem of considerable length in the group to which it belongs. It has a meaning and value apart from the questions of its origin and its mode of production" (1957, p. 159). A nationalistic argument informs the metanarrative here, in that *Beowulf* thus testifies to a long English history of imaginative creativity. Second, readers are reminded that the poem is an "epic," a term which at least implies breadth and grandeur of vision, even if readers fail to recognize that epic can still be adduced as the premier narrative genre. Third, as an epic the poem demands focus on the "great deeds of its warrior hero." At one level, this involves depictions of qualities popularly associated with the idea of the heroic: courage, loyalty, strength, endurance, passionate attachment to causes and a willingness to sacrifice oneself for them, an altruistic concern for the well-being of dependents, and a strong feeling of obligation towards anyone who has acted in such a way as to further the hero's cause. When this is put together with the idea of myth, the "meaning" of the text moves into that space where heroes exemplify a particular human role within a permanent cosmic struggle between good and evil, and retellers are then more apt to favor fantastic over historical modes as the appropriate narrative genre.

We have centered this chapter in a consideration of the representation of the hero in versions of *Beowulf* partly because of the poem's status, but mainly because retellings of Beowulf's battles against his monsters are symptomatic of a more pervading interest in the competing metanarratives whereby heroic figures represent universal values by suggesting either a sociohistorical or a (quasi-)spiritual context for the human will to power and propensity towards violence. Regardless of their purposes or differences, all modern retellings of *Beowulf,* or parts of it, place events within some kind of other world, a heterocosm, which can be clearly distinguished from our own everyday reality. This heterocosm can be one of two kinds: a world separated from our own by time and place, as in historical fiction, or a paracosm, some sort of parallel universe, a world of magic, of the supernatural, of the imagination. Perhaps this is because, as Rosemary Sutcliff argued, "the thing that makes the Hero cannot thrive in the Modern world" (1965b, p. 12), though this may have always been so. As Hume suggests, "We find it easier to credit heroes who are different from us than heroes who are just like us" (1984, p. 91). Heroes inhabit a world which is often similar to the one we know, but because it is a heterocosm it is never the same. Their habitus is irrecoverably other and yet is enterable as a kind of inner world which assures its readers that heroic lives are exemplary in their acts of raw courage, their faithfulness and strict adherence to a social code, and the strange individuality which prompts them to risk and sometimes lose their lives on behalf of others but in quest of personal renown. Campbell (1968, p. 29) argues that the effect of the hero's penetration of psychic depths is a "transfiguration of the world":

> Life no longer suffers hopelessly under the terrible mutilations of ubiquitous disaster, battered by time, hideous throughout space; but with its horror visible still, its cries of anguish still tumultuous, it becomes penetrated by an all-suffusing, all-sustaining love, and a knowledge of its own unconquered power. Something of the light that blazes invisible within the abysses of its normally opaque materiality breaks forth. . . The dreadful mutilations are then seen as shadows, only, of an immanent, imperishable eternity.

Through this humanist and religious view of how the meaning of sociality is transformed by individual endeavor, Campbell attempts to reclaim a sense of the hero's function which gets back past nineteenth-century conceptions of the heroic derived by combining classical literature with modern European ideals of individuality and eminence (Featherstone, 1992, p. 168). MacIntyre makes a careful distinction between the individualist fiction of aristocratic *self*-assertion and "forms of assertion proper to and required by a certain *role*"—identifiable in "Homer and the sagas"; thus, "the self becomes what it is in heroic societies only in and through its role; it is a social creation, not an individual one" (1981, p. 122). The tendency to misrepresent the hero in modernity lies in the possibility that the hero will rise above sociality, and any social effects of his actions will become incidental. Rather than being seen to be necessarily grounded in any social role, the hero's power will be located in his uncommon individual qualities as a person, and his almost boundless desire to test these qualities against impossible challenges or overwhelming odds. In this context, the tension which surfaces between the hero's articulated sociality and an exemplary individuality is potentially of great significance for retellings of heroic literature for young readers.

*Beowulf* is a particularly interesting example because it presents itself to most would-be retellers as an artefact always already interpreted. This is because of its cultural status in Anglophone societies in general, and in particular because, at least until the end of the 1970s, almost anyone reading English at a university would have had the opportunity to study it. We don't wish to suggest that retellings engage in any complex way with critical controversies—indeed, they don't, and usually greatly simplify issues apparently central to the source text, but they do happen to replicate two interpretive differences within non-allegorizing readings of the Old English poem: first, the question of whether Beowulf's heroic significance is universal or historico-social; second, the question of whether the relationship of Beowulf to the monsters is one of contrasts or of doubles.

An originary moment for later retellings of the poem is the significance asserted by Ebbutt in her *Hero-Myths and Legends of the British Race* (1910), a popular collection in its time. According to Ebbutt, Beowulf, "who may even be considered an historical hero," is

> this grand primitive hero who embodies the ideal of English heroism. Bold to rashness for himself, prudent for his comrades, daring, resourceful, knowing no fear, loyal to his king and his kinsmen, generous in war and in peace, self-sacrificing, Beowulf stands for all that is best in manhood in an age of strife . . . [his] life is a struggle against evil forces, and [his] death comes in a glorious victory over the powers of evil, a victory gained for the sake of others to whom Beowulf feels that he owes protection and devotion. (pp. 1–2)

Ebbutt's account drastically simplified what the poem is about, though versions of the metanarrative informing its apprehension of the heroic life and its polarization of good and evil will continue to emerge in later retellings of the text for young readers. This moral reformulation of the poem in socially-directed, militaristic, and imperialistic terms, though, is shaped by and perpetuates the early twentieth-century ideology described from another perspective by Girouard in *The Return to Camelot*: "How gentlemen lived and died was partly determined by the way in which they believed knights had lived and died. All gentlemen knew that they must be brave, show no sign of panic or cowardice, be courteous and protective to women and children, be loyal to their comrades and meet death without flinching" (1981, p. 7). Towards the other end of the century, Potter's discussion of Sutcliff's *Beowulf* (1961; a.k.a. *Dragon Slayer*) begins with an equivalent account of the source text, but with the moral weight shifted to qualities framed as an exemplary individuality. The "totally evil" monsters and "the virtuous hero" are still polarized, but Beowulf is now described as "idealistic . . . always pure, always in action what he declares himself to be, always honest and always consistent with himself" (1985, p. 108). The differences here reflect ideological differences between the two periods, but in both accounts the poem is simplified thematically in a comparable way and its re-presentations are envisaged as performing an exemplary function for the benefit of a diminished society. For Potter, the difficulties facing a writer trying to turn *Beowulf* into "a volume of literary excellence for the young reader" lie in the diverse and allusive contents, the overarching sense of fate (OE *wyrd*), and the "subjective setting." Sutcliff's achievement, it is argued, lies in her development of a unifying structure by means of a landscape metaphor contrasting spatial heights and spatial depths, and this structure enables successful mediation between "an ancient, rich culture and children relegated to the society of today" (p. 110). What is transmitted from that "ancient, rich culture" remains unclear, however.

## BEOWULF, RETELLINGS, AND PROBLEMS OF INTERPRETATION

It is not our purpose to offer a reading of the Old English *Beowulf* here, but we do want to give some indication of other challenges facing would-be retellers. The metanarratival implications of the issue we have already raised, that of the distinction between individuality and sociality, is pivotal. A reading of the poem may stress that Beowulf as heroic individual is pitted against inimical cosmic forces, and hence the significance will be abstractly ethical and universal; the hero is ennobled by his own awareness that his victories are only a temporary holding back of the dark. Conversely, it may be argued that the problems of life in a heroic society derive from more historico-social causes—that is, that the structures of everyday life designed to promote social cohesion are self-contradictory and destructive (Berger and Leicester, 1974, p. 41). These interpretations are not mutually exclusive, and a reading (or retelling, for that matter) need not choose between them, but their respective bases are ideologically distinct. In fact, neither enters retellings for young readers unmodified: Crossley-Holland offers the former in his 1982 retelling, but it is modified by the interrogative dialogic relationship with Keeping's illustrations, which forcefully deconstruct the good/evil polarity. Turner (1992) attempts the second, but by entirely omitting Beowulf's fights against Grendel and his mother he loses the metaphoric link between Beowulf's early deeds and death in the fight against the dragon. Other retellings reflect a more optimistic metanarrative of heroic individuality.

As Berger and Leicester point out, both interpretations center on the hall—meadhall, gift-hall—as site and source of social life, "a widely visible center of protection, solidarity, reciprocity, and celebration" (1974, p. 37). But the existence of the hall brings into being the very conditions which are opposite to its aspirations: isolation and exile, treachery, greed, and envy. In order to bind men to him by wealth and the exercise of power, the lord of the hall must hoard wealth and power, and in so doing he creates enemies. Turner picks this up in his expansion of the description of the death of Hygelac, reported in lines 2354–2359 in the Old English,[4] though he transforms it into the more palpable expenditures of "raising armies, building castles and winning wars." Hence the raid takes place because, "The Gaut-king had money, of course, but he did not have enough to carry out his plans. Having been a pirate before, however, Hygelac was experienced in the art of getting rich quickly" (p. 15). The flippant use of cliché draws attention to the moral condemnation of military expansionism, but doesn't begin to get at the underlying social pressures.

The original poem symbolically embodied these pressures in Grendel. It tells how at the completion of his hall, Heorot, King Hrothgar distributed treasure at feasts (lines 80–81), but that at a later time kinstrife would break out and the hall be burned (lines 81–85). These contrasts are then gathered together as Grendel is introduced (line 86ff.), impatiently enduring

> a time of frustration:
> day after day he heard the din of merry-making
> inside the hall, and the sound of the harp
> and the bard's clear song. (Trans. Crossley-Holland, 1968, p. 34)

It is not just that, as a creature of the dark, Grendel hates all men and all joy, as Sutcliff puts it (1961, p. 10), but that his existence is the complete antithesis of what the hall represents and a reminder of how fragile its social basis is. He is the Outsider defined by the hall's creation of its Insiders—the isolate, the exile. As a descendant of Cain, his being is blighted because of his ancestor's failure in reciprocal gift-giving with his Lord and subsequent recourse to kinstrife and fratricide. Not surprisingly, perhaps, retellings make little if anything of this psycho-social possibility, but work the contrast in the more universal terms of good/evil opposition. Only Crossley-Holland suggests the fragility of heroic social structure, which he does not so much through the depiction of Grendel but by retaining and developing a sense that Beowulf is also a threat to social stability: his generous heroism almost overreaches Hrothgar's capacity to reciprocate it, so that Hrothgar seems tempted to dispossess his sons and name Beowulf heir apparent (1982, pp. 21–22). Further, Berger and Leicester argue that the first conversational exchange between Beowulf and Hrothgar is a verbal duel hinging on alternative definitions of Beowulf's mission (1974, p. 47). Hrothgar seeks to define the hero "as a proper object for the king's friendship and munificence," while Beowulf "threatens to swell his ethos and the value of his offer . . . beyond the limits of adequate repayment." Crossley-Holland deftly catches the effect of this difference in the brief exchange in which Beowulf declares he will fight Grendel without weapons. Here Beowulf breaches conversational turn-taking principles to override Hrothgar's objections and to "swell his ethos" (1982, p. 11).

More often, however, Beowulf is depicted as an uncomplicated, exemplary individual struggling against simply delineated hostile forces. It is thus also not surprising that the five retellings of *Beowulf* examined by Potter all "suppressed the heavy sense of brooding fate" in the source text (p. 108). On the one hand, the Old English term *wyrd* has proven particularly hard to define, and seems better served by Payne's paraphrase as "the living experience of the human consciousness with the intractable" (1974, p. 34, n. 2) than by deterministic notions of "fate." On the other, the suggestion that what a hero strives to achieve finally results in his defeat requires complex representation if it is to avoid mere nihilism—the reception of Cormier's *The Chocolate War* is an index of the problem and challenge. Instead, retellings seek to incorporate an inspirational or social outcome for heroic behavior. In Sutcliff's version, for example, the habitus in which a warrior might battle against monsters is primarily a temporal heterocosm, described so as to evoke a sense of historical actuality, and governed by a recurrent alternation of sorrow and joy. This rhythm is established through the story of Grendel and his mother, and mitigates the implications of Beowulf's death by balancing the idea of a fully achieved life against the dire implications of his death for his people, now once more vulnerable to external depredation. It is a narrative which does not strain for cosmic significance, but seeks a simpler revelation of the mystery which may lie behind the everydayness of things. The effect is a certain diminishing of the source in ways not to everyone's liking. Mills taxes this version with diminishing the poem's mystery, darkness, and heroism,[5] with an urge "to explain, to make ordinary and understandable" (1986, p. 78) and contrasts it unfavorably with the Keeping/Crossley-Holland version. The greatest difference in the impact of the two versions derives, as Mills notes, from the great artistic and imaginative advances made by Keeping in the twenty years between the versions, and from the dynamic relationship between his pictures and Crossley-Holland's text. In the earlier version Keeping had illustrated Sutcliff's text, and the pictures were often literal and consonant, doing nothing to upset the simple polarizing of hero and monsters, and of light and dark, which carry the significance. For the later version the illustrations were made independently of the text (Martin 1993, pp. 143–144) and from a philosophical position quite different from Crossley-Holland's, so that the final product works like the best kind of dialogic picture book. We will say a little more about this reversion below.

A more straightforward exemplary hero appears in Turner's *Beowulf's Downfall,* one of the oddest of modern retellings. Presumably because the principal purposes of his version are to open a window on the distant past and to provide an easily followed story line as a "literacy resource," Turner made the astonishing decision to omit the story of Grendel. The result is an account of Beowulf's life in two parts; about half the book grounds the life in "history," and the remainder deals with the rousing of the dragon and Beowulf's death. For the first part of the story, Turner has taken the legendary and/or historical elements which notoriously inhabit the margins of the Old English narrative and moved them to the center. The impression of historicity is then reinforced in a number of ways: the narrative voice is factual and often rather flat, it is apt to foreground gaps in what is known, and it uses frequent attributive expressions to indicate that some specific details have little or no truth value. The result of these strategies is plausibility, even when the actual history is inauthentic. Apparently careful distinctions between the knowable and the unknowable, and between fact and belief, thus form the ground upon which the exemplary life unfolds. At the same time, most of the language is also evaluative, as in the information that "Shieldings and Inglings were both greedy for wealth, power and fame, so there was war between their two nations" (1992, p. 7), a formulation which not only effectively falsifies history through its simplistic cause-and-effect relationships but also presents it as always already moralized. A better gesture towards explaining the constant movement of peoples across northern Europe during the "Dark Ages" can be found at a moment in Sutcliff's *The Lantern Bearers,* when one of Aquila's Saxon masters remarks, "All men—all peoples—rise in the east like the sun and follow the sun westward. That is as sure as night follows day, and no more to be checked and turned again than the wild geese in their autumn flighting" (1981, p. 64). This is again a simple explanation of the pressures of land use and population increase that cause whole peoples to move, but it hints at a process more complex than the moralistic "greedy," and it is articulated by a character caught up in that process and whose limited understanding can only grasp it as a process of nature.

Turner has also attempted to make the Beowulf story more accessible by assigning Beowulf a normal royal childhood, in which he learns "all that a young prince should know" (p. 9). This of course contrasts with the "ash-lad" motif present in the Old English *Beowulf* and rendered in various ways in modern versions, and lays down a simpler relationship between individuality and sociality: it is easy to assume a causal relationship between Beowulf's education in "good dress, good manners, good speech and the ancient wisdom of the gods" (p. 9) and his deep sense of responsibility towards family and community. With the elision of the Grendel story, the problematic business of the swimming match with Breca also disappears and with it Beowulf's early unruliness. Even his great strength is attributed rather than recorded ("It was said that Beowulf was easily as strong as thirty ordinary people" [p. 11]), and the one mighty deed described at some length, his escape from the Franks after the death of Hygelac, his king, is as much imputed as reported: "In later days it was widely told. . . . It is said that . . ." (p. 17). Throughout his life, then, Turner's Beowulf is a bastion against disorder, seemingly the only person of rank not aspiring to kingship. These same qualities are depicted in other versions, but in Nye, for example, they are the background against which the more symbolic actions of monster-slaying are played out, rather than the prime focus as in Turner. When the second half of Turner's reversion takes up the story of the dragon and Beowulf's downfall, however, the shift from historical to fantastic discourse tends to reinvest the story with some of the classic heroic characteristics, and hence its value as cultural capital begins to outweigh the more specific effects of moralized (pseudo-)history. The language is now heightened in various ways: by interspersing expressions reminiscent of Old English kennings or other compound epithets—the dragon is "hoard-guarding" and a "destroyer of nations," for example; by syntax which seems archaic—"The thought of do-ing battle was pleasing to that ancient serpent"; and by stretches of text con-taining a high incidence of alliteration, as in "When at last the *d*ay was *d*one, Hringboga would *d*elay no more. His *h*eart *a*ched for battle-*a*ction, and so he *i*ssued *f*orth, *f*laming from the mound" (p. 23).[6] There are also some modern colloquialisms ("Wiglaf . . . was up to it," p. 25) which seem in-tended to anchor the fantastic in reality, but which can have a rather jar-ring effect. Extreme register shift is difficult to control in heroic discourse, and Turner is less skillful than Nye, for example.

## THE HERO PARADIGM

The outline shape of Beowulf's career corresponds at many points with hy-pothetical paradigms for a heroic life. Thus he has an unpromising youth but proved himself as an adult; his adventures in Denmark include key threshold crossings, in the night battle against Grendel and the undersea battle with Grendel's mother; after his return he eventually ascends the throne of his native land; he eventually falls when evil (re)enters the kingdom in the form of the dragon; he is buried on a hilltop. In *The Hero with a Thou-sand Faces,* Campbell suggested that heroic narratives conform to a "monomyth," a "standard path of mythological adventure" (1968, p. 30), which is always a version of the paradigm of *separation-initiation-return.* An important aspect of this argument is that the paradigm does more than describe a common, superficial structure, but points on to a significance that is both hieratic and inward. Thus,

> the first work of the hero is to retreat from the world scene of sec-ondary effects to those causal zones of the psyche where the difficul-ties really reside, and there to clarify the difficulties, eradicate them in his own case (i.e., give battle to the nursery demons of his local culture) and break through to the undistorted, direct experience and assimilation of what C.J. Jung has called "the archetypal images." (1968, p. 17)

This transference of adventure to a psychic plane is very obvious in Nye's depiction of the fight with Grendel, and its nature as an adjunct to the he-roic role is addressed by feminist reconceptions of the hero whereby the tra-ditional archetypal male hero is displaced by a female hero. Monk (1991) defines this as a contrast between the *sword-hero* and the *mage-hero*. In Lawrence's *The Warriors of Taan* (1988) and Bates's *The Dragon's Tapes-try* (1992) female heroes achieve comparable illumination through feminist transformations of fantasy motifs. Lawrence's Elana suffers a kind of death when she spends months with the stone-wraiths in their subterranean world and emerges "thin from starvation" (p. 195) and, initially, caught up in a mystic catatonia: "She lives, but not with us. She is deaf, dumb and blind to all around her. Lost inside herself" (p. 217). Unlike the pre-texts for the motif of the subterranean journey—in, for example, Tolkien's *Lord of the Rings,* Garner's *The Weirdstone of Brisingamen,* or the heterotopian labyrinths of Gothic fiction (see Botting, 1993)—Elana's experience is not a test of warrior courage against claustrophobia, orcs, and the like, but of patience and endurance in negotiation with other beings. Her dislocation is temporary, and she emerges with the wisdom to rule her world, just as Beowulf's experiences in Denmark equip him to rule the Geats. Bates's Marwen—more overtly a mage-hero than is Elana—wins out in a confrontation of will and knowledge with a dragon, at the price of a meeting with Death ("The Taker"), which also turns out to be a passage into a more complete fullness of being.

The heroic structure described by Campbell is an affirmation of transcendent meaning, in which the essence of the self and the essence of the world are one (p. 386), and monsters represent "the dangerous tyrant Hold-fast . . . the hoarder of the general benefit" (p. 15). Campbell saw that in the contemporary world "the long-inherited, timeless universe of symbols has collapsed," that the ideals of "the hieratic pantomime, making visible on earth the forms of heaven" had been replaced by the ideals of "the secular state, in hard and unremitting competition for material supremacy and resources" (p. 387, and see chapter 3, above). This must have seemed especially evident at the end of the 1940s when *The Hero with a Thousand Faces* was first published, and the book is framed by Campbell's awareness that the past cannot be revived. This change does not, nevertheless, mean the end of the hero, but a transformation of the role: "The modern hero-deed must be that of questing to bring to light again the lost Atlantis of the co-ordinated soul" (p. 388), to make contemporary life spiritually significant.

## THE HERO PARADIGM IN DISNEY'S *THE LION KING*

Many studies have plotted the shape of the traditional hero's career, though not always with Campbell's intense focus on a spiritual dimension or Jungian approach to archetypes. This perhaps in part explains why Campbell's work has itself been influential on text production, especially for children, and especially in fantasy of the 1960s and 1970s (there were three printings of the second edition of *The Hero with a Thousand Faces* between 1968 and 1971). Natalie Babbitt has acknowledged Campbell's importance (1987), and it seems evident in Lloyd Alexander's *Chronicles of Prydain* (Stott, 1992,

p. 44) and Ursula Le Guin's *A Wizard of Earthsea* (Cech, 1992, p. 86). More recently, now filtered through the influence of Vogler (1992), the "monomyth" has been used to structure Disney's *The Lion King*, albeit as part of a wider cultural bricolage that runs from the Muppets to *Hamlet* and *The Aeneid*. As we remarked about some other allusions in children's film in chapter 3, reminiscences of other texts in *The Lion King* enter and remain as bricolage, in that they are functionally inert for the film's audience. The hero paradigm is nevertheless such a palpable frame for *The Lion King* that the film can be used as a convenient text for outlining the paradigm, but it also illustrates how the paradigm does not express an unchanging metanarrative. There is also a serendipitous link with *Beowulf* in that both texts draw, ultimately for similar purposes, on the Old Testament myth of Cain. Grendel is a direct descendent of Cain, and Scar is named for the sign engraved on his face, neglects his religious duties, and commits fratricide. The story of Cain evinces a metanarrative about the tenuousness of civilized order in the face of a human propensity for mayhem, though *The Lion King* develops this more fully than most *Beowulf* retellings. Its presence is all the more unsettling here because in both texts the agent of evil is the monstrous double of the hero, though again *The Lion King* makes more of it. As Kroll says, writing of *Beowulf*, "The kinds of battles for civilization fought by Beowulf must be fought again and again, by Wiglaf and by others. The struggle is never over, never entirely won, because every man must overcome his Cain-like propensities and because every man must die" (1986, p. 129).

*The Lion King* evokes that unending process by beginning and ending with a song about "the circle of life," that is, about being within temporality. The song is quite explicit about its message, ending with the assurance that time will bring us all to our place within "the circle of life," through our experiences of both hope and despair, and our adherence to faith and love. The Tim Rice/Elton John song emerges over an "authentic" African improvisation, which is background to the film's vivid opening sequence of animal herds in a beautifully depicted, though iconic and geographically conglomerate, African landscape. As the Western words and tune take over, the scene shifts to highly anthropomorphic animals at Pride Rock, the symbolic focal point of the kingdom of Mufasa, the reigning lion king and Simba's father. The opening moments of the film are a potent eliciting of habitus, grounding the ancient "lion, king of the beasts" idea in a landscape extraordinary for its sense of actuality, even hyperreality, as large numbers of birds and animals are depicted in their everyday practices. That this opening hits its audience with the most brilliant animation ever seen on the large screen is part of its assertion of the ultimate "reality" of the narrative so introduced. From a logical or biological perspective the effect asserted is out-rageously appropriative, as natural, African scene is transformed by visual and auditory codes into social, Western significance. With the song's em-phatic closing refrain, the camera "pans" from Mufasa and Rafiki, the royal baboon-priest, to the hero-to-be, Simba, as a newborn cub cradled between his mother's front paws. In gestures reminiscent of Christian baptismal ritu-als, the priest anoints Simba and then lifts him up and displays him to the other animals, his future subjects, who all make obeisance. This scene is pre-cisely repeated at the close of the film, just before it cuts to the title and cred-its, as Simba's cub is in turn displayed on the final repetition of "the circle of life." The repeated scene conveys two aspects of the monomyth. First, herohood is not just achieved, but predestined (Campbell, p. 319), a point simply but effectively made by the filmic conventions of camera movement and focus, as well as the priestly ritual; the path Simba must "find" is al-ready unwinding. Second, but more obliquely, the "circle" encompasses the unstated death of the hero by the identification of Simba and Mufasa: it implies completion of the pattern without upsetting its preschool audience with a tragic ending.

In his youth, the hero is often unpromising: a male Cinderella, like Beowulf, or ideologically unsound, like Simba, whose infantile concept of kingship equates with tyranny and makes him susceptible to the wiles of his evil uncle, Scar. An even more widespread motif repeated here is that of in-fant exile and return (Campbell, p. 323); the exile is commonly prompted by the death or murder of the father, and is accompanied by attempts on the infant's life: Scar does believe that he has caused Simba's death as well as Mufasa's. As Campbell puts it, "the child of destiny has to face a long period of obscurity" (p. 326), which is a time of danger or disgrace (Simba clings to obscurity in the mistaken belief that he is responsible for his father's death); but he also finds one or more helpers. Simba, dying in the desert, is rescued and befriended by a meerkat and a warthog, who take him to a para-disiac land, reminiscent of the Garden of Eden or the Land of Cockaigne. The film introduces a variant on the myth here, since this landscape repre-sents a utopia of adolescent indolence and solipsistic self-gratification, of liv-ing as if there were no moment but the present. As the meerkat puts it: "No rules, no responsibilities, and—best of all—no worries." Food is always ready to hand without any effort, and the boys spend their time in typical homo-social activities such as hanging out, belching, and farting. It is also the "boys' own" adventure of The Coral Island and the like. Once Simba has reached physical maturity, he encounters the summons to adventure through a chance meeting with Nala, his childhood friend and betrothed. Nala sums up the call in one word, "responsibility," thus confronting Simba with, in Babbitt's words, "the lesson the hero must learn before he can become an adult" (1987, p. 150). Incidentally, Nala's function here is reminiscent of a common female function in relation to homosocial freedom, that is, to assert responsibility, domesticity, civility, and so on.

The meeting with Nala discloses a further aspect of the myth: with the overthrow of the rightful ruler, the country becomes desolate, a wasteland. Campbell's summation of this point seems remarkably like a pre-text for the "Circle of Life" song: "from the standpoint of the cosmogonic cycle, a regular alternation of fair and foul is characteristic of the spectacle of time. . . . The golden age, the reign of the world emperor, alternates, in the pulse of every moment of life, with the waste land, the reign of the tyrant" (p. 352). The film makes these contrasts visually explicit. "The Circle of Life," however, has invested the process with more accessible significant shape by grounding its key terms in a well-known biblical passage: "there remain faith, hope and love, these three; but the greatest of these is love" (1 Corinthians 13:13).

The hero must make a significant contribution to society by wresting rule from the tyrant, but before he does he usually undertakes a night-sea journey, a journey to the underworld, or the like. Simba replicates the journey of Aeneas to the underworld, and thereby a classic revelation of national destiny. In the *Aeneid,* Aeneas follows the Sibyl into a cavern, and then

> In desolate night they walked on through the gloom,
> Through Dis's homes all void, and empty realms,
> As one goes through a wood by a faint moon's
> Treacherous light. (VI, ll. 371–374)

Vogler comments that mentor/shamans "travel to other worlds in dreams and visions and bring back stories to heal their tribes. It's often the function of a Mentor to help the hero seek a guiding vision for a quest to another world" (1992, p. 58). So just as the Sibyl guides Aeneas, the mystic Rafiki leads Simba through a weird, night-lit tunnel formed by boulders and gnarled trees (Virgil's simile now becoming the primary landscape) to a pool of water where he is to see Mufasa. Simba sees himself, but of course Mufasa lives on in him, and Mufasa's spirit speaks to him from the sky (the scene is also a version of Hamlet's meeting with his father's ghost). Thankfully, the injunction for Simba to fulfil his destiny by following his father's example is much less imperialistic than the *Aeneid*'s "Roman, remember by your strength to rule / Earth's peoples. . . . To pacify, to impose the rule of law" (VI, ll. 1151–1154), though its implications are not entirely dissimilar.

After such an encounter the hero is ready to face the tyrant. As soon as Simba crosses back into the Pride Lands, he finds confirmation of the desolation caused by Scar's rule; at the same time, the wind freshens, and rain clouds sweep across the sky from behind Simba towards Pride Rock. The hero of destiny is here linked with the ancient concept of sacral kingship, which is also evoked in *Beowulf*: that is, the well-being and fecundity of the land is homeopathically tied to the goodness or wickedness of the ruler (James, 1960, chap. 4; MacCulloch, 1911, p. 253; Turville-Petre, 1964, pp. 192–193). A modern audience does not need to be able to recognize the sources of such ideas to pick up the film's message that rule is the domain of those born to rule. The message, heavily inculcated by verbal and visual signs, is driven to the end of the film, through the continued depiction of the nature of the villains and through the aftermath of their destruction.

Scar, usurper of the throne, illustrates a particular modern nuance of the metanarrative which explains the existence of evil. He is a thoroughly un-American figure. His creators have drawn on Hollywood conventions for representing villains, and, significantly, these were also broadly used in depicting Jafar, the villain of *Aladdin*. The convention is shaped by what Hawkins has termed "the stereotype of the cultured Nazi villain" (1990, pp. 14–15), grounded in a "traditional hostility to the aristocratic, élitist, European tradition that so many Americans had originally crossed the ocean . . . to get away from."[7] Citing Bowen's characterization of the typical "Hollywood Nazi" as "Smooth, suave and cultured, with a predilection for classical music and paintings, knowing the best wines and the histories of their occupied chateaux," Hawkins goes on to suggest that any male character displaying comparable cultivation was apt to be "marked as villainous and/or as un-American, if not unmanly." Such Nazis tended to be played by British actors with upper-class accents, and "merged into the general stereotype of the cultivated villain as played in a host of Hollywood films by the self-same British actors, from George Sanders and James Mason on to Terence Stamp in *Superman II* (1981) and *Alien Nation* (1989)." To which we would also add Jonathan Freeman in *Aladdin* and Jeremy Irons in *The Lion King*. Scar's accent, along with his assertion that he has the brains of the family but is "at the shallow end of the gene pool" in brute strength, type him as "educated, cultured, un-American, evil. Or as ineffectual or effete" (Hawkins, p. 15). These characteristics are sharply evinced in his first appearance, especially in the camp voice and body language displayed during his conversation with Mufasa. Alongside this muted homophobia, another perturbing convention, surprising to find here and in *Aladdin*, is the equation of color with evil: both Scar and Jafar are marked for blackness, in contrast to the "good" characters. In *The Lion King* the identification and pejoration of an underclass is underlined, not particularly obliquely, by the allocation of recognizably Afro-American and Hispanic voices to Scar's henchmen, the hyenas.

Simba's adolescent time-out separates him from aristocracy, making sure that any smooth edges are roughened. His two companions, Timon and Pumbaa, are ignorant of his origins; the world of physical indulgence equates him with the virile, nonintellectual American male. This structure is more obvious still in *Aladdin* because of the threefold identification of Aladdin as the destined one "whose worth lies far within, the diamond in the rough," and the film's romantic focus on who will get the Princess. But the spirit of Mufasa assures Simba that he is "more than he has become," and a small romance element is also enabled in *The Lion King* by Simba's separation, as he and Nala can now properly fall in love when they meet again as young adults. The prince can thus marry the girl next door. Hawkins has made the interesting suggestion that the sexual and national chauvinism of the Hollywood "anti-intellectual man's man" is "conspicuously atavistic," and this element has been cultivated in response to post–1960s feminism. *The Lion King* is particularly pertinent to this argument, as the shuffling between anthropomorphic and animal characteristics implicitly posits the argument that certain kinds of power relationships—men over women, rulers over ruled, whites over people of color—are natural and only evil will stem from other arrangements. The representation of females in *The Lion King* is utterly atavistic inasmuch as they have few rights or functions beyond reproduction and food gathering.

The final confirmation of this naturalness of structure is presented in the film's presentation of the penultimate moment in the hero's career, his return home and accession to power. Campbell argued that the hero who overcomes the perils of desire and fear, and moves beyond both selfishness and altruism, is "reborn in identity with the whole meaning of the universe" (p. 386), and this idea is strongly suggested by action, use of palette, and soundtrack. As Simba and his companions confront Scar and the final battle begins, lightning sets fire to the veldt so that the battle rages in the midst of quasi-purgatorial fires. At the moment of Scar's death, rain begins to fall, the fires are quenched, and the dry river beds begin to flow. Then Simba ascends Pride Rock as King, the clouds part and Mufasa's voice intones "Remember. . . ." Finally, the color changes from the dark blues and greys of the wasteland to the bright blues and greens of fecundity. The hero and his world are indeed one.

## MONSTROUS DOUBLES

The climactic sequence of *The Lion King* contains some key moments which double earlier moments. This doubling process actually begins when Simba attacks Nala in defense of his friends, and she "pins" him in a replication of a childhood game depicted near the beginning of the film. A little later, she gently mocks Simba by repeating some of his childhood words. During the battle, Scar attempts to kill Simba in exactly the same way he caused Mufasa's death, and then when Simba corners Scar he repeats Scar's own words spoken to the young Simba. Such doublings create neat structural symmetries and dramatic ironies, and imply that order and justice infuse the "circle of life." A more potent doubling, though less precisely articulated, is Scar's function as the monstrous double of Mufasa. They are brothers, and we have already indicated ways in which they are opposites, but the narrative doubling is effected through their parallel deaths in relationship to Simba. Each falls from a cliff when attacked by another lion, each death is linked with the hyenas, and Simba is indirectly involved (Mufasa is made vulnerable to Scar's attack because he is trying to protect Simba; Simba flings Scar from the cliff to be torn apart by the hyenas). There is a further analogy here in Bettelheim's interpretation of the stepmother phenomenon in fairy tales. He writes that "the typical fairy-tale splitting of the mother into a good (usually dead) mother and an evil stepmother" allows a child to preserve an all-good mother but still express anger (1978, p. 69). In a comparable way, Mufasa and Scar may here stand for the good and bad aspects of the father. Bettelheim's Freudian readings of fairy story have generally influenced subsequent retellings, so the analogy here may not be entirely coincidental. The doubling to produce the light and dark sides of the parent is, moreover, a Bettelheimian turn to an observation in Campbell, that "the work of the hero is to slay the tenacious aspect of the father (dragon, tester, ogre king) and release from its ban the vital energies that will feed the universe" (p. 352). Campbell goes still further to suggest that Hero and Monster are aspects of the same force, thus pushing interpretation to a highly symbolic level. On a simpler plane, the adult lions offer alternative possibilities for Simba's own development. The motif of the monstrous double occurs more widely in narrative, of course, but its endemic presence in hero narratives inspires its use in *The Lion King* and is a crucial suggestion for examining reversions of *Beowulf* (a text which Campbell himself doesn't discuss). It has long been a critical commonplace that the monsters in *Beowulf* are doublings of the hero, with all that implies about the metanarrative presumed to be driving the poem, so a reteller of that work may have to decide how to handle this aspect.

In her study of the Old English poem, Kroll reviews the long-standing scholarly recognition of what she refers to as "the doubles paradigm" and argues that it "both accounts for the curiously equivocal elements in the hero's nature and deeds and highlights the human dilemmas that make the preservation of political order problematical" (1986, p. 122). It is also possible, on the other hand, to interpret Beowulf's encounter with Grendel, for example, as a polarization of hero and monster, and hence of civilization and chaos. Parks (1993), arguing that the *Beowulf* poet's outlook is thoroughly homocentric (pp. 5–6) and a "vindication of human courage in the face of a hostile world" (p. 16), rejects the view that Beowulf's heroism contains an element of monstrosity. Retellings of *Beowulf* are thus susceptible to influence from the metanarratives underlying diverse contemporary critical interpretations. This has been most evident in relation to John Gardner's adult retelling, *Grendel* (1971). Gardner was himself a teacher and scholar of medieval English literature, and *Grendel* achieved dual status as a novel and as an interrogative reading of *Beowulf*. Hume adduces such elements as Gardner's incorporation of antiheroic descriptions of battles, for example, and comments that they function as "a shocking but useful addition to the heroic interpretation of facts long accepted as near-ideal by romantic critics" (1984, p. 89); she also notes the impact of the Vietnam War on *Grendel*. *Grendel* has not had an apparent influence on re-presentations of *Beowulf* for children, however, and of those which seem to have most in common with it, Nye's is earlier and Keeping seems to have independently evolved his own late twentieth-century view of the monstrosity of heroism for his 1982 illustrations (cf. Martin 1993, p. 143).

The polarization of hero and monster underpins Sutcliff's historicism, but is even more characteristic of anthology "Beowulf" retellings such as Spearman (1981) or Philip (1995), which deal only with Beowulf's fights against Grendel and his mother, or Horowitz (1985), which extracts only the fight with Grendel. In Philip's rather truncated version, oddly positioned between retellings of the Greek myths of "Midas's Ears" and "Theseus and the Minotaur," Grendel is "an evil creature" and "a vile monster," and his mother is "even viler" (1995, p. 106). Mistry's illustrations depict them as a species of wingless dragon.[8] Each is quite summarily despatched by the hero. Spearman's much more interesting retelling appears between "David and Goliath" and "St. George and the Dragon" in a section which the introduction to the anthology suggests is about "men grappling with the forces of evil in the form of monsters or giants" (1981, p. 4). Such a context implies a symbolic reading of "Beowulf," and the retelling quickly establishes its polarity between civilization and chaos through a number of binary oppositions: Hrothgar embodies wisdom, patience, and stability in a violent and unsettled world; Heorot is built on solid land, in contrast to "the treacherous fenland" surrounding it; "man" in the hall contrasts with the "shapeless monster" in the fen; human "happiness and laughter" are opposed to the monster's "pain and misery," and so on. In addition to these oppositions, the extracted episode accentuates Grendel's anthropophagy. The Old English poem does not suggest that Grendel eats his victims until his final entry into the hall when Beowulf awaits him and watches him kill and eat Hondscioh. Modern retellings mostly extend the anthropophagy throughout the description of Grendel's depredations, doing so either by implication (Sutcliff; Crossley-Holland) or explicitly (Nye; Spearman; Horowitz). Thus Spearman reduces the number of Danes killed by Grendel in his first raid from thirty to two, but this is apparently to make the anthropophagy more credible, and it is now presented in detail by substituting at this point the later description of the death of Hondscioh (*Beowulf,* ll. 739–745): "he seized the two nearest sleeping thanes, wrenched off their limbs and drank their blood. Cramming lumps of flesh into his mouth, slobbering and moaning with anger, he turned and made off" (p. 106).[9] This evidence of monstrosity is graphically emphasized by Keeping's accompanying, concordant illustration, in which a humanoid figure covered in scales and tufts of hair holds a gory arm in one hand while cramming something into its mouth with the other (p. 107). On the other side, Spearman is very reticent in his depiction of Beowulf. There is neither physical description nor background, beyond the information that he was "famous for his strength and heroic deeds." He is scarcely mentioned during the fight with Grendel, and the later fight with Grendel's mother, which is now narrated more from Beowulf's point of view, focuses on action and offers very few indicators of Beowulf's thoughts or attitudes. That is, the significance of the story has to be derived from the polarity of good and evil, from the horrific depictions of the evil, and from the undemonstrative way the hero goes about his job. Out of this representation comes, first, an assurance that Beowulf's heroic deeds are exemplary of humankind's struggle against evil, and second, a confirmation of what the surrounding stories imply—that those deeds are one more symbolic embodiment of a divine will.

By contrast, Horowitz's hero/monster polarization includes a fuller articulation of Beowulf's heroic attributes even though Grendel is again the principal focused participant, and the story is called "The Grendel" (1985, pp. 159–164). The significance of this retelling, however, remains somewhat elusive. Up to a point, it pivots on the customary oppositions between light/ dark and joy/misery, encapsulated in emotive and explicitly figurative language. Grendel has here become "the Grendel" (whatever that might be) and is always pronominally *it*; there is no hint of pathos in his situation, and he is designated by a lexical set of terms such as "poison, hatred, bitterness, brutal, cowardly" and his very physical movement is often denoted by non-human or pejorative terms ("slither, limp, slunk away, come stealthily"). He is an agent of the dark, awaiting destruction by the light. Thus when Heorot is closed, "it was as if all happiness had come to an end in the reign of King Hrothgar. A shadow had fallen not only across Heorot but across the whole country and the emptiness of the banqueting hall soon came to be a fitting image for the hollowness in the heart of all Denmark" (pp. 160–161), but when Beowulf opens the door he appears as a figure "silhouetted against the light which could almost have been emanating from his own body. The dust formed a shimmering aura around him. The king trembled. Never had he seen a warrior so tall, so strong" (p. 161). But, as with other stories in the anthology, it is difficult to pin down a significance for "The Grendel" because of Horowitz's playful resistance to the linguistic conventions of hieratic discourse which pervade retellings of myth and legend, and his use of a more contemporary fantasy style, with extreme shifts between portentousness and flippancy, which often seems to push the text towards parody. The introduction of Beowulf seems excessively overworded, whereas his companion who is eaten by Grendel is rather offhandedly described as "this unfortunate youth" (p. 163). Further, there is less contextual impact on any story's significance in this anthology because selections are arranged according to place of origin: "The Grendel" occurs between quite iconoclastic versions of "St. George and the Dragon" and "The Marriage of Sir Gawain" (see chapter 5). These three stories do happen to be about monsters—in the first, a saint tames an anthropophagous dragon, and in the third a monstrous woman is rendered amiable and beautiful by "the kindness and understanding of a noble spirit" (p. 173)—but beyond that they do not form a coherent sequence. The retelling in "The Grendel" suggests a thematic outcome much like Spearman's because of the strong light/dark and hero/monster contrasts and the utter routing of the utterly evil, but the manner of the telling might also suggest that the whole episode is really a bit absurd, so that the overall effect is randomly deconstructive.

The only modern reversion of *Beowulf* which unequivocally embraces the notion of monstrous doubles is that of Keeping and Crossley-Holland, and then only in Keeping's illustrations. As we said above, Keeping evolved this insight independent of critical discourse around the poem, as distinct from Crossley-Holland, who is an Old English scholar in his own right. Keeping's interpretation turns on an apprehension of an element of pathos in Grendel and of a robotic quality in Beowulf and his companions (Martin, 1993, pp. 143–144), but other illustrating projects, both before and after *Beowulf*, have involved the idea of the *doppelgänger: The Strange Case of Dr. Jekyll and Mr. Hyde* (1967); *The Wedding Ghost* (1985); *Frankenstein* (1988). The upshot is, as Mills says, that "Beowulf and the monsters are shown as remarkably alike: clownish, ugly, ungainly. The heads of the monsters . . . after Beowulf has hacked them from the bodies, might just as well be the heads of any of the warriors of human kind. The pictures thus call into question any simple interpretation of the story as an encounter of good, the hero, with evil, the monster" (1986, p. 84). This crossover effect also dismantles the sharp distinction between Insider and Outsider, so that the illustrations present the monsters not as the forces of chaos, or of evil, or of the dark within the human psyche, but as victims of a brutish, aristocratic society which marginalizes and excludes the Other.

As we have said, the possibility that a hero contains something monstrous within himself is widely entertained in accounts of the Old English poem. Especially pertinent here is Dragland's claim that "to read *Beowulf* symbolically is to conclude that no man can be pure as long as he contains dark, monstrous forces within him, that no hall can be completely cleansed as long as it is the residence of impure men" (1977, p. 615). In effect, this formulation inverts the relationship of virtue and monstrousness as encapsulated a decade earlier by Nye's Beowulf, who throughout the story contends that good and evil coexist, but are separated by moral discrimination. An example is this speech addressed to Grendel's mother:

> Listen, She-evil, and I will tell You why this heart does not blush or blanch at the wicked worst You can do. It is because I, Beowulf, know myself. It is because I hold a Cain in me, but do not let him out. That man is truly brave who, feeling fear, yet puts his fear to use and plucks new courage from the fear itself. That man is truly good who knows his own dark places. (1994, pp. 56–57)

Nye, however, used the generally shadowy figure of Unferth to depict the monstrous double. Little is said about Unferth in the Old English poem, except that he is guilty of fratricide. His role is to challenge Beowulf's credentials and suggest he would be no match for Grendel; subsequently, the two become more companionable. Nye's Unferth, however, is a person so fascinated by, and indeed in love with, evil that he eventually becomes insane and dies attempting to embrace Grendel's mother. In this retelling, neither Grendel nor his nameless mother functions as Beowulf's monstrous other because hero and monsters are polarized as contrary. To recognize and acknowledge the evil in human nature enables sufficient strength of character to overcome it (1994, p. 24). Thus Nye's *Beowulf*, like Sutcliff's earlier retelling, structures meaning through oppositions of light and dark, and of good and evil. This Beowulf has something of the twentieth-century anti-hero about him: he is short of stature, myopic, and afflicted with dental caries, but these shortcomings help transform him into a modern hero because they make him self-reflective. He is consequently able to engage with Wealhtheow in metaphorical conversations about good and evil. He talks a lot. Wealhtheow, in turn, is developed from the shadowy figure in Old English to a kind of 1960s alternative culture hostess, blonde, beautiful, and intelligent, who so embodies the power of love as a mystic force—or the fantasy that a good woman has no being without her male partner—that she saves Hrothgar from Grendel by interposing her own body (1994, pp. 14, 34). The novel thus poses two kinds of virtue against evil: the negative virtue whereby the inner Cain is contained, and the positive virtue of love.

Negative virtue, and the power that enables it, are given symbolic embodiment in the fight with Grendel and through the nuance Nye gives to the question of why Beowulf refuses to use weapons. In Sutcliff, for example, he eschews weapons because "he knew that mortal weapons were of no use against the Troll-kind; such creatures must be mastered, if they could be mastered at all, by a man's naked strength, and the red courage of his heart" (1961, p. 34). Nye's Beowulf recognizes that swords have not prevailed in the past, but more significantly when he has Grendel in his grasp he causes him to self-destruct: "I do not fear you, Grendel. I do not fear, therefore I do not fight. I only hold you, child of Cain. I only fix you fast in your own evil, so that you cannot turn it out on any other. It is your own evil, Grendel, that undoes you" (1994, pp. 33–34). This difference reflects a substantial ideological difference between the Old English poem and modern retellings. Kroll, pointing out that the fight with Grendel is the only one of Beowulf's battles in which he goes unarmed, explains this detail in terms of monstrous doubles, "the idea of a personal second self who is separate from and yet shares the hero's vital nature." Thus "each [Beowulf and Grendel] faces his own capacity for destructiveness nakedly in the other" (1986, p. 123). Nye's retelling precisely negates such a possibility, accessing instead a modern convention especially prevalent in children's literature, namely that evil will be ultimately self-destructive.

Nye's representation of the positive virtue of love is much more problematic, in that it is hopelessly grounded in patriarchal constructions of femininity. It is embodied in Wealhtheow, and intensified by depicting Grendel's mother as Wealhtheow's monstrous opposite, and here Nye manifestly reproduces a masculine ideological fantasy about the dual nature of female otherness. On the one hand, femininity represents beauty, purity, and goodness, and on the other, evil, corruption, and death (cf. Morris, 1993, pp. 14–19). Keeping was later to observe of Grendel's mother that "she loves her son, so she must be capable of love. I can't see them as totally evil" (cited in Martin, 1993, p. 144), and he builds this into his humanoid representations of her. But Nye depicts her as a travesty of female form and female love, oozing "sticky mother's milk," with eyes in her breasts, in an expression of misogyny centered in a loathing for female bodily functions. Both Nye and Keeping (Plate 3) depict the fight in which Beowulf kills her in extraordinarily sexual terms. In Nye she is a combination of bad mother, virago, and succubus, the dark female force which threatens to emasculate male potency. Even Cain, it is told, was struck by lightning and killed as punishment for having sexual relations with her (p. 56). The effect is accentuated by the capitalization of the female pronoun throughout the section, which effectively makes her *Woman* as well as Grendel's mother. The threat posed to patriarchal heroism by female sexuality in the following extracts scarcely needs to be pointed out:

> Her tentacle arms . . . closed about him tenderly. For a moment he succumbed, seduced by gentleness. Then, struggling to free himself, he found he could not. . . .
>
> There was no escaping, none, from these spongy, intangible fingers that pulled him on, on, on, irresistibly insistent, coaxing, maternal. . . .
>
> Slowly She began to draw him down into the heart of the cave.
>
> Beowulf snatched at his sword. Its jewels were sticky from Her vile embrace. . . .
>
> She kept on drawing him down into the dark, sucking at his skin, making kissing and swallowing noises, Her arms winding and unwinding about him like sinewy, swollen snakes.
>
> Beowulf screamed with fright. (pp. 55–56; our ellipses)

Once he regains his composure, Beowulf talks her to the point of death, as he had earlier done with Grendel. Other retellings retain the detail of the huge, ancient sword which Beowulf fortuitously finds in the cave and uses to kill the "sea-wolf" (OE *brimwylf*), but Nye defers this until Beowulf subsequently needs it to defend himself against the "undead" Grendel. Grendel's mother is not here granted a hero's death, by the sword. Through the power of negative virtue, especially the "contained-Cain" motif, Beowulf asserts his own inviolability, self-containment, and positive masculine self-identity, and as he chants a litany of masculine self-creation which effaces women— "I am Beowulf, son of Beowulf" . . . "I am Beowulf, father of himself" . . .

*Plate 3. The Fight between Beowulf and Grendel's Mother. Taken from* Beowulf *by Charles Keeping and Kevin Crossley-Holland, by permission of Oxford University Press.*

"I am Beowulf, who am myself"—Grendel's mother, now called "the monster," is reduced to helplessness. Her eyes, those eyes in her monstrous female breasts, flicker and close, and Beowulf turns the sex act that is death back against her: "Gently, carefully, with a stroking softness that was nearly pity, Beowulf put his hands about her neck, and strangled Her" (1994, p. 58). Nye's retelling predates such watershed rereadings of male discourses as, say, Kate Millett's *Sexual Politics* (1969), but we nevertheless do not think it unfair to highlight its misogynistic element, because its patriarchal assumptions at these points serve as a reminder that such assumptions are symptomatic of heroic metanarratives. We remarked earlier of *The Lion King* that its replication of a heroic paradigm enabled an interpellation of female characters within conservative reproductive and domestic roles, and that too can be read as symptomatic. The masculine self-generation which enables Beowulf to defeat Grendel's mother is also what enables Simba to defeat Scar. Heroic narratives hinge on the hero's active engagement with events and experiences, leading to the discovery of positive self-identity as masculinity, and perpetuate a masculine model of rivalry and competition as the normal pathway to that self-identity.

Keeping does not seem to have theorized about this aspect of heroic representation beyond the recognition that Grendel and his mother might not necessarily be monsters just because they are Outsiders, and that to be a hero is another kind of interpellation. He sought to make the latter point through the depiction of helmets: "Once you get everyone with helmets on it doesn't matter whether they are Saxons or police or yobs on the beach at Margate: they are just helmeted people" (cited in Martin, 1993, p. 144). The struggle between Beowulf and Grendel's mother thus became the subject for one of Keeping's most expressive illustrations, in which (and Keeping himself would not have put it this way) the marginalized female is locked in an ambiguously sexual/agonistic embrace with a metonym of phallocentric patriarchy. Her face in three-quarter profile expresses pathos rather than ferocity, counterpointing the text's description of her as "coated with her own filth, red-eyed and roaring" (p. 32). Her nakedness, the sinuous curves of her body, her thinness suggested by the sharply delineated ribs, and her breast flattened against Beowulf's chain mail, all combine to connote vulnerability rather than monstrosity. Her mouth opens wide above Beowulf's helmet, presumably to bite, but on what? Beowulf, for his part, is anonymous hero. His face is concealed, so the visual impression is predominantly of mail coat and helmet. But this is a curiously unadorned helmet, having only the shape but not the ornamentation of the helmet worn by the coastguard on page 8, and backed by the arm and hair of Grendel's mother it becomes an optical illusion, a visual ambiguity that hesitates between a representation of a penile glans and a representation of a helmet.[10] What in Nye was a triumphant celebration of patriarchal ascendancy is here much more complicated: it is no longer clear which figure is the hero, and which the monster.

## RETELLING THE STORY OF THE HERO: A FEMALE HERO PARADIGM

Nye and Keeping, in their different ways, bring us to the flip side of heroic discourse, and so to the insight that metanarratives do not occur simply or singly. And regardless of whether the retelling of a hero's career orients it towards exemplary sociality or exemplary individuality, it is still apt to be symptomatically patriarchal. Actions are performed by male characters, but female characters, insofar as they have a presence, have a passive relationship to events, responding rather than initiating. Robert Irwin, commenting on retellings of *Arabian Nights* stories, has suggested there is a need for retellings which may act as "a counter-weight to Campbell's unhealthily obsessive preoccupation with heroes and heroic destiny" (1994, p. 234). Such a counter-weight may be found in narratives oriented towards female experience which rather than retelling stories constructed around the male hero paradigm, with its misogyny and monstrous women, dismantle the monomyth and reconfigure heroic narratives around a female hero paradigm. That is, at the time of writing we were unaware of any retelling of *Beowulf* which, from a feminist perspective, attempts to disrupt or expose the socially and politically conservative discourses associated with the male hero paradigm, but there are novels which focus on the paradigm in settings modeled on the so-called heroic societies of the early Middle Ages.

It is an obvious point, often made, that masculine heroic paradigms cannot be transformed by gender reversals, such as merely allotting the hero's role to a female character (e.g., Cranny-Francis 1990, p. 84). Vogler notes that in his usage, "the term 'hero' . . . like 'doctor' or 'poet,' may refer to a woman or a man" (1992, p. 17), and he accordingly uses "he" and "she" randomly in his exposition of the heroic pattern. But this ignores the probability that "she" is just being assimilated to the male hero paradigm. If the notion of heroism is to be retained at all, its essential significance is in need of transformation. A female hero will have a different starting point and arrive at an alternative outcome by inhabiting a different mode of existence. An attempt by Jezewski (1984) to map a traditional female hero career in parallel with Raglan's "hero trait patterning" (see Raglan, 1990, p. 138) inevitably resulted in a very different paradigm. Starting from Greek mythology, Jezewski generated a paradigm consisting of eighteen traits, which she then tested by applying it to other female heroes from various cultures and periods. All of the female heroes she studied conformed with a range of eight to seventeen of these traits. This finding is suggestive for female heroes in children's fiction, but nevertheless seems to us to have some limiting elements. A significant pattern which underlies the twenty-two traits of Raglan's hero paradigm is that singly or in combination they separate the hero from everyday experience. Five of Jezewski's traits—relating to physical appearance, sexual relationships and reproduction—belong to what is commonly represented as everyday female experience. Their importance lies rather in the implication that a female hero does not have to become a pseudo-male. Second, the inclusion of "the Andromeda theme," which builds in a situation whereby a significant male rescues the female hero from interpellation within a restricted female function, is a crucial denial of agency. It occurs in less than half of Jezewski's examples, and is arguably a residual patriarchal strategy for ceding only a qualified heroism to female figures. Moreover, the "Andromeda theme" typically provides a male character with the opportunity of a morganatic marriage—that is, with the fantasy of gaining social rank, a kingdom, wealth, and so on, by winning a desirable, high-ranking female. In the literature we are concerned with there is more likely to be an "Ariadne theme," that is, an episode in which the female hero in some way rescues the principal male character (without necessarily suffering Ariadne's fate). This rescue may be implemented by physical or magical prowess, healing power, political acumen, or influence shaping the male's intellectual and emotional growth.[11] The male character may be of higher rank than his rescuer, and the incident does not necessarily lead to marriage.

Female heroes in heterocosmic children's fiction do conform to a great extent with the rest of Jezewski's traits, though are also marked by some of Raglan's male paradigm traits. We think that this is because authors are not writing out of any sense of a recognizable female hero paradigm, but are rather writing against the male paradigm. Thus, based on the female heroes in Lawrence's *The Warriors of Taan* (Elana) and Bates's *The Dragon's Tapestry* (Marwen) and those from novels to be discussed in later chapters—Lee's *The Black Unicorn* (Tanaquil); Pierce's tetralogy, *The Song of the Lioness* (Alanna); McKinley's *The Outlaws of Sherwood* (Marian and Cecily)—we suggest, tentatively, that the following modified version of Jezewski's paradigm is emerging as the female hero paradigm in contemporary heterocosmic children's fiction.[12] It now has only fourteen constant traits:

1. Her parents are of aristocratic or mage stock (or both).

2. Unusual circumstances surround her conception and/or birth.
   2a. As an infant, an attempt is made to kill her (this trait is probably a conscious quotation from the male paradigm. If evoked, it is likely that the next stages in Raglan's paradigm will also be evoked:
   2b. She is spirited away, and
   2c. Reared by foster parents in a far country.
   2d. On becoming an adult, she will return or go to her future kingdom).
3. During childhood and adolescence she is thought to be lacking in beauty and/or talent,
4. But she is confident that destiny intends a significant world role for her: her story will pivot on the emergence of her innate qualities.
5. She is upheld in her quest by a like-minded, unusual sisterhood, a network of female helpers.
6. She uses men for political purposes (in the widest sense of "political").
   6a. At some stage she adopts a male disguise (a specific political use of masculinity).
7. She also controls men in matters of love and sex (she is not entirely interpellated by conventions of romantic desire).
8. She performs tasks usually ascribed to the masculine domain (including the climactic victory over the king, monster, giant, dragon, demon, etc., which is the focus of evil and opposition in the story).
9. Her story contains the "Ariadne theme," and hence:
10. The subsequent development of this theme whereby the principal male becomes her partner or consort.
11. There are conflicting views of her goodness.
12. She becomes a ruler.
13. She prescribes law.
14. Her death is uneventful and may not be mentioned as part of her story.

What characterizes heroic female narratives in children's fiction, both in fictions seeking to transmute heroic paradigms and in those derived more from romance, is the concept of strategic identity—that is, female characters begin by inhabiting interpellated "female" roles but recognize the nature of their interpellation and subsequently construct for themselves alternative possibilities. Traits 3 and 4 are very pertinent here. The character's development is narratively marked by such elements as the disclosure of innate magical powers whose expression has been stifled or masked by patriarchal social thinking, or a movement from silence to speech, or achieving political identity and agency. It also goes without saying that conventions of narrative, especially focalization, are used to effect a reader's empathetic alignment with the female hero.

Although Elana and Marwen both display twelve hero traits, the two books are quite dissimilar and have different orientations towards the male hero paradigm. Bates pays little overt attention to the male paradigm, but constructs a female reversion of it. Lawrence evokes it directly as socially destructive and undesirable and takes up the Western construction of the hero as normatively male, asking whether a female hero must necessarily be inferior or complementary to the male. *The Warriors of Taan* moves to a utopian outcome whereby aggression and the will to power are contained by female-inspired communal sociality. The novel's heterocosm is a distant planet which has been invaded and overrun by peoples from Earth. The native society is a quasi-medieval society; it has an agricultural and pastoral economy, and a pretechnological culture, free of influence from the culture or technology of the Earth invaders. It is largely split along gender lines into two contesting "parallel cultures," sisters and warriors. The warriors resemble an early medieval Germanic heroic culture in their organization, artefacts, and engagement in a life broadly given over to drinking, boasting, and fighting. A warrior's self-identity depends on asserting his place above others in a hierarchy. We remarked in chapter 1 that epic discourse in children's literature is apt to affirm hierarchical social order, but works with a feminist agenda resist such an outcome. Lawrence constructs a pejorative view of warrior culture by depicting its futile, mindless violence, and misogyny, and through the confusion in the mind of Prince Khian, one of the novel's two focalizing characters, who almost loses all because of his desire for "patriarchal approval" (1988, p. 211). In contrast, the sisters insist that "status is meaningless" (p. 76) and cultivate development of the self within a wider sociality, in a sense of service first to the sisterhood and through it to the world. They are thus depicted as sharing a strong sense of community based on mutual respect for one another's skills, shared experience, and bonds of affection (that is, the basis for trait 5 of the paradigm). The "oldwives" in *The Dragon's Tapestry* represent a comparable community.

Lawrence also depicts the sisters as rather Machiavellian, evoking trait 6 as a general necessity. From the outset it is said of their reverend mother that, "Devious, manipulative, she would use whoever she could to further the aims of the sisterhood and safeguard the future of the planet" (1988, p. 8). Elana, the principal focalizing character with whom readers are most closely aligned, learns to recognize and accept this manipulativeness, so that by the time she herself has become reverend mother at the novel's close, she is ready to loose it on the rest of the universe. This is an interesting recognition that the alternative to violence is probably not rational discussion, and that a politics of opposition to a patriarchal gender ideology may require subversive strategies.

The Warriors of Taan reconstructs assumptions about heroism by means of a double-stranded, double-focalized narrative which contrasts male and female hero paradigms and invests female models with authority as the female perspective develops from an oppositional to the dominant position. Throughout this process, reader alignment remains firmly with that female perspective. The Dragon's Tapestry, now set in a recognizably sword-and-sorcery, nontechnological heterocosm, deconstructs the male hero paradigm more obliquely by presenting the female paradigm as, in part, a parodic reversion of it. Bates's feminist agenda is less obvious than Lawrence's insofar as characteristic feminist language and concepts are transmuted into the discourse of fantastic narrative, where their meaning remains as a trace to be reinstated as the female hero paradigm emerges. In other words, particular structures and motifs shape the novel's outcomes according to the assumptions and values of a feminist discourse. Marwen's childhood, for example, is subject to patriarchy, so that its ignominious aspects are attributed to her outcast status as an illegitimate child, whereby she continues to bear the punishment for her mother's sexual transgression. But as an apprentice "oldwife" (that is, as a witch figure, shaman, healer, and sustainer of tradition), her resistances to her community's attitude towards the functions of an oldwife are resistances to interpellation as female. Oldwives are expected to be modest, submissive, self-deprecating, apologetic about their power; they speak in soft voices and whispers. Marwen is expected to accept her restricted choices passively, to bear her sufferings stoically, and to accept punishment for perceived transgressions when small acts of magic go awry.

The patriarchal ideology Marwen struggles against is figured on two levels: first, on the personal level in the misogyny of her cousin Maug, for whom she is "something that lived and breathed without a soul" (p. 114), and whose mixed contempt and lust for her always made her feel diminished; and second, in Perdoneg, the dragon, who is driven by a vengeful will to power, and whose only effective opponent is Marwen. The dragon is less clearly a patriarchal figure, except inasmuch as the will to power is depicted as masculine, though this aspect is also cued when Perdoneg's desire to draw Marwen into his kingdom of death is given a sexual nuance: his voice "was caressing, even lustful" (p. 149); "Perdoneg's yellow eyes met hers lustfully" (p. 169).

Like many young characters in fantasy literature, Marwen is unable to focus her innate capacity while a young girl. She is filled with what in other contemporary fantasies is referred to as "wild magic," which is equivalent to a female sexual power often exhibited as deviance by the central female characters in adult fiction (see, for example, Jones's *A Sudden Wild Magic*). The novel implies this equivalence both by the circumstances of Marwen's birth and when, having been sentenced to death by exposure as punishment for her deviant magic, she narrowly avoids being raped by the three young men (led by Maug) who escort her into the wilderness. The outbreaking of wild magic, and the need to learn how to control it, is roughly equivalent to episodes in the early life of a male hero in which he tests the boundaries of his strength. A good example is the Breca episode in *Beowulf*, which in Nye's retelling Beowulf recounts with a smile, "as though all this struck him as great foolishness now" (1994, p. 26). In Marwen's case, learning to use her magic is likened to passing through the narrow opening at the center of an hourglass: "The higher your powers, the narrower become your options to use it [magic], for you come to know that every slight breath of magic moves the winds and the world" (1992, p. 24). But once she has passed through that aperture—that is, once she has faced and defeated the dragon which threatens to destroy her world—she finds "another expanding world in the next chamber" (p. 179). In another area, the novel's romantic subtheme is also fed by this interrelationship of sexuality and magic. Marwen and Prince Camlach (first linked by the novel's use of the "Ariadne theme") share a mutual desire, though Camlach does early on reject her when he learns she is "soulless." At the close of the novel, although it is foreshadowed that the two might marry in a sequel (as they do), Marwen refuses or at least postpones marriage to study and pursue her career and duties as the wizard she is in process of becoming.

Thus an important and central feminist turn Bates gives to her reconstructed paradigm is her identification of Marwen's quest as a quest for agency. There is a famous paradox in *Beowulf* that recurs in medieval Germanic hero narratives:

> Wyrd oft nereð
> Unfægne eorl,   þonne his ellen deah
> (Fate [Wyrd] will often spare an undoomed man, if his courage is good) (ll. 572–573)

In other words, a hero can be the agent of his destiny. In Ve, Marwen's world, an oldwife weaves a tapestry for every newborn child, and this tapestry contains images which are symbols of the child's destiny; a life is deemed well-lived if the tapestry is judged to have been fulfilled. The tapestry is rather like Wyrd as "the living experience of human consciousness with the intractable," but its symbols are also projections of contexts of heredity and environment. Marwen has never seen her tapestry: it was hidden by Grondil, the oldwife who fostered her, and later burned by her fosterfather. Her local community believes her never to have had a tapestry, and therefore to be "soulless," which is a simple metonymy for her marginality as an illegitimate orphan female and the social discourse which denies her agency: "In those days the people told her about herself, as a mirror did. They had defined her, had given her size and form, had erased her with one word: *soulless*" (pp. 164–165). Her quest centers on her desire to have her tapestry rewoven, though she does not realize until late in the novel that every action she performs is part of the reweaving. This is apparent to readers, since the weaving and with it the symbols of the tapestry were fully described in the opening chapter. At a crucial turning point, when Marwen understands that the best way to evade the dragon seeking her is to go towards it, she achieves a significant insight into the operation of the tapestry:

> Sometimes, or perhaps always, it was the knowledge of one's tapestry, not the fact, that made it true. The tapestry was not the thief of agency, it did not rob her of making her own life: it was a guide, a map to a place that was already within her heart. (p. 125)

Bates is here looking for a way to narrativize complex, abstract ideas about choice, agency, and desire. The restatement of "not the thief of agency" as "did not rob her of making her own life" is indicative of what she is trying to do within the constraints of a novel for young readers, in which she can't draw on the disruptions of language and form used in adult feminist fantasy.

The epigraph for the novel's chapter 10 proposes, "Intelligence is the stem and stalk upon which agency blooms" (p. 106); that for chapter 11 says, in part, "The essence of magic is not so much in the spell but in the words themselves" (p. 116). Knowledge and language combine when, at the climax of *The Dragon's Tapestry*, Marwen defeats the dragon not merely by summoning magical power but through language. As she speaks the knowledge she has gained in her quest to confront the dragon, her utterances are literally depicted as a development of *voice*. At first her voice "sounded small and weak in the face of the dragon" (p. 169), and it is "a still quiet voice," "whispered" and "trembling," until she has gathered the whole picture; then "she was elated, stunned, shaking with her own power. 'Go, dragon, back to your prison,' she commanded in the language of creation, not knowing she knew the words" (1992, p. 172). At this point Marwen has most fully achieved female agency, and is rewarded in the next chapter by a confrontation with "The Taker," the female figure of Death who has been pursuing her throughout her quest. Instead of taking her life, as Marwen expects, the Taker discloses the contents of her lost tapestry.

By the end of the twentieth century the legacy of the heroic literature of the early Middle Ages can be said to have bifurcated. On the one hand, it has been perpetuated as an aspect of cultural conservation, as a form of nationalism, as an expression of perceived archetypal human experience, and even as a conservative shoring up of patriarchal ideology. These uses tend to efface specific historical differences in favor of some sense of "eternal human values." On the other hand, and much more recently, a small literature has begun to emerge which seeks to deconstruct and reconstruct versions of the hero paradigm in order to affirm and celebrate female experiences and values.

NOTES

1. In the literature we are examining through most of this chapter such a heroic function is almost invariably the province of male characters, so we will generally use the pronoun *he.*

2. A useful standard account of these issues can be found in Marina Warner, *Alone of All Her Sex* (1976), especially chapter 9.

3. This note is not included in all editions of Nye's *Beowulf*, and the different forms in which it appears have interesting peritextual implications. We have quoted from the 1994 version, which stresses the original's stature and categorizes it as a "mythic story." Earlier versions of the note associated *Beowulf* with "old myths and legends" and detailed the texts of the poem, both in Old English and Modern English translation, which Nye consulted. It seems that by 1994 there is more need to invest the source text with authority and value than the retelling. Cultural value cannot be simply assumed.

4. The raid into Frisia in which Hygelac was killed took place about the year 521, and is the only historical fact in *Beowulf*. Beowulf himself probably had no historical existence. See R.W. Chambers, 1959, pp. 2ff.

5. Oddly enough, one of the problem areas, the change of the swimming match against Breca to a boat contest, which Mills describes as "a weakening . . . in the interests of rational credibility" (1986, p. 76), has been a subject of controversy amongst *Beowulf* scholars. Robinson (1974), seeking to stress Beowulf's physical limitations and vulnerability rather than superhuman qualities, argues that the Breca episode is a tall story, exaggerated by Unferth in his role of Jester, and part of a flyting, and that at least part of the adventure takes place in boats. Greenfield (1982) reasserts the more widely accepted reading.

Ebbutt, Sutcliff's source for most of the detail and much of the language of her retelling, unambiguously presents the episode as "a swimming contest in the ocean" (1910, p. 12).

6. Old English poetry, of course, used alliteration as a structural principle. The assonance of "heart . . . ached . . . action" is roughly equivalent to permissible Old English practice; the distribution of the alliterating syllables was regulated, however, rather than random as here.

7. These conventional cultural constructions of "evil" are given further em-

phasis by visual allusions in Scar's *Anthem* to Leni Riefenstahl's Nazi propaganda film, *Triumph of the Will*.

8. Peter Dickinson had so argued in his delightful mock history, *The Flight of Dragons* (London: Pierrot Pub., 1979).

9. The description here paraphrases Crossley-Holland's translation: "The monster . . . hungrily seized / a sleeping warrior, greedily wrenched him, / bit into his body, drank the blood / from his veins, devoured huge pieces" (1968, p. 53).

10. In his first attempt at these illustrations, Keeping had been much more explicit about the nudity of Grendel and his mother, but was persuaded by the publisher to be more concealing (Martin 1993, p. 143). The double image in this scene apparently went unremarked because it is symbolic rather than literal.

11. The role of Janet in the *Tam Lin* folktale has a similarity to this theme, but Janet embodies too few of the other hero traits for the paradigm to apply in her case. See the discussion in chapter 7.

12. The six female heroes mentioned exhibit the following traits:

| Elana | Marwen | Alanna | Marian | Cecily | Tanaquil |
|-------|--------|--------|--------|--------|----------|
|       | 1      | 1      | 1      | 1      | 1        |
|       | 2 [2a-d] | 2 [2a-d] |      |        | 2        |
| 3     | 3      | 3      |        | 3      | 3        |
| 4     | 4      | 4      | 4      | 4      | 4        |
| 5     | 5      |        | 5      | 5      |          |
| 6     |        | 6 [6a] | 6 [6a] | [6a]   | 6 [6a]   |
| 7     | 7      | 7      | 7      |        |          |
| 8     | 8      | 8      | 8      | 8      | 8        |
| 9     | 9      | 9      | 9      | 9      |          |
| 10    | 10     | 10     | 10     | 10     |          |
| 11    | 11     | 11     | 11     |        | 11       |
| 12    | 12     | 12     | 12     |        |          |
| 13    |        |        | 13     |        |          |
| 14    | 14     | 14     | 14     |        |          |

In some cases the traits are metaphorical. For example, traits 2 and 2a-d apply to Alanna in that she was born a twin, and escapes interpellation as a docile female by changing places with her brother, disguising herself as a boy, and undertaking warrior training at the royal court. Although she later refuses to marry the prince, trait 12 applies because she inherits her tutor/mentor's fiefdom.

AN AFFIRMATION OF CIVILIZATION
AGAINST BARBARISM

ARTHUR AND ARTHURIANISM IN MEDIEVALIST
AND QUASI-MEDIEVAL ROMANCE

*Arthur: "A Romano-British war-leader, to whom, when the Barbarian dark-
ness came flooding in, the last guttering lights of civilization seemed worth
fighting for."*
—Rosemary Sutcliff, *Sword at Sunset* (1963)

*Some man who knew those days had to set down the truth about them in
good black ink; there are altogether too many tales of magical swords and
great round tables going about already.*
—George Finkel, *Watch Fires to the North* (1968)

Another rich source of medieval themes and motifs has been romance, especially the romance traditions centering on Arthur and Camelot. There is
a thriving industry in adult fantasy which uses this material for quite diverse
purposes, and another in children's literature which overlaps with the former
but also has its own distinctive attributes, shaped by the familiar metanarratives of retold stories. The uses of Arthuriana in children's literature
thus follow the typology we have identified in earlier chapters, but now also
largely correspond with most of the categories Raymond H. Thompson
(1985) identified for Arthurian legend as a whole. As Thompson pointed out,
spatio-temporal *setting* is always the pivotal categorizing element. Significantly, retellings for young readers are grounded in reproduction of late
medieval Arthurian stories (that is, what we will refer to as the Malorian
tradition) and historical fiction revolving around a fifth-century Arthur,
whereas over half of Thompson's survey is devoted to fantasy, a relatively
minor domain within the children's literature.

The primary group, both chronologically and numerically, consists
of retellings of stories about Arthur and his knights, eclectically put together
from Thomas Malory's fifteenth-century *Morte Darthur* (itself in part a com-

pilation) and various other medieval sources (notably Geoffrey of Monmouth; *The Mabinogion,* for "Owain" and "Gereint and Enid"; the works of Chretien de Troyes; Godfrey of Strasbourg's *Tristan and Iseult;* and the separate poems *Sir Gawain and the Green Knight* and *The Marriage of Sir Gawain and Dame Ragnell*). The pattern for retellings thus derives ultimately from Malory, but is established in modern practice by Howard Pyle's *The Story of King Arthur and His Knights* (1903), which is as much a reversion as a retelling, and especially Roger Lancelyn Green's *King Arthur and His Knights of the Round Table* (1953). Green is as influential on subsequent retellings as is Malory, and particularly on the representation of mood and atmosphere, since his is a postromantic Arthuriad with Gothic nuances not found in Malory. In such gatherings the history of Arthur functions as a frame within which other stories can be set, sometimes loosely, but often bound more closely by a consistent site of narrative enunciation and by metanarrative.

A second and very important group consists of historical fictions set in premedieval Britain in the period of Anglo-Saxon incursion and settlement, and hence Arthur is depicted as a Romano-Celt defending his native land against barbarian invaders. These narratives have their source in the work of historians and archaeologists pursuing a historical Arthur on the basis of the histories of Gildas (who wrote in the middle of the sixth century) and Nennius (early ninth century). A good example of the kind of source material available to children's authors in the later twentieth century can be found in Geoffrey Ashe (ed.), *The Quest for Arthur's Britain* (1968), although the most significant works of historical fiction had been published by the end of the 1960s in the works of Treece, Finkel and, especially, Sutcliff.

Third, there are various forms of fantasy which use material that is vaguely medieval, and not specifically Arthurian, belonging to what Moody has described as an "accumulating fantasy of a quasi-medieval period" (1991, p. 187). This is the realm of sorcery, and of supernatural events and supernatural creatures, such as dragons and unicorns. The works may be further subdivided into three groups. They may be entirely set in an archaic world subject to magical or supernatural forces, and hence be a form of so-called high fantasy, as in Tamora Pierce's *The Song of the Lioness* tetralogy; this subgroup is most likely to be influenced by attempts in adult writing to reconfigure the habitus of sword-and-sorcery fantasy to produce a feminist perspective. Next, characters from the contemporary world, usually children, cross over into a pseudomedieval paracosm, in such novels as Alan Garner's *Elidor* and Catherine Fisher's *Fintan's Tower.* Or, finally, there are ironic versions of one or other of these subgroups, such as Susan Price's delightful *Foiling the Dragon* (1994).

Fourth, where adult Arthuriana is transposed into science fiction (as in, for example, C.J. Cherryh's *Port Eternity*) children's literature has developed a subcategory of postdisaster fiction in which the world, destroyed by nuclear, ecological, or other disaster, reverts to pretechnological social forms which are recognizably medieval. The category originated with Peter Dickinson's *The Weathermonger* (1968), in which Merlin plays a central role. Thematically, this category parallels that of the historical fictions insofar as both pivot on a struggle between civilization and barbarism, and both are apt to be fables about the nature of modernity.

Finally, there is a small fifth category of contemporary realist fictions which incorporate Arthurian material as an exemplary model, in a way which self-consciously reflects the characteristic purpose of the area in children's literature.

Within and between these categories, texts may function differently in the kinds of meanings they produce, but all prompt the common question, Why is there such an attraction for this particular kind of medieval material? Linda Yeatman (1991, p. 173) suggests that it is because it contains "all the best ingredients for good stories—magic, action, adventure, clash of characters, jealousy, love"; because it depicts a time of dramatic change when the old wisdoms of magic and ancient religions were being replaced by the new beliefs of a more modern society; and because of the fascination offered by a "vision and dream of perfection" undermined by the flaws of the main characters. These are plausible reasons for the appeal offered by the Malorian tradition, and Malory's own contrasts within the *Morte Darthur* between the Arthurian "then" and his own fifteenth century indicate that he was himself aware of these qualities. They do not entirely explain why authors have been drawn to historical fictions about post-Roman Britain, however, and the explanation for this seems to lie elsewhere. On the one hand, within a narrative frame which assumes a movement towards tragic closure, in national or cultural terms if not in personal, there is a greater freedom to invent episodes, incidents, and characters than the Malorian tradition seems to allow—though Pyle certainly felt free to invent new matter. On the other hand, it is no coincidence that this category develops in the second half of the twentieth century. In part this is because of the ready availability of semipopular histories such as Ashe's, but it also seems to be a response to the cataclysms of two world wars and the challenges to traditional culture posed by modernism and postmodernism, especially where this is perceived as the growth of a materialistic culture with little sense of past cultures and values, a new "barbarism."

As we said above, Arthurian retellings in the second half of the twentieth century formulate their shape and purpose largely under the influence of Roger Lancelyn Green's *King Arthur and His Knights of the Round Table*. Green's was an ambitious, new syncretic version which reshaped the corpus by combining selections from Malory with other works and aspiring to a new sense of unity through a single structure and metanarrative.[1] A secondary influence comes from Rosemary Sutcliff's innovations in her trilogy *The Sword and the Circle* (1981), *The Light Beyond the Forest* (1979), and *The Road to Camlann* (1981), especially the first volume. *The Sword and the Circle,* however, already shows the influence of Green's retelling, and the two authors share a common metanarrative whereby the Arthurian story functions as an account of the recurrent human struggle between civilization and barbarism. Both enunciate this struggle metaphorically as a contest between light and darkness, as when Green describes the Arthurian era as "that brief period of light set like a star of Heaven in the midst of the Dark Ages" (p. 81).

Green is quite overt about his purpose, which closely conforms to the Western metaethic in its conjunction of coherent, unified form, cultural heritage, and moral perspective. In his introduction, he explains that he "endeavored to make each adventure a part of one fixed pattern—Arthur's Kingdom, the Realm of Logres, the model of chivalry and right striving against the barbarism and evil which surrounded and at length engulfed it." He is quick to point out that this is "only the bare foundation" on which is reared "a fabric consisting of all the best-known adventures, exploits and quests" of the Arthurian story (1953, p. 11). It is a totalizing process whereby materials from disparate sources are rendered coherent and unified. Green achieves his purpose formally through his representations of character, setting, and motivation, but the unity is finally one of significance. Two examples of his strategy which were to prove especially influential are the elevation of Morgana le Fay as the focus of the dark force, powerful through "her beauty and her magic wiles" (p. 73),[2] and his transformation of the story into a Gothic discourse.

An aspect of cultural heritage which pervades the metanarratives of Green and Sutcliff is nationalism. Most retellings of the Arthurian story have originated in Britain, which is perhaps in itself hardly surprising but proves to be a context in which the story is constantly transformed into a parable for modern times whereby British culture is under siege from external military and cultural onslaughts. As we will argue in the next chapter, the story of Robin Hood can also function in this way. Thus ethics, exemplary behavior, and nationalism become inextricably intertwined. We will briefly demonstrate it here by citing the ways Green and Sutcliff transform the code of ethics laid down in Malory for the Round Table knights, a code which deals exclusively with standards of personal behavior. Green reproduces Malory's clauses, but frames them within "the Order of Chivalry," *national* honor, and exemplary behavior which transcends boundaries of time and place. It now begins:

> I lay upon you all the Order of Chivalry. All of you, and those who will sit afterwards at this Table, are the knights of Logres, and for the glory of Logres, the Realm of Righteousness, do not ever depart from the high virtues of this realm. (p. 63)

The terms are then reaffirmed by an exhortation from Merlin, added at the end:

> "Do you even so," said Merlin, "that the realm of Logres may endure for many years as an example to all the men of after time. For be you sure that, though you all die, its fame and its example shall live for ever." (p. 63)

Sutcliff's version is shorter, combining elements from Malory and Green:

> And that evening Arthur received the oaths of all his knights of the Round Table, that always they would defend the right, that they would be the true servants and protectors of all women, and deal justly in all things with all men, that they would strive always for the good of the kingdom of Britain and for the glory of the kingdom of Logres which was within Britain as the flame is within the lamp, and that they would keep faith with each other and with God. (1981a, p. 66)

In this case, the change of proportion seems quite significant, as about half the oath now deals with exemplary nationalism, and in conjunction with the central figure of light against the darkness. Further, the order of the material implies that it is nationalism which enables "faith with each other and with God." In drawing attention to this aspect of metanarrative, it's important to qualify it. Both Green and Sutcliff eschew the rampant imperialism of Arthur's European campaigns which Malory found in the fourteenth-century alliterative *Morte Arthure*, and instead of trying to incorporate versions of this story they rather expand the function of another major aspect of the metaethic: the ethics of individual subjectivity as explored in quests and tests centered on personal behavior, especially as found in *Sir Gawain and the Green Knight* and *The Marriage of Sir Gawain and Dame Ragnell.*

Focus on personal dimensions of ethics and behavior has developed a particular nuance, however. There is a tendency for modern medievalism to be refracted through versions of Gothic mode originating in the eighteenth and nineteenth centuries, by means of which a concern with the dark places of the mind and imagination, the paranormal, and the irrational are grafted onto medieval stories. This tendency is most apparent in quasi-medieval or sword-and-sorcery fantasy, but—once again under Green's influence—it also pervades retellings. The concern with the dark psyche is articulated quite explicitly in "Enchantress," the last story of Dickinson's *Merlin Dreams,* with its Gothic setting intensified by Alan Lee's illustrations, when the child-hero, Dan, defeats the enchantress by defining her: "Your name is all the names in the book. All our names. You are us. You are our dream. You are our nightmare" (1988, p. 161). This incident well illustrates how medieval story is used in the modern age to express psychic states untrammeled by technology and material reality—that is, to express our dreams and nightmares, psychic states in which, in Varnado's words, the supernatural becomes "a symbol of our past rising against us" (1987, p. 26). To achieve this, though, modern story has to recast the medieval and even invest it with "inauthentic" motifs: vampiric enchantresses, for example, derive not from medieval literature but from a postmedieval horror of anthropophagy (the word *cannibal* itself originated in the sixteenth century) combined with a modern apprehension that evil arises from the dark side of the human psyche rather than from external, demonic promptings.[3]

A particular attribute of Gothicized medievalism is the use of Gothic mode to intensify the emotive mystery attributed to things medieval. This appears in selections of content and focus, and is marked by the representations of setting, specifically by lexical choices in combination with lexical density. Malory's lexically spare prose is thus heavily augmented. For example, Lancelot's adventure at the Chapel Perilous is an episode fraught with mystery and terror, which readily lends itself to Gothic modifications. The adventure begins when Lancelot follows a questing hound to the castle of Sir Gilbert. A comparison of how Malory and Green describe his arrival illustrates how Malory is Gothicized:

> [T]he brachette . . . wente thorow a grete marys [marsh], and ever sir Launcelot folowed.
> And then was he ware of an olde manor, and thydir ran the brachette and so over a brydge. So sir Launcelot rode over that brydge

that was olde and feble, and whan he com in the myddys of a grete halle there he seye lye dede a knyght that was a semely man, and that brachette lycked his woundis. (Malory, Book 6:14)

[A]cross a great marsh they went and came at length over a bridge to an old manor-house whose crumbling walls, half hidden by ivy, went down into a weed-grown moat.

Into the great hall ran the brachet, and there Launcelot saw a knight lying dead: and the brachet went and licked his wounds and howled dolorously. (Green, 1953, p. 108)

Gothicizing is not simply a matter of loading the prose with lexically dense items, and Green's description in this example is actually shorter than Malory's. Rather, it is a matter of selection. Malory dwells on the point at which Lancelot emerges from the marsh and crosses the bridge, using the bridge's state of disrepair to alert readers that he is entering morally ambiguous ground. The dead knight's wife is a sorceress ("a wicked sorceress" in Green), and the need to counter her revenge on her husband's slayer motivates Lancelot's journey to the Chapel Perilous. Green transposes the perceptual order of manor and bridge, deletes the information about the bridge, and instead describes the manor using a register characteristic of Gothic ("crumbling," "half hidden," "ivy," "weed-grown"), thereby evoking different associations. Similarly, he deletes Malory's positive comment on the dead knight's appearance, which sustains the ambiguity of the situation, and supplies instead an aural Gothic effect ("howled dolorously"). The strategy is characteristic of how Gothic writing controls character-focalization: the characters seem to be focalizing objects and events, but the narrative defines the resulting response. The conjunction in Malory's version of the empty space of the marsh, disrepair, and death contains the seeds of Gothic, perhaps, but there is none of the emotive language, and the subjective response of the audience is not as controlled.

The tendency of Gothic writing to load the discourse with signifiers indicating darkness, eeriness, fear, and a sense of things happening just beyond the threshold of perception, becomes even more evident in the account of Lancelot's experiences inside the Chapel. Where Malory says that Lancelot "sawe no lyght but a dymme lampe brennyng," Green has "one dim lamp which cast weird shadows beneath the low stone arches" (1953, p. 110). And in Malory, when Lancelot cuts a piece of cloth from the shroud of the corpse he finds there, "then it fared undir hym as the grounde had quaked a lytyll; therewithall he feared." In Green, "the floor moved as if an earth-quake had shaken the chapel, and the lamp swung, creaking dismally on its chain until the shadows seemed to writhe and clutch at him. Sir Launcelot knelt awhile in fear." In these examples, Green's Gothicizing additions to his source simultaneously make the scene more immediately present to the senses and determine the nature of emotive response. When, in turn, Sutcliff reworks Green, she goes still further in inscribing response within depiction: "the pavement tilted under him as though the earth had quaked beneath the chapel, and the lamp swung on its chain, casting weird shadows about the place so that for a moment it seemed full of dark wings. . . . And Sir Lancelot's heart sprang racing into his throat" (1981, pp. 105–106). These modifications of Malory accord well with Varnado's observation that the "haunted castle," the "unifying ideogram of Gothic literature," contains a peculiar mixture of sacred and profane symbolism that constitutes a "har-mony of contrasts": darkness, silence, and sublimity of structures lit by an occasional glimmer of light "suggest by analogy the realm of existence that lies hidden behind the world of material reality" (1987, p. 32).

The doubleness of vision and sense of realms of existence that lie ambiguously between the everyday world and other worlds meshes with a particularly important element of the Arthur story: the doubleness (or even duplicity) of its close. That is, there is a final narrative cataclysm in which Arthur perishes, with all that is implied about order and social anarchy, and there is a promise of his return, which enfolds the past eternally into the present and asserts that human time is always a dialectic between the light and the dark, good and evil, and that human beings can always look be-yond any present social or moral debility to a resurgence of positive condi-tions. Muriel Whitaker (1977, p. 153) has argued that this dialectic appeals to modern audiences because of an attraction to heroic defiance and doomed love, and to dreams of order and a sympathy with hopeless causes: "we may see in the story of Arthur how the tragedy of the human condition where good intentions are too often thwarted by malign fate can be combined with the hope of another chance." Later in this chapter we will examine how these themes are explicitly reworked in contemporary realist fictions.

HISTORICAL FICTIONS

The quest for a historical fiction about Arthur, as opposed to retold romance, really begins after the 1939–45 world war. It had been made possible by his-torians publishing between the wars, especially Chambers (1927) and Collingwood (1937). A clear example of the influence of this work is the use made of Collingwood's argument that a Romanized *Comes Britanniarum*

("Count" of the British provinces) is likely to have created a force of cavalry capable of routing the Saxon warriors (1937, pp. 322–323). The Saxon invaders were infantrymen, with little or no body armor and with little tactical discipline: "Against such an enemy, a small force of ordinary Roman cavalry, resolutely led, must prove invincible." This argument ultimately lies behind the "romance of cavalry" which plays such a large part in the fictions of Sutcliff and Finkel, and most recently in Anne McCaffery's expansion of the motif from Sutcliff's *Sword at Sunset* in her historical novel *Black Horses for the King* (1996)—a rather weak historical romance mainly about horseshoes.

It also seems likely that in the postwar years there was a nationalist motive for retelling the Arthur story from a more historical base, as it now becomes an account of the struggle to sustain sovereignty and civilization in the face of invasion from Europe. A similar motive again underlies retellings of the Robin Hood legend. Treece, for example, while insisting that his version is not "history," envisages a British audience and describes the book as "an adventure story, about people rather like ourselves—all except those who were more like Apache Indians [sic] and gangsters—and, of course, it is about the 'growing pains' of our own country" (1954, p. 9). The implicit comparison here with Hollywood films underscores the book's framing contrast between civilization and order, on the one side, and barbarism and chaos, on the other. Sutcliff saw the demise of Roman Britain in similar terms, and commented that "the disintegration of the Roman Empire and the onset of the Dark Ages contain truths for our own time. . . . We have the same uncertainty the Romans must have had whether the light would show up again at the end of the tunnel" (cited in Carpenter and Prichard, 1984, p. 506).[4]

Authors who would write this kind of historical fiction have few actual facts to go on, apart from what archaeological evidence discloses about general cultural conditions. Ashe suggests, following the (eleventh-century) *Annales Cambriae,* that records of a strictly historical kind yield nothing more tangible than that Arthur (almost certainly as leader of the British) fought at the battle of Mons Badonicus in C.E. 516 or 518 and died at the battle of Camlaun about twenty years later (1968, p. 43). There may also be some substance in the account given by Nennius of Arthur's twelve battles. Ashe argues that "because the names are obscure, they are likely to be genuine" (1968, p. 40). Barber is much more circumspect, and thinks that the "irreducible minimum of Arthurian fact" is that "Arthur was a hero of the Welsh, celebrated in their literature by the eighth century" (1973, p. 24). Sutcliff, going well beyond the "strictly historical," gives the available sources as ancient chronicles, known history, Welsh Bardic tradition, and "the leas lying at the bottom of legends and folktales" (1965b, p. 26); from these the "historical" Arthur is reconstructed in historical fiction. Sutcliff offered such a reconstruction in *Heroes and History*, but in her enormously influential adult novel, *Sword at Sunset*, not only engaged in creative surmise but also chose to retain crucial framing elements from later tradition. As she puts it in her prefatory author's note:

> Certain features I have retained from the traditional Arthurian fabric, because they have the atmosphere of truth. I have kept the original framework, or rather two interwrought frameworks: the sin which carries with it its own retribution; the Brotherhood broken by the love between the leader's woman and his closest friend. These have the inevitability and pitiless purity of outline that one finds in classical tragedy, and that belong to the ancient and innermost places of man.

Since virtually everything in the novel is fiction anyway, there is little reason not to follow such a course. Our interest, then, is not in whether or not Sutcliff was justified in her decision, but in the evocation of the Western metaethic through key concepts of her formulation here: "the atmosphere of truth," sin and retribution, "the ancient and innermost places of man," "traditional . . . fabric," and "classical." In her conception, the metaethic in all its ramifications is encapsulated in her retelling of the Arthurian story, notably in its patterned narrative, its expression of significant and universal human experience, its link between "truth" and cultural heritage, and its ethical dimension. The double perspective—the suggestions that the narrative is historically possible or plausible, and that it expresses universal human experience—is typical of historical fiction, but also powerfully reinforces the metaethic. Sutcliff's recurrent metaphor of the struggle of the light against the dark becomes the key: the struggle focused in the figure of Arthur is a struggle not for territory, or personal or ethnic survival, but a struggle between civilization and barbarism, light and dark (and Sutcliff's metaphor has later influences, surfacing again as the heart of Susan Cooper's *The Dark Is Rising* sequence).

In its handling of traditional material, *Sword at Sunset* also employs a strategy common to the major Arthurian historical fictions for younger readers—that is, Treece's *The Eagles Have Flown* and Finkel's *Watch Fires to the North*—to enable the reuse of elements from later tradition. The works flaunt a self-conscious paring away of elements identified as legendary accretions. Thus Treece disposes of the Round Table legend in a little scene in which Arthur solves a tension over precedence by throwing "his great round shield" on the ground and asking the petty kings present to place themselves about it:

> Then, when they looked up at him enquiringly, Artorius smiled back at them and said, "Who is at the head of this table? No man, for each has his own place, neither higher nor lower than another's." (p. 121)

Because Lancelot is a French addition to the Arthurian story, Sutcliff retained the adultery by devising an affair between Guinevere and Bedivere (Guenhumara and Bedwyr). Finkel describes a "curious relationship" between his Gwenyfer and one Olans, a foreign recruit (of Gothic birth, but the name is obviously an echo of Lancelot, and here his younger brother is "Glahad," the grail knight); but the point of introducing it is to raise rumors of adultery in order to dismiss them (1968, pp. 232–233). Some time after Arthur's death, Gwenyfer and Olans are married, as part of an aftermath which generally debunks various supernatural and numinous elements of the tradition—Arthur's disappearance to the Isle of Avalon; his future return; the magic associated with Excalibur (pp. 308–309). The purpose of anchoring the story in historical realism is to tie the narrative's significance more closely to everydayness, to the exemplary function of historical fiction.

Treece's *The Eagles Have Flown* overtly discards the Malorian (and Tennysonian) tradition in favor of a mix of adventure story and historical realist strategies which at the time, and even now to some extent, distinguished his retelling from other retellings for children. This is most evident in the detail and grittiness of his descriptions of death and fighting, in his often unsympathetic characterization of Arthur, and in his use of his two focalizing characters, the boys Festus and Wulf, to register emotional responses. For example, Arthur's summary execution of a suspected tax evader is presented as follows:

> [T]here was only the blubbering of the ragged old man, who still knelt in the road, asking for mercy. Wulf recognized the voice of Artos; he was laughing in a strange manner, but it was not a laugh that he liked.
> "Did you see what happened, Festus?" said the Jutish lad [Wulf].
> Festus was shuddering, his head held low as though he tried not to see anything else that might happen. (p. 47)

The language now feels dated and a little awkward, but the process is clear enough, as within a brief sequence the text quickly establishes a moment of sympathy for the victim and then presents a twofold response to his undescribed death. It is not immediately obvious that Artos himself performs the execution at the moment he laughs, and readers have to work to determine this. Wulf's response to the laugh marks it pejoratively, and Festus is sickened by what he has witnessed. Treece's purpose here in part is to depict Artos as himself primarily a barbarian and to incorporate this representation into one of the major themes. Throughout the novel Treece sets up oppositions between the Romans (who stand for civilization) and both the Saxons (that is, the barbarians) and the British Celts (who have reverted to tribalism and savagery). Arthur is represented as a barbarian who becomes more Roman, and by representing both the Saxons and the British as barbaric, Treece valorizes the cultural capital associated with "Latinity"—that is, with a classical education, where "Rome" becomes a metaphor for an idea of culture, justice, and the kind of behavior which will guarantee "a free Britain" (p. 49). What Treece here exemplifies is what Bové has described as a humanistic dependency on the demonic in culture, and the antithetical need to sublimate it (p. 260). Bové argues that the outcome of this dependency is fascism, though in children's literature it is rather consciously subsumed into the metaethic as a bulwark against fascism and/or anarchy. This is perhaps more readily apparent in the Malorian retellings, especially Green's, where the demonic appears explicitly as sorcery or general absence of the ethical values which enable Camelot, and is more evident still in Tolkienesque medievalism or Alan Garner's novels. A good example is Garner's *Weirdstone of Brisingamen,* where the united struggle of children, dwarfs, and wizard is specifically against a demonic, fascistic will to power in society, but the juxtaposition of Cadellin and Grimnir, the white and black wizards who are brothers, denies that this can be collapsed into a simple binary opposition (see Philip, 1981, pp. 24–25).

Historical Arthurian fiction of the kind we have been discussing seems to have been a short-lived genre, arising from a confluence of historical research and postwar mentality. Its successors, if they can properly be called that, are works which are set in Romano-Celtic Britain, but develop this setting in different ways.

One possibility, as seen in the retellings by John Matthews and Bob Stewart in *Legends of King Arthur and His Warriors* (1987; as a children's book, *Tales of Arthur,* 1988), is to retell Celtic legends associated with Arthur. In effect, those which are identifiable precursors of stories familiar from the Malorian tradition are now stripped of later, medieval accretions. This is a different process from the debunking we have pointed to in the historical fictions, since its objective is not realistic narrative but cultural au-

*Plate 4. Merlin as Leader of the British. Illustration by Richard Hook/Linden Artists, in John Matthews and Bob Stewart,* Legends of King Arthur and His Warriors, *Blandford Press (London), 1987. Reprinted by permission of Richard Hook.*

thenticity, retelling stories "in our own words but faithfully as far as possible to the spirit of the times" (1987, p. 12). The full-page illustration opposite the book's title page says much about its metanarrative (see Plate 4). In the foreground Merlin stands, arms spread and uplifted in a conventional magic-working gesture, in a blaze of fire within a circle of standing stones; behind him, in muted blue, brown and grey, is a collage of fighting men, a panoply of warriors spanning the millennia and ranging from a prehistoric figure dressed in skins and wielding a stone axe to twentieth-century soldiery.

Ideals, aspirations and symbols transcend time and place, gesturing toward universal human experience. At the same time, because the conventions for representing "wizard" are here isomorphic with those for representing "Old Testament prophet," especially Moses—the full-length white robe, the rope belt, the long white beard, the staff (reminiscent of a shepherd's crook), the arms raised (now) in benediction—the figure is a hieratic symbol of transcendent spiritual leadership. What is signified here is expressed in another way in the introduction, in which the authors move swiftly from a so-called "factual foundation" to symbolic significance: "On a historical level Arthur tried to revitalize and unify a British culture, and out of this obscure historical period emerge legends and mythical patterns of human unity, even of spiritual vision, which are unquestionably holistic. The fight against savagery, the order of honorable warriors, the Round Table, the essential significance of feminine power, the ultimate quest for truth in the form of the Grail . . . all attempt to fuse historical and imaginative elements together and pass them on to future generations" (p. 14). The impulse behind this is very much the same metaethic we have been adducing throughout our study, but the formulation here is quite remarkable in its assumption that the metaethic is an independent, transcendent entity which shapes cultures.

How the authors put this assumption into practice in the retelling of stories is clear in Stewart's inventive, carefully structured, and wittily told version of "The Beheading Game," an ancient legend lying behind the often retold fourteenth-century narrative *Sir Gawain and the Green Knight* (in Green; Sutcliff [1981a]; Morpurgo; Yeatman; et al.). In Stewart's remaking of the story, the significance derives less from the thematics of the story itself than from its framing and narration. We have summarized the intricate frame-within-a-frame structure in the table below. (See Table 5.1.) Myrddin (that is, Merlin) embodies the metaethic which enables and informs the story at every level, from issues of power and governance in the actual world to metaphorical expressions of ethics and the sacred bond between people and territory. The narrative is quite explicit about its purposes, and perhaps even about its extraordinarily strong expression of the connection between the metaethic and the nationalism which has pervaded modern Arthurian retellings at least since the publication of *The Eagles Have Flown*.

In the story as told here, the test is to cut off the giant's head and then receive a return blow on the following day. In conformity with the folktale rule of threes, two warriors undertake the challenge, but lack the honor and courage to endure the waiting through twenty-four hours for the return blow, and each in turn flees; for the climactic third occasion, the king's special hero arrives at court and fulfils the quest. Instead of being beheaded, he is lauded

TABLE 5.1. Structure of Stewart's *The Beheading Game*

| Outer frame | Inner frame | Story |
|---|---|---|
| The court of the Emperor of the West in the fifth century. The emperor feels vulnerable because he knows his power is illegitimate. Myrddin as ambassador from Ambrosius seeks trade, assistance, and support (this includes the "cavalry motif" of historical fiction). As grand manipulator of metanarratives, Myrddin has also gathered information about the state of decayed Europe. He has a vision of British imperium, which will at least be realized as legend, because "the bards would eventually sing as if his dreams had become history." Indeed, there is more "truth" in metanarratives than in historicity (p. 166). | The emperor tries to humiliate Myrddin by demanding he entertain him with a story from his native land, because "Everyone knew that Britain . . . had no writing or literature of its own; everything had been borrowed from the civilization and influence of Rome" (p. 160). In his telling, Myrddin incorporates and makes fun of all the attendants in the room, so that the emperor sees the tale as "an allegory of his futile wars against the invading tribes from the North" and realizes it has "some other subtle meaning" (p. 162). | The Beheading Game is primarily a test of honor and courage, but the giant who initiates the game is a fertility figure, a tutelary deity of the land, a guarantee of the "sacred nature of kingship" (p. 162). His final act is to prophesy the coming of Arthur "as an example to the world" (p. 165), an event already foreseen by Myrddin (p. 166). |

by the giant as "incomparable for valor, for courage, and for fair play" (p. 165). These virtues are then attributed forward to Arthur and, more importantly, to what is represented by the idea of Arthur, as exemplary for the world. The double frame for the beheading story is a British story, told in thinly veiled mockery of the European emperor and his court, and together with the fact that Myrddin tells it in an immaculate classical Latin which the semibarbarian emperor recognizes but cannot reproduce, constitutes "Britain" as a repository of values and knowledge in an age when morals and learning are decadent. An apparent motive in the endeavor by Matthews and Stewart to recover and reinstate culturally authentic Arthurian stories, then, is to transmit a version of unity and spirituality which might again be an inspiration for a decadent world.

An unusual modification of the metaethic in Matthews and Stewart (not evident in *The Beheading Game*) is the inclusion of "the essential significance of feminine power," through their argument that in Celtic culture heroes were "inspired, advised, trained and finally claimed by female power"

(p. 80). They argue that the role of women has been heavily corrupted in the Malorian tradition. However that may be, modern retellers have made little headway against the endemic connections between female virtue and passive submissiveness, on the one hand, and wickedness and female agency on the other. We will return to this question below, in an extended analysis of retellings of *The Marriage of Sir Gawain and Dame Ragnell.*

The combination of history and magic in the Matthews and Stewart project has been attempted by other retellers of the Arthur story. John Emlyn Edwards, in *The Adventures of Arthur Dragon-King* (1984), set out to devise a new set of adventures, obliquely patterned on a combination of Green and the historical novelists, with Arthur as protagonist but framed by an epic contest between the white magic of Merlin (on the side of Arthur and Britain) and the black magic of Morgana le Fay (on the side of the Saxons). It remains quite unusual to attempt to graft new stories to the legend in books for young readers, perhaps because to do so contravenes the domain's function to transmit cultural heritage, although it is a widespread practice in adult fantasy writing. This book claims to be "an adventurous reconstruction from the British viewpoint of how the Arthurian legend was born in a Dark Age Britain abandoned to invading Saxon hordes," and purports to "recount the long-lost [that is, invented] deeds of a real Arthur, the youthful Dragon-king" as opposed to "a retelling of the twelfth century chivalric myth" (foreword, pp. 7–8). The result, however, is a rather mediocre book mixing parody of conventional versions of Arthurian romance, Treece's depiction of Arthur, and "boys' own adventure" stories.

A conjunction of the historical realist and Malorian traditions has led to the emergence in the late twentieth century of retellings which are mainly versions of the medieval sources but firmly place the early part of the narrative in the time of the Anglo-Saxon invasions, and hence ground the narrative in a kind of historical actuality. Lister (1992; 1988) and Morpurgo (1994) maintain the "Saxons" as Arthur's principal foe throughout his early career. Morpurgo, in particular, has integrated the "historical" material as a semivisible part of the narrative fabric. He invokes the cavalry motif (p. 32), tells of a three-year campaign against the Saxons, Picts, and Irish, and in describing the final defeat of the Saxons alludes to the battle of Mons Badonicus (he doesn't name a specific location): "There is a swathe of red earth all across the West Country to mark the place where we met them, hunted them down and destroyed them" (p. 33). His Camelot, when first introduced, is reminiscent of a hill fort such as South Cadbury Castle[5]— "I had built there a hilltop castle, surrounded by marshes and safe from the world." The transition into a predominantly Malorian story is made by adapting a strategy devised by Lister (pp. 38–39), whereby a campaign against King Rience of North Wales—"a bloodthirsty savage" (p. 34)—is causally linked to Arthur's first meeting with Guinevere.[6] From this point on, the story line in both Lister and Morpurgo draws on various events and incidents to be found in Malory (though Morpurgo's actual source is clearly Green).

The impression of historical grounding in these narratives is only partly a matter of content, however. In addition, it is carried by framing and register. Both writers give their retellings a unified narrative voice by representing the whole as retold to a modern audience by Merlin (Lister) or by Arthur himself (Morpurgo), and in both cases this enables an intense emotional engagement with events and characters. The effect is further enhanced by the pervasive use of a discourse which mixes demotic and epic registers and hence mediates between the otherness of events and the familiarity of emotions and responses.

## QUASI-MEDIEVALISM

One of the obvious attractions of the Middle Ages is its otherness. The kind of premodern (especially precapitalist and pretechnological) societies found in medieval romance, and in modern imaginings of the Middle Ages, furnish a medium through which modern fantasy can express powerful ideological positions. Although such societies may be depicted as racked by political conflict (a conflict generally framed in terms of the struggle of the forces of Good against the will to power of the forces of Evil), they are nevertheless societies to which clear principles of order, justice, and morality can be attributed, usually as principles reinstated by events of the text. Such reinstatements inevitably function as models or aspirations offered to the modern world. An example which beautifully encapsulates this process is Tanith Lee's *Black Unicorn* (1991), a fantasy set in a premodern, medievalized secondary world typical of sword-and-sorcery fantasy: society is governed by an absolute monarchy; the main characters live in castles; labor is organized by guilds; there is no electricity or combustion engines; and the soldiery is armed with spears, swords, and bows (though there are cannon). The novel interconnects three narratives of positive growth: the development of an agential subjectivity for the protagonist, Tanaquil; the freeing of "the city" from its official founding and sustaining political myth, which is only a form of false consciousness; and the return of the unicorn to the "perfect world" of which Tanaquil's "badly made" world is but an imperfect reflection. The story of the unicorn has a structure reminiscent of the structure of the story of Arthur: it is a story of foundation marred at the outset by evil means, of death and passage to the "summer country" otherworld of Celtic tradition, Avalon. Tanaquil's brief visit to that world of perfect Platonic form (chapter 11) evokes the "summer country" but also reflects the pervasive influence (often via C.S. Lewis and Tolkien) of George MacDonald's *Phantastes* on modern fantasy. When McGillis says that *Phantastes* is about "identity," that "it deals with the struggle to attain consciousness and to overcome self-consciousness. It reconciles opposites" (1992, p. 60), he could also be describing *Black Unicorn*, in which Tanaquil's development of her own "identity" (agential subjectivity) mediates male and female, mother and father, mechanism and magic, desert and city, solipsism and intersubjectivity, child and adult. She begins as a figure conventional in modern fantasy: she is trapped within her own solipsism as the only child in an isolated desert fortress, alone with her preoccupied, eccentric mother and with no inkling of her father's name. She has no apparent future because she is the child of a sorceress but appears to be without magical powers. Her development of agency is figured by the disclosure of genuine power of an unexpected kind, the power to *mend* things so that they never break or malfunction again. The disclosure figures a growth from childhood to adulthood, a significance obliquely stressed throughout the novel by the frequent reminders that she is sixteen, but it also figures a power to retransform her world and resist the force of entropy. Her ability first manifests itself in a dramatic way when she unintentionally "mends" the unicorn by assembling its skeleton, thus setting it on the way to physical resurrection, and later when she uses her power to mend the gateway between the worlds to enable the unicorn to go back. This novel astutely balances the relationship between the growth of an individual identity and the need for individuals to act in the public good, and as such it reflects a thematic concern underlying more explicit retellings of medieval material.

Lee's *Black Unicorn* also draws attention to an aspect of Arthurian retellings quite prominent in popular adult medievalism but generally absent from versions for children, namely, recastings of the stories to present female perspectives and to express a sense of female power. Moody suggests that this literature principally conforms to two of the types of retelling we have set out above, historically oriented fantasy and a constantly evolving image of a quasi-medieval world (1991, p. 187). The attraction of the former is that it "offers the woman writer the opportunity to reevaluate women's history from her own perspective in regard to the interpretation of evidence," and "it substantiates the 'strong' female heroine as something more than science fiction—a heritage" (p. 187). In particular, women writers often restore the pagan background as an integral part of the legend, and concentration on the magical elements and the Celtic background enables the creation of strong and mature female characters and female perspectives (p. 191). The paradigmatic text here remains Marion Zimmer Bradley's *The Mists of Avalon* (1982). Moody argues that "women can be seen in positions of power and active in society only when the early Christian notions of their place are removed through either matriarchal respect, religious sorority, or by being in possession of knowledge" (p. 192).

Why such an approach has not spilled over into writing for children may be a subject for some speculation, but can at least in part be explained by pointing to three factors. The cultural conservation function of children's retellings, together with the propensity for biblical exegesis to shape the process of interpretation and a general wariness about confronting Christian structures in children's literature, means that writers are more likely to pursue the strategy of Lee and Tamora Pierce and set the story in a quasi-medieval paracosm with only vaguely articulated religious beliefs. Second, historical fiction has tended to be nationalistic and written under the shadow of an assumption that history is about great men, governance, and battles, and that women's roles are at best ancillary. Third, the powerful female figures discernible in the Malorian tradition are the sorceresses, and these are invariably tinged with evil. It seems likely that this situation is perpetuated by the persistent and powerful influence of Roger Lancelyn Green's version, in which the malevolence of sorceresses is a primary cause of many dire events, and as such functions as a unifying element by imposing a common pattern on various stories. The enhanced role of sorceresses is more than a structural element, however, in that it is closely connected with Green's Gothicized discourse. The response might have been expected to come from modern feminist Gothic, but this has not yet made much impact on literature for young readers, apart from such notable works by Tanith Lee as *The Castle of Dark* (1978).

A medievalist pastiche which does introduce a female warrior as principal character is Tamora Pierce's *Alanna* (1983), the first volume of a distinguished sword-and-sorcery tetralogy. This subgenre, which might be called "feminist sword-and-sorcery fantasy," demonstrates perhaps more clearly than any other how modern cultural paradigms are grafted onto the metanarratives which are implicit in source texts. The habitus of *Alanna* is defined through contrasted locations and their architecture, journeys, class-based codifications of behavior, educational structures, and, interacting with all of these, the effects of Alanna's gender-switching within a tightly gendered habitus. The novel is essentially the first part of a *bildungsroman,* in which a twist is added to the cinderlad story of such (ultimate) pre-texts as Malory's

"Tale of Sir Gareth."[7] It begins with Alanna and her twin brother Thom exchanging places when they are sent from home at age eleven to further their education in appropriate domains. But since it is Alanna, not Thom, who wishes to train for the knighthood, she easily persuades him to allow her to take his place, while he goes off eventually to study sorcery.

In the course of the novel a feminist agenda emerges overtly from time to time, though the function of such overt moments seems to be to sustain a reader subject position which might be considered broadly feminist. Alanna's moments of self-doubt, for example, illustrate this function, as when she reflects on her defeat of the despicable bully Ralon, who had attempted to make her life miserable. To beat her older and larger opponent, she had undergone secret training in hand-to-hand combat:

> No matter what Myles said, she had used fancy tricks to beat Ralon, that was all. She was still a girl masquerading as a boy, and sometimes she doubted that she would ever believe herself to be as good as the stupidest, clumsiest male. (p. 88)

But readers cannot agree with this judgment, both because the discourse of bully-and-victim has already evinced unequivocal reader alignment in relation to the two characters and the terms of Alanna's self-disparagement are too overstated ("fancy tricks"; "stupidest, clumsiest"). Moreover, the impulse here to generalize the doubt beyond the specific instance, indicated by "sometimes," tends to shift readers towards a more general (and habitual) favorable assessment of Alanna's performance. This assessment is sustained discoursally by a strategy, pervasive in both narrative and conversation, whereby Alanna is designated by her own name and feminine pronominals in narrative and speech reporting tags, but referred to by other characters by her assumed name, "Alan," and masculine pronominals. The passage cited above continues:

> The door opened. "Sir Myles. You beat me here." It was Prince Jonathan. "How's Alan?"
>
> Myles stood. "I think he's tired. Alan, I'm going, but I wish you'd think about what I said."
>
> "I always think about the things you tell me," she admitted.

The admiration and respect most characters show for "Alan" exists in a dialogic relationship with the constant textual reminders that she is always still "Alanna," and that neither she nor the text's narrator ever think of her as

"Alan." In other words, while Pierce has followed sword-and-sorcery practice in constructing a female hero by situating her within a conventional male role in a conventional structure—training in the Code of Chivalry and other aspects of cultural heritage designated as parts of a male domain— she constantly reasserts Alanna's femaleness and hence, it can be argued, deconstructs such gendered classifications.

Alanna's individuality is not only established by her sex and mastery of the male domain, but also by her Gift, her capacity to work magic, and especially the power of healing, which tends to be nuanced as a female art. The recuperation of the witch figure as a healer is so widespread in modern literature there is no need for us to go into it here. More pertinently, Alanna's Gift has been enhanced because she has been singled out by "the Goddess." The nexus between her female and male skills is graphically made during the climax of the novel, when Alanna goes with Prince Jonathan to confront the vampiric demons which prey on the Bazhir people. (These creatures are a cross between ifrits and demons, since the novel has here appropriated an orientalist discourse; we will further discuss this aspect of the incident in chapter 8.) Realizing that she is female, the demons try to exploit that by, literally, laying her bare to Jonathan: "She doubled over in pain. It was over as swiftly as it began, with one difference. Her clothes were gone. All she wore was her belt and scabbard" (p. 222). Here the novel ironically evokes those very *un*feminist sword-and-sorcery heroines who stride around dressed in a G-string and a brass bra, and goes on, albeit a little coyly, to depict Alanna's shifts between feelings of embarrassment and her sense of power: she "tried to cover herself with her hands"; "she shouted, 'I may be a girl, but I can defend—or attack!—as well as any boy!'"; "she whispered, blushing a deep red." Pierce seems to be invoking a kind of visual pun here on the virgin warrior's naked female power: as a devotee of the Goddess, she perhaps reflects how "the magic of the Goddess dwelt more in the reality of her flesh than in her garments" (Walker, 1983, p. 706). Once she is reclad, now in Jonathan's tunic, male and female, Alanna and Jonathan, then combine to defeat the demons in a series of magical duels, but, most importantly, these culminate in a mystic sword fight in which Alanna defeats the most powerful male demon after she has experienced an influx of power from the Goddess. This final battle, bringing the first volume of the *bildungsroman* to a close, thus shapes Alanna's initiation into maturity within a double framework: an evocation of transcendent female power and, rather more obliquely, an assertion of female sexual power.

Such sword-and-sorcery feminism has extensively transformed its medieval antecedents. In doing so, it carries out substantial cultural work over and above its capacity to entertain. It depicts a quasi-medieval habitus whose boundaries are more strictly regulated than those of our own more loosely defined habitus, through class and gender structures and the chivalric code.[8] At the same time, the boundaries seem infinite because of the pervasive presence of the paranormal as many-faceted, mystic religions, experienced by the main characters as moments of profound transcendence. It can thus offer an intense combination of material and spiritual aspiration, within a teleological structure which affirms female power both materially and transcendentally. Along the way, it accesses and deals with a multiplicity of ethical and moral questions which arise in everyday human relationships, and such questions can be resolved precisely because they arise within a framework of defined social and religious paradigms.

### REWRITING WOMAN: *THE MARRIAGE OF SIR GAWAIN AND DAME RAGNELL*

The widespread modern project to redefine the role of women in medieval(ist) romance can involve a more complex struggle with older metanarratives than evidenced in *Alanna*. A story which raises some significant contemporary issues, especially concerning gender representation, is *The Marriage of Sir Gawain and Dame Ragnell,* one of the most frequently retold Arthurian stories. It has been incorporated into Arthurian cycles, anthologized in collections of legends, handled separately as a picture book, told as a feminist folktale and as a feminist romance, and told parodically. There are various reasons why the story invites retelling, including the broad contrasts between the roles of the characters, the lure of depicting the "monstrous" Ragnell, the centrality of gender relations, the challenge of overturning a sexist narrative, and the comic possibilities, but beneath all other attractions is an endemic conflict between a narrative frame which limits the possibilities of meaning and a stubborn openness of significance. This openness is fostered by the variety of sources drawn on by modern authors. Retellings ultimately derive from a fifteenth-century English romance (henceforth referred to as *Gawain and Ragnell*) or a fragmentary related ballad (both printed in Bryan and Dempster, 1941); there is some influence from an analogue retold by Geoffrey Chaucer as the *Wife of Bath's Tale;* a fourth version, an analogue in John Gower's fourteenth-century *Confessio Amantis,* has not been used by modern writers, though its moral seems to be reproduced by Pyle in his very eclectic account of Gawain's adventures (1903, p. 311). Modern retellings are not always based directly or exclusively on an early text, however, but may be mediated through two important subsequent versions, those of Ebbutt (1910) and Green (1953). Thus versions published after 1960 fall into three groups. First, reversions which are creative variations on *Gawain and Ragnell:* for example, Phelps (1981), Rosen (1984), and Philip (1987), although Philip and Rosen also drew on the *Wife of Bath's Tale.* Matthews (1995) belongs here, but as a retelling which has made minimal changes to *Gawain and Ragnell.* Second, texts which derive from the ballad, but have drawn partly or wholly on Ebbutt: for example, Garner (1969), Hastings (1985), and Sutcliff (1981a), although Sutcliff's version has also been influenced by Green. Finally, texts which derive from either *Gawain and Ragnell* or the ballad but also draw extensively on Green's imaginative reworking of these:[9] for example, Troughton (1972), Horowitz (1985), and Yeatman (1991). Horowitz's rather unsatisfactory version also makes extensive use of the *Wife of Bath's Tale,* and Yeatman borrows from Sutcliff.

The basic story elements are as follows: King Arthur falls into the power of a malevolent knight, Sir Gromer Somer Joure, who spares his life on condition he return on an appointed day with the answer to the question, "What do women most desire?" With the help of Gawain, he assembles a large number of possible answers, but none seems definitive. Just before keeping his appointment, Arthur meets Ragnell, a hideously deformed old crone, who offers the correct answer in return for marriage with one of his young knights (or, as in *Gawain and Ragnell,* she specifies Gawain). Gawain readily saves Arthur by agreeing to the marriage, and Ragnell discloses the answer (which, in *Gawain and Ragnell,* ll. 468–470, is that "Women desire sovereignty . . . to rule over the manliest men"). On their wedding night, when Gawain overcomes his revulsion and makes some kind of husbandly gesture, Ragnell is partly freed from an enchantment and turns out to be exquisitely beautiful, but can only be so for twelve hours a day. Gawain's final test is to choose which twelve hours, and when he asks Ragnell herself to choose (that is, gives her the sovereignty) the enchantment is entirely removed. Ragnell then explains how she came to be enchanted (by her stepmother in *Gawain and Ragnell,* the ballad, and Ebbutt; by Morgana le Fay in Green, Sutcliff, Yeatman, and Horowitz; by Sir Gromer in Rosen, Phelps, and Philip; by her sister in Troughton).

The primary attraction lies in the story—the characters and events—but several elements can be presented in various ways so as to modify the attitudes and consciousness of the characters and to vary the relationship between narrator and audience. This affects the moral significance of the outcome, especially involving assumptions about gender and class. In particular, these variations are crucial determinants as to whether a retelling engages with the underlying antifeminism of the early versions. It may seem a paradox that in dealing with a story which pivots on the issue of gender relations, at most only two of the eleven retellings even attempt to use the story to elicit a perception of gender relations which differs significantly from that informing the fifteenth-century text. This probably happens because narrative point of view is focused on the plights of Arthur and Gawain, rather than of Ragnell, even when an outcome most closely affects Ragnell. Because the story pivots on her surprising transformation, she must remain a mysterious figure, always an object of male gaze and never herself a focalizer. Other factors also militate against any radically different significance. The frame of the story may be so endemically antifeminist that no retelling can really overcome this: the effect is produced not only by narrative perspective but also by the sequence of events and the outcomes. Further, any retelling will tend to replicate the schema for male-female relations assumed in romance and in the notions of chivalry which tend to be taken for granted when handling "medieval" themes. Hence it would be inadmissible to offer, say, "a room of her own" as the answer to Sir Gromer's question. The patriarchal perspective of chivalry and romance is obvious in one common presentation of Ragnell's answer, whereby she whispers it to Arthur but it is withheld from readers. This motif follows the *Wife of Bath's Tale* rather than *Gawain and Ragnell*, where the answer is spelled out in detail. Arthur's response is revealing:

> He vowed with great bursts of laughter that this was indeed the right answer. (Ebbutt, p. 272)

> Then the King caught his breath in laughter, for it was such a simple answer, after all. (Sutcliff, p. 231)

> And then Arthur knew with absolute certainty that he had nothing more to fear. (Hastings, p. 13)

> At once the king smiled for he knew she had the true answer to the riddle. (Yeatman, p. 120)

> Arthur, seeing at once it was the true [answer], breathed a sigh of relief from the depths of his heart. (Philip, p. 42)

This strategy assures readers that the still undisclosed answer is a universal truth, so when Arthur then uses it to save himself that "truth" is doubly confirmed. Even when, as in the five versions just cited, the structure is linked with the less confrontational answer given in the ballad, that is, that "All women desire to have their own way," the implication is that female agency is a social aberration, and hence the texts reinscribe a patriarchal schema. Rosen's version is unusual because she directly confronts this schema by attributing Arthur with incredulity at Ragnell's answer, which was "contrary to all his beliefs" and "upsetting to his notion of the natural order of things." Just as men desire to be "subject to the will of their King, their sovereign," so women "wanted to be ruled by men, to be subject to their laws and protection" (1984, pp. 20–21). Rosen makes the point several times in different ways, so that Arthur even tells Sir Gromer it is an idea he finds "hard to take seriously" (p. 26), but this overinsistence doesn't in itself overturn the schema. To begin to do this, Rosen needed to redefine the meaning of *sovereignty*, specifically to dispense with the issue of dominance, though simply changing the meaning of Ragnell's answer wouldn't have such an effect. There is also need to address the terms of Ragnell's disenchantment—that she remain loathsome "until such time as the finest knight in the kingdom would marry me and yield to me sovereignty over himself and all he possessed" (p. 35). Because these issues aren't taken up in the retelling, the foregrounding of the question of dominance tends merely to reinforce the conventional gender relations of the original early English texts.

Other story elements also effectively reinforce an antifeminist metanarrative. In seven versions, Arthur seeks out Sir Gromer because of the arrival at his court of a disheveled damsel who claims that Gromer has imprisoned her partner and molested her (Ebbutt, Green, Garner, Troughton, Sutcliff, Horowitz, Yeatman), and all except Ebbutt and Garner subsequently reveal that the damsel was sent to deceive Arthur. As far as we have been able to determine, the loose narrative thread of the damsel as catalyst for action seems to be Ebbutt's innovation, perhaps to reground the story through motifs of chivalry and female vulnerability (the damsel obliquely indicates that she has been raped by Sir Gromer). The motif of female duplicity is then introduced by Green, who further reinforces it by borrowing a detail from *Sir Gawain and the Green Knight* and identifying Morgana le Fay as the villain behind the deception (a detail repeated by Sutcliff, Yeatman, and Horowitz). The effect here of Green's general expansion of the role of Morgana is to evoke a conventional contrast between the wickedness of powerful women and the virtue of subject women. The intersection of gender and power here then becomes more specifically focused in the concept of the "ugly woman," as Ragnell follows a trajectory from social outcast to feminine ideal.

Because desirability in women is measured in physical appearance and social grace, Ragnell comprehensively fails; in men it lies in actions and behavior, especially as demonstrated by Gawain. Some versions draw on the ballad to further enhance Gawain's behavior towards the ugly Ragnell by contrasting it with the ungracious behavior of Sir Kay (Ebbutt, Garner,

Sutcliff, Hastings). When Ragnell first appears in the medieval romance, she is described by means of a conventional inverted blazon, or parody of a portrait of a beautiful woman (her face is red, instead of her lips; her teeth are yellow, instead of her hair; her mouth is large, instead of small; her breasts are huge and pendulous, not small and high; and so on). The joke is thus literary and rhetorical, and doesn't work in modern literature, so modern descriptions instead run the gamut from set-piece evocations of a physical horror (Hastings, Horowitz) to muted descriptions which suggest that Ragnell experiences anguish and suffering (Green, Sutcliff, Matthews). The most extreme example appears in Horowitz, both because of the casual ordinariness of the language and because there is an assumed close and confidential relationship with readers: "he realized that she was without doubt the ugliest woman he had ever seen. She really was incredibly ugly. . . . Her skin was the color and texture of rice pudding and her hair would have looked better on a camel . . . she was horrendously fat" and, when she looks at Gawain, "The horrible woman grinned at Gawain and ran a wet tongue over her lips" (1985, pp. 167–168). A correlative for this display of appetite appears in Horowitz, and in three other retellings (Green, Philip, Rosen), as versions of Ragnell's gross eating habits during the wedding banquet (based on *Gawain and Ragnell*). The horror is increased because Ragnell wields the power of life and death over Arthur, and her price is Gawain's person. Horowitz redirects the ending by basing the bedchamber scene on the "pillow-sermon" from the *Wife of Bath's Tale* and by deleting both the physical catalyst for Ragnell's transformation and Gawain's final test, thus dispensing with the formal structure whereby the answer to the two puzzles is the same. By reducing Ragnell to any normal young and beautiful woman, Horowitz's text is the clearest in its correlation of, on the one hand, assertiveness with female ugliness and, on the other hand, female beauty with docility and submissiveness. There is a comparable effect in the Hastings version, for example, in which an extreme of ugliness contrasts with an extreme of almost ethereal beauty, both emphasized by Wijngaard's graphic illustrations. When physical undesirability is constituted as grounds for pity, as in Hastings or Philip, it further intensifies the effect of reinforcing youth and beauty as cultural norms.

In three of the early analogues the transformation of Ragnell is specifically sexual and takes place at the moment the young man turns to her in bed with a resolve to consummate the marriage. The exception is Chaucer's *Wife of Bath's Tale,* which rather effects a thematic interchange between sexual acts and speech acts, sexual power and verbal power. Here the young knight's inability to consummate the marriage emphasizes the symbolic function of the old woman: she is Woman as Man fears she might be—unattractive but, or perhaps because, sexually voracious, assertive, demanding, and verbally powerful. When confronted with female sexual aggression he is stricken with sexual reluctance, and this dysfunction leads to the old woman's "pillow-sermon," a verbal consummation of the story (see Stephens and Ryan, 1989). Most modern retellings of *Gawain and Ragnell,* with the exception of Rosen's, follow Ebbutt and Green in omitting the sexual reference, though a more satisfactory alternative is to commute it to a kiss, which then brings the incident into line with a folktale disenchantment motif. This happens in Troughton, Philip, and Phelps, and is especially important as part of Phelps's more general reframing of the story as a folktale. Rosen includes an extended pillow dialogue, comically framed by Gawain's reluctance and by the fact that, as a bashful virgin, he only has a "general-if-foggy impression" of what sex entails (Rosen is inverting another stereotype, of course). However, moved by Ragnell's arguments and by his sense of chivalry and duty, "he turned, intending to take the hideous hag in his arms" (p. 33) and finds her beautiful, "exquisite beyond belief." Uniquely, the marriage is consummated before Gawain is faced with the next dilemma, a fact which exacerbates Gawain's problem. Oddly, though, despite "trying to see the problem from every point of view" (p. 35), Gawain doesn't here see it from Ragnell's point of view—a crucial addition to the story already made by Green: "With you is the greatest suffering, and you alone must choose which you are most able to bear" (Green, p. 174). In a sense, Rosen might have missed a crucial move here, but unless Ragnell is endowed not only with point of view but actual agency, the move only has the effect of diminishing her power. That is, Gawain must not only cede the decision to Ragnell, but in doing so he must recognize her right to exercise her own free will. Only Phelps (p. 44) seems to have grasped this. The issues of Ragnell's point of view and agency are evident in the four versions where Gawain only relinquishes power of choice to Ragnell after he proposes, and she forcefully rejects, one option and then the other (Ebbutt, Garner, Sutcliff, Hastings). To write the scene in this way avoids the narrative stasis of extended soliloquy or represented thought, but the cost is to imply that Ragnell has browbeaten Gawain into yielding up the decision to her, into yielding *sovereignty.*

We remarked earlier that Phelps has been the only author who sets out to change the fundamental significance of the story's pivotal utterance, the answer to the question, "What do women most desire?" The story's most recalcitrant element is the premise that there is a universal, transcendent answer, not an answer arbitrarily chosen from multiple possibilities. The early versions list the rejected possibilities, and they are inevitably a catalogue of female "vices," which, needless to say, must pale into insignificance beside the great vice of wanting to rule over men. Modern retellings which include a list generally mix together diverse answers, and sometimes show that they are relative by indicating a source, such as "the ladies of the court, pretty as peacocks . . ." (Hastings, p. 10). But the effect of a list such as "pretty clothes, lovely jewellery, happiness, love, beauty, comfort, long life" (Yeatman, p. 118) will still be determined retrospectively by the ultimate desire "to have her own way" (Yeatman, p. 121). Phelps, who strategically doesn't include such a list, tackles the problem of producing a feminist reversion in a number of ways which pivot on the careful semantic phrasing of the answer Ragnell gives Arthur: "What a woman desires above all else is the power of sovereignty—the right to exercise her will" (p. 40). She rephrases this when Gawain relinquishes the final choice to her as "the power of choice—the power to exercise my own free will" (p. 44). In short, sovereignty is not a matter of ruling or being ruled, but the power of choice, the having of agency. Phelps's representation of other components underpins this central shift, and these modifications are in turn reinforced by genrically redefining the story and situating it within a collection of feminist folktales (see chapter 7, below, for further discussion of Phelps's collection). Ragnall's enchantment was worked by Sir Gromer, her stepbrother, because he thought her "bold and unwomanly" for defying him: "I refused his commands both for my property and my person" (p. 44). To break the spell, she had to achieve "the 'impossible' condition": first "persuade the greatest knight in Britain to willingly choose me for his bride," and then be given "the power to exercise my own free will." In other words, she had to form a relationship based on sexual equality. Crucially, at the moment Ragnell invites the disenchanting kiss, she commends Gawain because he has "shown neither revulsion nor pity." The folktale kiss, now motivated by neither desire nor pity, is itself transformed into a new significance. Throughout her retelling, Phelps has carefully shifted the significance of each of the components of the story and brought them into a new alignment.

*Gawain and Ragnell* is a story about *desire*, its forms, and its social construction in the context of male/female relations. The shape of the story is a teleological structure which pivots around a question that discloses a basic masculine fear, but leads to an outcome which (implicitly) assuages that fear by suggesting that women would be content with *sovereignty* in name but not in fact (and really not even in name, since the story closures of most retellings habitually ignore any ramifications, implicitly representing woman by a schema of subjection). Any version will thus turn out to reinscribe an element of antifeminism inasmuch as it will evoke female desire as unreasonable and unrealizable. Only Phelps has successfully thought this through, and by reshaping the answer to the question and resituating the story genrically has radically transmuted the story's significance.

## POSTDISASTER QUASI-MEDIEVAL FICTIONS

In the modern popular imagination, insofar as anybody thinks about it at all, the "real" Middle Ages, as opposed to the Arthurian fantasy, is a period of squalor and ignorance between Roman civilization and the new civilization of the Renaissance. It always has something of the "Dark Ages" about it, more characterized by loss and lack than by inventiveness, and by a clinging to outmoded beliefs and superstitions than by creativity. One of the more daunting punishments that could be meted out for the human folly that might bring on global disaster through nuclear war or ecological degradation is a reduction to social conditions typical of the Middle Ages. The subgroup of postdisaster fictions which envisage such a scenario thus apprehend a Middle Ages in which everyday life is often bleaker than in the quasi-medieval worlds of neo-Arthurianism or sword-and-sorcery fantasy, but which can be paralleled in Arthurian literature, either in descriptions of the Waste Land in Grail narratives (see, for example, Lister, 1992, p. 62) or in historical fiction. Thus Bedwyr, narrator of *Watch Fires to the North,* depicts degraded forms of existence to which people were reduced after the collapse of Roman *imperium:* "Here in Britain, with bent backs and matted hair, living in holes in the ruins that stank worse than any bear pit at the circus, were people descended from Romans like ourselves. There is doubtless a moral in all this, but I am not wise enough to see it" (1967, pp. 173–74). Readers, presumably, *are* wise enough to see the moral. In a similar vein, Tigg, the young protagonist of McGowen's *The Magician's Apprentice,* grows up amongst "swarming, poverty-ridden, hovel-dwelling people . . . who seemed to spend their lives in a steady grip of rage that frequently flared into curses, blows, and violence" (1987, p. 14). Although this could be a vision of urban poverty at any historical time, it typifies the dark side of quasi-medieval societies.

At the same time, however, the bleakness of everyday life may be redeemed by an ethic of community values and responsibility which contrast with the destructive egocentricity of the twentieth century or its continuity into oppressive regimes of the future. It is thus possible to identify a genre of postdisaster quasi-medieval fiction, characterized by a habitus which actively rejects social formations and technological artefacts reminiscent of the predestruction (that is, late twentieth-century) world and embraces values of community, loyalty, and altruism. The contrasts are explicit in the earliest works in the subgenre, such as Peter Dickinson's *Changes* trilogy (of which *The Weathermonger,* 1968, is the first postdisaster novel for young readers), or John Christopher's *Prince in Waiting* trilogy (1970–72), or his *Wild Jack* (1974). Thus the rise of technophobia in *The Prince in Waiting* is attributed to a link between technology and mass destruction: "Our ancestors made machines and the machines destroyed the earth, causing earthquakes and volcanoes that killed men by the hundreds of thousands. That is why the Spirits decreed that the making of machines was an abomination" (1983, p. 62). The outcome, however, is not necessarily a better society.

Christopher himself acknowledged that he found "a special appeal in aspects of the feudal ethos," but also expressed the hope that he managed "to point out the disadvantages of adhering to a narrow range of values" (Gough, 1984, p. 94). His comment encapsulates the opposing potentialities of the genre. On the one hand, a dream of chivalry, in which individual prowess and loyalty were combined and infused with a spiritual quality, can be invoked as a source of optimism for an imagined society rising out of the ruins of global disaster. Medievalism thus imagines a second chance for humanity by reconstituting a moment in time before people embarked on the course that led to modern technological society, a time when spiritual values were prized over material, and people were other-focused rather than self-focused. An overt example of tradition reconstituted is found in Lee Harding's *Waiting for the End of the World* (1983), which begins with the sentence: "Manfred decided he would make a longbow." In doing this Manfred is proving his fitness as a vessel for receiving communications from the past, and does so by exercising a craftsman's skill and patience now commonly associated with past ages. The bow, made from "Yew, the magical yew of olden times" (1983, p. 4), is a channel between Manfred and the past, which he glimpses as shadowy armies which "could be traced to a common source: the historic battles of Crécy and Agincourt" (p. 76). At the end of the novel, as three of the characters set out in search of a safe haven distant from the urban dystopia typical of postdisaster fictions, Manfred walks "with all the confidence of knowing that the ancient world was intact inside him, and how it had enriched their lives. A chosen future stretched before them, and they would shape it with care" (p. 206).

On the other hand, there are two negative possibilities. First, the "return" to a quasi-medieval world may be seen as a failure of imagination and a lost opportunity to imagine a new society rising out of the ashes of the ruined world. Such imagining is, of course, very hard to achieve, as many other types of postdisaster fiction wittingly or unwittingly demonstrate— consider, for example, the controversy prompted by Louise Lawrence's vision of an improved, mutant race in *Children of the Dust* (see Parker, 1992). Instead, texts project a postdisaster future which is still homocentric and merely nostalgic for a Golden Age that never was. Second, it is suggested that a nontechnological or antitechnological world has no automatic purchase on moral superiority. This view is expressed in Dickinson's *Changes* trilogy. While aversion to machinery produces cleaner air, it might also be simply self-destructive, preventing social evolution. Dickinson satirizes the ideal of community patterned on a small, largely self-sufficient village by depicting its Luddite inhabitants as superstitious and irrational, intolerant, and cruel.

A propensity for postdisaster fictions to be satirical is well demonstrated in Graham Oakley's *Henry's Quest* (1986), an exceptionally subtle picture book with complex interactions between its text and illustrations. The disaster (which is not referred to in the text) has reduced Henry's society to rural idiocy. It is a small community, cut off from the rest of the world by surrounding forest, and living amongst the vestiges and debris of a long-vanished twentieth century. Every illustration is replete with ruined and disused artefacts, or artefacts which have been displaced for other uses—a car shell serves as a pig pen, the case of a television set as a rabbit hutch. The point is made that even after a cataclysm there could be no such thing as a fresh start, so Henry's society bases its cultural formations on the two books remaining to them, which therefore become their cultural heritage: *King Arthur and the Knights of the Round Table* and *Aunty Mabel's Fairy Tale Book*. The quasi-Arthurian quest declared by Henry's king is a quest to find petrol, that is, to find a key to past technology. When the journey Henry undertakes brings him from his own pastoral world into a society that is a social Waste Land, a pastiche of all that might be considered decadent in twentieth-century postmodern culture, the book's satire sharpens: its targets are the materialism and solipsism of late twentieth-century society and, perhaps taking a cue from *The Weathermonger*, utopian and New Age imagined alternatives. Henry is an innocent fool who survives outrageously because he lacks the will to power which, it is implied, is the human failing which *is* the disaster.

These issues have been thematically available to the genre since *The Weathermonger*, an allegory about the abuse of power, about how drastically the world might be changed if absolute power fell into the wrong hands. That there is always a tendency for this to happen is suggested by the glimpses the novel offers of the "normal" world, which imply that power is always in the wrong hands. The military, in particular, who send the children on their dangerous quest, have little interest in anything beyond the exercise of power, and readers will readily agree that, at the end of the novel, the children are wise in concealing all they learned. The message is a strong one, even though the explanation for England's reversion to the Middle Ages can be regarded as too factitious—the awakening of Merlin under the wrong circumstances. In Green's *King Arthur*, Merlin lies "in his dark tomb . . . until the day of his awakening, when the Circle of Logres shall be formed once more in this island" (1953, p. 67). To engage critically with Green's meta-narrative, Dickinson remakes this so that an insignificant man named Furbelow discovers the sleeping place of Merlin and attempts to master him by inducing a morphine addiction; the actual consequence is that in his morphine-inspired dreams Merlin recreates a distorted version of his own lost era. Furbelow had mistaken an accident for an access of power, and rather than enslaving Merlin he had become ensnared in a relationship of mutual slavery. His own entrapment in the castle built by Merlin suggests a kind of escapist solipsism, in its disregard and essential lack of interest in what is happening to the world beyond the castle walls and the forest.

Merlin's role is more than that of catalyst, however, inasmuch as it also has a broad metafictive function which enables the novel's ironic interrogation of medievalism. In other words, Merlin's drug-induced fantasy state causes him to confuse himself with the myths about him and hence to create a fantasy world to replace reality, and this has implications for some modern impulses to reconstruct reality. While the desire for a less industrially polluted world has continued to grow throughout the late twentieth century, that does not invalidate the novel's critique of the widespread 1960s desire for "dropping out," a rejection of the technology and social structures of mid–twentieth century Western society, a rejection which found one voice in Tolkienesque medievalism: "a tendency to try to return to the modes of living and thought that characterized the Dark Ages" (*The Weathermonger*, p. 32). Put more bluntly, the book suggests that the dream of putting back the clock has its origin in a kind of madness (the book was also written, of course, at the end of the psychedelic sixties). However, the dream is realized, and its consequences shown, right from the opening chapter depicting Geoffrey and Sally condemned as witches (that is, the social deviants perhaps most readily associated with medieval societies) and stranded on the drowning rock. The effect is also seen in the return to inefficient modes of agriculture and inappropriate education systems, such as the compulsion to speak only Latin at school (p. 113).

Medievalist postdisaster fiction subsequently developed as an identifiable, if small, subgenre within a larger genre of postdisaster fiction, but specifically Arthurian nuances are uncommon. The larger genre was particularly prominent in Australian children's literature throughout the 1980s, and the output included several examples of the medievalist subgenre (see Stephens, "Postdisaster Fiction," 1992b).

## CONTEMPORARY REALIST FICTIONS

In contrast with the ambivalence of postdisaster medievalisms, contemporary realist fictions use medieval motifs for exemplary purposes, constructing stories in which characters map their own behavior onto Arthurian figures and themes. The pre-text is normally Malorian Arthurianism, but Gene Kemp in *The Turbulent Term of Tyke Tiler* depicts classroom activities in which the Malorian and historical traditions are brought into opposition. In chapter 6, the pupils' regular teacher, Will Merchant, takes them on an excursion as part of their study of eleventh-century English history. Exeter, where the novel is set, is palpably rich in history, and the teacher presents it not just as facts and artefacts but as narrative to be engaged with imaginatively: "Never did any kids live in a place where there was so much history. Wherever you go, wherever you tread, adventure, tragedy, romance has gone before you. And they are all around you, still. I want you to get the feeling in your bones" (1984, p. 58). He goes on to conduct a very interactive lesson about the siege of Exeter by William the Conqueror in 1066, using questions and answers to connect past and present, but leaving many gaps through which, by filling, readers enter the text. The lesson concludes with the children staging a mock battle which continues to interrelate past and present: "Pithead, beside me, made a rude gesture of defiance, as Sir called it, and we rushed down shouting into battle" (1984, p. 63). The object of the lesson is not just to teach history, but to develop the pupils' sense of place and tradition, and of the value of standing up for a cause and against oppression. But there is more than that. When a bystander interjects, "Who won?" an answer is given by "a very old man" sitting on a nearby park bench: "We won, of course. We always do. And we beat the Boers and the Germans." This reply misses the point of who "we" are in history: 1066 saw the last successful military conquest of England, and the teacher now shifts the conversation by pointing out that the question of winning and losing is less significant than the fact that the country was changed forever. We will examine in our next chapter how stories of Robin Hood often use conflict between "native" Saxons and Norman "invaders" to figure twentieth-century conflicts, and this discloses a curious tendency in English children's literature. A similar phenomenon appears in the Arthurian historical fiction, where "we" are now the Romano-Celts, trying to fend of the invading "Saxons." More curious still, both phenomena can be depicted by the same author in different books, as in the cases of Green and Sutcliff. The teacher in *Tyke Tiler* implicitly refuses to use history in this particular kind of way.

Three chapters later (chapter 9), the pupils' student teacher, Jenny Honeywell, launches an extended Arthurian project in the Malorian tradition (Tennyson's *Idylls of the King*, T.H. White's *The Sword in the Stone*, and other unspecified texts). As well as reading, the pupils "did a terrific mural on the wall, with forests and castles and lakes, with knights in armor with their pages and ladies in mediaeval dresses" (1984, p. 78), and the project culminates in a readers' theater performance in which Tyke's friend Danny plays Sir Galahad. Kemp includes a little skirmish between teacher and student teacher, when Merchant introduces the topic of the historical Arthur, defending Britain "against the barbarians," and this leads on to pose the question of the relative value of facts as opposed to ideas and imagination. The earlier scene demonstrated the imaginative force of facts, but as Danny modifies his behavior to become pure of heart like Galahad, the novel also argues for the therapeutic force of exemplary texts.

Galahad thus functions as a model of integrity in *Tyke Tiler*, but Katherine Paterson, in *Park's Quest*, goes further in using Malorian Arthurianism as both archetype and exemplar. Park, the title character, mirrors the attributes and experiences of several knights—Gareth, Gawain, Perceval, Galahad, and even Balin—so that a quest for self-identity unfolds into a narrative of emotional and spiritual healing. Park is a "fair unknown" like Gareth, but with the crucial difference that whereas Gareth knows his own name but conceals it until his exploits create a substance for the name, Park feels that he has a name empty of significance. In this he is perhaps more like Perceval, who did not even know his name until after he had seen the Holy Grail and had failed to "ask the question" which would have healed the Fisher King. Park knows almost nothing about his dead father, or his father's background, and it is only when he goes to his grandfather's house for the first time that he eventually learns his parents had divorced and the Vietnamese girl who is his uncle's stepdaughter is in fact his own half-sister.

Paterson incorporates a parallel Arthurian thread not as a coherent narrative strand, but as Park's stream-of-consciousness transposition of events into an Arthurian context. Thus in chapter 1 he links himself with Gareth at the outset of his quest, mocked and spurned by Linnet; in Chapter 3, when he has taken himself to the Vietnam Memorial, he links his desire to touch his father's name inscribed on the black stone with the moment in Malory at which the Grail appears in the hall at Camelot (1990, pp. 30–

31). At such points, an indented paragraph contains a paraphrase in an archaic, epic register drawn from Malory, Roger Lancelyn Green, or other texts. Chapter headings also prompt readers to see the primary narrative as an expression of an Arthurian archetype; Park's description of his grandfather's house as "Castle under Curse" (chapter 7) is a prompt that his grandfather, crippled by two strokes, is in the role of Pelles (the Maimed King, or Fisher King) and that the property is figuratively a Waste Land. In a metaphorical parallel, when Park "takes up arms" and shoots and wounds a crow, he replicates "the dolorous stroke" struck by Balin (though, thankfully, the pun implicit in the novel is nowhere articulated):

> Now Pelles the maimed king lies wounded with a wound unhealable in the hall of Castle Carbonek, until Galahad the pure knight shall come to cure him after many years. (Green, 1953, p. 46)

When Park first looks at the wounded crow it reminds him of his grandfather (p. 121), symbolically giving expression to his earlier feeling that somehow he, Park, was responsible for his father's death and grandfather's illness (p. 94), though he would prefer to see Thanh as scapegoat because she was Vietnamese, a "geek."

Paterson brings these elements together in a closure fraught with significance. Creeping out in the middle of the night to feed the crow, Park and Thanh—now bonding as brother and sister—decide to take their grandfather for a ride in his wheelchair to the spring. Here two crucial events coincide; left alone with his grandfather, and at last beginning to communicate with him, Park recognizes a particular grief in his suffering. Here there is an implicit contrast with Percival, who failed to "ask the question" when at the Grail Castle; Park asks the question:

> "You think you killed him," Park said softly. "You think it's your fault."
>
> Between his fingers, he could feel his grandfather's head move forward and back. He was nodding yes. (p. 141)

As the two embrace, Thanh returns with the news that the crow has recovered and flown away—a very obvious recuperation of the emotional and spiritual waste land all the characters had been drawn into by past events. Thanh fetches water from the spring, and the novel concludes with a close paraphrase of a passage from Green, but not set out as one of Park's Arthurian reminiscences:

| Then they took the Holy Grail in | Then Galahad took the Holy Grail |
| their hands and drew away the cloth | in his hands, drew away the cloth, |
| and drank of the Holy Wine. And | and drank of the Holy Wine. After |
| it seemed to all who saw them | this he rose from his feet and set |
| that their faces shone with a light | the Grail upon the altar: and it |
| that was not of this world. And | seemed to all who saw him |
| they were as one in the company | that his face shone with a |
| of the Grail. (Paterson, p. 141) | great light. (Green, p. 246) |

Paterson's changes are slight, but enough to transform the structure into a representation of a mystical group communion rather than of a priest officiating at mass. It is still a religious moment, nevertheless, as the wording "a light that was not of this world" insists, but an intersubjective moment which is produced when human communication and human love transcend barriers and differences. One of the novel's epigraphs is from Sutcliff's *The Sword and the Circle,* and it includes a favorite Sutcliff metaphor: "We shall have served our purpose; made a shining time between the Dark and the Dark" (Sutcliff, 1981, p. 260). As remarked earlier, this is one of the major ideological points made in Arthurian retellings, but these realist fictions use Arthurian motifs as a guarantee that individuals have always made a significant difference.

The notion that a version of Arthurian ideals and models can inform behavior in everyday life is expressed particularly clearly in Clare Bevan's *Mightier than the Sword,* a novel for middle primary school readers in which stories of the Round Table overlay, in elaborate schematic detail, an "everyday" story about saving a village pond and its surrounds from being destroyed to make way for a housing development. Action in the world is an outgrowth from the class teacher reading his pupils *The Tales of the Round Table* (1989, p. 9),[10] which the children then incorporate into a game of their own, devised by Adam, the narrator, in which each adopts the name of an Arthurian character. In this heavily patterned text roles self-select because the children's own names echo or are anagrams of the names of their Arthurian counterparts. An effect of this repetition, or double perspective, is that as the threat to the pond and its trees forces the children in the novel to realize that these things are their cultural heritage, so too the Arthurian story is instantiated as cultural heritage. Hence a more or less plausible realistic narrative about a local issue expresses universal human experience. *Mightier than the Sword* is a good book to end this chapter with, since its use of Green's Malorian retelling to produce a schematically patterned narrative, an interchange between the everyday local and universal human experience, an affirmation of cultural heritage, a victory of civilization over barbarism, and an exposition of ethical, socially focused behavior, demonstrates how fully a traditional story can be reworked to mediate the Western metaethic to very young readers.

## NOTES

1. Widespread critical acceptance of arguments that Malory's *Morte* is a unified work with a single vision and purpose postdates Green's retelling, so the impulse to produce a coherent, whole work is understandable. In his then definitive edition of Malory, Vinaver had described the work as "a series of separate romances each representing a distinct stage in the author's development from his first timid attempts at imaginative narrative to his consummate mastery of his last great books" (1947, I, p. vi). Reviewers questioned this thesis, and scholars began exploring arguments for unity, but these did not culminate until around ten years after the publication of Green's retelling: see Bennett (1963), Lumiansky (1964), and Moorman (1965).

2. We attribute this effect to Green, but it has perhaps been reinforced by White's *The Once and Future King* (1938); although, in general, White has had negligible impact on children's versions.

3. This oversimplifies the temporal contrast, of course. A similar point can be made by comparing Ballantyne's *The Coral Island* with Golding's reversion in *The Lord of the Flies.* In *The Coral Island* anthropophagy marks the state of being primitive, savage, not-European; *Lord of the Flies* suggests that civilization is only ever a veneer, and would collapse without its structures of authority (cannibalism is here displaced into the link between the pig-cult and the murder of Piggy). See further chapter 9. To some extent, the same message is found in the story of King Arthur and the Giant of St. Michael's Mount (retold by Malory from the alliterative *Morte Arthure*): the giant's inhuman monstrosity resides in acts of rape and pillage, and eating children. This story is rarely included in children's versions, however; there is a summary version in Lister (1992, pp. 40–42), for example.

4. One would not expect to find overt analogies, though there are some reminiscences of modern political discourse; for example, in *Sword at Sunset,* Arthur uses the "domino theory" of military expansionism when trying to persuade a local prince (whose territory was modern Lincoln) to supply warriors to wage war against an Anglo-Saxon war party mustering in (modern) East Yorkshire: "If we stand alone, state and princedom and tribal hunting run each within our own frontiers—state and princedom and hunting run, we shall fall one by one, each within our own frontiers. It is only if we can stand together that we shall drive the Saxons back into the sea" (1987, p. 83).

5. South Cadbury Castle is often identified as the site of Camelot. Alcock and Ashe's account of excavations at South Cadbury strengthened this propensity, especially their conclusion that around the year C.E. 500, "The lord of Cadbury was a person as much like Arthur as makes no matter: a person living on a site traditionally picked out as his home, in the traditional period, with resources on the traditional scale, playing at least a part of the traditional role; a person big enough for the legends to have gathered round him" (Ashe, 1971, p. 147). Morpurgo's marshes are perhaps borrowed from nearby Glastonbury, however.

6. The apparent borrowing from Lister here is symptomatic of the extremely complex intertextual relationships of modern retellings of the Arthur story—often too complex to trace. Any attempt to trace sources, however, might yield two usual kinds of information about metanarratives: that is, which versions, and hence metanarratives, a particular retelling has engaged with; and what significant variations have been chosen or invented. In this example, Sutcliff (1981, pp. 46–49) had juxtaposed Royns with Guinevere by the simple expedient of following Malory's sequence but deleting the

whole book of "The Knight with the Two Swords"; Lister subsequently reworked this as cause and effect. In context, Morpurgo's retention of the detail that Royns (now "Rience") has "A many-coloured cloak, trimmed with the beards of all the kings he had conquered and killed" (p. 34) associates him with the retribalized, barbaric Celts depicted in the historical fictions of Treece and Sutcliff (1965)—Morpurgo's description of the cloak as "many-coloured" can be taken as a reference to parti-colored Celtic fabrics. That Arthur defeats Royns is Sutcliff's addition and is part of his imposition of order and civilization on British society; in Malory (and Green) Royns is actually defeated by Balin and Balan.

7. By the end of the volume, and subsequently, Spenser's Britomart emerges as an obvious precursor. Her charmed lance anticipates Alanna's magic-charged sword.

8. Such regulation and the conventions for breaching it can be readily paralleled in children's literature in the school-story genre, of course.

9. Green rather curiously comments that the story "seems never to have been retold," but his version has many coincidences with Ebbutt's.

10. The novel is narrated by Adam, a child disabled by spina bifida, who thinks he is a kind of reincarnation of Arthur. The teacher's readings are then presented as Adam's remembered summaries, though they are in fact yet again based on Green; the crucial promise that Arthur will return "when my land has need of me, and my realm shall rise once more out of the darkness" (1986, p. 101) is a direct quotation (Green, 1953, p. 277).

*My book is based on authority throughout.*
—Roger Lancelyn Green, *The Adventures of Robin Hood*

*Herne . . . held out a longbow. "String it."*
  *"Why?"*
  *"To give it purpose."*

—Richard Carpenter and Robin May
*Robin of Sherwood and the Hounds of Lucifer*

The stories of Robin Hood exemplify the whole range of reversions in a particularly illuminating way. On the one hand, because there is no single, fully
integrated story coming down from antiquity, the legend can both sustain
and provoke a diversity of representations. But on the other hand, because
a multiplicity of stories has been in circulation since at least the eighteenth
century, there has been a tendency to contain the growth of the legend within
the bounds of the already told. This tendency might be explained either, first,
as cultural conservatism (the responsibility of the present to remember the
past); or second, as an attempt, within the belief that the stories have some
basis in history, to control their significance by asserting historicity and constructing a coherent, quasi-historical narrative expressing significance and
insight into human experience; or third, as the culmination of a process of
rewriting "a mode of symbolic contestation as an arcadian dream, acceptable because irretrievably in the past" (Stallybrass, 1989, p. 63). In other
words, the impulse is to mold the story fragments into some kind of metanarrative whose details are fixed in time and place but whose significance
transcends the constraints of setting and the particularities of incident and
character. We have been arguing that in retold stories in children's literature

the metanarrative which shapes both story and significance generally expresses a socially and politically conservative ideology, and this is especially so with Robin Hood stories, where the situation has been reinforced by the conservative historicizing of the corpus. There have been some attempts to invent new characters and new adventures, though the main forum for such additions has been the television series. (*The Adventures of Robin Hood*, the late fifties series starring Richard Greene, ran to 143 episodes; the cult series of the eighties, Richard Carpenter's *Robin of Sherwood*, subsequently novelized, embedded known stories within a framework of newly created stories; and Tony Robinson's comedy series in the late 1980s mixed traditional and new stories.) Our concern here is with written versions, however, and attempts to produce such books as Donald Suddaby's *New Tales of Robin Hood* (1950) have been relatively few compared with the very large number woven out of and around the "traditional" stories found in the ballads composed through the fifteenth to eighteenth centuries.[1] Nevertheless, story innovations of any kind still tend to be subordinated to a universalistic metanarrative, and no works illustrate this better than Suddaby's.

The two quotations placed as epigraphs to this chapter together encapsulate the essence of Robin Hood retellings. As a body of traditional matter, "based on authority," the legends are reproduced as part of the literary baggage of (mainly) Anglophone culture. By assuming the authority of "authority," a retelling such as Green's also implies that the socio-cultural values overtly or covertly imparted by the text are in fact innate, absolute, and universal. That is, by implying that the stories themselves, together with their narrative forms and significance, are reproducible, such a reversion is also implicated in a cultural process. The extreme here is represented by a group of texts which adhere closely to a particular selection of the ballads and which would be best classified as replications rather than reversions, though even these are highly selective in matters of detail and its significance. The point is, though, that the same double reproduction examined in earlier chapters is evident in Robin Hood reversions: the *story* from the past is being reproduced, but it is a selective version wherein the *values* reproduced are an expression of the particular cultural interests within which the author is situated. Hence the importance of our second epigraph: any particular Robin Hood story is always like the unstrung bow, and an author will string it "to give it purpose." What, then, are the "purposes" of Robin Hood reversions?

## DETERMINING SIGNIFICANCES

As argued in earlier chapters, retold stories always carry at least a double potentiality, in that they can encode a traditional view of cultural transmission or, by implicitly stressing difference, can show that the significance of story is relative to the culture which reproduces it. Because they are grounded in the past, their common inclination seems to be towards conservatism—socially, culturally, and politically—in the assumption that the present is shaped by the past and by universal and absolute values inhering in the past. In children's literature, in particular, such assumptions also often incorporate the further assumption that the present is either an affirmation of or a lapse from the values of the past. An examination of such children's literature also discloses palpable evidence that the cultural heritage being transmitted in this way carefully selects out those elements from the past which are currently deemed desirable and eliminates others. An obvious example is what happens in modern reversions of material in two ballads which contain versions of the death of the Sheriff of Nottingham. The late medieval *A Gest of Robyn Hode* is the source of the frequently retold story of the dealings between Robin and Sir Richard at the Lee. In the *Gest* these culminate in Robin's rescue of Sir Richard from death at the hands of the Sheriff and in the death of the Sheriff himself, the latter in effect assassinated by Robin. The ballad of *Robin Hood and Guy of Gisborne* ends similarly, so that after Robin kills Gisborne and rescues Little John, John kills the fleeing Sheriff in the subsequent melee:

58
But he cold neither soe fast goe
    Nor away soe fast runn,
But Litle John, with an arrow broade,
    Did cleave his heart in twinn. (Dobson and Taylor, 1976, p. 145)

The Sheriff's slaying in the *Gest* is carried out in a more cold-blooded way:

347
Robyn bent a full goode bowe,
    An arrowe he drowe at wyll;
He hit so the proude sherife,
    Upon the grounde he lay full still.

348
And or he myght up aryse,
    On his fete to stonde,
He smote of the sherifs hede,
    With his bright bronde.

"Lye thou there, thou proude sherife,

   Evyll mote thou cheve: [= you were bound to have a bad end]
There myght no man to the truste
   The whyles thou were a lyve." (Dobson and Taylor, p. 104)

Modern versions, shaped by a desire for coherence and order, do not preserve both versions of the sheriff's death. More importantly, those which preserve either motif invariably do so in a form which mitigates its ferocity and/or links it with an expression of ethical or social value. The trend was perhaps set by Pyle (1883, p. 320), who carnivalizes the incident by having Little John shoot the Sheriff in the buttocks. In Hayes's retelling for younger readers (1989, p. 66), the assault is mitigated still further, so that John now merely gives the Sheriff a hard kick. Compare, though, the following five versions of the Sheriff's death at Robin's hands:

1. Robin said aside to his lady: "Madam, the Sheriff is gone." And he jerked a thumb downwards at the damp sward.

"I reckoned it must be so," said Maid Marian. "Where did you get him?"

"In the Houndsgate," said Robin. "The right place. Oh!—and through the heart with the first arrow from my new bow." (Oman, 1939, p. 208)

2. The next instant the grey horse was almost a-top of him [Robin]; the two swords rang sharply together, hissing and grinding; then Robin sprang in under the other man's guard, his blade flashed forward and up, and the Sheriff of Nottingham flung up his arms, and crashing to the ground, lay still.

Robin stood for a moment looking down at the fallen man. He would not have slain the sheriff for any wrong done to himself, but a wrong done to a friend was another matter. (Sutcliff, 1950, p. 161)

3. And when they reached Nottingham, there were the sheriff and his men, with Sir Richard bound among them, marching down the street. . . .

And with that, Robin bent his bow. *Twang*, an arrow flew. The sheriff fell to the ground. He was dead. . . .

The sheriff's men, seeing their master lie dead, had little heart for a fight. Robin's merry men soon drove them off. . . . (Manning-Sanders, 1968, p. 137)

4. [The Sheriff besieges Sir Richard's castle.] No-one knows who it was that killed the Sheriff. It happened at night, while he was walking round the camp, encouraging his men. An arrow aimed from the castle walls struck him between the shoulder blades and passed clean through his heart, and when he fell his men took fright and one by one departed to their homes in Nottingham. (Miles, 1979, p. 111)

5. During the battle, Robin let fly an arrow that severely wounded the Sheriff, and without a leader, the soldiers soon disbanded and fled. (McSpadden and Hildebrandt, 1990, unpaginated, illustrated, for younger readers)

While Oman preserves the incident, she distances it in several ways. First, it becomes reported by Robin himself within the dialogue with Marian, rather than anonymously narrated, and so presents the outlaw point of view. Such a restriction of point of view is common in Robin Hood narratives. Second, attitude is controlled by the mixture of bluntness, in the described gesture, and the wordplay provoked by Marian's question: the evoked cliché ("shot down like a dog")[2] and the syllepsis ("In the Houndsgate . . . through the heart") simultaneously disclose and mitigate the information that the sheriff was apparently shot down in cold blood. An alternative method is adopted by Manning-Sanders, who frames the incident with the information that Sir Richard was present (this only emerges subsequently in the *Gest*), makes the death swift and clean, omitting the need for the sheriff to be finished off with the sword, and finally shifts focus to the behavior of leaderless men in contrast to "Robin's merry men" (a potent cultural concept in itself). So while her version is not vastly different from the *Gest* in its story details, it is nevertheless still subjected to two major propositions informing most Robin Hood retellings; namely that Robin, despite being an outlaw, has little blood on his hands, and that perhaps the major theme of the legends is the nature, quality, and effects of leadership. These propositions also emerge, in different ways, in the other three extracts, especially obviously in the McSpadden and Miles. Sutcliff relocates the incident to the forest as part of an ambush and pitched battle, places Robin at a disadvantage (he is on foot, the sheriff mounted), presents the fight largely through the clichés of battle ("swords rang sharply . . . his blade flashed . . . lay still"), and concludes with an ennobling reflection over the corpse, stressing the altruism which motivates Robin's actions. In chapter 5 we remarked on some of the ways the ideology of heroism and nationalism in Roger Lancelyn Green's 1950s Arthuriad was influenced by national mentalities in the aftermath of World War II. We would now suggest that in the second half of the twentieth century, retellings of the Robin Hood legend, with its amenability to representations of chivalric behavior and of the defense of the weak and ruled against tyrannical rulers, disclose the same ideological impulse which has been used to motivate and justify military excursions into East Asia, the Falklands, Latin America, and the Middle East.[3]

## The Modern Metanarrative of Robin Hood

In his discussion of fifteenth-century pre-texts, Bessinger (1969) detected some contradictions in the constructions of Robin Hood which mark the beginnings of his reshaping into the popular hero of modern tradition. Such a contradiction is not in itself surprising, and Raymond Williams has reminded us that the social processes which shape a tradition are not systematic but can generate alternative and even antagonistic versions of it (1981, p. 187). The stories about Robin Hood and the modern reversions in children's literature present scholars with as perfect an example of such processes as might be imagined. It shows a clearly discernible metanarrative, a smaller alternative tradition, and certain key points at which ideological assumptions and decisions can be examined. In addition to such choices as those informing accounts of the death of the sheriff discussed above, retellers must also choose between alternative but traditional possibilities with a potential for vastly different implications. Key moments of possibility include the class origins of Robin; the circumstances of Robin's outlawry; the class origins of Marian, and her relationship with the outlaws and Sherwood; the presentation of setting, especially the idea of "merry England"; the functions of the royalist ideology commonly attributed to Robin since the time of the *Gest* (whereby Robin punishes the wicked amongst the social elite, but remains loyal to the true monarch), and firmly established in the modern tradition by Pyle and Gilson (*Robin of Sherwood*, 1958; first edition 1940); the presentation of the arch-villain and arch-enemy Guy of Gisborne (the character always permitted to die); and the existence of alternative (and, since Pyle, alternate) endings. If to this list is added such generic choices as that between novelistic or illustrated narrative, or that of any mix of historiography, legend, fantasy, and adventure story, there would seem to be an infinite number of ways of retelling the story. But although each retelling is different in its own way from all the others, two somewhat surprising conclusions emerge from our reading of about forty of them: first, despite the range of possible choices, the retellings on the whole are culturally and ideologically uniform and conform to a universalistic metanarrative; and second, the significant ideologically alternative texts, namely Trease (1934; revised, 1966) and Carpenter et al. (1984ff.), construct their oppositional stances not by reworking traditional stories but by inventing new ones.

Modern retellings are far too many to permit an exhaustive account, so the following discussion will concentrate on key issues and some symptomatic texts. Versions may be classified into two types. The first type, which further subdivides into three subgroups, comprises most existing texts, and is characterized by a shared conservative metanarrative (Table 6.1). The subgroups here are first, novelistic renditions with a developed sense of coherence and an inclination towards inventiveness (these embody the metanarrative at its most powerful); second, *replications,* which are characteristically episodic in structure and re-present a traditional selection of ballads; and third, illustrated and comic books which repeat the cultural assumptions of the conservative metanarrative, but usually focus only on a narrow selection of incidents.

The second type—the "alternative" reversions—is very small, consisting of Trease's *Bows Against the Barons* (1934) and the novelized spin-offs from Carpenter's television series (1984ff.). These works are very different and widely separated in time, but what they share is a politicized, radical narrative stance which refuses the transcendent order on which the majority metanarrative finally rests. These narratives seek to exploit the play of difference between their versions and the traditional motifs and outcomes in order to suggest that new social formations will think about old narratives in new ways, reforming them not just into new shapes and plots, but into new significances. In an oblique way the discussion of the Robin Hood ballads as an expression of peasant discontent in Maurice Keen's *The Outlaws of Medieval England* (1961) also belongs here. Keen recanted this view in the 1977 reprint, acknowledging that it had been thoroughly demolished by subsequent scholarship, but not before it had entered popular and academic discourse (see, for example, Coggeshall [1980], where Keen's arguments of 1961 are simply reproduced without question).

There is a third kind of text, which frames its retelling of the stories within an antiromantic and purely antagonistic stance and in doing so discloses an opposing metanarrative. We are aware of only one clear example, that found in Rex Dixon's *A Book of Highwaymen* (1963), a recount of pseudo-history rather than a narrative fiction. This is an eccentric reading, but very instructive, in that whereas its Robin Hood is a remarkable travesty of the legends, the process which produces that travesty discloses how the ideology of a particular culture at a particular moment will selectively reinterpret material for its own ends. Dixon recognizes only some elements of the common metanarrative—the motif of leadership, for example, as in "Good men, and bad, will always follow a strong and inspiring leader, for the world is full of followers but scarce in true leaders." (p. 81), but invariably interprets them as being pejorated in the Robin Hood reversions. (The quotation above continues, "The prowess of Robin Hood spread and drew to him men who zested for good living and high rewards for little effort: men without conscience. . . .") He constructs his account by presenting selected and modified motifs as historical fact and then subjecting them to a realistic and moralistic reading. Thus, "Robin Hood is often portrayed as being of high birth and related to the Earls of Huntingdon. In fact he was the son of a poor shepherd" (pp. 79–80). Dixon's own metanarrative revolves around honesty and the so-called Protestant work ethic, so of Robin's skill with "bow and sword and stave" he writes, "Had these talents and qualities been directed into some honest purpose, there seems little doubt that this young man would swiftly have risen to great accomplishments" (p. 80). This metanarrative, needless to say, is an interpretation of culture prevalent in the boom years of the early 1960s, when it was imagined that there might be enough for all and that by sheer talent, without recourse to dishonesty, one could be anything one wanted (a possibility scarcely open to "the son of a poor shepherd" during the economic chaos of late twelfth-century feudal England, by the way). At the other end of Robin's life, ravaged by "heavy drinking. . . , consorting with gay ladies, insufficient sleep, irregular and often vilely prepared meals" (p. 90), the prematurely aged outlaw, "ill and brooding with depression and remorse," is accidentally killed when a nun bleeds him and can't stop the flow! So perish all enemies of church, state, law, aristocracies, and a well-ordered bourgeois lifestyle!

A central motive for this reading, it seems, is a belief that young readers read literally, perceiving only story and not significance, and in a rather simple-minded way apply what they read to other situations. Hence, "The young mind absorbs the colorful myth of Robin Hood and there is danger of the myth's twisted morals being applied to modern criminals" (p. 78). The paradox here is that traditional details have been twisted under the influence of a different metanarrative, and there is still an expectation that the young mind will create its own reversion of any Robin Hood text by using Dixon's reading to confront the common metanarrative. This is an interesting point, though, since in its crude way the Dixon rereading makes overt the impulse underlying all metanarratives.

We now turn to the details of the common metanarrative we have been referring to.

## STORY AND SIGNIFICANCE IN THE METANARRATIVE

Table 6.1 sets out the seven key events of the metanarrative: the left-hand column extrapolates a *story* frame, and the right-hand column seeks to bring out the kind of cultural assumptions which inform the discourse through which that frame is narrated. Sometimes the latter is quite apparent through overt moralizing or register choice, but mostly it is left implicit. The cultural significance perceived or assumed in an event is, of course, a matter of interpretation. What is offered here is not the whole sum, and any significance is apt to be nuanced differently under the impact of changes in context. For example, the motif of hostility to foreigners will not have the same meaning in Carpenter (1984) as it had in Sutcliff (1950), and neither will the conceptualization of the nature of evil. Written in the aftermath of World War II, Sutcliff's *The Chronicles of Robin Hood* could hardly fail to access the recent experiences of a continental enemy and a very materially present evil. If one were inclined to feel skeptical about this claim, a glance at the book's closing sentence should dispel any doubt:

> [Robin Hood and his men] lived on in the hearts of the people; and indeed they still do, even to this very day, because they stood for freedom and justice and kindliness, and all those things which are dear to the English people. (p. 280)

Winston Churchill's speech writers would not have put it very differently. But the Carpenter series, written over thirty years later, is more apt to be a text in which, as J.C. Holt has put it, "Robin is taken over as an expression of present-day social malaise or discontent" (1989, p. 199). Implicitly, though this is very hard to prove, what in Carpenter is identifiable as foreign threatens a loss, under the impact of EEC Europeanization and of global culture, of that essential Englishness so easily assumed by Sutcliff; and evil, though it takes social forms as the petty tyranny of the Sheriff or the brutal stupidity of the stereotypical military mind evidenced in Gisborne, is also a transcendent force embodied in imported forms (the diabolism of Simon de Belleme; the cruel fanaticism of the Templars). Against it Robin pits not his faith in the Virgin Mary (as in the metanarrative) but his faith in the English forest spirit Herne the Hunter (often evoked in British children's fantasy literature since the early 1970s).[4] This shift in focus has important implications for the depiction of Robin's altruism and for the grounding of his social vision.

TABLE 6.1 The Key Events and Cultural Significance of the
Robin Hood Metanarrative

| Key Events | Cultural Significance |
|---|---|
| 1. A young man is forced into outlawry. | Any society should be governed under the rule of social and political justice. |
| *Options:*<br>He is from either the noble or yeoman class;<br><br>he is driven from his land by unscrupulous men [usually foreigners] *or* he crosses the king's foresters | The natural or freely chosen leaders of a people will not oppress them.<br>It is important for a culture to preserve its native forms and traditions, and to resist foreign influences. |
| 2. He gathers and leads a band of similar victims of persecution, and formulates a code of ethics. | Freedom is won by adhering to high ideals under the guidance of a charismatic leader. |
| 3. The outlaws engage in a struggle against the forces of corruption.<br><br>*Options:*<br>Any of the traditional stories can be used, modified, or combined to form an episodic series of adventures; new incidents may be invented. | Resistance to authority can be morally sanctioned when that authority is corrupt, self-seeking, repressive, etc. Such resistance may go as far as violence and killing. |
| 4. Marian comes to live in the greenwood (optional motif, but usual in twentieth-century versions)<br><br>*Options:*<br>Like Robin, Marian may be of noble birth (usually) or of the same class as Robin; Robin may rescue her from an unwanted marriage; they marry, *or* she remains a virgin until Robin is restored/raised to her rank). | Love is a special form of desire which may override social conventions and expectations; it symbolizes the individual's freedom of choice. Marian's presence in the greenwood may also signify something about the social roles of women. |

| | |
|---|---|
| 5. Robin fights a climactic duel with Guy of Gisborne, and kills him (optional; usual in replications, rare in illustrated books). | As the embodiment of evil, Guy evokes the hope and belief that such evil and malice will always be defeated in the end. The duel in the forest, fought without witnesses, symbolizes the naked struggle between light and dark, good and evil. |
| 6. Robin meets the King, is pardoned and raised/restored to a position of honor. Reparations are usually exacted (such as fighting in the King's army, or training his archers). | Society finally rests on a transcendent authority (stronger, more charismatic) capable of reimposing the just rule of law and integrating the deviant back into the whole. The appropriate reward for loyalty to the state is to be raised above one's previous class or station in life. |

*The narrative may end here, or proceed to:*

| | |
|---|---|
| 7. Robin returns to Sherwood and his old life, eventually to be murdered by the Prioress of Kirklees. *Options:* Robin's followers drift away and he wearies of court life and leaves; the King dies/departs and Robin's old enemies return to power: the cycle begins again. | Ambivalent: freedom is precious, but contingent. The texts may cultivate a romantic longing for the pastoral world, but can it be had at the expense of social responsibility once the carnival life of the forest should have ended? *Or*, the power of evil is never finally defeated. Robin is a figure of eternal vigilance and struggle. |

## How Robin Became an Outlaw

The various options available to a writer for representing this incident offer several ways by which immediate audience sympathy with Robin may be evoked. These are the options:

### Option A

Robin is a Saxon, and suffers persecution as part of the general oppression and dispossession of Saxons by Normans. Introduced to Robin Hood stories via Walter Scott's *Ivanhoe*, this motif often appears as the base cause underlying more immediate causes of Robin's outlawry, but in other cases—especially where Robin is a member of the old Saxon nobility—it is a sufficient cause in itself, and is so represented by Gilson and Green, and initially by Groom. Gilson's *The Adventures of Robin Hood* (first published in the early years of World War II) is a celebration of Englishness. Thus chapter 2 depicts the Saxons at a feast in honor of "the natal day of Maid Marian" (Robin's *sister!*), where "the board literally groaned beneath the weight of the good Saxon fare, whilst both wine and ale flowed freely" (pp. 13–14). Robin becomes an outlaw when his father is killed during an unprovoked attack on their home by a horde of Normans. In Groom, Robin returns from the crusades to find his house and lands in the possession of a "Norman usurper"; the story then picks up Option B (displaced version—see below) when Robin rescues a deer poacher from the King's Foresters. Finally, in Green's very eclectic *The Adventures of Robin Hood* Robin is depicted as a Saxon nobleman who secretly, in the guise of "Robin Hood," assists the poor and oppressed, selling off his lands to raise money for this purpose. The profligate Robin who had appeared in Martin Parker's ballad *A True Tale of Robin Hood* (1632; Child, 1888, III, pp. 227–233) and in Thomas Love Peacock's *Maid Marian* (1822) has thus become a model of charitable altruism. Green motivates this behavior by introducing hostility between Norman and Saxon into an otherwise obvious reversion of the first four chapters of *Maid Marian*. It is encapsulated by Guy of Gisborne (to whom Green transfers the function of stopping the wedding between Robin and Marian) when he declares: "Why, the very act of calling yourself Earl of Huntington in right of your mother's Saxon forbears shows you as a traitor: the old Saxon earls were deprived and outlawed for refusing to obey their rightful King, William of Normandy" (p. 30).

What can be surmised about the point and effect of this motif, and about its survival into recent versions such as McKinley's (1988)? In our table, we suggested that the metanarrative discloses a complex cultural significance here. Although Robin becomes an outlaw, there is no suggestion that he poses a threat either to the rule of law itself or to social hierarchy. Hence it becomes a convenient fiction to portray the oppressors as foreign invaders rather than natives, since this gives the outlaws a quasi-external focus for their actions and reduces the possibility of textual depictions of them as engaging in *class* warfare or as mere anarchists. These reversions seem to us to be posited on the assumption that a nation has a natural ruling class which rules altruistically because that is its essential nature and function. The assumption is never explicitly articulated as theme because its ideological presence is anterior to the text's production and, as with so many ideological presuppositions, it remains intangible and invisible. It can be glimpsed, however, whenever the more nationalistic versions express "public school" values. Thus Gilson begins his story of Robin Hood with a potted history that sketches the rise of British civilization from the Neolithic age to the Norman Conquest, and the rise of a people who learn "to have common interests and ideals, and to fight for the same common cause against a common foe, from Agincourt to Ypres" (p. 8). He concludes, "For thus, as we said in the beginning of our story, was our England formed and molded; and thus, because of the deeds of which we have now told, does Robin Hood, even to this day, stand for something that is English" (p. 128). In between, Gilson can describe Robin in language that would not be out of place in *The Fifth Form at St. Dominic's* or *Stalky and Co.* Its social ideology shines through with no need for further explication:

> [Robin] is the first example that we know of, in either history or legend, of what we call a "sportsman": he could accept defeat at the hands of a better man than himself without bitterness or jealousy; no man had ever a greater sense of justice; and he could see humor even in adversity. Thus is his memory typical of all we know as English: true ever alike to friends, himself, and his given word, he and his merry men lay in hiding by woodland path and highroad to waylay Norman abbot and prior, baron, knight and sheriff, that he might assist the poor; and though never a day passed when he did not break the law, he had his own code of honor that he lived up to all his days. (pp. 26–27)

*Option B*

Robin is falsely accused of poaching deer (Sutcliff; Miles; Hayes), and so from the outset is a figure of wronged innocence. The effect might be intensified, as in Sutcliff's *Chronicles,* by glancing at the motives of his enemies: "[Robin] knew that the Abbot of St. Mary's hated him because he had never scrupled to speak plainly his opinion of the fat churchman and his ways, and he knew also that the abbot had long coveted his little farm with its rich corn and pasture" (p. 5). The Abbot's role here is derived from Parker's *True Tale,* but there the motive is that Robin had borrowed money from the Abbot to support his lavish life-style and had not repaid the debt (stanza 9). Sutcliff's reworking is symptomatic of her heavy-handed directing of audience attitude: the language encoding the motives of "the *fat* churchman" turns the register of religious practice and belief against him to expose his hypocrisy ("hated, never scrupled, coveted"), while contrasting his fatness and the littleness of Robin's farm. It should also be noted that this is the same Abbot whom Robin is later to foil in his attempt to gain the lands of Richard-at-Lea, and whom Robin robs of twice the amount of Sir Richard's debt. The connection was not made by Parker, but many of the modern versions exploit or construct such linking threads, thus achieving both an impression of structural unity and a sense of moral shape and purpose, and thereby enhancing the significance of the metanarrative.

*Option C*

While on his way to an archery contest Robin is mocked by a band of foresters, demonstrates his prowess with the bow (usually by shooting a deer), and in the ensuing altercation kills one of the foresters (Pyle; McKinley; McSpadden). This motif presents the writer with a moral difficulty: in Pyle Robin expresses immediate remorse (pp. 18–19); but McSpadden describes the action as a "just cause" because performed in self-defense and upon an enemy who had profited from the death of Robin's father, and two sentences later has linked Robin with "other men who had been unjustly accused." What seems to have disappeared during the century between these two texts is the possibility of an action being mitigated by remorse. In this regard, McKinley is the most interesting of the three. In her radical reconstruction of the character of Robin so that he conforms more to the modernist antihero than to the type of the superhero, she has created a character who is touchingly vulnerable. The chain of events that leads to his outlawry is an unfortunate product of the malice of the drunken, bullying foresters lying in wait for him and simple bad luck. An important strategy in McKinley's reconstruction of Robin is to deprive him of the usual heroic skill with the bow (he's better with a staff), so that his accidental victory in the impromptu archery contest proposed by his tormentors only serves to antagonize them even more, and prompts the standard incident whereby one of them shoots at Robin and provokes his disastrous response:

> He had aimed for Tom Moody's right leg. He had aimed neither well nor carefully, and he took no thought for the consequences, should he succeed at so tricky a shot—or should he fail. But he was nonetheless appalled as he saw the feathered shaft appear as if by magic in Tom's broad chest, as he heard the man's hoarse cry of pain and terror. Tom looked down a moment, and clutched at the great spreading red stain around the thing that grew now so abruptly from his breast; and then his knees buckled, and he fell forward on his face and lay still. (p. 13)

What is immediately striking about McKinley's text is its capacity for getting past all the narrated derring-do and enabling the characters to focalize incidents and events. This is unusual, because the ballad origins and then the later affinities with blood-and-thunder adventure stories have conspired to construct a particular mode for narrating Robin Hood stories: characters are seen from outside, and reactions and responses are stated within narration rather than explored through inner mental processes or dialogue. In contrast, the effectiveness of the above extract lies in the switch at the third sentence from Robin's *narrated* unthinking state to his focalization of the unbelievable. Whereas some of the language belongs to the heavily dramatic—even melodramatic—register many retellings inherit from the ballads (especially "appalled" and "hoarse cry of pain and terror"), and the final two clauses are expressed in quite conventional language, the word set expressing perception and response ("appalled, saw, heard") introduces a new dimension of feeling into the Robin Hood stories. How different this is becomes more apparent if we compare the same moment in Pyle, a comparison which McKinley's text, as a reversion of Pyle, makes virtually obligatory:

> The shaft flew straight; the archer fell forward with a cry, and lay on his face upon the ground, his arrows rattling about him from out of his quiver, the gray goose shaft wet with his heart's blood. Then, before the others could gather their wits about them, Robin Hood was gone into the depths of the greenwood. (p. 18)

This scene is pictured entirely by its narrator, in keeping with Pyle's practice of presenting action with as little introspection as possible. The action is a simple temporal and causal sequence ("the shaft flew . . . the archer fell. . . . then Robin Hood was gone"), and this is deviated from only with the central focus on the arrow in the heart. But any impact this might have had is negated by the simultaneously clichéd and overworded language: Pyle never calls an arrow an arrow if he can call it a "gray goose shaft," and the "heart's blood" cliché compounds the effect. McKinley takes the scene, repeats enough of the language to evoke Pyle, and then transforms the language of that crucial moment into "the feathered shaft," "the thing that grew now so abruptly from his breast," and "the great spreading red stain." That is, instead of a moment of stasis she represents a moment of process as perceived by a mind making sense of what it sees even while it refuses to fit precise words to what it sees. This is a major shift in narrative strategy within the corpus of Robin Hood retellings, and a direct consequence of it is that the significances emerge less from narrator commentary or the registers selected for narrating events and more from character perceptions and interactions. This is, nevertheless, primarily a change at the level of discourse, in that although McKinley offers her readers a compelling, innovative reversion of the Robin Hood legend, her outcomes and significances still fall within the cultural sphere of the common metanarrative. She does succeed in redefining some of the cultural markings of that metanarrative, nevertheless.

## Option D

The shooting of the deer, the first crisis point in this group of retellings (except for McKinley, who does not use the motif), is in itself a sufficient crime to merit outlawry. Both Trease and Carpenter incorporate this motif, though in a displaced form. Carpenter combines it with Option B (false accusation), inasmuch as it is not Robin who commits the crime but his slow-witted stepbrother, Much, and with Option C, since it is the Norman Gisborne who catches them, and "He considered the native English to be hardly human, and enjoyed hunting them whenever they were foolish enough to break the forest laws" (pp. 10–11). This combination of all possibilities emphasizes that there is no legal or political action available to "the native English," and so they will inevitably situate themselves outside the bounds of law and politics. Trease had presented a comparable situation half a century earlier. In *Bows Against the Barons* the deer is killed by the sixteen-year-old peasant lad Dickon, who then flees to Sherwood and joins the outlaws. The displacement of the motif here is part of a wider displacement of point of view, in that Trease uses Dickon for the unusual strategy of telling a Robin Hood story from the perspective of a minor character. While such a strategy is commonplace in historical fiction, which Trease is following as a model, it still remains virtually unparalleled in Robin Hood stories.[5] The effect is that characters, settings, and events are depicted with an experiential quality determined by Dickon's focalization of them, and this is very different from the narrator-focalized depictions which are the norm in other texts. The method proves particularly useful for Trease's depiction of Robin as an egalitarian mentor rather than a heroic warrior.

## MEN IN GROUPS AND THE IDEOLOGY OF LEADERSHIP

At one point in McKinley there is a reference to how Little John "had resisted—and never quite given up resisting—the presence of women in the camp" (p. 189). The remark is part of McKinley's recognition that in Robin Hood stories the outlaw band, as a wholly or substantially male group, shares the major characteristics of other secret societies, political parties, military organizations, and the like, insofar as they are generally reluctant to allow collegiality to women. If women are admitted at all it is as affiliates, and they are then allotted subordinate or subservient roles or, in the case of Marian, given special status in the role of leader's consort. The ballads are a rich source for examining male bonding and the formation of male societies through patterns of ritual and initiation. More importantly, because subsequent versions of the legend have been developed within the story frames supplied by the ballads, there has been little reason (or room) to make significant changes in the depiction of the social structure of Sherwood. The pattern was largely set by Pyle. Marian exists only as a fleeting thought in Robin's mind (pp. 15, 16, 239), and virtually the only women in Pyle's text are barmaids, apart from a queen who belongs to a different category anyway. Women exist as an audience for male performance (p. 37), but they then tend to be slow-witted—"Women do not take a joke so quickly as men" (p. 235). They may be objects of fleeting desire, as with the "plump and buxom lass" who serves in an inn and whom Little John momentarily finds more interesting than food (pp. 283–284), but food *is* more important. Allan-a-Dale's wife is the ultimate object of desire, and worth fighting for, but since she's Ellen-o'-the-Dale (p. 149) she is really only Allan's specular other, and is not mentioned again after the wedding on page 185 until pages 339 and 342. (Of course this is a product of Pyle's pre-texts, but McKinley's exploration of these characters shows how an imaginative writer can dispense with the texts of the past in order to confront this problem of cultural coding.) Subsequent retellings have often given a more substantial presence, if not role, to women, though we are still waiting for a *Robin Hood* in which Marian is principal focalizer or even first-person narrator. To date, McKinley remains the only writer to have used female focalization.

The problem has been compounded by the existence of one apparent exception, the seventeenth-century doggerel ballad *Robin Hood and Maid Marian,* which (via Ritson's *Robin Hood*) is the source for the story of how Marian came to Sherwood, and versions of it appear in Sutcliff, Green, Miles, Hayes, McSpadden, and so on. But this story of how Marian disguised herself as a boy and fought a duel with Robin is through and through a complex of literary and cultural stereotypes. We will discuss the duel as a narrative schema later in this chapter, with reference to Robin and Guy of Gisborne. More important here is the element of disguise, a recurring motif in the stories which, as Nagy has argued (1980), functions to define the liminality of the outlaws' existence, the flexibility of subjectivity when an individual is removed from his or her normal social formation. Disguise can also function as a transition from a socially constructed self to a true self, a process explored most fully in McKinley's representation of Will Scarlet's sister Cecily. Marian is usually depicted as fleeing an unwanted marriage, so her disguise initially conceals her function as an object of desire. More importantly, her duel with Robin (who is usually also disguised!) allows her entry into outlaw society to be assimilated to the standard rite of passage through which most of the main outlaws have passed: Little John, Will Scarlet, Arthur-a-Bland, Friar Tuck. The duel is also followed by the ritual sharing of food. The paradigmatic example of a rite of passage followed by initiation into a male society, and a universal favorite in retellings, is that of Little John. He fights Robin on a narrow bridge spanning a stream (a standard symbolic boundary), the two quickly develop a mutual admiration based on prowess, and then John undergoes a ritual initiation involving much horse-play, practical jokes, dousing with beer, a mock christening, and the bestowal of his new by-name. Pyle's merry version, in particular, is a representation of a male group at its coarsest play. The duel with Marian, the apparent major exception to the all-male rule, has been narratively shaped by literary and cultural convention in such a way that it serves to affirm that rule. It is also always kept significantly separate from the pattern, though, by being invariably narrated without any of the humor which characterizes the duels fought between the group's dominant males.

In *Men in Groups* (1971, p. 144), Tiger argued that males prefer to be with high-status males and devise such initiation rituals to affirm the group's status and quality by demonstrating the worthiness of its recruits. What is it, then, in the Robin Hood stories, that gives Robin first place in a high-status group? In the second story of Suddaby's *New Tales of Robin Hood* a stranger, Gilbert of the White Hand, attempts to join the outlaw band, is taken for a spy, and is in danger of losing his life. At this point the following scene takes place:

> "Quiet, men!" Little John was thrusting his great body through the crowd, and all fell silent in his presence. "Robin alone deals with strangers to Sherwood."
> "Yes, I alone!"
> The leader stood tense and aloof, a few paces from the angry throng.
> "Does anyone doubt my authority?" Robin Hood went on in his gentle, even tones. (pp. 42–43)

The one man who does offer resistance is thoroughly beaten by Robin and banished for three days, under the threat that "My orders are that you be killed if you are seen within three days from now." Two weeks later, in the course of his impulsively begun but carefully executed campaign to win back Gilbert's rightfully owned castle, Robin entrusts the same man with a major responsibility, and thereby "Robin displayed his wonderful knowledge of the human mind" (p. 57). Now what Suddaby has done in this story, in a very crude fashion, is to bundle together the seven main features which are stereotypical of that fictive concept known as "Robin Hood": a charismatic projection of authority; physical prowess in a male group; an impulsive acceptance of physical challenges; generosity to anyone needing help; sound organizational skills; a readiness to overlook past differences; and a capacity to make shrewd assessments of people. For most purposes, this bundle of features *is* the Robin Hood of virtually any modern version. Each feature is a positive term, though as a bundle they are a specifically male grouping. In terms of the proposed metanarrative, then, it can be argued that Robin's strength as leader of an alternative society is that his qualities as a leader conform closely to what Western cultures assume to be mainstream leadership qualities. Actual figures in power in the stories, such as the Sheriff or Prince John, display few or none of these qualities, though they are normally embodied to a heightened degree by King Richard (with Carpenter's *Robin of Sherwood* being the only exception). One difficulty with such a paradigm is, of course, that it is a male one for a male world; a second difficulty is that it doesn't just function to define by binary opposition the absence of desirable qualities in the evil or false leaders, but also marginalizes most people in a society; and third, because it is presented through the characteristic overnarrated and underfocalized discourse of the Robin Hood stories, it is rarely interrogated as a set of values. The notable exception is McKinley's *The Outlaws of Sherwood,* the most successful interrogation of the traditional male base of the Sherwood culture.

## MALE BONDING IN "MERRY ENGLAND"

The opening words of the prologue to Pyle's *Merry Adventures*— "In merry England in the time of old"—draw immediate attention to a significant element of setting for male society in modern Robin Hood stories. Situated in a forest in an imaginary place in an imaginary time, outside the bounds of normal society, the outlaws are enabled to get on with what it is presumed male groups prefer to do: being heroic, hunting, fighting, playing sport, and doing lots of eating and drinking. At the same time, it is a setting tinged with the nostalgia of nineteenth-century medievalism in that, again in Pyle's words, "The good old days have gone by when such men grow as grew then; when sturdy quarterstaff and long bow toughened a man's thews till they were like leather" (p. 104). The focus on heroic male behavior becomes emphasized in a truncated reversion such as Louis Untermeyer's (1964), which is restricted to a retelling of four incidents (based on Pyle). Untermeyer begins by conceding that "Robin Hood was an outlaw. There was no question about it," but swiftly moves to a remarkable, even exemplary, catalogue of the traits of the lovable rogue male: "he was . . . a wrongdoer, a rascal, a scamp, a ne'er-do-well, a breaker of the king's law. Most of all, he was a happy-go-lucky adventurer. He and his band of merry men made Sherwood Forest ring with their gladness, their games, and their gleeful songs" (p. 180). The rest of the narrative can be read as an expansion of this account, and the significance of the four incidents emerges as follows:

1. *Robin's conflict with the foresters, killing of the first deer, and outlawry* (pp. 180–182). On his way to a sporting contest, Robin is waylaid by "rough-looking fellows" who mock his manhood; he behaves with restraint, proves his skill, and kills one of his tormentors in self-defense. Having fled to the forest, he gathers the oppressed and homeless into "a small but wonderfully united army" and dresses them in their uniform of "Sherwood green."

2. *The meeting with Little John* (pp. 184–185). This episode exemplifies the mix of courage and good humor which epitomizes the camaraderie of the outlaw band, and the emphasis on the physical attributes necessary to join (strength, and skill with staff and bow). Untermeyer also includes the renaming as a sign of admission to the group and the popular motif, "He was baptized with a pot of ale."

3. *The capture and rescue of Little John* (pp. 185–188). Captured by the Sheriff's men when his disguise is inadvertently revealed by a begging dog, John is sentenced to be hanged. The incident illustrates on the one hand John's courage in undertaking a dangerous mission and in his request to fight the Sheriff's fifty soldiers single-handed instead of being hanged, and on the other hand the loyalty, daring, and enterprise of the outlaw band who rescue him. Of particular interest here is the obviously manly demeanor of Robin when he spares the wounded Sheriff (in yet another reversion of this moment): "'You deserve to die,' said Robin. 'But I am in no mood for revenge. Besides, I do not kill cowards. Go home and nurse your wound.'" The two reasons given for sparing the Sheriff are mildly unconnected statements of position which don't arise compellingly out of the episode itself. In part, they have their meaning intertextually through their evocation of other Robin Hood stories and general hero lore which portrays the hero both as merciful rather than vengeful and as fittingly contemptuous of cowards. In other words, the significance of the incident lies in its implications about the nature of heroic action.

4. *The coming of the disguised King to the forest* (pp. 188–190). This summary version encapsulates the dreams of male society. It includes lavish feasting ("a lordly haunch of venison . . . liberal flagons of cream ale"), a display of physical skills, and mutual buffeting between the King and Robin. It concludes with translation to a higher order male group, as the outlaws enter the king's employ and Robin achieves the ultimate male bond, becoming one of the king's favorites, accompanying him everywhere in war and peace. "The king never tired of his company"; with that last sentence, Untermeyer has gone well beyond his source in Pyle.

Untermeyer's text can thus be seen as a quintessential statement about an idealized male society, existing somewhere in the past, but evidencing forms of exemplary behavior with implications for contemporary readers. Thus the preface to his collection offers readers the standard humanist justification for the retellings, that is, that "These stories have survived, not because they are based on fact, but because they touch on fundamental traits of human nature" (p. 9). Readers can expect to derive a timeless cultural or moral significance from the particular narrative discourses.

The relationship of readers to significance through discoursal evocation of setting was at times directly explored by Pyle. A particularly good example occurs early in the text with the account of a Tinker who sang "an ancient ballad of the time of good King Arthur, called the Marriage of Sir Gawaine, which you may some time read, yourself, in stout English of early times; and, as he sang, all listened to that noble tale of noble knight and his sacrifice to his king." This complicated maneuver orients the addressed audience towards the evoked story in a position comparable to that of the represented audience towards the sung ballad. The story of the Marriage of Gawain and Dame Ragnell (see chapter 5) is itself not actually told here, though: instead we are given a general approbation of the deep past ("ancient . . . early times"); an assumption that sacrificing oneself for royalty is a privilege; and possibly even that the older language was better, since Pyle uses one of his favorite praise-terms for it ("stout"); and finally a suggestion that readers themselves "may" seek a first-hand acquaintance with the texts of "merry England," thus entering the deep past on its own terms. His book claims only to offer them escape into a world of "innocent laughter" where "flowers bloom forever and birds are always singing" (p. 3), but this is an escape frequently replicated by characters within the book who flee to the greenwood to escape the drudgery of the workaday world (Arthur-a-Bland, Midge the Miller's son, Will Scarlet, Friar Tuck). Indeed, the author's invitation to the reader—"Will you come with me, sweet Reader? I thank you. Give me your hand" (p. 4)—is replicated on page 41, where in inviting the Tinker to join his band Robin collapses together the Golden World and the land of milk and honey of the Bible:

> Thou shalt share all with us and lead a right merry life in the greenwood; for cares have we not and misfortune cometh not upon us within the sweet shades of Sherwood, where we shoot the dun deer, and feed upon venison and sweet oaten cakes, and curds and honey. Wilt thou come with me?

In this way, Pyle's *Merry Adventures* stands as the pinnacle of the process whereby, to quote Stallybrass's formulation once more, a mode of contestation is rewritten as an arcadian dream. It has been an influential rewriting and has itself had to become a site of contestation in recent years as modern versions—both the fantastic romance of Carpenter and the blended romance and realism of McKinley—have sought to overturn the arcadian dream. After all, as Kingsley Amis's Dixon long ago asserted, "The point about Merrie England is that it was about the most un-Merrie period in our history" (*Lucky Jim,* 1954, p. 227).

As remarked earlier, two versions which contest the ideological constructions of "Merry England" settings are Carpenter and McKinley. Carpenter's versions are actually quite hostile to the past, or rather to what the past represents. They are intensely antimonarchic and anticlerical (and thus Christianity and Diabolism are depicted as opposite means to the same ends; that is, power, dominance, material wealth). The series evokes a transcendent essential Englishness which is embodied as a pagan spirit of place, focused in the mystic figure of Herne the Hunter and hostile to such cultural superstructures as kingship, Christianity, and the rule of law. That is, it stands in clear opposition to the values and ideological assumptions of the common Robin Hood metanarrative. It expresses this opposition through its use of setting and frame, in its original stories, and through its reworkings of some of the traditional stories, as when the contest for the silver arrow (*Robin of Sherwood,* pp. 48–55) is redrawn as a struggle between Norman and Saxon for possession of Herne's arrow, which the Sheriff recognizes as "a cult object. . . . Like a scepter or a cross. An English thing. A symbol. Magic" (p. 44). It is also apparent in the marriage of Robin and Marion [sic]. In most versions the marriage is celebrated after the king's return and Robin's (re)elevation to the nobility, and thus functions as a metonymy for a return from nature to culture (and hence the end of Sherwood days). In contrast, Carpenter's version presents a marriage in supernature:

> That night Herne called to his son again, and Robin took Marion deep into the forest and made her a crown of white hawthorn blossom. They knelt together in the moonlight and waited for the forest god.
>
> At last they saw him, his antlers silhouetted against the moon, looking down at them in silence and holding up his hands in a blessing as old as the forest itself. Robin took Marion's hands in his and promised to love her until the day he died. Then he folded her in his arms and kissed her. And when they looked again, Herne had vanished. (p. 67)

The Christian ceremony is present here as a palimpsest, visible in the structure of kneeling, blessing, promising, and kissing, but has been evoked in order to be displaced by the setting (both time and place), by dress, and by the presiding deity. The hawthorn coronet—symbolizing May, magic, sexuality, and fertility (Grigson, 1975, pp. 180–181), the god's antlers, and the twice-mentioned moonlight, in particular, conjure up the older and more elemental ground being alluded to directly by the description "as old as the forest itself." These strategies of evocation and replacement are very symptomatic of the way in which this group of books inscribes its counterideology. It should be noted, however, that Marion is here still constructed largely as object: things happen *to* her and, despite assertions to the contrary within the texts, she never seems to shed her female otherness within the male group. Indeed, at the end of the third series she had become a nun, and in the unmade final series the ultimate fate in store for her was to be raped and killed by Gisborne (Turner, 1989).

Although McKinley's *The Outlaws of Sherwood* develops many strategies which forcefully dismantle the masculinist assumptions of the traditional "Merry England" setting, its ideological grounding finally seems to waver between contradictory positions, largely because of the felt need for a romantic outcome. This might seem a pity, because her dismantling strategies are particularly effective. There are at least six of them. First, Pyle's arcadian perpetual summertime is subjected to a realistic re-presentation: the outlaws have no permanent shelter, are exposed to bad weather, and suffer head colds in winter; and the period of outlawry is realistically brief, extending for only "a year and a half" (p. 287), by which time it had become virtually impossible to sustain. Far from an idyllic Eden, Sherwood is a hard place in which to live and hide, so that rather than uniting the homeless and dispossessed into an army of "seven score of wyght yonge men" (*A Gest of Robyn Hode*, p. 288) or "almost a hundred men" (Untermeyer, p. 181), Robin's principal concern is to relocate them safely within normal society and to restrict his numbers to fewer than twenty. Second, camaraderie amongst the outlaws often parodies traditional motifs, as in the following conversation:

> [Robin] "I shall go ask him what he wants, if you will show me the way."
>
> "I would come too," said Little John. "He might want knocking in a stream to cool his anger."
>
> "I will come too," said Much, "to fish him out again, and to reassure him that not all of us have this queer craving for hurling folk in water." (McKinley, p. 109)

In retrospect, the exchange has a complex irony over and above the reminiscence of Pyle and the joke about male pranks and initiation rituals, since the person referred to is a young *woman*, Cecily, dressed and passing as a man. Moreover, McKinley has introduced this invented character immediately after telling an analogous story, that of the rescue of Marjorie, Alan-a-dale's beloved, from an enforced marriage, which is what Cecily is fleeing. There are plenty of clues that "Cecil" is Cecily, but the narrative refers to her as "he" and it is seventy pages before her identity and situation are clearly revealed. The effect at that point is then to force a retrospective rethinking of those pages, especially the social meaning of readers' responses to the engaging and promising youth we have known as "Cecil." Third, as the examples of Marjorie and Cecily illustrate, the representation of Sherwood is extended so that it also functions as a refuge for women seeking to elude the social construction of woman as disposable property. This is made especially clear in the rescue of Marjorie, since here McKinley represents two parallel and equivalent acts of theft: while half the outlaws are stealing the bride, the other half are plundering her father's house. Fourth, from chapter 10 (and hence for two-thirds of the novel) Cecil(y) functions as one of the principal characters, gradually emerging as the major focalizer. Scenes and events are thus continually presented from the perspective of an introspective female subjectivity in the process of becoming, a strategy which is McKinley's most innovative contribution to the genre. Fifth, the patterns of male bonding are displaced by an emphasized social concern and conscience, by a group loyalty and love which cuts across gender, and by the pervasive, romantic representations of heterosexual love.

Finally, Robin himself is a transformed and somewhat decentered character. Most obviously, he is not a superhero—we can compare Carpenter's Robin who is reinvested with some superhero quality through his adoption by Herne. McKinley's Robin is often quite bumbling; he is cautious, sometimes to the point of indecisiveness; his physical prowess in some areas is below ordinary ("It was common knowledge when I was a forester that I could hit the broad side of a barn only if it wasn't walking away too quickly" [p. 143]); and he is not as quick-witted as Marian, nor as idealistic as Marian or Much. He keeps his band together not by derring-do but because he is caring and careful. As a result, his self-concept is frequently in conflict with the self constructed and invented by the perceptions of others. Thus McKinley shows that "Robin Hood" is an *idea* constructed in people's attitudes towards him— that is, they imagine the Robin they want or need. In this respect she has incorporated into the novel a replication of the process by which all representations of Robin Hood are produced: a core figure is subjected to a variety of cultural and ideological reinscriptions. To the Sheriff, he is "the devil himself, or at least devil-inspired" (p. 120); and a very pertinent example is that offered to Cecily by the anonymous goodwife at Nottingham Fair: "He's an elemental, of course, child . . . Robin Hood is one of the old gods come back to save England from the Normans" (p. 194). A cross-reference to the Carpenter series seems unavoidable here, especially through the anachronistic, modern fantastic use of the signifier "an elemental."[6] Above all, though, McKinley's Robin Hood is a young man unwittingly and unwillingly propelled into an ultimately hopeless situation, from which he is fortuitously rescued by a *deus ex machina,* the return of King Richard at the crucial moment. It is here that the ideological relationship between *The Outlaws of Sherwood* and the metanarrative becomes ambiguous, in that having thoroughly interrogated the tradition and the practices of authors working within it, the book at its close collapses back into the paradigmatically romantic ending of comedy, with a noble king distributing rewards and property and disposing marriages. That the marriages between Marian and Robin and between John and Cecily are morganatic only reinforces the return of the old paradigm.

## The Fight with Guy of Gisborne

The final battle between Robin and Guy of Gisborne has a very special status both for what it discloses about male values and for its connection of these to notions of transcendent value. When the overall assemblage of characters in the Robin Hood narrative is perceived as various fragments of a male culture, Guy represents its darkest aspect. Whereas John is Robin's closest companion and friend because he is his "good" mirror-self (or, better, specular other), Guy stands on the other side as a socio-psychic element which needs to be expunged, a dangerous and frightening impulse to violence. Hence Robin's fight with Guy can be compared usefully with the fight with Little John, both narratively and ideologically. Since the eighteenth century, as part of the process of absorbing Robin Hood into elite cultural paradigms, the good-humored duel with Little John has gradually become the better known of the two, though the fight with Guy originated perhaps two centuries earlier.[7] The latter has become the most heavily moralized of any incident in modern versions, but because these versions still draw on the contents of the ballad they retain one of the incident's most interesting motifs, Robin's temporary adopting of the horsehide outfit and with it the role of Sir Guy. In the ballad the immediate point of the disguise is to rescue Little John from being hanged by the Sheriff, but it has an attraction which extends beyond that. For example, the complex mirroring of Robin, John, and Guy is implicitly recognized in Julian Atterton's *Robin Hood and Little John* (1987), in which Robin and John disguise themselves as Guy and one of his soldiers in order to rescue an imprisoned maiden. Carpenter also reflects the motif in *Robin of Sherwood* (p. 88), when Robin enters Nottingham Castle wearing Guy's clothes.

The ballads with which the two incidents originate are examples of a common narrative schema, the ritualized, and somewhat formalized, conflict between two men in an isolated spot. It takes many forms, such as meetings between wandering knights in romances or shoot-outs in Westerns, and Robin's fights against John and Guy epitomize the variant occurring in Robin Hood narratives. Pyle explicitly evokes the schema when he says of Robin and John, "Never did the Knights of Arthur's Round Table meet in a stouter fight than did these two" (p. 22). The similarities and divergences in the two ballads are evident from the table on the following page.

The significance of the duel with John is easily expressed: while John is victorious, the fight becomes a mutual testing of manhood, and Robin comes out all the better for being gracious in defeat. But the fight with Guy is less tractable. The ballad "Robin Hood and Guy of Gisborne," first printed in Bishop Percy's *Reliques of Auncient English Poetry* (1765), is both fragmentary and cryptic, and supplies no motivation for the meeting or the implicit, anterior hostility between the men. It does, however, contain elements of similarity and difference: both are outlaws (so also in Pyle, but rarely afterwards); both belong, though in different ways, to the world of nature (Robin in the greenwood; Guy clad in his horseskin, complete with head, mane, and tail). But they represent antithetical values. Guy is murderous, has done "many a curst turn" (stanza 34, Dobson and Taylor, p. 144), and merits the necrology pronounced by Robin over his corpse:

"Thou hast beene traytor all thy liffe,
Which thing must have an ende." (stanza 41)

Robin is justified by the implicit intervention of "Our Lady deere" (stanzas 39–40), and he is given the witty remark, when exchanging clothes with the corpse, "If thou have had the worse stroakes at my hand, / Thou shalt have the better cloathe" (stanza 43). A way to preserve the balance and antithesis between the two men in more recent versions appears in the handling of social class. If noble birth is attributed to Robin, he must inevitably draw Guy with him (Green, Stinnet), though it is has in fact become more usual to situate Guy in a higher social class than Robin (Carpenter, Hayes, McKinley, Miles, Sutcliff). This conforms ideologically with the modern metanarrative, being grounded in the assumption (or at least expectation) that standards of behavior and morality rise with social class and are both innate and cultivated. One of its clearest expressions is in Green, when, Guy having shamefully and dishonorably attempted to shoot Robin rather than fight him fairly, Robin reproaches him. The text then continues: "Sir Guy flushed a little at Robin's words, for seldom indeed can those who are nobly born crush out the last flicker of the honor which is their birth-portion" (1956, p. 199). The higher morality of the outlaw also emerges when we consider how later versions have found it necessary to moralize each stage of the basic schema outlined above and to ameliorate Robin's role. This happens within a twofold frame of moral abstraction. First, we are shown a

TABLE 6.2 Robin's Fight with Little John compared with Robin's Fight with Guy

| Robin and Little John | Robin and Guy |
| --- | --- |
| Robin, seeking adventure, meets a stranger in the forest. | Robin, troubled by dreams, goes in search of a stranger. They meet. |
| They fight. | They fight. |
| Robin is knocked into the water. | Robin trips and falls. |
| Help arrives (from the other outlaws, but is not accepted). | Help arrives (from the Virgin Mary, effective by implication). |
| Robin and John become friends; John is "baptized" and renamed. | Robin kills Guy, disfigures the corpse. and exchanges clothing; Robin rescues John, who kills the Sheriff. |

particular example of the eternal struggle between good and evil, and hence the characters are depicted accordingly. In McKinley, for example, both are described as "uncanny" (1989, pp. 194, 199), and the coincidence of the term is then remarked by Cecily (p. 199). When first introduced, Guy is marked by such descriptors as "paid assassin," "bloodthirsty," and child-killer (pp. 198–199). Second, the incident functions as an articulation of the moral situation in which the good man feels he must kill, that is, when faced with an evil enemy who threatens his life. The fight normally takes place in Sherwood, as in the ballad, so Miles's version (1979) is very unusual in that Robin travels for many days to enter Gisborne's estate in order to visit retribution upon him for the murder of Marian's father. Here are two symptomatic descriptions of Guy's death:

> Robin's blade entered cleanly over the other's black heart, and with a choking cry, Sir Guy of Gisborne dropped his sword, and staggering back, crashed to the ground.
>
> The outlaw stood over him, breathing quickly, and looked down on his fallen foe.
>
> "A swift death, and a cleaner one than you deserve!" said he, quietly. "Howsoever, there you lie, Sir Guy of Gisborne. No more will you torture humble folk who have no defence against you. Slain men, and men branded and mutilated, the aching hearts of women, and little children left alone in the world—all these are avenged, Sir Guy; and so I thank the sweet Mother of Our Lord!" (Sutcliff, *The Chronicles of Robin Hood*, p. 248)

> Then suddenly it was over. Maddened by the look of pity in his opponent's eyes, Sir Guy took a lunge at Robin's head. And in that moment, Robin's sword found a gap in the horsehide cape. Sir Guy fell lifeless to the ground.
>
> "It was kill or be killed," said Robin soberly.
>
> (Hayes, *Robin Hood*, p. 63)

Different as these may be, they share a firm narratorial control of audience response. In Sutcliff this is achieved because narrator and Robin share the same perspective, made evident in the very obvious shared moral orientation of the narratorial "black heart" and Robin's catalogue of avenged wrongs, and in the repeated use of Guy's full title. The latter, in contrast with "Robin" and "the outlaw," also emphasizes the inversion of values Guy has embodied. Finally, Robin concludes his antinecrology by grounding the moral justification of his action in a notion of transcendent justice. Hayes achieves a comparable effect in the contrast between Guy's rage and Robin's sense of pity. In both passages the actual moment of penetration is expressed as if Robin himself is not an active agent—"Robin's blade entered"; "Robin's sword found a gap"—and the speech reporting tags on his responses indicate an absence of passion ("quietly"; "soberly"). The implication of each, perhaps, is that Robin is a cipher enabling the operation of some form of transcendent justice. Such a position is also implied, though again very differently, in McKinley's version. Hopelessly outmatched by Guy, who is better armed, stronger, and more skillful, Robin is only able to defeat him because Guy is disarmed by a dagger thrown by Cecily (1988, p. 250):

> And then, like the bolt of lightning Tuck had not been able to pray for, a dagger came flashing through the leaves—flashing *down,* where Guy could not see it, standing as he stood with his back to one particular tree at the edge of the clearing . . . it did what it needed to do.

The evoked, but unavailable, divine intervention has now become the historical process of cause and effect which has brought Cecily to Sherwood, allowed her to develop her physical skills, and placed her in that "one particular tree." The moment discloses one of the ideological cross-currents in *The Outlaws of Sherwood,* the combination of realism and romance so as to produce a strongly teleological interpretation of events which culminates in the advent of the king. To that we now turn.

ORDER, HIERARCHY, AND FREEDOM: THE RETURN OF THE KING AND ROBIN'S DEATH

The social and political conservatism of the Robin Hood metanarrative usually appears at its most overt in accounts of the meeting between Robin and King Richard, the moment at which Robin's moral, social, and political struggle is vindicated. This scene allows full vent to pervasive aristocratic ideals operating in a society whose proper rulers are both feudal and paternal. Robin, a type of king in Sherwood, is usually shown to embody and practice those ideals, so that in Richard he finds a kindred spirit who extends paternal forgiveness to the outlaws and is then an appropriate liege lord to preside over the dismantling of Sherwood's alternative society and the redisposition of its members. Such an outcome is always already anticipated in narratives which present Robin as a dispossessed noble. Green (1956) offers one of the clearest examples in an early speech uttered by Robin, a speech which expresses the significance of Robin Hood stories much more accurately than the better-known oath about robbing rich oppressors to help the poor, protecting women, and so on:

> We are all comrades and brothers, though me they have chosen to be their leader and their king—not because I am by right an Earl, not merely because I have the gift of a steady hand and a clear eye and so can shoot an arrow further and straighter than most men, but because one must rule and I come of a race of rulers (though we are but slaves now to our Norman masters). . . . My friends in Sherwood have chosen me king, and a king in Sherwood I shall be, my first care for my followers, but our first care for justice and mercy and the Love of God. And in this I hold that we commit no treason: when Richard comes home from the Crusade this reign of terror and of evil against which I fight will end. Cruel, lawless John will oppress us no longer, nor his friends and followers use us without right or justice, as slaves not as free men. (p. 42)

The hierarchical pattern evoked here is the real "authority" on which Green based his book—the rhetoric by which conservative governments have always asserted their right to rule. The whole argument is grounded in the incontrovertible assumption that freedom should be the inalienable right of each individual. But what are the conditions of this freedom? As each stage of Robin's argument moves from a lower-order concept to a higher, freedom is seen to exist in a symbiotic relationship with a particular kind of hierarchical authority. And since a hierarchy implies a pinnacle, all rests on the assumption that "one must rule." Robin is qualified not (just) because he has rank and ability, but because he belongs to the class which has a hereditary (and unquestionable) right to rule. The repeated assertion that his men have "chosen" him to be king is thus semantically very interesting, since it constitutes not a choice between possibilities but a choice to accept a version of the status quo. At a higher level this is also reflected in the "choice" between Richard and John as ruler. Only Trease and Carpenter offer versions which envisage a different possibility, expressed in the shout of Trease's serfs, "No baron! No king!" (1968, p. 101), and in the discovery by Carpenter's Robin that Richard is as self-seeking and untrustworthy as any other ruler. The kind of freedom these two books seek to imagine is very different from other versions, which are content rather to explain freedom as the difference between just and unjust rule. In other words, texts which replicate the metanarrative, whether wittingly or unwittingly, are politically programmatic in a specific way. Further, the "end" of the "reign of terror

and of evil" can also be inscribed as an indefinitely deferred possibility—
"when." Although many versions (especially for younger readers) end hap-
pily at Richard's return (Gilson; Manning-Sanders; McGovern; McKinley;
Oman; Stinnet; Storr), the return may also be represented as always momen-
tary, because the struggle is endless. Hence the need to follow the *Gest* and
Pyle and graft onto it the alternative ending, Robin's betrayal and death
(Green; Hayes; Miles; Sutcliff). The most detailed reworkings of this type
are the overtly conservative and nationalistic versions of Green and Sutcliff,
produced during the Cold War period immediately following World War II.
Its most overt expression, however, has to be that with which Miles concludes his "historical" account (1985, p. 123):

> [Robin Hood] was one of the first in a long line of men and women
> who believed that freedom is more precious than life itself. After cen-
> turies of struggle, that freedom has been handed down to you and
> me. It has been a long and up-hill battle, but for us and for our chil-
> dren it is won. Now we have the task of guarding it and of bringing
> it to others. And if Robin were alive today he would be among the
> first to help us.

Such didacticism in fiction would be apt to produce critical outrage, but this
is history, told with the conservative assumption that historiography exists
for its moral lessons (the passage is followed by an authenticating epilogue
which tells of the discovery, and loss, of "Robin's cave" in the 1820s). There
is a telling comparison between the process of argument here and that which
Green attributes to Robin, though Miles's logic is perhaps less transparent:
the particular stands as an example of a higher order general principle; "we"
now occupy that particular place, first with a responsibility to the principle
itself and "our children," and then with a responsibility to transcend self-
interest and extend what has been won to others. Then, with the easy assumption of the final sentence that the writer knows the meaning of history,
the argument folds back into a circle which, if examined, ought to be self-
destructing. In Miles's previous chapter, Richard comes to the forest disguised
as a monk, defeats Little John in a wrestling bout, then reveals his identity
wearing "his white surcoat, with the blood red cross of the Crusaders on
its front" (pp. 113, 116; Ambrus's illustration of the figure dominates pp.
116–117). The Crusades represent a potential problem for modern Robin
Hood narratives (and for didactic historiography), since they are a monu-
mental example of the folly of trying to export an ideology. They are usually not a problem because they happen elsewhere, so it is a curious tactic

on Miles's part to foreground them here. The purpose, we take it, is to get the same effect as Green gets when Robin argues that the basis for his authority does not rest simply in his hereditary right: the king in his turn is subject to a higher order. Robin's paternal "first care for my followers" is in turn subsumed into the higher order, communal concern for "justice and mercy and the Love of God." But the good thus pursued is then folded back into a political vision, much as happens in Miles, with the difference that Robin's vision is national whereas Miles, apparently, is advocating the exporting of freedom (since it's already the prerogative of "us and our children"). Is it carping to point out that since World War II the West has had a sorry record with its attempts at "bringing [freedom] to others"? Miles finds the idea of the Crusades quite unproblematic (though unsuccessful, Richard "had won great glory" in "the Holy Land" [p. 112]), and presumably he finds modern analogies equally unproblematic, though there is nothing in the text itself to force the connection. We think the argument is self-deconstructing, regardless of our own disapproval of a children's book which implicitly advocates international adventurism.

What most of these books have in common is a sense of hierarchy grounded in a notion of transcendent aristocracy. Thus a constant element in the story is its royalist ideology. While the idea of King Richard is its inspiration, those humanist virtues which Western cultures have linked with gentility remain dominant. That is, within an ideology that places *gentility* and *baseness* as polar opposites, gentility is the *norm* from which some characters fall away and towards which others rise. Gentility is defined as nobility of birth and/or behavior, and its representatives are the King and the remnants of the Anglo-Saxon nobility; baseness is likewise constituted by birth, occupation, and behavior. Robin Hood and his fellow outlaws, as good yeomen and loyal subjects of the crown, maintain an upwards trajectory. Prince John, the Sheriff, and Gisborne, as Normans and degenerate nobility, are on the downwards path. The outlaws of Sherwood had been represented in the *Gest* as the true king's loyal subjects, so the dominant modern representation has a long antecedence. Writing of the relationship between loyalty and the misrule of outlawry in early modern versions, Stallybrass (1989, p. 69) identified three specific functions, which we think are replicated in modern versions for children. First, the threat of misrule is contained by representing it as the antithesis of rule. In most versions the king's adventure in the forest requires him to play out another identity, which he undertakes in a holiday spirit. Hence he disguises himself, feasts with the outlaws, and takes part in some form of sport in which he is victor (in Green he successively knocks down John, Tuck, and Robin) or delivers the penalty, thus establishing his position at the top of the male hierarchy. The transition from misrule to rule is marked when he appears in his proper clothing and the outlaws fall to their knees before him (in Miles, Robin's dog even licks his foot, "as if she recognized true majesty when she saw it" [p. 116], as a surrogate for utter abasement). The king usually reintegrates the outlaws into society, often by cataloguing their crimes and exacting reparations in the form of service (redirecting their skills into either fighting in the Crusades, or training the king's archers, or acting as foresters, or, in Robin's case, being or becoming a good aristocrat). Second, because the return of the king sets a temporal boundary to the period of outlawry, dissolves the band, and destroys the idea of Sherwood, misrule is reduced to a seasonal and "mythic" moment rather than a permanent possibility. This is articulated quite clearly whenever the king refers to the stories about Robin Hood which have drawn him to the forest. Sutcliff, for example, includes an interplay of rumors and attitudes in an extended conversation between the king and several knights (pp. 200–203). Third, monarchy is presented as a source of *license* rather than of control. A king who is "chosen" by his "comrades and brothers" rules by consent—hence the importance of portraying him as a man of the people, ready to mess about in the forest, dress up in lincoln green, trade blows with the outlaws, and enjoy the joke of eating his own deer. Stallybrass argues that because both monarchy and misrule are elided within "the ideological construction of England as a band of brothers," political and social hierarchy also seem to be effaced.

It is only an illusion, of course, and many children's versions dispense with it, preferring to represent freedom within an overt royalist and nationalist ideology. The Stinnet/Kimberly comic-book version (1990) is a perfect example. Here Robin is represented as a fair-haired squire (he owns a substantial property and employs workers) who comes into conflict with authority by trying to protect peasants against the depredations of the Sheriff and Guy (both swarthy and suspiciously Mediterranean-looking). Throughout the story he is the model of a paternal and feudal leader. At the end, he inspires a peasants' revolt, but his leadership of it passes implicitly to a mysterious stranger who is, of course, the disguised king: hierarchy exists naturally amongst the forces for good. Robin's reward, as ever, is to be made a count and allowed to marry Marian, a suitably aristocratic wife. More interestingly, McKinley attempts to subvert the pattern by dispensing with the scene in Sherwood, reinserting the meeting with the king into sociality by setting it within a castle; here the outlaws are entirely at the king's mercy, but are allowed some scope to negotiate their future. As suggested earlier, it is an uneasy ending, and McKinley's Richard is manipulative and whimsical. He is offering "tricky choices" (p. 292), not free choice, and in each case the outlaws choose the army in order to stay together rather than live comfortable lives apart. The book's closing lines return us ambiguously to the hierarchy seen in Green and Miles, now inverted so that it appears as a top-down hierarchy but also subjected to the effect of end-focus which suggests that the last item is most important (p. 298):

> "Health and victory," said the Lionheart; and they all drank.
> "And to the king's mercy," said Robin.
> "And to comrades," said Cecily.

Few stories have been retold as often as Robin Hood's, and it is a curiously depressing experience to read thirty or so of them. Retellings may in general tend towards socially conservative ideologies, but here, with only a few exceptions, the process is unrelieved and systematically programmatic. The texts resoundingly confirm what we have also seen in earlier chapters, that previously told stories can be so ideologically encumbered by a deep structure metanarrative that transformations of particular details can seem in effect no more than superficial tinkering. Hence attempts to subvert the metanarrative, such as McKinley's, may meet with only partial success if they operate within a largely intractable genre or mode, or fail to transform its implications. Effective re-readings are difficult to achieve unless, as with Carpenter, old stories are embedded within entirely new frames. Even there the books are apt to suffer from the notorious left-wing failure to imagine a revolution which enables a transformation in the roles of women. In the main, though, Robin Hood emerges as a paradigmatic Tory voter, and that is the role model he usually offers young readers, the place to which the narratives' invitation into the greenwood finally leads.

NOTES

1. See especially the selection in *Rymes of Robyn Hood,* edited by R.B Dobson and J. Taylor (1976).

2. Part of the mitigating effect will also be intertextual, as many readers, recalling the melodramatic death of a later outlaw, Alfred Noyes's highwayman ("shot down like a dog on the highway"), may be apt to access the romantic hostility to authority figures inherent in such a scene.

3. Compare, for example, a newspaper item about a British soldier in the Falklands war cited in Fairclough, *Language and Power,* 1989, pp. 52–53. The ideas stressed are altruism, leadership, and the notion of a job to be done. These ideological positions became more sharply focused when Robin Hood was transposed into the *Green Arrow* adult comic series, where his avatar—a sociopolitical liberal—fights to uphold the existing political and cultural formations of the U.S.A.

4. Most notably in Susan Cooper, *The Dark Is Rising* (1973), Penelope Lively,

*The Wild Hunt of Hagworthy* (1971), and, more recently, Jean Morris, *The Troy Game* (1987). For the background, see Michael John Petry, *Herne the Hunter: A Berkshire Legend* (1972).

5. Another example is a small-format picture book, *Robin Hood,* by Joan Collins and Richard Hook (1985), which tells the story of the silver arrow from the point of view of an eight-year-old. The child is also named Dickon, perhaps in acknowledgment of a debt to Trease for the strategy. (The details that Robin here disguises himself as an old man, and his disguise is seen through because he has a young man's hands, seem to derive from Carpenter [1984, p. 54].)

6. *Elemental spirits* are a personification of natural phenomena (*OED, elemental,* 4.). The use of *elemental* as a substantive, in the sense of "an entity or a force which is regarded by occultists as capable of producing physical manifestations" (*OED, Supplement*), dates from the late nineteenth century, and in the late twentieth century has been commonly used in fantasy games of the "Dungeons and Dragons" type.

7. The available evidence indicates that "the main elements of the story of Guy of Gisborne were present before the end of the middle ages" (Dobson and Taylor, p. 140), whereas the fight with Little John is probably an early seventeenth-century invention (ibid., p. 165).

# FOLKTALE AND METANARRATIVES OF FEMALE AGENCY

*Intelligence is the stem and stalk upon which agency blooms.*

—Martine Bates, *The Dragon's Tapestry*

Folk literature poses a particular challenge to anyone who desires to conserve or retell stories drawn from traditional sources, in that the metanarratives of the traditional societies within which, broadly speaking, folk narratives evolve often incorporate world views antithetical to those preferred by many members of modern societies, and especially by those people keen to disseminate contemporary forms of humane values.[1] Moreover, the conventionalized forms of folktales—for example, the formulaic beginnings and endings, the general recourse to character stereotypes, the recurrent patterns of action—tend to reinforce existing metanarratives and so make it difficult to reshape the stories without recourse to more drastic processes of revision, such as parody, metafiction, or frame-breaking. These more drastic processes are often employed in reversions of the relatively small number of "fairy" tales—usually derived from the collections of Perrault or Grimm—which are still widely known in modern Western society. Our discussion here is not concerned so much with reversions of the modern "canon" as with how editors and writers have sought to recover and disseminate a wider range of folktales in an attempt to recuperate one of the more recalcitrant elements of folktale—gender bias and its effect on the representation of female roles.

In her brief introduction to *Wise Women: Folk and Fairy Tales from Around the World,* Suzanne I. Barchers relates that to assemble her collection she examined over four thousand folktales and found only a hundred with "female heroes who showed intelligence, perseverance, or bravery" (1990, p. xii). From these, sixty-one "were selected carefully to represent the best of the heroic women." Phelps likewise refers to examining "several thousand" folktales to find the forty-six she rewrote for her two volumes, *Tatterhood* (1978) and *The Maid of the North* (1981). This actual scarcity has been further accentuated by the virtual hegemony of the *Grimms' Tales* in Anglophone popular culture. As modern scholars have detailed, the Grimms' editing of the tales furthered a tendency in early modern Europe for powerful folktale heroines either to be deprived of their power or for their power to be transformed into evil witchcraft (Bottigheimer, 1987, pp. 19, 76–77; Zipes, 1983 and 1986a). In making the selections they have, Barchers and Phelps both position themselves on one side of a long-running debate about whether or not folktales present negative gender role models. In fact, the issue of gender makes folktale the focus for the most acrimonious debate to have taken place over any category of retold stories. It is now widely held that, as Zipes puts it, "It is no longer possible to ignore the connection between the aesthetic components of the fairy tales, whether they be old or new, and their historical function within a socialization process which forms taste, mores, values and habits" (1986a, p. 2). We agree with this view, but we are also aware that these formative effects are not empirically demonstrable, and that the debate finally depends on ideological positions and logics derived from those positions. Attempts to ground arguments in surveys of attitudes (see, for example, Stone, 1985) remain essentially anecdotal, only pointing to the possibility that role and gender representations in folktale reinforce the effect of these representations within other cultural formations. Many authors, nevertheless, have retold and invented folktales under the assumption or at least hope that their work can make a difference to social practice, and our focus in this chapter is on texts of this kind, rather than on the work of retellers more concerned with some of the other presumed functions of folktale, such as preserving tradition, transmitting universal values, or stimulating the imagination of audiences. For this reason, we do not intend to rehearse well-known arguments here (for a summary see Stone, 1985 and 1986; Zipes, 1986a, pp. 1–36), but will briefly consider some points salient for the process of retelling folktales.

## READING FOLKTALE: UNIVERSAL VERSUS GENDERED EXPERIENCE

The debate about folk/fairy tales and gendering has pivoted on two related issues, and these have clearly affected the process of retelling: first, on familiar diverse theories about culture and human experiencing of it; second, on notions of how readers make sense of texts. In other words, the argument about folktale is implicated within major theoretical concerns of the later twentieth century. The first issue can be reformulated as the difference between assumptions about the supposed universality of human experience and assumptions that human experiences are culturally relative. The second pivots on the kind of understanding critics (and, importantly, authors) have about the possible alignments readers might make between their own sense of selfhood and experience and those represented textually. Naive "reader-identification" theory (Stephens, 1992a, pp. 68–69; Lesnik-Oberstein, 1994, pp. 110–114), especially of the 1960s and 1970s, has been influential in both the literature and the criticism, though this is too blunt a tool to take discussion very far. Nevertheless, it is clear that consumers and compilers of folktale collections have thought in simple identification terms, as when Minard, author of the first significant collection of folktales with female heroes, cites as catalyst for her endeavors a mother's protest that "She did not want her four-year-old daughter . . . identifying with Snow White, the Sleeping Beauty, or Cinderella" (1975, p. vii). On the other hand, this notion of "identifying with" is perhaps only a misapprehension of a more complex process. Folktales are a specific discoursal genre and, although more writerly retellings shade into other modes such as romance and types of fantasy, what seems to us to be the crucial point is repetition of motifs and social formations across a multiplicity of texts. This is what feminist critics of the genre are more apt to be concerned with. Individual tales do induce empathetic alignment with focused characters, of course—though we wouldn't call this "identification"—and because there is a kind of intertextuality which operates throughout the genre this might be presumed to have a cumulative effect in constructing particular social formations. As Oring, for example, has pointed out (1986, pp. 127–129) folktale characters are not complex and do not develop; interactions between participants are likewise limited and formulaic; and action is often stereotyped and repetitive (as with the reliance on threefold repetition in Western folktales). This can have the effect of depicting human experiences and social structures as generally homogeneous. Ultimately, though, one can only envisage this as tending towards an outcome in social practice if, despite the otherness of settings and character functions, the world depicted can be mapped onto the everyday social world inhabited by audiences—that is, if it coincides in some way with other constructions of experience in everyday culture. This brings us back to the difference between universal meanings and culturally specific meanings.

Bettelheim's *The Uses of Enchantment* (first published in 1975), which was widely influential for at least a decade, is apt to be cited as representing the quintessential modern universalist position, and arguments center on a small group of "fairy folk tales," what we might think of as the modern popular canon. Bettelheim's decision "to concentrate on a few still-popular fairy stories . . . some well-known favorites" (1978, pp. 14–15) tends to have confirmed the parameters of the corpus earlier designated by Lieberman as "those which have affected masses of children in our culture," that is, "the best-known stories, those that everyone has read or heard, indeed, those that Disney has popularized" (1972, pp. 383–384). Both sides in the debate accept the view that stories can "affect masses of children," but they differ about the nature of the influence, and particularly about the kind of rite of passage that is being depicted.

Bettelheim is quite specific in the claim that fairy tales do not differentiate male and female pathways, and argues that "Even when a girl is depicted as turning inward in her struggle to become herself, and a boy as aggressively dealing with the external world, these two *together* symbolize the two ways in which one has to gain selfhood: through learning to understand and master the inner as well as the outer world. In this sense the male and female heroes are . . . aspects of one and the same process which *everybody* has to undergo in growing up" (1978, pp. 226). Hence Bettelheim consistently reads fairy tales as maturational rites of passage which deal with "universal human problems" and thereby help children to find meaning in life: by transcending the confines of the self, by overcoming oedipal dilemmas, sibling rivalries, and childhood dependencies; and by developing a sense of self-worth and moral obligation (1978, p. 6).

Feminist critics are usually much more skeptical about the supposed universal and essential values in fairy tales, and argue rather that they offer boys and girls different developmental paradigms which are products of gendered social practices. Hence Bettelheim's dictum that "It is the characteristic of fairy tales to state an existential dilemma briefly and pointedly. This permits the child to come to grips with the problem in its most essential form" (1976, p. 8) can be turned on its head into the claim that fairy tales "reduce a complicated process of socialization to its essential paradigm" (Rose, 1983, p. 209). An issue here which remains unresolvable is whether the impact of the tales comes from their story structures—where boys are shown as active, clever, resourceful, and courageous, and girls as passive, pretty, dependent, long-suffering, and self-sacrificing—or their symbolic significances, and hence whether readers align or differentiate between textual representations and cultural experience. Stone (1985, p. 127) argues that if fairy tales do reflect rite of passage experiences they nevertheless offer sexually stereotyped pathways for both boys and girls. Thus female lives are represented as revolving around, competing for, and winning male attention, and hence the emphasis falls on beauty, passivity, and dependence on outside forces. In other words—and this is the objection to Bettelheim—the rite of passage laid out for females is socially determined, conservative, repressive, and limiting. The same view is expressed by Rowe, who subscribes to the general view that folktales are one of culture's primary mechanisms for inculcating roles and behaviors, symbolically portraying basic human problems and social prescriptions, but now argues that the glorification of passivity, dependency, and self-sacrifice as female virtues suggests "that culture's very survival depends upon a woman's acceptance of roles which relegate her to motherhood and domesticity" (1991, p. 348). That is, women are encouraged to internalize a patriarchal construction of female functions and the notion that conforming to this construction brings the rewards of marriage, wealth, and well-being. As we have said, such a position drastically changes the terms of the underlying premise—that folktale texts function to help children find meaning in life by teaching that they can transcend the narrow confines of self-centered existence and make a significant contribution to sociality. Meaning, subjectivity, and sociality are represented through and as endemically gendered structures.

These contradictory positions point to the way retold stories always carry at least a double potentiality, in that they can reproduce a traditional view of cultural transmission or, by implicitly stressing difference, can manifest how the significance of story is relative to the culture in which it is told. Because their roots are in the past, the common inclination of retold folktale has tended towards conservatism—socially, culturally, and politically—in the assumptions that the present is shaped by the past and that universal and absolute values inhere in the past and its texts. In children's versions, in particular, such assumptions also incorporate the further assumption that human nature is essential and unchanging, and that the present is therefore either an affirmation of or a lapse from the values of the past. As we will see, an examination of such children's literature also discloses palpable evidence that the cultural heritage being transmitted in this way carefully selects out those elements from the past which are currently deemed desirable and eliminates others.

To explore these matters further, in this chapter we will sample four main types of retelling, all of which have a well-established place in the long history of retelling stories: folktale anthologies of stories with positively presented, active female heroes; framed collections; genric intertextuality; and novelizations.

## FOLKTALE COLLECTIONS AND FEMALE HEROES

From the mid-1970s folktale collections began to appear which bring together only stories in which female characters are central and manifest agency

through cleverness, resourcefulness, courage, perseverance, and related qualities; there were several such collections during the next twenty years. The
number of stories in each of the seven collections we are concerned with here
ranges from sixty-one (Barchers) to five (Leeson),[2] and amongst them they
include a total of one hundred and twenty-two separate stories. This is rather
more than the hundred mentioned by Barchers, and is certainly not exhaustive.[3] Only nineteen tales appear in more than one of the seven volumes, with
the most frequently included stories being "Clever Manka" (x5), "The Husband Who Was to Mind the House" (x4), "Kate Cracker-Nuts" (x4), "Molly
Whuppie" (x3), "East of the Sun, West of the Moon" (x3), "Tam Lin" (x3),
and "The Mastermaid" (x3). These in turn have frequently appeared in more
general folktale anthologies, but cannot be said to constitute a recognized
alternative to the popular canon. As a group, nevertheless, they are indicative of the kind of values advocated in these collections.

A question which immediately faces any compilers of such a collection
is whether to reshape the tales in order to advance their objectives, and so risk
incurring the charge of "violating the objectivity of the folklore collector by
imposing one's own language and bias on the narrative" (MacDonald, 1982,
p. 18). The earliest collection, Rosemary Minard's (1975), is conservative
in its approach to the text of the selected tales: hers is a compilation of
"found" texts, all of which were reproduced without modification, but most
were already literary retellings. She prints Walter de la Mare's retelling of
"Molly Whuppie," for example, which seems very literary when compared
with Joseph Jacobs's version (itself a rewriting of a Scottish pre-text to make
it more like standard Southern English). Thus de la Mare overtly brings out
the similarity of the tale's opening with that of "Hansel and Gretel" and "The
Babes in the Wood," articulates well-meaning motives for the behavior of
the Giant's wife, and ameliorates the violence by having the giant lock up
his daughters rather than murder them (though, curiously, the changes make
Molly's subsequent behavior towards the giant and, especially, his wife even
more problematic). Minard's is the only example in this group which consists entirely of "found" tales, reprinted without further editing, though other
volumes may include a proportion of such tales, and retellings are not always directed towards a feminist outcome. The assumption which grounds
Minard's collection is that a hitherto undiscerned metanarrative will emerge
if tales of female heroes are simply brought into conjunction: folktale traditions already incorporate gender-positive attitudes and values, but these have
been rendered invisible by the patriarchal assumptions which otherwise pervade folktale and dominate other kinds of collection. What Minard offers
instead is the most straightforward example of a compilation based on the

assumption that aggregated acts of empathetic alignment with focused characters will disclose an alternative social practice—that is, that a metanarrative emerges from macrodiscoursal patterns and effects. She also subscribes to a common attitude towards folktale in Western culture, that is, that it is part of children's "cultural heritage" (1975, p. viii). Further, when she reproduced classic versions of tales which "have existed for hundreds, perhaps thousands, of years as part of the oral tradition of earlier civilizations" (ibid.), she was deliberately evoking the traditional connection of the oral tradition with the cultural transmission of the past and of a society's knowledge and construction of the past. These evocations of heritage and tradition serve to affirm that the situations depicted within the tales are not fanciful propaganda, but reflect a reality which exists outside the text.

Another important feature of Minard's collection is the practice of drawing widely on the international folktale repertoire, and this practice is replicated in other volumes. There has been a long and continued history of national collections, but these in turn are drawn on for international collections which explicitly or implicitly assert the universality of human desires, aspirations, and experiences. The pattern was firmly set by Andrew Lang's "color" fairy books, both by the catholicity of their contents and by Lang's own sense that the similarities between "stories of the remotest people" were attributable partly to diffusion and partly to "the uniformity of human fancy in early societies" (*Orange Fairy Book,* pp. xii, xiii). It is only a small step from there to interpreting such products of "human fancy" as signs of essential common humanity, and hence to valuing folktales for their universality (see also Burne, 1987). This is still so in the modern era—for example, Joanna Cole in her introduction to *Best Loved Folktales of the World* cites the oral origins of folktales and continues, "the stories express the wishes, hopes and fears of many people, rather than the concerns of a particular writer, and they deal with universal human dilemmas that span differences of age, culture, and geography" (1982, p. xvii). By reproducing the practice of internationalizing—even though the motive for doing so may be the lack of resources within specific national groups—the compilers of "feminist" collections effectively appropriate the principle of universal experience and hence assert the universality of the newly disclosed metanarrative.

The most obvious example of this effect amongst the feminist collections is Leeson's *Smart Girls* (1993), a small volume for young readers, consisting of one tale from each of England, Ireland, Norway, the Ukraine, and Egypt. Leeson has also rendered the collection more homogeneous and so emphasized the universality of the theme in three other ways: first, by retitling the tales, so that each is now named for its young heroine; second, by choosing tales in which the heroine triumphs through her own courage and/ or intelligence; and third, by retelling tales in which issues of gender are obviously imbricated with issues of class. In each tale the heroine comes from a less powerful socio-economic stratum than the men with whom she has to deal. This little gathering of narratives thus constructs a readily identifiable metanarrative, whereby the mental capacities of individual heroines enable them to achieve agency despite stiflingly patriarchal and otherwise unfavorable social contexts. Mary is a servant girl whose abilities gain her wealth and social prestige. Fionna's intelligence and foresight enable her to steadily better her situation and to shield her husband and father-in-law from the King's intention to kill them. Kari thwarts her father and their wealthy, powerful neighbor in their attempts to bully and trick her into marrying the neighbor. Marusya engages in a battle of wits with the local Squire and wins comprehensively. Zaina, daughter of an impoverished street vendor, refuses to allow the Sultan's son to use the power of his sex and position to harass and bully her and induces him to abandon his sexist and classist attitude towards her in favor of equality within marriage. In each of the three stories in which the heroine marries, however, she does so not as a reward for what she is or does, but because of her own agency.

The metanarrative of *Smart Girls* is not only a product of the processes we have outlined, but is further shaped by microdiscoursal aspects of Leeson's retelling. Because he was prepared to make substantive changes to his pre-texts, Leeson's volume, together with those of Phelps, represents the most radical approach to assembling a feminist collection. For example, a comparison of "Mary," the opening story, with the first recorded version of its pre-text ("The Dauntless Girl," reprinted in Briggs, 1970 A1, pp. 204–206; Philip, 1992, pp. 382–385) shows that Leeson has developed setting and motivation, and varied the ending. The revisions are a departure from the oral style of the pre-text, and of orally transmitted folktales in general, which avoid narrative embellishment and attention to motivation (Philip, 1992, p. xxxiii). The point of Leeson's setting is to emphasize Mary's courage, since to reach the village from the house where she first works as a maid she now has to pass through "a dark wood," past "the ruined church where gravestones glinted white in the moonlight," and through "gloom" and "shifting shadows" (1993, p. 11). We remarked in chapter 5 on the gothicizing of stories retold for children since the 1950s, and this seems a clear example of that influence entering retellings of folktale (perhaps now enhanced for this genre by the influence of Jean Cocteau's 1946 film *La belle et la bête*). It here replaces the frisson of fear which the pre-text develops around the episode of Mary's midnight trip to fetch a skull from the charnel house. Leeson transposes that episode into comic discourse, especially in drawing attention to the frustration of the "village lad" who had been paid to hide in the charnel house and impersonate a ghost; in the pre-text this role is taken by the sexton, and when Mary locks him in he dies of fright before his co-conspirator can arrive to release him. Leeson develops Mary's motives for action by his unique handling of her two trips in the first part of the tale: both are made the objects of a bet, and both times Mary silently notices that she is being exploited by her employer. This becomes the motive for her to change employers when she is offered another position. In the pre-text there is only one bet, and Mary's employer gives her his winnings. In her retelling of this tale (as "Fearless Mary"), Susan Price has Mary first assert that the prize is by rights hers and then take it (1986, p. 15). Mary turns the tables on the employer class in her next adventure, when the ghost of her new employer's mother leads her to find two hidden bags of gold, with the instruction that the small one is for her and the large one for her employer. In the pre-text, she reverses the terms of the instruction, and her master marries her in order to get both bags. Leeson includes the reversal, but now has Mary suggest the marriage, as the culmination of her developing control over her situation. Hence the two halves of the story both pivot on her courage but contrast insofar as, in the first, her courage is exploited and she is without agency, and in the second, she exploits it for her own betterment. Price's version develops Mary as having still stronger agency: she is rewarded for both acts of courage in the first half, she accepts the offer of a new position not out of discontent but because her courage has become a desirable resource and she can negotiate a tripling of her salary, and at the end she takes the larger bag of gold and embarks on a life of independence. Both endings are a far cry from the ending of the pre-text, in which not only has Mary no evident agency in the question of marriage, but also "[the Squire] got both bags of gold, and he used to stick-lick her whensoever he got drunk. And I think she desarved it, for deceiving the old ghost" (Briggs, p. 206). We said earlier that retellings are apt to select elements from their sources which are currently desirable and to eliminate others, and modern versions of "The Dauntless Girl" afford two very obvious examples in omitting the death of the sexton and at the close replacing an archaic moral justification of domestic violence with Mary's accession of agency.

Modern reversions of a folktale, such as Leeson's or Price's, retain the basic set of characters and events, but transform them into a literary artefact. The oral narrative voice is replaced by a literary narrative voice; motifs are redirected so that the story is more obviously thematic in its orientation; the empathetic participants display a more developed inner psychological motivation, are designated by name rather than by function, and act within more fully articulated settings; and the terms of the outcome are substantially modified. The result of these changes is that the tale now more precisely accords with a metanarrative which asserts that exploitation of another on the basis of assumed superiority of sex and class is morally and socially wrong, and any act which subverts this is permissible.

Collections which shape a metanarrative both macrodiscoursally—by means of a unifying frame and recurring themes and motifs—and microdiscoursally—by attention to the language, structure, and significances within individual components—are still the exception. Thus Minard's implicit strategy for constructing an ideological, metanarratival effect is replicated in two other collections which treat their pre-texts conservatively: Alison Lurie's *Clever Gretchen and Other Forgotten Folktales* (1980) and Barchers's *Wise Women*. *Clever Gretchen* is a collection of fifteen tales retold by Lurie "freely in [her] own words" (1980, p. xii), but with the apparent purpose of making the tales aesthetically accessible in the hope that such stories of heroines who "are not only beautiful and good, but also strong, brave, clever and resourceful" may become as familiar as those of the popular canon. About half of the tales in *Wise Women* are reprinted without change, while the rest have been retold to varying degrees, at times in truncated form. There is, of course, no compelling reason to reshape a tale which already promotes the desired metanarrative, and even Phelps, the most interventionist compiler of a larger collection, reprints nine tales in *Tatterhood* in the form found in source texts, as well as retelling a further seventeen. Again, not all reshaping is specifically designed to promote the metanarrative of female agency, but may have more direct aesthetic or structural purposes. This difference is illustrated by retellings of "The Mastermaid," for example.

After "East of the Sun, West of the Moon," "The Mastermaid" is the most popular Scandinavian tale with a strong central female figure. It appeared in Lang's *Blue Fairy Book,* from which Barchers reprints it. Most reversions of it are based on Asbjörnsen and Moe (1969, pp. 50–61), from which it is reworked by Lurie and by Phelps (in *Tatterhood*), both in shortened form. The story in the pre-text is episodic and fantastic, breaking into two halves in a familiar morphology. In the first half, a wandering prince takes service with a giant, performs three tasks with the help of the Mastermaid, and then, again with the Mastermaid's intervention, escapes the castle and the pursuing giant (whom the Mastermaid thwarts by throwing down magical objects), and returns with her to his father's kingdom. The prince is the focused and focalizing character for this part of the tale. In the second half, with the Mastermaid's role shifted from helper to hero as she takes over as focused and focalizing character, there is a further period of testing when the prince is bewitched and forgets the Mastermaid, and she creates the conditions for his disenchantment. The second half is problematic, because in demonstrating her prowess with a magic wand stolen from the giant the Mastermaid causes the death of an old woman whose cottage she has appropriated. She then agrees to marry, in order to deceive and rob, in turn, the Constable, the Attorney, and the Sheriff; after the prince is disenchanted, the witch responsible for his state is "torn to pieces between twenty-four horses." Lurie gets around this problem by writing a reversion confined to the first half of the story, which she further reshapes by deleting a brief segment in which the prince, contravening the giant's interdict on exploring the castle, enters three other rooms before finding the Mastermaid, and by depicting the prince's attempts to perform the first two tasks without the Mastermaid's advice. The latter changes emphasize the difficulty of the tasks and hence the value of the Mastermaid's wisdom in knowing the tricks necessary to perform them. In the pre-text, the prince's first sight of the maid is of "a Princess . . . so lovely, that the Prince had never seen anything like her in his born days" (Asbjörnsen and Moe, p. 51); in Lang "princess" became "like a king's daughter." Both Lurie and Phelps excise the nexus between physical attractiveness and princesses: in Lurie this moment reads "a girl so lovely that he had never seen her like" (p. 36), and Phelps goes still further with "a handsome bright-eyed young woman," who, in accordance with Phelps's practice, also has a name, Maj. The pre-text is a transitory evocation of the motif of the "captive princess in the tower," and then the effect is ironical because it is the prince who is in danger and needs saving. The story has a potential to be reshaped as a mutually supportive adventure, but insofar as the maid's role in the first half of the tale is mainly advisory, her function is the standard one of "helper" or "donor," so her role is in need of further modification. The prince remains consistently inept throughout, though this is not necessarily a good way to impart agency to the female character, since it may amount to no more than role reversal. Barchers argues that in general female heroes are not posited on male victims (though some of the men happen to be in danger, ridiculous, evil, or spineless), and many of the tales depict male and female as equally persistent and enterprising (p. xii). In Asbjörnsen and Moe's "Mastermaid," however, the princess advises and the prince actualizes, and she takes a more active role only during the escape and subsequently when she emerges as the focused character. So by retaining only a trace of the irony playing over the prince-princess roles, omitting the pursuit, and then entirely omitting the second half of the tale, Lurie's reversion reduces the maid's agency by restricting her actions to little apart from the helper role. The desire for a better structured and more concise narrative eliminates the problematic elements in the maid's story, but only at the cost of her agency.

Phelps reads "The Mastermaid" as a story about "the adventures of two young people in love" which imparts two deeper significances: Maj and the prince function positively as a couple, and "heroines may indeed have more wisdom and knowledge than heroes, and heroes need not be tradition-ally heroic nor excel in all things to be loved" (1978, p. 159). She reshapes the narrative "for the sake of a more compact story" (p. xviii), but the rather drastic changes made in her version of the second half of the tale also en-hance the deeper significances. This part of the tale is only one-fifth the length of the equivalent section in the pre-text, a reduction achieved mainly by omitting the encounter with the old woman and the three marriage contracts. Hence Maj now uses the giant's wand to renovate an abandoned, derelict cottage, and is then depicted in the guise of the good witch who performs her healing functions from a place on the margins of society: "she trans-formed the hut into a comfortable cottage with a garden of herbs and veg-etables and a clutch of plump hens. Very quickly she became known around the countryside for her powers and skills" (p. 154). It is this reputation, rather than the frightening experiences of the men of law, which brings Maj to the attention of the palace when the carriage of the prince's bride-to-be is immobilized. Finally, and most crucially for articulating the significance Phelps perceives here, the disenchantment scene is substantially changed. Maj arrives at the palace bringing a golden apple (or ball) and a gold cock and hen. Here are the two versions of what she does with them:

> [She] put them down on the table before her, and the cock and hen began at once to peck at one another, and to fight for the golden apple.
> "Oh! only look," said the Prince; "see how those two strive for the apple."
> "Yes!" said the Mastermaid; "so we two strove to get away that time when we were together in the hill-side."
> Then the spell was broken. . . . (Asbjörnsen and Moe, p. 61)

> Maj laid the gifts on the table before him. The gold hen pecked the golden ball over to the cock, and he with his beak returned it to her. Back and forth it rolled.

The prince was fascinated. "See how they share the ball, each with the other!"

"Yes," Maj replied, "just as you and I shared danger in escaping from the giant."

He looked at her in surprise for he did not recognize her. Then he picked up the golden ball. At once the giant's enchantment was broken. (Phelps, p. 155)

There can be no doubt that the analogy in the earlier text is ill conceived, in that the pivotal notion of striving has to override the fact that the birds are competing rather than cooperating, and the image implies that relationships between males and females are inherently contentious. Indeed, the maid's maltreatment of her would-be husbands has already indicated as much. The use of an apple as the object of contention can also evoke the association of apples with Eve, and the tradition that conflict between the sexes originated in Eden. It is not surprising to see the problem addressed in a modern retelling, and accordingly Phelps has substituted a ball for the apple, thus introducing *play* in place of the other connotations, and, more importantly, linked it with the further substitution of *sharing* for *striving*. In contrast to Lurie's reshaping of the tale, Phelps has used her omissions and changes specifically to further the metanarrative of the collection.

The combination of macrodiscoursal and microdiscoursal elements to reshape a collection so that particular tales might more overtly embody the perceived metanarrative produces a collection at the other end of the spectrum from Minard's. *Tatterhood,* however, is not the paradigmatic example of this strategy, because Phelps took the process still further in her second volume, *The Maid of the North.* In her introduction to this volume, Phelps follows others in alluding to the centrality of the oral tradition, but now to remind readers that "Each generation shaped the tales according to the values of the times, adding or subtracting details according to the teller's own sense of story," and to claim for herself "the traditional storyteller's privilege" (1981, p. xi). As part of this privilege, Phelps has assembled an international collection of tales more varied than that of any of the other collections, ranging beyond the usual repertoire to include some stories from other genres, notably romance (see our discussion of her "Gawain and the Lady Ragnell" in chapter 5). She has also taken large liberties with individual stories, as in her drastic retelling of the Grimm story "The Twelve Huntsmen," in which, once again, details have been reshaped so that the main female figure is seen to act with more deliberation and agency, and the path to the outcome is radically changed. The tenor of the collection is set by the title story, with which it opens. Phelps has extracted and reassembled this from the *Kalevala,* but the biggest transformation is not the representing of the tale as a discrete narrative but its focus and point of view. If one reads the same material in, for example, Irma Kaplan's *Heroes of Kalevala* (1973), the implied audience alignment is with the male heroes competing in their courtship of the Maid of Pohjola; in Phelps's retelling the perspective of the Maid or her mother predominates when either is a participant in events. Such a realignment within the narrative is a crucial aspect of the overall discoursal strategy.

## FRAMED COLLECTIONS

Another way in which a gathering of stories may be subordinated to a metanarrative is by embedding within a framing narrative, so that the significance of the embedded stories may be transformed both by the impact of the frame and by modifications of individual stories. This is an ancient procedure, of course, and we have already drawn attention to it in previous chapters in relation to retellings of Bible story, myth, Arthurian romance, and Robin Hood stories. It is less commonly found as a strategy for retelling folktales, and John Gardner's admirable *In the Suicide Mountains* (1977) remains almost unique as an example of the type with a focus on gender. Susan Price's more recent *Head and Tales* (1993) is another fine example of a framed collection, but less apposite for our purpose here because its focus is more consistently on issues of class than of gender. One of the principal strengths of a frame-driven bundle of stories is that focused issues, such as gender, can be articulated within a wider ideological context, and the framed stories need not be subjected to microdiscoursal modification. Gardner follows his pre-text quite closely (in contrast to Price, who substantially rewrites individual tales). *In the Suicide Mountains* depicts a deeply humanistic quest for identity, carried out in despite of a society which strictly subjects its members to conventional roles. The three main characters—Chudu, a dwarf; Armida, a blacksmith's daughter; and Christopher the Sullen, the country's Crown Prince—all feel alienated from society because of the behavioral patterns attributed to or imposed upon them. They meet by chance in the Suicide Mountains, where they have all gone intending to kill themselves. The Suicide Mountains are thus implicitly defined as a habitus in which existential angst seeks resolution.

The narrative unfolds according to two key principles: that the manifest surfaces of things do not necessarily constitute reality, and that meanings are attributed, found, and controlled by means of stories, especially rumors, lies, (auto)biographies, folktales, and fables. The story thus begins,

"In a certain kingdom, in a certain land, there lived a dwarf who had an evil reputation" (p. 3), and goes on to detail how Chudu is ostracized because of his difference, and is made the scapegoat for all ills that occur in the village, even though his evil reputation derives from "lies and fictions." He is in fact the victim of a racist discourse. Armida and Christopher, on the other hand, are victims of gendered discourses. Armida has learned in early adulthood to imitate femininity. The role models imposed upon her by her stepmother, especially the heroines of books (p. 21), are "flimsy and graceful, helpless and fluttery" (p. 22), whereas Armida is "mannish—complex and quick of mind and as strong as a gorilla" (p. 64). The consequence of this clash between extreme socialization and her earlier unfettered selfhood is a fractured subjectivity. Christopher, for his part, has little aptitude for the folktale roles of male hero and prince. In learning to interact and cooperate, and to share mutual respect and love, each also learns to recognize the individuality of the others and to negotiate the social roles and functions into which he or she is interpellated from time to time, without becoming subjected to them. Gardner, evoking the Western metaethic, suggested in *On Moral Fiction* that good art should present "valid models for imitation, eternal verities worth keeping in mind, and a benevolent vision of the possible which can inspire and incite human beings toward virtue" (1978, p. 18), a stance we have continually identified in most impulses to retell stories for young audiences. *In the Suicide Mountains* sets out to present such a vision by contrasting positive and negative examples.

This story about how to embrace difference and otherness consists of many other stories, so that as well as including the histories of the main characters Gardner borrows from Russian folktale in order to embed four hypodiegetic (or second-degree) narratives (see Rimmon-Kenan, 1983, p. 91). Three of these tales ("Marco the Rich and Vasily the Luckless," "The Secret Ball," and "The Miser") are narrated by the Prince's adversary, a bandit disguised as a saintly abbot, and the fourth ("Misery") by a baby into whom the bandit is transmogrified after being killed by Armida, Christopher, and Chudu. These folktales closely follow their pre-texts (Guterman, 1945) and their significances have not been substantially adapted in the retelling, but they nevertheless develop a complex thematic relationship with the framing story. We will focus our discussion here on "The Secret Ball," because it has a strong relevance to gender issues and because "The Dancing Princesses," the Grimm variant of the tale (1987, no. 133, "The Worn-Out Dancing Shoes"), is one of the lesser members of the Anglophone popular canon.

Gardner frequently draws attention to the processes and practices of storytelling, continually nudging his readers to think about them. The Prince's response to the first and third tales—"It's an interesting story . . . I don't understand why you've told it to us" (pp. 80, 135)—prompts readers to seek their own answers, and even more so once Armida identifies the abbot's explication of the first as "hackneyed lecturing" (p. 81). It is important for readers to recognize that the lessons the abbot draws from his tales are partial and self-interested. On the simpler level, the abbot's first moral that "Things are not always as they seem" (p. 81) mocks the three travelers with his own disguise and has a central function in the outworking of the frame story. His second moral, drawn from "The Secret Ball," is that because human beings have consciousness and free will "our human business is to clarify, that is, sort things out, put the good with the good and the evil with the evil and the indifferent with the indifferent" (p. 99), but in using this as an argument to persuade Christopher to attempt to kill a dragon, the abbot harnesses existentialist humanism in the service of tyranny. What the framing story obviously does here is remind readers that the meaning of a story is fluid and apt to change according to context. By positioning readers to interrogate how a particular narrative is subordinated to and serves a larger purpose—in effect, the abbot's metanarrative—*In the Suicide Mountains* also empowers its readers to interrogate metanarratives more generally.

The embedded tales can be said to share, for example, a perception that individuals can make a difference to their own lives, and they do so operating in a world which turns out ultimately beneficent for a person who acts in order to create his or her own life, especially when those actions have a positive effect on the lives of others. Thus Vasily, ordained by a mysterious trio of old men to receive all of miserly Marco's wealth, miraculously escapes Marco's attempts to murder him as an infant, and achieves his destiny on his last quest by placing the needs of others before his own. The poor peasants in "The Miser" and "Misery" better their lives by taking positive action in the face of adversity. "The Secret Ball" is more problematic, however. Because the empathetic focus is aligned with the "needy nobleman" who discovers the secret of where the princesses go and how they wear out their shoes, the tale's implicit misogyny seems to remain unaddressed, and it remains an unmitigated "taming of the shrew" type in which the king's undutiful daughters are put in their place, signified by the subordination in marriage of the youngest to the socially inferior nobleman. Further, Gardner makes small additions to the story so that the roles of the "helper" and the "adversary" affirm that gender hierarchy is divinely ordained. While it is the nobleman who is instrumental in the discovery, he is the instrument of a divine power, operating through the mysterious old woman who at a first meeting advises him to make his peace with God, and next day gives him

"Saint Krasna's invisibility cap" (in the source text she simply gives him "an invisible cap" [Guterman, p. 224] at their only meeting). The adversaries are not only the princesses themselves but also "the accursèd king," whose realm they visit each night (p. 97). Because folktales rarely offer any motivation for an action beyond need or desire, there is no explanation for the princesses' behavior, but it is not difficult to see that the tale pivots on the patriarchal urge to contain the transgressive female sensuality figured in the nightly dancing "till their shoes were torn to shreds" (p. 98). Readers must also draw on traditional associations between women and demons here, though perhaps what lies behind this version of the tale is Russian folk epic, in which "women are always presented as sly and demonic; they represent evil of some kind, and the hero does battle with them" (Vytkovskaya, 1992, p. 113). Containment is reached when the nobleman reveals the secret and the king "ordered the passage to the underground kingdom to be bricked up, and married his youngest daughter to the needy nobleman." This double containment is seen to be a "proper" outcome in the closing sentence added by Gardner: "From the beginning, the nobleman expected nothing of his wife, but as the years passed she gradually became all that his heart could have asked for" (p. 98).

Can the framing story, in which Armida has learned that it is possible for a woman to be free and independent, overturn the significance of this tale in which women are overtly deprived of any responsibility for their own lives? We think this is possible, but the kind of resistant reading necessary requires very sophisticated readers. The cue, as often here, lies in the immediate framing. The story is presented as a moral *exemplum* within the abbot's attempt to persuade Christopher that an effective way to commit suicide would be to attempt to kill the dragon, Koog; the episode in which the dragon is killed, by Armida, deconstructs the kinds of gender roles asserted in "The Secret Ball" and further emphasized in Gardner's retelling. Before the story begins, doubt is suggested by Armida's overt positioning of herself, as she "watched through spread fingers, more and more suspicious" (p. 92). Her attitude draws attention to the abbot's sophistry at this point—for example, the logical slippage in his argument that Christopher's will to suicide is the same as "indifference to life," and then that "God loves the man who's indifferent about himself, the charitable man. That's the kind of fellow God looks after" (p. 92). "The Secret Ball" is introduced as an illustration because the needy nobleman exemplifies such an "indifferent" man. Armida's suspicion draws attention to a recurring concern in Gardner's works, the danger of allowing reason to overthrow "the creative impulses of the imagination" (Merrill, 1984, p. 170). Although Christopher does decide to fight the dragon, he does so not for any reason the abbot has suggested. Rather, he does it in response to the role constructed within traditional story, that is, because he feels interpellated by the role of dragon-slayer: as he says to Armida, "It feels really fine to be battling a dragon, with a beautiful maiden looking on. No fooling. It's the kind of thing a prince *ought* to do" (p. 108). But Gardner has evoked the stereotype in order to dismantle it, as often happens in other modern dragon-fights. Armida devises a plan to draw the dragon from its cave and distract it long enough for *her* to close in and kill it; Christopher's role in this plan is to play his violin. Out of all this framing context, and especially Armida's functions within it, it is not all that difficult to see that "The Secret Ball" is embedded as a negative *exemplum* or antitype. It represents the kind of storying and the kind of social practice which *In the Suicide Mountains* sets out to destroy.

Before leaving this topic, we would like to make a brief comment on the ways in which two retellings (of the variant version) of "The Dancing Princesses" take up the unaddressed question of why the princesses behave as they do and hence the corollary question of why this behavior needs to be changed. We mentioned earlier that the Grimm version is a less familiar member of the popular canon, and this version, the usual source for retellings in English, lies behind Robin McKinley's retelling in *The Door in the Hedge* (1981) and the 1984 television production for Shelley Duvall's *Faerie Tale Theater*. These versions also illustrate how the fuller articulation of folktales in modern versions is achieved through conjunction with romance or fantasy genres. The television version, written by Maryedith Burrell, is the more straightforward of the two. Its assimilation to romance enables the gorgeous costumes, magical settings, and gentle humor present in much romantic fairy tale, though here at the price of cuteness and preciosity. But there is also clearly a strong awareness that the behavior of the young women needs to be explicable, and the version draws on popular psychology to invert the theme of undutiful daughters reduced to submission, so it becomes a tale obliquely about the dangers of sexual repression. As summed up in the packaging blurb, the moral is now that "[an] overbearing king learns from his daughters that being overprotective is as unwise as being too permissive." The underground world and its dancing princes are a reifying of powerful, repressed erotic desires. Each princess opens the portal in turn, reciting the attributes of her ideal lover. When the princesses enter the gondolas which carry them to the "fairy-tale" pavilion, the narrating voice explains that they "floated off into their own private dreams." Thus it becomes more significant for the tale to disclose *why* they go than *where* they go, so part of the soldier's disclosure is the advice to the king to "trust your daughters and give them a little freedom." Inevitably, the soldier will not claim his reward—marriage with the daughter of his choice—unless she has already fallen in love with him, and the outcome is reached through a romance cliché: the eldest daughter, who has led the others into the underground world and has apparently been most resistant to the soldier's gentle humanity, confesses that she is indeed in love with him. This transmogrification of folktale into romance evokes again the debate we reviewed at the beginning of the chapter: under the guise of a more liberating message, this retelling has offered its audience the same message as found in contemporary adolescent romance. As Christian-Smith sums it up, feminine sexuality is dangerous, sexual desire must be self-regulated and properly channeled, and the proper channel is heterosexual romance; young women must learn to accept a subordinate role, making do with whatever degree of autonomy they can get (1990, pp. 40–42).

In contrast, McKinley draws on elements of fantastic Gothic mode to flesh out motivation, setting, and atmosphere, so that the psychic depths reified by the princesses' descent underground to the dance suggest a more complex range of possible meanings. The old woman ("helper") who gives the soldier the cloak of invisibility also explicates the plight of the princesses, who are held under an enchantment enabled by a taint of witch's blood inherited from their mother. The princesses are thus innocent of intent, though arguably guilty of being female through an analogy with the doctrine of original sin. The text employs Gothic horror to insist that the land the princesses visit is the realm of nightmare, "the palace of haunted dreams at the heart of the black lake" (p. 199), and represents inexpressible anxieties and fears. Dance, normally a patterned social ritual which both expresses and contains sensuality, is perverted so that grace and beauty disclose an underlying horror, a disclosure which perhaps suggests that the princesses' "dreams" embody subversive desires which threaten female socialization. Or perhaps the perversion of the dance figures an aberration within the psyche, the inner source of feelings, emotions, desires. Moreover, the princesses experience their state as entrapment, and although they know that every day's dancing brings closer the release of their demon partners from the depths into the world, they can do nothing "but watch the sands of their own time running out" (1981, p. 156). There is an allusion to some forbidden knowledge here which the text declines to identify but rather characterizes in the dance music as "the emptiness of the void" (p. 198) and "something more than silence; something unnameable, and better so" (p. 208). Gothic mode once again generates a sense of unease by loading the discourse with signifiers indicating darkness, silence, eeriness, fear, and a sense of things happening just beyond the threshold of perception. Significantly, the soldier's task is to confront the terror, which he does by each night penetrating further into the demon world and by looking inward at his own fear—"the steady and knowledgeable fear of an old soldier who dares face an enemy too strong for him" (p. 199)—and then to *name* it by disclosing and describing in detail where the princesses go. The tale is thus transformed into a Gothic fantasy in which the characters enter a forbidden other realm and, by escaping it and returning to reality, experience psychic growth through the exposure of forbidden and transgressive desires. Nevertheless, the structure of events and setting in the pre-text necessitates that the tale will always pivot on female transgressiveness and male rescue, and this is accentuated by the switch of McKinley's version into romance mode at the close. It seems probable that the only effective means to counter this effect is that chosen by Gardner—that is, by wrapping a frame around the tale to promote resistant reading. We will come back to some of the implications of rescue from the otherworld shortly in an examination of the reverse situation offered in the "Tam Lin" story.

## GENRIC INTERTEXTUALITY

We will make only a brief mention of this third type, as these are no longer folktales but rather original creations which have a general intertextual relationship with folktale schemata, are not indebted to particular tales, and no longer pretend a direct connection with oral tradition.[4] A symptomatic example is Jane Yolen's *Tales of Wonder* (1983), in which are gathered together thirty "literary fairy stories," as Yolen describes them (p. ix). Writing of this kind is confluent with various fantasy genres, especially medievalist romance and sword-and-sorcery, and will often appeal to both adolescent and adult readers. For example, the "truly modern fairy tales meant for mature, adult readers" in Del Ray and Kessler's *Once upon a Time: A Treasury of Fantasies and Fairy Tales* (1991, p. vii) were commissioned from writers of fantasy for the adult market (Brooks, Cherryh, McCaffrey, et al.), but would be readily enjoyed by adolescent *aficionados* of fantasy. *Once upon a Time* was conceived as a genric, rather than thematic, collection, and has no particular agenda with regards to gender representation. The ten stories are predominantly androcentric, however, though two and sections of two others are focalized by women, and several major female characters demonstrate intelligence, perseverance, and courage. To this extent the collection probably reflects a pervasive impact of the women's movement on literary fairy tales and fantasies, rather than any conscious intentions. Collections for young readers in which all the tales include central female characters are still surprisingly rare, and the gathering of five superb original stories by Robin McKinley in *A Knot in the Grain* (1994) remains a rare treat.

## NOVELIZATIONS: RETELLINGS OF "TAM LIN"

Finally, as with other types of traditional stories, folktale materials may be transformed by novelization. In order to do this, writers have recourse to one or both of two main procedures, elaboration and combination. As with other kinds of story, folktale is expanded into novel by elaborating common elements of literary fiction: main characters may be more complex, the motivation for their actions will be a little more than stereotyped, and experiences may be depicted as having subjective or introspective impact and consequence; both social and physical elements of setting may be more detailed and specific; reduplicated events or actions may be individually elaborated so as to stress difference rather than similarity; and the positioning of audience towards characters and event may be more complicated. McKinley's *Beauty* (1978) is an excellent example of this first procedure. Second, folktales may be combined, whether by drawing on several analogues or variants of a single tale-type, or by joining unrelated tales. For example, in *The Girl Who Sat by the Ashes* (1919), written before the twentieth-century popular canon had emerged, Padraic Colum expands the "Cap o' Rushes" tale episodically by drawing on other "Cinderella-type" tales, by borrowing folk motifs from other sources (such as a "riddle-solved" motif from a variant of "Clever Manka"), and by inventing incidents. He does not, however, elaborate character or motivation beyond simple folktale stereotypes. By the end of the twentieth century, with knowledge of folktale increasingly restricted to the popular canon, writers are more apt to produce the kind of bricolage effect we have noted in other contexts, incorporating explanation as well as allusion (that is, characters within the text will often read and so summarize the relevant pre-text), and developing fictions by means of both elaboration and combination.

The story of the dancing princesses introduced the motif of human beings caught in a struggle for possession on the boundary between this world and an otherworld. This condition of liminality—defined in McKinley's version when the captain of the guard remarks to the soldier that, "each of us walks at the edge of a dangerous border, and makes believe that he is the guardian of it" (1981, p. 190)—is a common theme in Celtic folklore, and when pivotal it renders a folktale ideally suitable for expansion as fantasy fiction. A tale which has been widely retold to illustrate female resourcefulness and courage is "Tam Lin." This story of a young man snatched into the otherworld of faerie and reclaimed by a determined young woman has been reproduced or retold by Barchers, Lurie, and Phelps (1978); there are some notable picture book retellings, especially that by Cooper and Hutton (1991); many more elaborated versions have been written, notably by Moray (1965) and Vinge (1986); and there are two novel-length versions for young adults: Diana Wynne Jones's *Fire and Hemlock* (1985) and Lucy Sussex's *Deer Snake* (1994).[5]

The two novels are complex, and it is not our purpose here to offer extended readings but to consider the tradition and context of retelling of those "heroic mythical events" from which the novels have been developed. Jones has written that her objective was "to write a book in which modern life and heroic mythical events approached one another so closely that they were nearly impossible to separate" (1989, p. 134), and Sussex has also produced such an intertwining. Some version of the "Tam Lin" story has existed since at least the mid-sixteenth century, but modern retellings are based on sources from the eighteenth century, principally nine versions of a ballad printed in Child's *English and Scottish Popular Ballads* (I, 1882, pp. 335–358) and Joseph Jacobs's retelling in *More English Fairy Tales* (1894). All modern retellings reproduce the central story schema of a mortal who is taken by fairies, meets a young woman (usually named Janet; otherwise Margaret) at a well, and is reclaimed by her before he can be sent to Hell as part of the fairies' due "teind" or tithe. To win Tam Lin, Janet must await the fairy host at an ancient cross at midnight of Halloween/Samhain, pull Tam Lin from his horse, and hold on to him while the fairies cause him to shape-shift. Briggs comments that the ballad is "a compendium of Scottish Fairy beliefs" (1970, A1, p. 502), which in itself is an explanation both for its popularity as a retold story and a widespread practice, presumably with child audiences in mind, of eliminating one or both of two story constituents: that is, the patriarchal interdiction Janet breaches in going to the well and her consequent sexual relationship with Tam Lin and resulting pregnancy. Thus an ameliorated version appears, for example, in Jacobs, in Manning-Sanders's reworking of the border ballads (1959), in Jarvie (1992), and in the feminist collections of Barchers and Phelps. Barchers's source for the story was an anthology of myths and legends for younger readers, and so she seems content to reproduce a story of heroic altruism depicting a "wise woman" within a textual context dedicated to transmitting traditional culture. Phelps reshapes the tale so that it becomes a story of true love overcoming apparently insuperable barriers. The two novels of Jones and Sussex both follow the modified version in postponing any romantic attachment between the protagonists until after the defeat of the otherworld powers, though the issue of sexuality otherwise pervades both books. A particularly interesting treatment of these issues is found in Cooper and Hutton, where Cooper's narrative about a young woman asserting her agency against the pressures of a confining discourse of femininity ("I am not a flower waiting to be picked. I would rather do my own picking!") is brilliantly complemented by Hutton's illustrations: many of these depict restless movement, and at key moments they are allusively symbolic. Thus the first meeting between Margaret and Tam Lin is a version of Eve plucking fruit for Adam in Eden, and when in the series of transformations Tam Lin becomes a snake, the scene is reminiscent of Hutton's own representation of Eve and the serpent in his *Adam and Eve* (1987). As we suggested in chapter 2, the Fall is a pivotal example of boundary and transgression; here, the symbolism and strong sexual charge of Hutton's scenes can be interpreted as challenging and recuperating the significances for female agency and sexuality attributed to the Fall (see the discussion of *Adam and Eve* in chapter 2).

"Tam Lin" may be a compendium of fairy lore, but it is first of all a story about the boundaries of sexual desire. Most commonly, the consequence of breaking an interdiction in folktale is an imminent disaster which the transgressor must recuperate. In Janet's case, she recuperates her sexual transgression and pregnancy by "winning" the child's father. Jones demonstrates her understanding of this principle in *Fire and Hemlock* by blending the story with others, but especially "East of the Sun, West of the Moon," which furnishes the pattern for recuperating a broken interdiction. Retellings which retain the interdiction and pregnancy have the potential to question the social bases of the interdiction, exposing it as an expression of patriarchal attempts to control female sexuality and, at a deeper level, of the ambivalent attraction/repulsion felt towards "wild" sex and embodied in the Fairy Queen. Janet, at a crucial moment in her life—the onset of adulthood and hence nubility—is confronted by a socially imposed interdiction (do not go here; do not do this) which contains her sexuality. It may seem folly to disobey the interdiction, but well-being, effective individual agency, and even—for Tam Lin—life itself depend on the action. Folktale form and content are used to examine the importance of free will and choice in human life, while insisting that individuals must take responsibility for the consequences of their actions.

The modern retellings which most explicitly, at times even heavy-handedly, take up these questions are Moray's and Vinge's. One reason these are interesting to compare is that the impact of the women's movement in the two decades between the texts becomes very evident, and this in turn throws light on *Fire and Hemlock* and its concerns. Moray and Vinge share a perception that Tam Lin is already embodied as a trace in Janet's mind. In

Moray this is because Janet had known Tam Lin as a child before he was taken, and this enables him to inhabit her dreams. What she experiences, then, is an outflowing of something that has been repressed, through the recovery of a "memory" that consumes the subject with an insatiable desire. Janet not only displays steadfastness and bravery, as the Fairy Queen puts it, but also a quality of vision and imagination which enables her to transcend the mundane world and wrest something for herself and her people from the imagination. Significantly, Moray has enhanced this focus by suppressing the motif of the Hell-tithe. Vinge's Janet (here Jennet) is rather engaged in a confrontation with patriarchy, and from the perspective of a psychoanalytic feminism Vinge has accordingly elaborated Robert Burns's version of the ballad (Child, 39A).[6] Thus the prelude to Jennet's meeting with Tam Lin occupies a third of the story, where Vinge adds a misogynistic priest, and develops a strong sense of female power through the symbolism of Jennet's contemplation of her own image in her mirror and of her "dead" mother's portrait. The conjunction of mirror and portrait, of Jennet's likeness to her mother and her mother's gaze "filled with longing, as if she were searching for something she had lost and would never find again" (p. 185), form the ground of Jennet's discontent with her patriarchal society, a discontent which leads to Tam Lin, the confrontation with the Fairy Queen, and the knowledge that she can choose and shape her own life. An amusing and important modulation in the close of this retelling is that, once reclaimed, Tam Lin is just a man, and a self-interested and self-regarding one at that—the "magic" has gone. With this touch, Vinge radically reforms the tradition of "Tam Lin" retellings. What Jennet has won is not romantic love but individuation, a sense of her own unique subjectivity: "When she looked into her mirror, she would never see someone else there again" (p. 212).

Vinge's retelling is contemporary with *Fire and Hemlock,* and has not evidently influenced *Deersnake* (though Sussex often seems to be writing against both Vinge and Jones). Jones has acknowledged her own awareness that "feminism . . . was slowly changing the climate of opinion" at the time she was working on *Fire and Hemlock,* and that to produce an acceptable hero she accordingly needed "a narrative structure which did not simply put a female in a male's place" (1989, pp. 134, 135). The key term here is "structure," since for most of the novel Polly is depicted as either in a "male" role in her fantasy game with Tom Lynn, where she imagines herself disguised as a boy, or matching herself to a feminine schema. The text stresses her physical attractiveness, long hair, blondeness, and soft-hearted compliancy (see Rumbold, 1995, pp. 121–126). Moreover, her pre-teen tomboy phase is brought to an abrupt end when she one day looks in a mirror and discovers "a wild, gawky figure," knees scabbed and grubby, hair unwashed, and face with "a sulky look" (1985, p. 88). As Rumbold points out, the mirror here positions readers as much as it positions Polly, so readers will accept the presupposition that Polly has been made miserable by her departure from female-gendered behavior. From here on, Polly is conscious of maintaining an appearance approved by males. The structure of the novel, however, allows Polly to act at the close in ways which are not marked for gender. She does not save Tom by holding on, but by letting go, by renouncing him and so forcing him to use his own strength and resources in the final confrontation. This, in effect, leaves them free to start afresh.

Another important structural element is that much of the novel is shaped by Polly's efforts at age nineteen to remember her childhood relationship with Tom, the memories of which had been effaced by the Fairy Queen. While this attempt to retrieve lost memories is narratively functional, and conveniently reunites Polly and Tom when she is old enough for an adult relationship, it also evokes the link between the otherworld and the unconscious which we pointed to in "The Dancing Princesses" and in the "Tam Lin" retellings by Moray and Vinge. In most retellings of "Tam Lin" the predatoriness of the fairies, whether or not it is explicitly a sexual predatoriness, is shown to be a repellent, self-gratifying lust and far inferior to the power of love based in mutuality. It is always an abuse of power, and remains so whether it is imagined as an external and otherworldly force or as symbolic of unchanneled or misdirected human desire. In *Fire and Hemlock* the Hell-tithe is replaced by the motif of the Fairy Queen and her consort living off the lives of the young men she snares. It is paralleled in the everyday world in the possessive desires of Ivy, Polly's mother, by which she allows her partners no privacy and no personal space and so destroys any basis for relationship in mutuality. In another way, the destructiveness of wild desire is translated into the various ways Laurel and her minions attempt to get at Polly: in Laurel's playing on Polly's sensibility and then effacing her memory; in the attempts by Morton Leroy, Laurel's consort, to kill Polly; and in the attempt of Seb, Leroy's son, to gain power over Polly by trying to marry her.

*Fire and Hemlock* reworks its traditional material with an orientation towards a sense of universal human values, moral insight, and cultural tradition. The books of traditional literature which Tom sends Polly as he tries to get around the interdiction that he cannot disclose his bond with the otherworld are quite a comprehensive bibliography of this literature. At the same time, Jones has attempted to address the issue of social, especially gender, construction through such cultural formation. Sussex goes much further, however, when she uses the "Tam Lin" story in *Deersnake* to illustrate the abuse of power for the purpose of sexual exploitation. Drawing on the ballad "Thomas the Rhymer" and the ballad version of the medieval romance *Sir Orfeo* as well as "Tam Lin," Sussex gives a strong new twist to retellings by uncovering a social schema until now left implicit or displaced by the link between faery and the unconscious—the schema of the dissolute rake reformed by the love of a good woman. She does this by intertwining three parallel narrative strands and splitting the Tam Lin figure into its two primary aspects of victim and sexual predator.

The framing strand deals with a group of middle and senior secondary school students whose negotiations of male-female relationships are disrupted by Mori, a corrupt school teacher, who supplies hallucinogens to these students and then seduces them, and who in this way attempts to seduce Kate (the novel's Janet figure). It is during a drug party at Mori's house that Martin (the victim aspect of the Tam Lin figure) is snatched into Annwfn, the Celtic underworld. Kate's mother has returned to study and is dating one of her tutors, Tom Burdekin, who represents the predatory side of the Tam Lin figure and also has designs on Kate. Because of her justified dislike and distrust of Burdekin, Kate has left home to live with Gray, her novelist aunt, and is eventually vindicated when her mother finds Burdekin's "boast book" of photographs of his young "conquests." These two everyday world strands are then glossed by the parallel with the behavior of the mistily presented inhabitants of Annwfn, for whom their captives are playthings, to be shape-changed, discarded, or forgotten at whim. In this way, Sussex imparts a social rather than psychological symbolism to the otherworld. Thus the Tam Lin depicted as Burdekin serves as a reminder that in the everyday world sexual dangers are far more likely to stem from predatory males with positions of authority vis-a-vis females than from female desire itself. This is in effect a strong riposte to Vinge's reworking of the situation. Vinge, as we said, also modified the "happy ever after" ending to suggest that it was a balance of gain and loss. Sussex pushes this further, too, in Kate's interrogation of the myth of romantic love and her desire to know "the endings beyond the ballads. What happened to Heurodis and Orfeo, True Thomas, Tam Lin and Janet" (1994, p. 199). What she learns is that representations are misrepresentations: "'Faeryland isn't even like fairyland,' I muttered, recalling that little in the ballad books had prepared me for the alien world of Annwfn" (p. 201), and the happy-ever-after ending for Janet and Tam Lin is at most implied in the ballad and imposed in retellings.

Sussex, however, isn't finally negative about relationships or texts. Rather, the point is that experience and textual representations of it need to be subjected to critical interrogation. A final way the novel brings this out is through a self-reflexive concern with novel writing. Kate's aunt is working on a novel throughout the book, but at the end abandons it to write a different book based on Kate and Martin's experiences, especially what happened when Kate entered Annwfn to rescue Martin. Sussex is using the common convention of a character at the end of a story setting out to write the story readers have just finished reading, but she does rather more with it: in part, the product will be a *roman à clef*, but Kate and Martin retain the power to edit and suppress details, in other words, the power to shape their own story.

Sussex's tough-minded rereading of the Tam Lin story picks up the alternative interpretations of inner and outer world we pointed to at the beginning of this chapter, and she implicitly aligns herself with a feminist position by stressing a social rather than psychological symbolism. This also gives a fresh nuance of meaning to some central assumptions pervading folktale retellings—the need to cross interdicted boundaries, for example, or that glimpsing and losing fairyland entails a sense of lost possibilities and diminished existence. Folktale and its various uses remain a site of struggle, as the books of Leeson and Sussex illustrate, even though there may be a general assumption in the children's literature community that the argument has been won. What Sussex deftly shows is that the argument is not won if it retains and does not address powerful disruptive elements in the tales themselves.

Folktales will continue to be mediated for young audiences through anthologies, retellings, and novelizations constructed so as to convey a sense of universal human values, moral insight, and some aspect of cultural tradition. The typicality of folktale narrative will continue to mask culture-specific elements, as the shape and meanings of particular tales will be produced within and through a discursive context apt to point to unarticulated metanarratives. A consequence is that there will always be a place for collections which introduce macrodiscoursal and microdiscoursal modifications in order to challenge the dominant metanarratives, and for novels which explore ways of representing traditional folktale materials so as to preserve these elements of the past while seeking ways to interrogate traditional metanarratives.

## NOTES

1. The labels *folktale* and *fairy tale* are used interchangeably, though in practice *fairy tale* is most commonly used with reference to the *Grimms' Tales*, Perrault, and other tales brought into association with these, or derived from them, and now usually written for children. In this chapter we will normally use *folktale*, except when discussing other writers whose preferred term is *fairy tale*.

2. Rosemary Minard, *Womenfolk and Fairy Tales* (1975); Ethel Johnston Phelps, *Tatterhood and Other Tales* (1978) and *The Maid of the North: Feminist Folktales from Around the World* (1981); Alison Lurie, *Clever Gretchen and Other Forgotten Folktales* (1980); Suzanne I. Barchers, *Wise Women: Folk and Fairy Tales from Around the World* (1990); Susan Price, *Crack a Story* (1990); and Robert Leeson, *Smart Girls* (1993).

3. The two volumes of "Fairy Tales" compiled by Angela Carter for Virago (1991, 1992) contain in all 104 folktales or folk anecdotes, the majority of which are not duplicated in any of the feminist collections prepared for young readers. We have consulted Carter's collection but have not drawn on it here because its purposes are too different: Carter did not herself retell any of the tales; the collections are not aimed at young readers; and, most importantly, Carter did not have such an overt feminist agenda and so did not restrict her selection to positively presented female protagonists, but ranged over the "clever, or brave, or good, or silly, or cruel, or sinister, or awesomely unfortunate" (1991, p. xiii). For example, from Bushnaq's *Arab Folktales* (1987) she reprinted "The Little Red Fish and the Clog of Gold" (a "Cinderella" variant), "The Woodcutter's Wealthy Sister," "The Girl Who Banished Seven Youths," and "The Princess in the Suit of Leather" (a tale of the same type as "All Fur" [Grimm, p. 65] and the English "Cap o' Rushes"); these are only marginally of the type favored in the children's collections ("The Girl Who Banished Seven Youths" is a distant variant of the Grimm "The Twelve Brothers," which appears in Barchers and Minard). Tales in Bushnaq more in tune with the metanarrative informing the children's collections would be "The Sultan's Camp Follower," "The Clever Minister's Daughter," and "The Girl Outwits Three Men."

4. For an extensive discussion of such texts, placed in the context of contemporary reversions of fairy tales, see Zipes, "The Contemporary American Fairy Tale," pages 139–161 in his *Fairy Tale as Myth* (1994). Zipes's analysis throughout this book of the social, cultural, and political implications of retelling fairy tales is generally pertinent to our discussion in this chapter.

5. Moray's version is in *A Fair Stream of Silver: Love Tales from Celtic Lore;* Vinge's in Robin McKinley (ed.), *Imaginary Lands*. Passing reference will also be made to Jarvie, *Scottish Folk and Fairy Tales,* and Manning-Sanders, *A Bundle of Ballads*. Versions for older readers not discussed here are Pamela Dean's *Tam Lin* and Tanith Lee's *The Silver Metal Lover* (the latter merged with the Orpheus story). Terry Pratchett's *Lords and Ladies* incorporates the "Tam Lin" story into a reversion of Shakespeare's *A Midsummer Night's Dream,* where he represents the otherworld inhabitants as sadistically playful in a way similar to Sussex (see the discussion in chapter 10, below). An illuminating, contrastive study of otherworld possession is offered in Dahlov Ipcar's splendid fantasy *A Dark Horn Blowing* (1978).

6. Hamish Henderson has described this as "one of the most famous ballad texts in the world. Burns drew on orally transmitted variants from the Borders and the [Scottish] South-West, but he tightened up the narrative and turned the ballad into a poem which reads supremely well on the printed page" (1975). This version is also used for *Deersnake,* though the motif of being taken by the fairies from beneath an apple tree only occurs in Child 39G (Sussex links it with *Sir Orfeo*); *Fire and Hemlock* uses the version compiled by Walter Scott in his *Minstrelsy of the Scottish Border* (Child, 39I), or Quiller-Couch's reworking of it in *The Oxford Book of Ballads* (1910).

# 8 THE IDEA OF THE ORIENT

## STORIES AND MOTIFS FROM *THE ARABIAN NIGHTS*

*There is a growing awareness that other cultures, non-European, non-Western cultures must be met by means other than domination, . . . and that the erotic and aesthetic fascination with "the Orient" and "the primitive" is deeply problematic.*

—Andreas Huyssen, *After the Great Divide*

The idea of the Orient enters children's literature in several forms; this chapter will focus on retellings of *Arabian Nights* stories and new stories derived from *Arabian Nights* motifs. The other principal orientalist forms are folktale anthologies; Kipling's Indian works, especially *Kim* (still the most extensively discussed orientalist work in children's literature); novels set in Asia, such as Katherine Paterson's *Rebels of the Heavenly Kingdom;* and, in the United States, Canada, and Australia, novels about the experiences of children of immigrant settlers from East Asia. In general, the orientalism of children's literature conforms to what Lisa Lowe has argued about orientalism in general—that it "consists of an uneven matrix of orientalist situations across different cultural and historical sites" and "each of these orientalisms is internally complex and unstable" (1991, p. 5). Even the more restricted field of retold stories evidences such a variety, but the works within it are nevertheless characteristically framed by the Western metaethic. Because the stories are strange, especially in their physical and social settings, and yet familiar, because so often retold within Western culture, it seems inevitable that a telling will be constructed so as to convey a sense of universal human values, moral insight, and some aspect of cultural tradition. To examine how this happens in *Arabian Nights* stories, we will focus mainly on stories about genies—or jinnis, as they are now often called. First, we will examine some retellings of the "Aladdin" story from versions of that rather amorphous text now generally referred to as *The Arabian Nights* (or *A Thousand and One*

*Nights,* and so on). Next we will consider modern stories which have a genie as an important character. Finally, we will return again to an example of sword-and-sorcery fantasy, since this omnivorous genre also exploits the Orient of the *Arabian Nights* for its otherness, especially its exotic settings and motifs involving magic.

The Orient depicted in the *Arabian Nights* is another medieval fantasy world, already constructed as a fantastic Other by that medieval world itself subsequently reconstructed as a fantastic Other by the modern West. At the same time, it is an Other which exists to be appropriated. This is very clear from, for example, the dust jacket blurb on Alderson and Foreman's *The Arabian Nights* (1992): "*The Arabian Nights* is a classic collection of popular stories. . . . They create a fabulous and fanciful world of sorcerers, sages and Jinnis, but also of ordinary people who find themselves in extraordinary situations." The version is then praised because it "strips the stories of their archaic prose and, in the best tradition of European folk tales, reveals an intimate and colloquial version of the tales," though they are still "faithful to their Eastern origins." This blurb discloses an essential split in representations of the Orient in children's literature: on the one hand, the reading subject is positioned in relation to an Other which is both exotic and able to be appropriated as familiar, both faithful to its origins and assimilated to the archive of European folktale. The blurb precisely fits Ali Behdad's account of nineteenth-century orientalism, in which he describes the desire for the Orient as "the return of a repressed fascination with the Other, through whose differentiating function European subjectivity has often defined itself since the Crusades" (1990, p. 39). In children's literature this process of defining subjectivity emerges more obviously in stories using motifs derived from the *Arabian Nights* than in actual retellings, but pervades both narrative types.

Genie stories effectively enter European literature in the eighteenth century, initially via Galland's French compilation which began to appear in 1704. Now, almost three hundred years later, they form quite an extensive genre in children's literature, as well as in film and television. In children's literature these belong to two main, often contrasting, discursive formations. The first of these consists of retellings of selected *Arabian Nights* stories, especially those which seem to have a timeless appeal within Western capitalist societies.[1] We mean, of course, the stories of Aladdin, Ali Baba, and Sinbad—those rather escapist, rags-to-riches stories which combine the unexpected gaining of unimaginable wealth with notions of the spiritual destiny of the individual, seen in, for example, the personal development of Aladdin from childish solipsism to social responsibility and romantic devotion to his wife, or in the faithfulness and intelligence of the slave girl Morgiana in the Ali Baba story. The second discursive formation is made up of newly invented stories built around three genie figures derived from the *Arabian Nights*—the genie of the bottle, the genie of the ring, and the genie of the lamp. Each of the three genie novellas written by Anne Fine, for example, uses a different one of these genies.[2] This second type of story is usually a vehicle for advocating altruism and modes of behavior shaped by a strong sense of moral value and responsibility, and therefore often functions as an interrogation or criticism of the forms and practices of contemporary Western society.

In both discursive formations genies are useful figures as the pivot for a story. One obvious attraction is the exotic culture these genies represent, and contact with that culture enables a drastic displacing of ordinary, everyday characters and their experiences. Genies are not human, but spirits of enormous power, often rather amoral, often bringing with them a frisson of danger. They originate in Islamic demonology, and are therefore comfortably separable from the demons of Christian Europe; and they belong to the realm of oriental fantasy, a make-believe, medieval world of magic, of immense wealth, of sensuality, of instant gratification of desire, and of sudden, irrational, and barbaric cruelties. For the modern invented stories, in particular, these elements invest the story with a sense of radical otherness against which Western humanist values are constructed as culturally normative.[3] They allow the representation of a social and religious system more highly structured and controlled than that of the decentered and largely relativistic Western societies, and hence allow or imply some definition of points of stability and instability, and patterns of value and belief, within those societies. Further, this cultural positioning is linked with a second major attraction in genies: they offer what we may call a broad intertextuality, whereby *any* particular invented story is brought into relationship with a three-hundred-year-old tradition of storytelling and a concomitant way of thinking about culture. Finally, as often, stories dealing with culture contact, or with encounters between self and other, contribute towards a sense of self-identity and a sense of cultural value.

The process of producing versions of the *Arabian Nights* for young readers has evolved under the influence of the Western metaethic, with little or no recourse to literary traditions in Arabic. In essence, the *Arabian Nights* is constituted by its nineteenth-century translations—in English, principally the Burton (1885–86), Lane (1839–41), Lang (1898), and Mathers translation of Mardrus (1899)[4]—and these have richly supplied modern redactors with the exoticism associated with the Orient, especially spectacles built around foreign settings, magical forces, alien customs and modes of behavior, the dealings of kings and sultans, passion, violence, and death. This body of motifs has much in common with the forms of exoticism we have pointed to in other sources for retellings, and like them it is subject to a calculated interplay between exotic and familiar, everyday elements. What retellers found in their nineteenth-century sources is a discourse characterized by outlandishness. Haddawy says of Burton, for example, that he created "an ornate, pseudo-archaic style that is alien both to the style of the Arabic original and to any recognizable style in English literature" (1995, p. xiii). Lane's translation, intended for family reading, involved much expurgation or rewriting of sections unsuitable for Victorian families, and cultivated a style Irwin has characterized as tending towards the "grandiose and mock-Biblical . . . pompously high-flown" (1995, p. 24). Of Mardrus's adaptation, Irwin comments that it was "a belated product of *fin-de-siecle* taste, a portrait of a fantasy Orient, compounded of opium reveries, jeweled dissipation, lost paradises, melancholy opulence and odalisques pining in gilded cages" (1995, p. 38), little of which is obviously usable in children's versions.

The desire to reproduce exotic incident and language in versions for young readers while also rendering the text accessible is well exemplified in an anonymous retelling of the Aladdin story in a collection illustrated by Edmund Dulac (1914).[5] A comparison of a significant moment in the story of Aladdin as retold in this edition and as translated by Haddawy from Galland reveals much:

> Well knowing that it [the lamp] would fetch a better price if it were clean and bright, she set to work to polish it with some fine sand; when lo, as soon as she started to rub the Lamp, the air before her danced and quivered and a chill gasp of wind smote her in the face. Then, looking up, she saw, towering above her, a being monstrous and terrible, with a fierce face in which gleamed fiery eyes beneath frowning brows. She gazed at this apparition with fear and astonishment. . . . (1914, p. 78)

> 'Ala al-Din's mother fetched the lamp, saying to her son, "Here it is, but it is very dirty. If it was cleaned, I believe it would bring more." She took water and a little fine sand to clean it, but no sooner had she begun to rub the lamp than a hideous demon of gigantic size appeared instantly before her and her son and said to her with a thundering voice . . . (1995, p. 95)

The 1914 version elaborates both incident and language, though the language is actually not particularly complex. Where in Haddawy the demon/ jinni is introduced immediately after the lamp is rubbed, the earlier writer interpolates an uncanny moment and elaborates the woman's sensory perceptions; when the text gets to the jinni he is described much more emotively—his size, for example, is expressed specifically in terms of a perceived threat. A heightened, epic-style language is striven for through the piling up of doublets (clean and bright; danced and quivered; monstrous and terrible; etc.), archaism (smote), word-order inversion (a being monstrous . . .), and the use of sound to emphasize a lexical set (fierce, fiery, frowning). This reproduction of the discourse assumed appropriate for *Arabian Nights* retellings in part reflects the practice of a past age, and in more modern narratives tends to fulfill more parodic functions, whether in retellings or spin-offs, but it does still appear in many retellings as a persistent trace employing linguistic devices of a different kind. Thus an equivalent heightened effect is created in McCaughrean's description of Badr al-Budur entering the baths, as focalized by Ala al-Din in his hiding place:

> A crunch of gravel, a snort of horses, the setting down of a palanquin— and then a fragment of sunlight broke from the brightness outdoors and pattered in through the doorway on tiny white feet and dressed in cloth of gold. Badr al-Budur at once cast off her veil.
>
> (1982, p. 165)

In this case the effect is achieved by lexical density, by the presence of non-English or slightly archaic terms ("palanquin," "cast off her veil"), by metaphor, by a hint of syntactic complexity, and by the narrative suspense which replicates the effect of an elaborate left-branching sentence. McCaughrean's version is not all like this, however, but also incorporates overt examples of nineteenth-century *Arabian Nights* discourse and everyday demotic English, often moving rapidly between its registers. As an example, we can turn to another significant moment, a conversational exchange between Ala al-Din and the jinni of the lamp:

> "Does your life content you, O ifrit[?]" asked Ala al-Din.
> "Content me, master? I often wish that I could say something different when I appear, if that's what you mean."
> "No, I mean do you enjoy being a slave? Do you enjoy being coiled up inside that lamp through all eternity?"

The ifrit scratched his head: "One gets used to anything in time, master. I don't mind being *your* slave. It was rather different working for this scoundrel [the magician]." (1982, p. 182)

This is a very significant cultural moment indeed, since it is perhaps the first time the Aladdin story has been reshaped by incorporating the modern "setting the genie free" motif, it is an early example of the influence of pantomime discourse (especially its register and humor) on a retelling of Aladdin, and the negotiation also draws on conventional British discourses of class. There is a large shift from the formality of Ala al-Din's first question (which would be expressed more demotically as "Are you content with your life?"), through the doubly self-reflexive joke in the ifrit's reply (interrogating both the role and the discoursal tradition), to Ala al-Din's demotic rephrasing of the question and the colloquialisms of the ifrit's final speech. The register shifting and evocation of other contemporary cultural discourses marks this as a distinctively late twentieth-century retelling mode, and other contemporary versions of the Aladdin story are really only variants of McCaughrean's innovations in plot and discourse. If all debts were paid, indeed, we would surmise that the 1992 Disney animated *Aladdin* owes much to McCaughrean, though it has been the role of the Disney film to naturalize the innovations, both in itself and through the various books which spin off from it.

## VERSIONS OF "ALADDIN"

"Aladdin and the Wonderful Lamp" has always been one of the best-known *Arabian Nights* genie stories, and the massive publicity associated with the Disney film undoubtedly reinforced its popularity. The Disney version, as so often with Disney versions of well-known stories, has also probably immutably altered the components, narrative shape, and range of significances of the Aladdin story. The motif of setting the genie free, for example, seems set to become the standard ending in all genres, at least for a while (see, for instance, Lattimore [1995], in which *both* ring and lamp genies are freed; it has also influenced the pantomime tradition, acting as a closural element in a pantomime production staged in England and Australia in 1995). We suggested above that the appeal of the Aladdin story might be sought in the way in which its components and outcome conformed with Western capitalist, rags-to-riches stories, and it is always revealing to look at how retellings handle this possibility and develop it within Western metanarratives. It can be seen most clearly in the Twin Books *Aladdin* (1994), a peculiar travesty of the story produced as an eight-page board book for preschoolers, with illustrations indebted to the Golden Book spin-offs from the Disney film. Reducing the story to 105 words, the version omits the magician (and hence all story elements associated with him), the ring genie, the Wazir's attempt to marry his son to the princess, and much else. The story is thus reduced to an "essential" outline:

1. Aladdin finds the lamp while "exploring a cave."
2. When Aladdin's mother attempts to clean the lamp, and so conjures the genie, the genie simply "gave Aladdin and his mother many more jewels, and made them rich."
3. Aladdin goes himself to ask to marry the Sultan's daughter, and is successful because he "was now a rich and handsome young man."
4. The marriage takes place, "and they were both very, very happy."

As we have said, this is a travesty, and yet the elimination of elements specific to the story has three main effects: the story is assimilated to a basic Cinderlad narrative in which the hero achieves the twin outcomes of romance or folktale—the money and the royal bride; the summary implicitly combines the sudden acquisition of wealth with assumptions about the destiny of individuals; and the process foregrounds the four components of the Aladdin story of most interest to the Western metaethic. What is noticeably missing, however, is the kind of obvious ethical dimension which makes Aladdin deserving of his good fortune. In the long Dulac/Housman version much had been made of the contrast between Aladdin's wastrel life before he acquired the lamp and the more sober life he led subsequently: "He no longer consorted with the ragamuffins of the street but selected for his friends men of standing and integrity" (p. 83), and he spent his days in the market observing the merchants and traders and learning their skills. A similar explicitness appears in Grabianski (1964): "Little by little he became accustomed to mixing with educated people and acquired their good manners and behavior," and he again learns from the merchants. In both versions this diligence has a primary plot function, in that the immediate consequence of Aladdin's education is that he learns the value of the jewels he gathered from the cave, but that also serves to reinforce the moral lesson. In more recent versions less is made of Aladdin's reformation: in Riordan (1983), over a five-year period "Aladdin changed from a foolish, idle boy to an intelligent, handsome young man" (p. 18), and in Alderson (1992) he simply "turned into a shrewd dealer" (p. 154). With the Disney version, he has become one of the meritorious poor. Thus the fantasy about unlimited gratification becomes framed by one of Western society's most cherished metanarratives:

the story of the Cinderlad who through a mixture of good fortune and judicious cultivation of his opportunities comes up in the world, and both attains vast wealth and marries a beautiful woman from a higher social class, after overcoming one or more rivals who already belong to a higher class but are much less worthy.[6]

This last change, along with some other significant changes in the Disney version, was anticipated in a picture book by Carol and Donald Carrick, another shortened version (1989, unpaginated). The Carricks quite obviously used the Western metaethic as the story's thematic frame, as the story becomes one of a boy's maturation into moral responsibility. This is effected by selecting and reshaping the story elements so that there is never anything blameworthy in Aladdin's behavior, and by interpolating direct moral comment. Thus Aladdin is a street urchin when the story begins, but the only mention of his father is that he has died; the usual pejorative account of Aladdin's childhood has been suppressed. This might seem an odd move for a moral narrative, but as with Disney it is a move which strengthens a particular kind of moral perspective, in that this is a story of a person who is essentially good: both versions eliminate the morally problematic situation whereby Aladdin does not deserve his good fortune. At the beginning of the story Aladdin is simply in a state of need which prevents him from fulfilling his responsibility: "When his father died, Aladdin had no way to support himself or his mother." Similarly, Disney's Aladdin is poor and hungry, but displays good-heartedness and generosity in his readiness to help the anonymous young woman in the marketplace (Kreider, 1992). After the genie of the lamp effects his escape from the cave (there is no ring or ring genie), the Carricks's Aladdin makes no further use of the lamp, but "glad that his life had been spared" he redirected his life so that he "studied hard and worked for his daily bread." The language here, through its combination of contemporary work ethic and biblical reminiscence, furthers the underlying teleology of the narrative. Next, Aladdin's behavior is generally freed from grounds for reproach. He does conceal himself in order to see the princess without her veil, but once he has fallen in love with her, his mother approaches the Sultan of her own volition, not at Aladdin's urging. The negotiation is straightforward, and the episode of the Sultan's attempt to marry the princess to the Vizier's son is deleted. Finally, the last encounters with the magician build Aladdin's character. Without the help of the ring genie, Aladdin's search for his missing wife and palace takes on the form of a quest extending over some (unspecified) years, and during his roamings Aladdin "saw how many suffered while others lived in splendor." This insight looks forward to the book's closing sentence, which tells how "From then on, he used the lamp wisely, and shared what he had with the poor."

While this moral narrative has much in common with the Disney version, ultimately the two are driven by different metanarratives. The difference pivots on the role of the genie in each. Each uses only the lamp genie, the Disney substituting a magic carpet for the ring genie. The Carricks, furthermore, greatly reduce the genie's role, so that he makes only five appearances. The effects of this diminution are that the otherness of the story is minimized, the operation of culturally alien supernatural forces is restricted, and the ethical orientation of the genie is changed. For example, the text is significantly silent about how the magician removed Aladdin's palace, and readers can only infer that he used the powers of the genie to do so. This seems to downplay the amorality of the genie, so that when at the end of the story he discloses that Aladdin's guest is the disguised magician who intends to kill him, this takes on the function of a morally positive act. In these ways the genie is adapted to the narrative's assumption that moral growth and well-being are interdependent.

Disney's genie has undergone a much greater transformation, now into a character who is funny, vulnerable, morally committed, and, above all, humanized. McCaughrean had done all this ten years earlier, but there was now a new impetus, no doubt because the film role was designed to give full expression to Robin Williams's comic talents. Essentially, however, it is a retrospective substitution into an *Arabian Nights* story of the type of genie which has evolved in modern children's fiction. The crucial components are the genie's humanity, his affection for Aladdin, the motif of the three wishes the genie can grant, and Aladdin's promise that his third wish will be used to set the genie free. Finally, another central change which discloses this version's very different underlying metanarrative is the conflation of the roles of magician and Vizier into a power-hungry politician plotting a coup against the Sultan. The projection of human power struggles as a black-and-white conflict between good and evil simultaneously fought out in the mundane and supernatural spheres implicitly evokes the religious aspects of the Western metaethic, and reflects its deployment for sociopolitical purposes. This Aladdin story is not exactly an allegory, but it is informed by the same metanarrative which informs the ideology and rhetoric of military intervention against totalitarian regimes: the Gulf War has been invoked as an obvious example.[7] Orientalism functions here to construct the forces of evil as the alien other, whereas Aladdin and Princess Jasmine are represented as essentially Western in their behavior and aspirations. Aladdin is the Cinderlad who rises in the world and exerts an influence for good through his innate ability, persistence, altruism, and capacity for love. Jasmine has been freed from the oriental tyranny of an arranged marriage, and at moments exhibits quite feisty behavior, but in fact, in a gesture of flagrant neo-colonialism, has been merely transformed into the female love object of a Western romantic paradigm. She is the prize for which the males fight and a metonym for the political power which is the ultimate objective, and so in most respects she is now *less* free than her oriental counterpart.[8] In her devastating, culturally informed critique of the film, Erin Addison argues that "Jasmine, the Arab woman, is the locus at which the colonial catalysis occurs, through whom the narratives of naive individualism, romance, and secularism pass into and unravel the fabric of Islamic culture" (1993, p. 6).

The genie, finally, despite his apparent great powers, is only ever a client until set free at the end. He is happy to work for Aladdin, whose aspirations are "good": after all, he wants to be a prince—that is, rich and socially eminent—only so he can marry the girl of his dreams, not for the sake of power and wealth in themselves. The genie is unhappy when working for Jafar, whose intentions are evil: he cultivates power for its own sake; he exiles or attempts to destroy his political opponents (Aladdin); he turns the Sultan into a marionette (that is, in political rhetoric he has become merely a puppet ruler); he is driven by lust and takes the princess as booty; he treats the genie as his slave; and he envisages no limit to his power. As a client/slave, the genie has no self-volition and is compelled to further the magician's evil ends. He can only assist in overthrowing the tyrant when Aladdin opens the way by inducing Jafar to desire ultimate power. Jafar's third wish, to be a genie himself, figures that assumption built into Western thought whose originary moment is figured in the myth of Satan's wish to be equal with God: evil creates the condition for its own destruction by overreaching. (There is a simpler version of this in the Carricks's *Aladdin,* where the magician dies by accidentally falling on his own knife!) Aladdin's third wish, needless to say, is not on his own behalf. He has been tempted to keep the genie enslaved, but resists and sets him free. But what is the nature of the genie's freedom? As he goes out to take his place in the world, wearing his Disney cap and garish Western clothes, carrying his golf clubs, he is as much a client as ever, but now a client of cultural rather than political hegemony. This shift is further accentuated in one of the spin-off books, Karen Kreider's *Aladdin: The Genie's Tale* (1993), in which the genie himself narrates the story of his own involvement (this strategy had also been anticipated, though with different effect, in the Faerie Tale Theater video, 1984).

The *Aladdin* movie is enormous fun, but there can be little doubt that through its underlying metanarratives the film is, in Noam Chomsky's phrase, implicitly engaged in "manufacturing consent" to a whole ideological bundle of social and political paradigms. In doing so, it makes very clear how such retellings function more generally.

There are numerous other retellings of the Aladdin story, but we will conclude this discussion with some brief remarks on the particularly interesting version by Brian Alderson in his *The Arabian Nights* (1992). The Disney version could be characterized by an extreme interplay between exotic oriental and familiar North American elements. In a comparable way, Alderson's version contrasts the exotic with specifically British elements, situating the latter primarily in a demotic narrative voice which transforms the story into iconoclastic comedy and goes well beyond McCaughrean in evoking the British pantomime tradition. For example, Aladdin's mother is given the stock pantomime name for this character, Mrs. Tuanki (a variant of the more usual "Twankey").[9] In this collection Alderson writes in a great range of styles. For some stories he draws on an epic register which echoes Burton, Alderson's main pre-text, in its formal syntax and archaic vocabulary; in others, the style is more demotic, using colloquialisms, dialectisms, and contemporary slang. This is the style used in "Aladdin." It could be illustrated from almost anywhere in the story, but this example, taken from the moment at which the magician asks Aladdin to pass him the lamp before being helped from the cave, is symptomatic:

> "But that's daft," said Aladdin, and went on arguing the toss until gradually he came to realize that there was more to this Lamp than he thought. His uncle obviously didn't want it just to read in bed with (and that was true, as we shall see). (p. 150)

The contrasts across the volume are further accentuated by Michael Foreman's illustrations, which pictorially match Alderson's narrative range. More specifically, Foreman also obliquely evokes the pantomime tradition in his illustrations for "Aladdin" by depicting the characters as if they were "overacting," for example, or by painting Aladdin's palace as if it were a stage backdrop. Pantomime tends to be quite self-reflexive in its juxtaposition of the wonderful and the everyday, and Foreman reminds us of this by his picture of the genie leaning against the door of the outside toilet ("the bog out back," as Alderson puts it) with a posture and expression of casual, amused wickedness, or by his final picture for the story, in which the ring genie, now in the conventional representation of "Wind," is helping Aladdin fly a kite. This illustration perhaps reminds us, if we hadn't noticed, that the whole retelling has been an exercise in "kite-flying."

An effect of the stylistic and pictorial playfulness in this "Aladdin" is that the story is metafictive to a degree unusual in retellings of the *Arabian Nights* for young readers, though this is a possibility always implicit in the tales and sometimes exploited in modern genie stories. A primary function of drawing attention to the processes of representation here is to accentuate how this particular mode of telling has moved the story outside the shaping influence of the Western metaethic. The values Aladdin lives by are more characteristic of modern urban youth culture: laid back, pragmatic, skeptical of the old metanarratives, forging its own ethic as it goes along. Readers need to turn to a modern genie story—Francesca Lia Block's *Weetzie Bat*—to find a comparable reworking of metanarratives.

## New Genie Stories

Modern stories which use genies as characters look back to the *Arabian Nights* to varying degrees, depending on how much a writer wants to cultivate specific intertextual effects. A book which includes some very precise examples of what happens to *Arabian Nights* stories as they are reshaped and which also includes both a clear and comprehensive appropriation of genie motifs and a cosmic good-against-evil conflict is Robert Leeson's *Arabian Nights* pastiche, *The Last Genie* (1993).[10] A pivotal example of how the narrative is framed by the Western metaethic can be seen in the book's climactic moment, when Alec Bowden, the child-hero, engages the Prince of Evil in a riddling competition. What is at stake, of course, is the balance of good and evil in the universe. Alec wins the competition by posing this lengthy riddle:

> What has no legs but travels swifter than a horse? What has no body but lives in all cities at once? What makes us laugh and cry in the same moment? What costs nothing but enriches all?
>
> What lasts but a short while but endures forever? What is easily forgotten but always remembered? What tells the truth when it seems to lie? What takes the poor wife from her cooking pot and the king from his council chamber?[11] He who brings it leaves it behind and takes it away with him. What is it? (p. 154)

The answer is "a story." Leeson's use of this riddle here not only resolves the crisis in this particular story, and not only functions as a testimony to the power of story itself, but also enacts the way story "lives in all cities at once" and "endures forever." It does this in the way the novel itself reflects and replicates the structuring frame of *The Arabian Nights,* and the way in which Alec's adventures, traversing vast tracts of time, place, and space, interact with particular stories from the *Nights*. The effect is that Alec's unfolding story becomes embedded within several of the *Nights* stories, but, at the same time, in a clever narrative interchange, *those* stories become embedded within Alec's story. The effect is rather like that of standing between two mirrors. Four of these connections are particularly interesting for what they suggest about the process of story-making.

The first involves the story of Sinbad: having been dropped into the sea by a flying genie and rescued by a passing ship, Alec notices how similar that event is to an incident in the story of Sinbad the Sailor, so he impersonates Sinbad, and tells his story as if it were his own, doing so at a moment in time before the Sinbad story had been imported into *The Arabian Nights*.[12] The book is here making an elaborate joke about the circulation and transmission of stories, but it also yields up a serious point about the circulation of meanings. An old story cannot be retold and heard and have the "same" meaning, because the "same" story has a different meaning when it is told in a different temporal or spatial context.

The second story is that of Ali Baba: Alec is several times attacked or imprisoned by a robber named El Jawan, who leads a band of forty thieves, until finally Alec (at this stage transformed into a donkey) brings Ali Baba to their cave. Again, there's a joke here about recurring elements in a plot, and how that particular narrative structure produces humorous effects, and there's a game with climax and closure. On the one hand, there's that pleasure readers take in having been conned, when light dawns as to where this recurring motif is heading; and on the other hand, the intertextual effect enables readers to enter the story and complete this strand for themselves, albeit on the basis of some obvious cues: the djinniah ("girl genie") Maimunah is impersonating Ali Baba's slave girl Marjiana ("Morgiana" in Burton et al.), and tells Alec, "I shall stay here to protect Ali Baba and his wife. It is written that El Jawan and the robbers shall be destroyed—boiled in oil" (p. 125). It is a very practical example of how any story shares its narrative space with a multitude of other stories, and how readers work out or anticipate endings and meanings on the basis of their own reading histories.

Third, when Alec seeks to "rescue" his own genie, Abu Salem, who is enclosed in a flask at the bottom of the sea, the story takes on the form of one of the oldest stories gathered into *The Arabian Nights,* "The Fisherman and the Jinni,"[13] with a crucial difference. In the *Nights* story the fisherman is financially enriched by events; in *The Last Genie* Alec himself is not the fisherman, but has to hand over all of his share of Ali Baba's treasure to pay a fisherman to fetch up the flask. That is, the novel repudiates the dream of infinite wealth, investing its values instead in the moral quality of placing the welfare of another before the interests of the self. This in fact is the dominant theme of all three of Leeson's genie books, just as it is also the dominant theme of all three of Anne Fine's. This particular moment in *The Last Genie* is not only another example of how a story drastically changes meaning when shifted into a different context, but also shows how a newer meaning can contest what might be thought of as the "traditional" meaning. This becomes especially manifest when, as here, the narrative is informed by a particular, but widely subscribed to, metanarrative of heroism: that is, that true heroism consists not in grandiose gestures or in superhuman courage, but in self-effacement in altruistic causes.

Finally, Shahrazad's story-telling—that intricate weaving and embedding of story within story in order to save her own life and to transform her husband—finds its equivalent in Alec's riddle, in that special story form (that is, metafiction) in which at the climax of the plot readers' attention is drawn to the narrative process whereby that climax is produced. In other words, at the moment of greatest pleasure in the story told, readers are reminded that this pleasure is actually derived from the process of telling. This is an important effect of intertextuality, as well, since the abundant allusions to and relations with other stories keep reminding readers that part of their task is to make connections, to place themselves outside the story and enjoy the narrative process for its own sake. This enables speculation about some of the more oblique connections. For example, the outermost frame for *The Last Genie* is a school excursion, which Alec is especially looking forward to because he's going with his English-West Indian friend Eulalia, his first "girlfriend." This adolescent presexuality seems a far cry from the dark interplay of sex and death in the *Arabian Nights* frame, though in fact in the course of *The Last Genie* there are as many threats to Alec's virginity as there are to his life. It is one of the novel's running jokes,[14] as Alec is relentlessly pursued by the sensual female genie Maimunah, is threatened with all forty thieves when he falls into their hands while disguised as a girl, and is even momentarily tempted while transformed into a donkey. An important qualification of this joke is the cultural otherness of the setting, the Orient of the *Arabian Nights*. This is particularly evoked when Alec is whisked off by Maimunah to her Palace of Delights, where he cavorts in a bath with twenty slave girls and banquets all day on delicious foods (pp. 45–50). At the same time, readers are reminded that this is a piece of exotica, and it has two important thematic functions within the novel. First, it affirms that the innocent, adolescent friendship with Eulalia is Alec's proper sphere, and this is tied off quite neatly in the closing pages by means of a pair of earrings which is all Alec has left from his share of Ali Baba's treasure, and which he is keeping for Eulalia. When Maimunah asks for one of them "as a keepsake" (p. 157) Alec has no option but to give it to her; when he presents the remaining one to Eulalia, it turns out to be a duplicate of an earring she has lost, if not the very same earring. To the extent that Alec's replicated gesture in giving the earrings suggests that the two girls are in some sense complementary, the ending throws backwards questions about the complexity of individual identities and our tendency to construct and interpret other people in terms of our own expectations and desires. The second function of the episode in the Palace of Delights is to foreground the nature of desire in the context of the perpetual human quest for love, for the lure of neither sensual delight nor vast wealth can turn Alec aside from his quest to save his friend, the third-class genie Abu Salem. Indeed, at the end of the novel when, as the price of victory, Alec demands that all djinns be set free from the metal—the rings, flasks, lamps—which binds them, he must accept that this also includes Abu Salem. That is, he must grasp the principle that one way love for another can be expressed is by setting the other free.

Haddawy has remarked that "the genius of the *Nights* and the secret of their appeal lies in their reconciliation of opposites. . . . they interweave the unusual, the extraordinary, the marvelous, and the supernatural into the fabric of everyday life, in which both the usual incidents and the extraordinary coincidences are but the warp and weft of divine Providence, a fabric in which the sacred and the profane meet" (1995, p. xvi). Traversing Europe and the Middle East on his flying bed and wearing his homely blue-striped pajamas, speaking in a flamboyant Burtonesque language but focalizing in demotic British, enduring comic humiliations and engaging in a cosmic struggle between Good and Evil, Alec is a hero who also reconciles opposites. The capacity of the incident of the earrings to bridge the fantastic and the everyday has an additional effect in linking the novel's close with Campbell's reading of the significance of an exchange of rings between Qamar al-Zaman and his beloved:

> The talismanic ring from the soul's encounter with its other portion . . . betokens a conviction of the waking mind that the reality of the deep is not belied by that of common day. This is the sign of the hero's requirement, now, to knit together his two worlds.
>
> The remainder of the long story of Kamar al-Zaman is a history of the slow yet wonderful operation of destiny that has been summoned into life. Not everyone has a destiny: only the hero who has plunged to touch it, and has come up again—with a ring. (1968, p. 228)

Irwin objects to Campbell's focus on resemblances rather than differences, and sees this particular reading as an example of his "unhealthily obsessive preoccupation with heroes and heroic destiny" (1994, p. 234). This may be so, but as we have argued throughout this book, Campbell's work has furnished metanarratives which pervade twentieth-century Anglophone retellings of traditional story, and *The Last Genie* is no exception. Maimunah's last words to Alec after he has given her the earring are, after all, "Go to meet your Destiny" (1993, p. 157).

The Western-based discursive formation informing *The Last Genie* is also the basis for George Selden's comic novel *The Genie of Sutton Place* (1973), with some specific differences attributable to the difference in time and place of its authorship. It is also a story about the irruption of a genie into a twentieth-century occidental community, where he forms part of an interrelated group of people depicted in the process of constructing subjectivity: Timothy Farr, the thirteen-year-old first-person narrator, is newly orphaned and is having his place in the world redefined; his maiden aunt and guardian, Aunt Lucy, is wealthy but leads a life devoid of affection. More extreme are the genie, Abdullah, and the ex-dog, Sam, whose subjectivities are being constructed from the extreme domains of "magic" and "animal." Importantly, if Abdullah is to become human and Sam remain human, Timothy must be willing to let the genie go, to give up "sure bets at the race track, automobiles, the latest clothes" (p. 172). The novel has implicitly prepared this moment by the motif of "there's no sense in doing by magic what you could do by hand" (a moral point shared by sitcoms like *Bewitched*), as it develops its central insight that true humanity resides in individual endeavor, in caring, and in the free, intersubjective sharing of love.

Selden mediates Greenwich Village through the *Arabian Nights* motifs—the genie entering an interface between "the life of man . . . no longer than the scent of jasmine on the air" and "the bondage of magic and the prison of immortality" (p. 169), and the transformation of Sam from dog to man (that is, reversing, for example, "The Eldest Lady's Tale" embedded in "The Porter of Baghdad," in which the lady's elder sisters have been transformed into dogs). In his use of these motifs, Selden illustrates a way in which children's literature uses the Orient differently from the nineteenth-century orientalism which still informs it. Behdad, discussing Nerval's descriptions of Constantinople, explains how Nerval's use of the fantastic stories of the *Nights* to mediate his experience makes "the 'real' experience of the city appear like a dream in which everything is thrown into an oblique past" (1990, p. 43). Selden uses the fantastic to affirm the everyday qualities of ordinary humanity, a state halfway between "magic" and "animal" (p. 169), but this is a culturally specific ordinariness, which can also be seen in the orientalisms of Ann Fine and, more parodically, of Robin Klein. The genie, Abdullah, becomes "Dooley," by the long-standing occidental habit of assimilating the alien by renaming it. Thus, despite describing "Abdullah" as "an interesting name," and despite the information that it has been in his family for "over a thousand years," Aunt Lucy simply puts it aside: "But we can't really call you Abdullah. I tell you what—we'll just call you Dooley—is that all right with you?" (p. 64). There is no irony in this renaming, as there might be in a more recent text, but rather Timothy describes it as "an inspiration." When Dooley finally becomes human, the price is that he will eventually forget "the palaces and mountains and towers" (p. 174). Sam, too, is absorbed into the everyday world of social chit-chat ("filling up pauses and making it all sound interesting," p. 175). And Timothy will give up being hugged by Dooley and Sam ("From now on it'll have to be man to man—handshakes and things like that," p. 172) and will return to the everyday world of adolescence: "Now that everything is normal around here, I'm sure that I'll have more fun at camp" (p. 175).

*The Genie of Sutton Place* is thus informed by a clearly definable, familiar, not particularly inexplicit, metanarrative: to be human is to share love and to inhabit sociality; there is some space for individuality and eccentricity, but this belongs on the margin of subjectivity, not at its center. The process of exposing the subject to an Other does not mean opening subjectivity to otherness, but using the idea of otherness to define the proper relationship of central and marginal behaviors and experiences—in other words, of defining an essential self within a particular social frame. It is perhaps for this reason that the novel shares Hollywoodizing tendencies with Aladdin stories, to efface the radical otherness of genies by stripping away the elements of danger, terror, and unpredictability and assimilating them to a recognizable cultural norm. The metanarrative thus frames and controls what can be desired.

In the discussion of Nerval cited above, Behdad argues that "the mediating function of the intertext that comes between the subject and the Other also provides the conditions of desire. . . . For the object of desire to be discovered by the subject, it must be absent or at least seem initially inaccessible" (1990, p. 44). In the books we are discussing in this chapter, the object of desire is not the infinitely deferred object which Behdad goes on to describe, but a metanarratively inscribed social state which is temporarily absent to the characters but present to readers. Absence is frequently defined through the construction and dismantling of recognizably false objects of desire. This is very evident in the simpler version of "setting the genie free" which is the narrative focus of *A Sudden Glow of Gold,* the third book of Anne Fine's 1992 trilogy. This is about a boy's encounter with a lamp genie who is empowered to bestow three wishes and who is under a curse "to serve one greedy, grasping master after another until you find one whose wishes are all for another, not for himself" (p. 151):[15] without knowing of the curse, the boy fulfils its terms and sets the genie free. As is usual in these modern stories, no material gain accrues to the child: instead, he learns that "the things which could not be bought or sold were more valuable than anything else." Conflict about the object of desire also pervades the excellent Australian/UK co-produced television series *The Genie from Down Under* (1996) which pivots on the wish of its two genies for freedom, to live within time, and to be human. At its close the series develops a further twist when love for another proves stronger than the desire for freedom.

Another pertinent variation on cultural meaning and materialism is Robin Klein's short story "Zarab-Hasaka" (in *Against the Odds,* 1989). This story uses contrast of cultures, times, and places as a form of commentary on contemporary social life, developing this on the simple principle of a repeated motif, grounded in double meanings. Every time Joanna Mullen asks the genie for something, he conjures up a version of it from his own culture—a culture very remote in time and place from the contemporary Australian suburbia in which the story is set. Thus "a dishwasher" for her mother turns out to be "a huge, toffee-coloured slave" (p. 76), and "a nice big caravan" is a camel train, "laden with vats of oil, wineskins and other household goods" (p. 80). The mismatching of wish and fulfilment are part of a process of comic cross-cultural commentary. The exotic participants are comic because they are so out of context, but they also suggest that the everyday lives of the Australian social group represented by Joanna and her family lack scope, imagination, and taste. This is most apparent when Joanna wishes for "some pet lizards": "Mrs. Mullen came and peeped cautiously around the door at the two large crocodiles slithering in and out of her beautiful blush-pink bathtub" (p. 82). The shift into Mrs. Mullen's point of view and the gratuitous over-description of the bathtub highlight that it is a tasteless artefact, confirming the genie's view that the Mullens were "lowly" people (p. 74). The overall pattern suggests that there is something narrow and dull about modern society, and that its characteristic consumer goods disclose how it exists at a remove from real, living and breathing things. Joanna's first wish, for "one whole wall of my room . . . filled up with . . . records" (p. 75), is disclosed as relativistic and solipsistic when instead of albums she is given historical records, stone tablets. These aren't just images of a past world, but a reminder that individuals inhabit more than a particular place at a specific moment, but a world which entails huge expanses of time and space. The story ends with a comic twist. Having persuaded Zarab-Hasaka to enter a new bottle, having thrown him back into the sea, and having disposed of all his gifts (the stone tablets, for example, are used "to pave the area around the barbecue" [p. 91]), Joanna and her mother promptly discover that a fondue lamp left behind by the kitchen slave turns out to be inhabited by yet another genie, and the process begins again. Having been touched by otherness, there is no way back. This implication about the inevitability of growth consequent upon experience links with two further metanarratives underpinning "Zarab-Hasaka": first, an assumption that the best life style is the fullest, richest, most interactive; second, an assumption that desire, especially impulsive desire, must be controlled by reason, or people become trapped in an endless cycle of desire and disappointment. This latter metanarrative may also tend to incorporate the contingent, somewhat classist assumption that unreasonable desire occurs more frequently in some social groups than in others.

The contemporary uses of orientalism we have discussed so far are all based on some kind of irruption of a fantastic "oriental" Other into a Western society. Finally, another kind of orientalism appears in fantasies set entirely in a secondary world which nevertheless replicates the actual world's distinction between Occident and Orient, though perhaps with some geographical rotation. Thus Diana Wynne Jones, in *Castle in the Air* (1990), and Tamora Pierce, throughout her *Song of the Lioness* tetralogy (1983–1988), both substitute a North-South distinction, though in each the Southern peoples are obviously mapped onto Middle Eastern societies. *Castle in the Air* has been discussed elsewhere (Stephens, 1992a, pp. 272–280), so we will here concentrate on Pierce, who indeed offers an exemplary case of how sword-and-sorcery fantasy appropriates things oriental as part of its repertoire and, assimilating them into its endemically hierarchical patterns of power, transforms the geographical space of the other into colonial space.

The principal (though not the only) oriental society in the tetralogy is that of the Bazhir, a nomadic people loosely based on the Bedouin. Their names, such as that of their spiritual leader Ali Mukhtab, immediately identify their origins. They are a people characterized by Arabic fatalism and elaborate ceremony: remarks such as "Alanna . . . felt too tired and dazed for the dance of manners that passed for conversation amongst the Bazhir" (*The Girl Who Rides Like a Man,* 1992, p. 11) are very telling in their cultural assumptions. The first encounter with this people, towards the end of *Alanna,* is brief but symptomatic, and quickly establishes them as a race old in knowledge (especially occult knowledge) but in a decadent phase. Said has pointed to a habit amongst orientalists of constructing, or representing, the Orient as culturally decadent, a bundle of fragments out of which a greater past can be deduced. Behind this habit is a Darwinian notion of the rise and fall of civilizations, and an assumption that Asian civilization had fallen and now had to make way for European powers to enter and intervene in order to give shape and purpose to chaos. Although in the third volume, *The Girl Who Rides Like a Man*, Alanna discovers there is much to be learned from the Bazhir, the novels nevertheless generally incorporate that occidental and colonialist attitude in the representation of the Bazhir. Thus the Bazhir's function in *Alanna* is to furnish a setting and a challenge within which Alanna can perform a major quest to mark her growth to maturity. The degeneration of the Bazhir from a pastoral to a nomadic culture is seen to have been caused by ten vampiric demons, known as the Ysandir: these are vampires of the type which drain "their victims of their spiritual, mental, physical, and life essences" (Bunson, 1993, p. 268), and are only loosely reminiscent of the ghouls and alguls of the *Arabian Nights*. The Bazhir have been able to contain and limit the depredations of the Ysandir, but the Northerners, Alanna and Jonathan, have the power to destroy them. Part of their conversation afterwards is very revealing. Jonathan has reassured Alanna that the "The Ysandir are gone forever," and she replies:

> "Doesn't it seem—well, strange—that a boy and a girl were able to destroy the Bazhir demons?"
>
> "You're forgetting," he reminded her gently, "we had help. Even the Bazhir demons couldn't stand against the gods."
>
> "I suppose so," she said dubiously.
>
> "I *know* so." (1992, pp. 236–237)

Now the overt intention here is to emphasize the power wielded by the pair as innate magical gifts and through divine infusion, but an inevitable consequence of this is to imply a cultural superiority: a boy and a girl, aided by "their" gods, achieve in an afternoon what an entire race has failed to do for immemorial time.

If this tendency were to be doubted, it becomes confirmed in *The Girl Who Rides Like a Man*. First, Alanna becomes shaman of one of the Bazhir tribes and in doing so revolutionizes their way of life, in particular their typically quasi-Islamic conception of female roles. She also becomes the focus for a shaman school which promises to share and spread knowledge amongst the Bazhir people. Throughout *Orientalism*, Said repeatedly makes the point that the Orient is depicted as needing the Occident to explain it to itself, and

Alanna's role here seems to replicate this exactly. Further, Jonathan then succeeds Ali Mukhtab as "the Voice" of the Bazhir, their supreme spiritual and political leader, who speaks both to and for them. Again, in terms of the unfolding of story, these achievements are part of the characters' development; they can also be perceived as an example of rank colonialism based on an implicit metanarrative of racial superiority. The fact that the people which here accedes to the authority of a colonial power is a people recognizable in our own world accentuates the novels' unwitting acceptance of colonialist paradigms apparently based on assumptions of racial and cultural superiority. Further, the complicity in these novels with a metanarrative of cultural superiority constitutes a context for reassessing their feminist agenda (see our discussion of *Alanna* in chapter 5). Pierce does not seem entirely unaware of the problem, but it does seem clear that in her depiction of Alanna's education of her female apprentices, Kourrem and Kara, she is attempting to instil a female consciousness that is essentially Western. In many ways they are already more Western than the tribe's males, in perhaps a textual manifestation of the pictorial convention of Westernized representation of Arabic women (see note 8). Alanna succeeds in persuading them to take their places amongst the men, but her recurrent attempts to persuade them to discard their veils raises a more complex issue of the relationship between sign and thing. Alanna is told that the cultural construction of an unveiled woman as a whore is too persistent amongst the Bazhir for Kourrem and Kara to contemplate conforming with her wish, but the issue seems to be just set aside when her discussion of it with Ali Mukhtab is interrupted by the arrival of visitors signaling a new phase in her life (pp. 123–124). Subsequently, when the girls are inducted as shamans (thus making it possible for Alanna to move on) her final protest—or is it reluctant acceptance?—is silent: *"They'll be good for the tribe,* she realized, *even if they do want to keep their face veils"* (p. 156). The problem in all this is that it is presented as a contentious issue without being worked through, and seems to end up being designated a cultural trait, a marker of a rather quaint otherness. As such, it cannot escape association with an endemic aspect of orientalist discourse, a thesis that "Islam is innately and immutably oppressive to women, that the veil and segregation epitomized that oppression, and that these customs were the fundamental reasons for the general and comprehensive backwardness of Islamic society. Only if these practices 'intrinsic' to Islam (and therefore Islam itself) were cast off could Muslim societies begin to move forward on the path to civilization" (Ahmed, 1992, pp. 151–152). In this light, it seems to us all the more a missed opportunity that no attempt is made to develop a connection between the veil as a sign and Alanna's more personal concern with clothing as a gender marker. The outcome of all this is that in this section of the tetralogy the feminism does seem to be conceived in accordance with a Western hegemonic metanarrative.

What we have pointed to here may seem a hostile account of a generally well-received text, as, more generally, some of the meanings we have teased out of many of the stories discussed in this chapter may seem surprising. But that is the nature of meanings which accrue around stories as they move through time and across cultures, and become subjected to the metanarratives of particular times and places. As we are arguing about the two kinds of genie stories, in the process of retelling, stories become a site on which rival metanarratives compete or on which we can discern shifts in social values. Thus the modern genie stories such as Leeson's are part of a widespread critique of modern materialism, whereas the retellings of "Arabian Nights" stories and the appropriation of oriental motifs into sword-and-sorcery narrative both tend to reproduce older ideologies.

## Notes

1. In this light, it is perhaps significant that the most popular—"Aladdin" and "Ali Baba"—were imported into the *Arabian Nights* by Galland from some other source (he claimed to have been told them by a Maronite Christian from Aleppo; the claim may be genuine). No authentic Arabic source has yet been found for either; ironically, Burton's translation, the ultimate source of many retellings, is based on a faked translation of Galland into Arabic (Haddawy, 1995, p. xii)!

2. Collected in *The Genie Trilogy* (1992). *A Sudden Puff of Glittering Smoke* is centered on a ring genie; *A Sudden Swirl of Icy Wind* on a bottle genie; and *A Sudden Glow of Gold* on a lamp genie.

3. This process has a long history outside children's literature. The authoritative study is still Edward Said, *Orientalism* (1978).

4. See Irwin, *The Arabian Nights: A Companion* (1995), pages 9–41, for a very informative discussion of translations and adaptations of *Alf Layla wa-Layla*, the *Arabian Nights*.

5. The text is possibly by Laurence Housman, who had produced an earlier *Arabian Nights* volume with Dulac and some editions of single tales. Dulac strove to imbue the illustrations with an oriental aura: as Whalley and Chester point out, he "used Persian and Indian miniature painting for his inspiration . . . deep purples and blues evoke an appropriately [sic] shadowy Eastern atmosphere" (1988, p. 155).

6. A version of this metanarrative is spelled out by Shelley Duvall in her introduction to the Faerie Tale Theater video, *Aladdin and His Wonderful Lamp* (1984): "Legend has it that good fortune smiles upon those who most deserve it. Tonight's tale, however, follows the adventures of a rather lazy young man who seems to stumble upon fortune. But what he does with his simple lamp proves him a most deserving hero."

7. Western enthusiasm for the Gulf War was, presumably, fanned by such propagandistic deployments of "Arabism" as found in Tom McGowen's postdisaster fantasy *The Magician's Company* (1988, p. 68). Here, the disaster of thermonuclear war and the subsequent destruction of civilization on Earth in the year 2003 (within fifteen years of the novel's publication!) is attributed to "war between the nations of the Pan-Islamic Brotherhood and the United States and its allies of Europe, Canada, the

Soviet Union and China." But not only is the threat of Islam powerful enough to produce a rapprochement in the Cold War, it is also a threat stemming from benighted fanatics: "this will be an all-out thermonuclear war, inasmuch as the fundamentalist leaders of the Pan-Islamic Brotherhood are firmly convinced that they have divine assurance they can use atomic missiles with no danger to themselves" (ibid.).

For a more extended discussion of the Disney *Aladdin* as a Gulf War narrative, see Phillips and Wojcik-Andrews (1996).

8. An implicit regressive element in her representation is skin color, since in comparison with the Wazir she is very fair. There is a coding here which originates in nineteenth-century orientalist art, whereby Arabic women are usually shown as lighter-skinned than Arabic men. See for example the curious pastiche in S.L. Alma-Tadema's *A Summer's Day* (1863). In this painting, with its oblique evocations of Middle Eastern splendor and decadence, five of the six women present (presumably in a harem) have peaches-and-cream complexions; two of these have red hair, and the ethnic association is accentuated for one of them by situating her against a background of pink flowers, and for two of the brunettes by adorning them with pink garlands. The sixth woman is Arabic, and draws back a veil to disclose her olive skin and hooked nose, which match those of the only male in the scene. This skin-color convention also appears in *Arabian Nights* illustrations—Grabianski's, for example.

9. Her name is actually from *Twankay*, a variety of green China tea. In traditional pantomime versions of "Aladdin," Mrs. Twankey is the production's cross-dressing role, the "Pantomime Dame." "She" is a gross and sexualized comic figure, whose behavior inevitably conjures up her name's echo, *wanky*. As Angela Carter puts it in "In Pantoland" (1994, pp. 100–101):

> Double-sexed and self-sufficient, the Dame, the sacred transvestite of Pantoland, manifests him/herself in a number of guises. For example he/she might introduce him/herself thus:
> "My name is Widow Twankey." Then sternly adjure the audience: "Smile when you say that!"
> Because Twankey rhymes with—pardon me, vicar; . . . they talk in double entendre, which is a language all its own and is accented, not with the acute or grave, but with the eyebrows.

10. The novel's pastiche combines *Arabian Nights* and contemporary Western narrative elements. Its outcome pivots on the "letting the genie go" principle, while many of the story elements are loosely—often parodically—derived from the *Nights,* and especially from "Qamar al-Zaman and His Two Sons, Amjad and As'ad," and the well-known stories of "The Ebony Horse," "Sinbad the Sailor," and "Ali Baba." "Qamar al-Zaman" is not retold in children's versions, but gave Leeson the names of his main djinn characters, Maimuna[h] and Dahnash, and such incidents as the comic threat of seduction by the Prince who turns out to be female (Haddawy, 1996, pp. 216–220; Leeson, 1993, pp. 94–95); Alec's misadventures are also roughly comparable with those of As'ad. This is the only *Arabian Nights* story discussed and partly reproduced in Campbell's *The Hero with a Thousand Faces.*

11. Some readers will recognize here an oblique invocation of Western cultural heritage, in that the pre-text is Philip Sidney's *Apology for Poetry:* "[the poet] cometh unto you with a tale which holdeth children from play, and old men from the chimney-corner, and, pretending no more, doth intend the winning of the mind from wickedness to virtue."

12. John Barth, of course, is responsible for the most complex and radical experiment with narrative and temporal displacements in relation to *The Arabian Nights,* in the first part of his metafictional novel *Chimera* (1972).

13. In Burton's translation, the Fisherman has the custom of casting his net only four times each day. Leeson (as also in the extensively restructured version by

Alderson and Foreman, pp. 17–31) assimilates this to the more Western "rule of three," but arranges them in his own climactic sequence. Before bringing up the flask, Leeson's fisherman first drags up "fish, seaweed, stones, bits of wood" (the third cast in Burton, "potsherds and broken glass"; the second in Alderson, "a large pitcher full of sand and mud, potsherds and broken glass" [conflating Burton's second and third]), and then "a dead donkey" (the "dead jackass" of the first cast in Burton and in Alderson).

14. The classic English pre-text, available only to adult readers, is Henry Fielding's *Joseph Andrews*.

15. The motif of the three wishes is widespread in folk literature, of course. For a fine example of intertextual storytelling using this motif to dismantle the dream of riches, see Bill Scott's "A Bogan is a Gnome, Third Class" (in *Many Kinds of Magic*, 1990)—an Australian story with Irish antecedents and cross-references to *Arabian Nights* djinns!

# 9 REVERSIONS OF EARLY MODERN CLASSICS

*When Hwel the playwright turned up with the rest of the troupe next day they told him all about it, and he wrote it down. But he left out all the bits that wouldn't fit on a stage, or were too expensive, or which he didn't believe. In any case, he called it* The Taming of the Vole, *because no one would be interested in a play called* Things that Happened on a Midsummer Night.

—Terry Pratchett, *Lords and Ladies*

In the preceding chapters we have been arguing that the relationships between a retelling and its pre-text(s) are, in the main, dominated by meta-narratives which are androcentric, ethnocentric, and class-centric, and whose purpose is to induct audiences into the social, ethical, and aesthetic values of the producing culture. Any retelling is oriented towards those meta-narratives and their informing metaethic in stances which are usually legitimating but may develop interrogative positions. Retellings and reversions of texts which are literary classics of modern high culture and can be identified as the work of particular, canonical authors have the potential to throw this process into sharp relief. They tend to be more self-conscious about the ways they elaborate their dialogic relationship with their pre-texts and more overt about their reproductive or interrogative purposes. This enhanced openness is characteristically visible in the tendency to cultivate an alternative or contrasting register, foregrounding a dialogue between the characteristically demotic mode of the reversion and the more hieratic or epic modes of the pre-text.

This chapter will focus on the processes of reproduction and interrogation in retellings and reversions of a bundle of literary classics spanning high culture and popular culture texts and texts intended for adults and for children. We will begin with re-presentations of Shakespeare's plays as, in effect, short stories for young readers. Our sample text will be *A Midsum-*

*mer Night's Dream.* Predominantly, though not exclusively, these reworkings seek to promote an appreciation of the plays as works of art and monuments of culture. The practice of reworking canonical texts highlights those cultural functions common to reversions and retellings in general that we have been discussing: the initiation of children into aspects of a social heritage, and the transmission of a culture's central values and assumptions, shared allusions, and experiences. One function of rewriting adult high culture texts, such as Shakespeare, for children is to popularize and make more accessible those cultural values seen to be embodied in those texts. These literary classics also represent cultural capital, and reversions of Shakespeare's plays in particular serve an especially powerful role in the initiation of children into high culture.

The rest of the chapter will examine some reversions of classic works of fiction of the early modern era: Defoe's *Robinson Crusoe* (1719), Stevenson's *Treasure Island* (1883), Ballantyne's *Coral Island* (1857), and Grahame's *The Wind in the Willows* (1908). Novels such as *Robinson Crusoe, The Coral Island,* and *Treasure Island* were in the eighteenth and nineteenth centuries regarded as popular culture texts. As the novel genre attained high culture status such texts have been endowed with canonical status within children's literature. Modern reversions seek to interrogate the basis of that canonical status by laying bare the ideologies which underpin the metanarratives of those classic texts. Hence some of the reversions we look at in this chapter are relatively simple retellings of high culture texts which in a sense make those "classics" of children's and adult literature more accessible to young readers and are instrumental in initiating young readers into a cultural heritage. Other reversions of canonical literary texts are overtly politicized and self-consciously call into question and undermine those cultural values underpinning the literary pre-text and the cultural heritage of which it is part, and hence interrogate the agenda of the canonical enterprise itself. Either way, these retellings and reversions of literary classics are situated in a dialogic relationship with their pre-texts.

Miles's *Favourite Tales from Shakespeare* (1976; 1983), McCaughrean's *Stories from Shakespeare* (1994), Birch's *Shakespeare's Stories* (1988; 1993), and Garfield's *Shakespeare Stories* (1985; 1988) are prose retellings of a selection of Shakespeare's plays. In this sense their primary function is to transmit cultural values. However, as we have been arguing, any retelling will be influenced by the cultural context in which it is retold and by the changes in register, narrative tone, and point of view which seek to ensure the accessibility of those cultural values and aspects of social heritage that a text seeks to inculcate. These retellings favor a demotic register in order to offer ready access to the ideas and values implicit in those "great" works, but we are also interested in how demotic register affects cultural transmission. Furthermore, it is a general characteristic of texts of this type that a retelling is a selection from an overload of data, which is then organized according to particular schematic hierarchies. Thus retellings of canonical literary texts have a double edge: they serve in the transmission of cultural values, but also shape those cultural values according to dominant metanarratives through processes of discursive and narrative selection and modification.

We will be comparing some of these fairly conservative retellings of Shakespearean texts with Pratchett's more radical reversion, *Lords and Ladies* (1992). Next we will consider some reversions of modern classics mostly written specifically for children: Golding's *Lord of the Flies* (1954; 1965)[1]— a reversion of Ballantyne's *Coral Island,* itself a reversion of Defoe's *Robinson Crusoe;* Leeson's *Silver's Revenge* (1978)—a reversion of Stevenson's *Treasure Island;* and Needle's *Wild Wood* (1981)—a reversion of Grahame's *Wind in the Willows.* These reversions have in common a subversive impulse: they seek to undermine and call into question ideological assumptions about class, gender, childhood, maturation, and human nature underlying their classic canonical pre-texts. A further aspect of this second group of texts is that they are all bricolage texts. As reversions of a range of literary and cultural texts, they frequently engage with a number of metanarratives and there are a range of generic links between the texts. They are all boys' adventure novels, incorporating common story and theme motifs, and they construct culturally specific notions of childhood and of masculinity. As Richards has suggested, "generic literature, relying as it does on the regular reuse of the same elements, characters and situations, functions as ritual, cementing the ideas and beliefs of society, enforcing social norms and exposing, labeling and isolating social deviants" (1989, p. 1). In this way, boys' adventure novels and their reversions, such as those which we discuss, have an important role in both the construction and interrogation of cultural metanarratives.

## RETELLING SHAKESPEARE

Despite attempts by postmodernist theorists and critics to dismantle the literary canon, Shakespeare still occupies a primary position within the cultural imagination as "the Great Bard" or "master storyteller" (Birch, 1988). Novelistic and prose retellings and reversions of Shakespeare's texts for children have three main interrelated cultural functions. First, they have a role in making Shakespeare accessible and popular. Second, they are instrumental in the continued canonization of Shakespeare and, simultaneously, in the construction of a canon of Shakespeare texts retold for children. The most commonly retold texts include: *Romeo and Juliet, A Midsummer Night's Dream, Twelfth Night, Hamlet,* and *Macbeth.* And third, reversions of Shakespeare texts perform a key role in the transmission of the culture's central values and assumptions to children. The central assumption that underlies and links these three functions is that Shakespeare is cultural capital. As Janet Bottoms argues in her examination of retellings of *The Tempest,* "It has been axiomatic among large numbers of educationalists, and among those political and cultural leaders who pronounce on education, that children should be taught Shakespeare" (1996, p. 73). Shakespeare, "the icon of a proper English education" (p. 74), is believed to give "access to something that is seen as the mark and property of the cultured and educated" (p. 73), a belief which is implicit in the commendations which introduce Birch's collection *Shakespeare's Stories:* the collection will "complement a young person's study and understanding of the original plays" and "help attract the reluctant and the intimidated to the pleasures of Shakespeare" (Birch, 1988).

However, there is a double-edged quality in the cultural and ideological enterprise of rewriting Shakespeare which is highlighted by the three main functions that we have identified—popularization, canonization, and cultural transmission. Typically, the introductions to collections of retold plays are characterized by appeals to the universality of Shakespeare's plays and to the essentiality of the stories they tell and the values they embody. Ideologically, such aims might be read in the light of a democratization of culture—in making high culture texts, such as *Hamlet,* accessible and popular, the boundaries between high culture and popular culture are breached. Alternatively, the same aims might be read as a form of cultural imperialism—in breaching the boundaries between high culture and popular culture from within the stronghold of high culture, assertions as to the universal appeal of stories looks suspiciously like an imposition of cultural values from above. This doubleness is implicit in the peritextual apparatus of Garfield's abridged version of *Romeo and Juliet* (1992). Garfield's edition opens with an account by Spottiswoode of the rebuilding of the Globe Theater and some of the similarities and differences between Elizabethan and contemporary theater. This account asserts Shakespeare's universality by establishing a continuity of tradition "from the time when the Globe theater was first built until today" (p. 7)—the building of the Globe becomes synonymous with an originary and authentic moment within cultural history. This idea is carried through in Garfield's introduction, which opens with an anecdotal comparison of Shakespeare and God—"Next to God . . . Shakespeare created most. In thirty-seven plays that are his chief legacy to the world—and surely no one ever left richer!—human nature is displayed in all its astonishing variety . . ." (p. 8). However, Garfield goes on to describe Shakespeare's plays as collective cultural property—"In the four hundred years since they were written, they have become known and loved in every land; they are no longer the property of one country and one people, they are the priceless possession of the world" (p. 8). In other words, Shakespeare's plays represent the pinnacle of high culture, but they are not the exclusive property of high culture—they are also "for everyone."

While the "language of Shakespeare" is frequently the feature of Shakespeare's plays most extolled and most frequently evoked in the ascription of high culture values to the plays, it presents a fundamental problem in the revision and rewriting of the plays for children and more generally in the popularizing of Shakespeare. Archaic vocabulary and syntax, the use of poetic forms, and dramatic dialogue limit the accessibility of the plays for children, and so in the process of rewriting story and character tend to be valued over the discourse, as in, for example, Miles's *Favourite Tales from Shakespeare*. Miles describes the stories which are "locked" and "hidden away inside the plays" as the "frameworks or skeletons that the poetry and the people who speak it are fastened to" (p. 8). For Miles, the process of rewriting the plays as prose stories, then, is one of dismantling or paring away and translating the kernel that is left into modern demotic narrative prose. The process of reconstruction then involves dressing the tales up with an abundance of social and technical details and contrastive descriptions which construct a historical context for the stories. The resulting tales bear little resemblance to their pre-texts, but Miles also points out that he is, of course, merely doing to Shakespeare what Shakespeare did to other writers . . . rewriting their stories. Thus the process of rewriting, adding, and altering continues a tradition in which Shakespeare was central. Miles also claims that he is trying "to turn [the plays] back into the kinds of stories he [Shakespeare] started out with" (p. 8) and that his changes are only of the kind which he thinks Shakespeare would have permitted. These claims are informed by assumptions about the universality of stories which are very similar to those we identified as informing the retelling of Bible stories and classical myth. The claims assume on the one hand that the "essence" of a story can be transmitted unchanged irrespective of the discourse, genre, and narrative forms in which it is encoded, and the historical and cultural context in which it is retold, and on the other, that Shakespeare, again along with the Bible and classical myth, represents some kind of authoritative standard against which the rest of culture is to be measured.

The translation of Shakespeare's dramatic dialogue into narrative prose has some crucial effects. The differences between drama and prose center on the key distinction between mimesis and diegesis, or between showing and telling. Drama is primarily a mimetic mode of representation, in that the story existents are generally shown rather than narrated. Narrative prose is usually a more diegetic mode of representation and there is usually a narrator who tells the story, though narrative prose of course also uses dialogue as a way of showing the story. Ostensibly, this difference accounts for many of the differences between the two genres, particularly the different ways that point of view is constructed and, in narrative fiction, the often powerful effect of narrative voice, the flexible presentation of incident and event through the use of summary and scene, and the range of modes for representing dialogue. In retellings of *A Midsummer Night's Dream* it accounts for the variety of ways the comic scenes are handled, especially the scene in which Bottom changes into an ass, and the different ways that the various groups of characters—the lovers, the fairies, and the mechanicals—are represented.

As Bottoms has noted, a crucial difference between the two genres is the treatment of point of view and voice. In drama a range of different viewpoints can be constructed via the voices of individual characters. Narrative prose is usually shaped by the voice of a single narrator. Alternative viewpoints will be offered through the use of focalization strategies and dialogue, but the narrator's voice frequently dominates and shapes representations of characters. The distinction is not always this clear cut, however, as Shakespeare's characters often have a narratorial function through the use of asides and direct address to the audience—Puck's final speech in *A Midsummer Night's Dream,* for example. Such strategies have a potentially metadramatic effect, though, interestingly, this potential is not frequently exploited in prose retellings of the plays. In the retellings and reversions of *A Midsummer Night's Dream,* Pratchett's *Lords and Ladies* is one of the few reversions to exploit the metafictive potential of its pre-text for thematic purposes. More frequently this metafictive potential is elided by the use of summary for the close of the story.

Bottoms has argued that retellings of Shakespeare's plays are shaped through processes of selection, organization, and "translation" by the values and interpretations of their new "tellers," by the agendas that govern the publication of new versions at certain historical points, by the development of children's literature, and by wider socio-historical movements (p. 74). Her study focuses on how different retellings of *The Tempest* reinterpret the play and how narrative strategies like structure, voice, and point of view construct interpretive subject positions for readers. Our approach builds on her work insofar as we see these strategies as also having a role in the construction of schematic hierarchies and metanarratives which shape the cultural values that are ascribed to the plays.

## Cultural Capital and *A Midsummer Night's Dream*

As we suggested earlier in this chapter, a characteristic of texts which retell classics is that they are a selection from an overload of data, a selection which is then organized according to particular schematic hierarchies. Shakespeare's plays present peculiar problems for prose retellings partly because of the complexity of the plots and partly because of the semantic density of the language—the tangible features of the cultural capital which is "Shakespeare." The ways in which these two features are dealt with are clear indicators of the metanarratives which drive retellings.

Typically, Shakespeare's plays have multiple interwoven plots; *A Midsummer Night's Dream* (Arden Shakespeare, 1979) has three. They center on the lovers and the court, the fairies, and the mechanicals. Retellings vary as to which are given the main emphasis, and especially which one frames the narrative. Furthermore, the order in which the plots are introduced affects the framing of the story and hence the metanarratives shaping the ideologies of the retelling. Shakespeare's version is hierarchically structured. Act one opens with Theseus and Hippolyta at the palace and introduces the tangled plot involving the four lovers, Hermia, Helena, Demetrius, and Lysander. This is followed by a scene depicting the mechanicals at Peter Quince's cottage. Acts two, three, and four are set in the wood, where the action is framed by the conflict amongst the fairies, which incorporates first the lovers plot, then the mechanicals plot (the scenes involving Bottom and Titania) and then the resolution of both these plots. Act five returns to the palace for the weddings of Theseus and Hippolyta and the four lovers, and the performance of the mechanicals' play, and closes with the scene involving the fairies. In this way the Theseus/Hippolyta plot frames the narrative and structures it according to a social hierarchy.

Most retellings replicate the basic shape of Shakespeare's version, apart from Miles, who changes it radically so that its function is to mediate and explicate cultural capital. The most common change to the structure of the story involves the order in which the plots are introduced and which plot the text opens with. Garfield's version opens with the lovers, then moves to the wood where the mechanicals are rehearsing—and where Theseus's marriage is mentioned in passing—and then to the fairy sub-plot. In this way, emphasis falls on the plots pertaining to the lovers and the mechanicals. In contrast, McCaughrean's version opens with the fairy sub-plot: to begin, "Something was wrong in the world of the fairies" (p. 33), replaces the position of Theseus in the hierarchy by Oberon and Titania, and so gives more emphasis to the supernatural ordering of human events in the everyday world and the convention whereby disorder in the social world (both of fairies and humans) is reflected by disorder in the natural world. This is a convention which is overtly parodied in Pratchett's *Lords and Ladies,* when in reply to Jason's list of the latest events in the natural world, such as "one of Mother Peason's hens [laying] the same egg three times and old Poorchick's cow [giving] birth to a seven-headed snake," Nanny Ogg answers "Been pretty normal, then" (p. 48). The exchange is indicative of Pratchett's systematic dismantling of conventional oppositions between nature and culture which underlie traditional interpretations of Shakespeare's plays, but it is also an aspect of Pratchett's complex metafictive play with ontological arguments. Whereas Shakespeare's fairies derive power from the natural world, Pratchett's fairies derive power from people's belief in them—the fairies exist because people think they exist.

Miles's retelling of the play deviates most strikingly from other retellings, especially in the framing of the tale and the ordering of the plots. The story is set in England and opens with a description of Peter Quince, who is a reader and storyteller as well as a carpenter. The stories of Theseus and Hippolyta, Thisbe and Pyramus, Oberon, Titania and Puck are incorporated into the narrative as stories which Quince tells, and the plot involving the mechanicals frames the tale. Then the other plots in the pre-text are all incorporated into the tale as elements within a dream that Bottom has the night before the performance of their play. Thus the retelling takes the dream motif from its pre-text—a thematic and metadramatic element in Shakespeare's play—and reconstructs it as a story element in the tale. The narrative also includes some long explanations of the cultural and geographical discontinuities which emerge from the confluence of setting and character— for example, how Oberon and Titania came to England from India and how Puck came to be in Athens. In this way, the setting and the framing of the narrative have an ideological function in that just as the other sub-plots are subsumed within the dominant mechanicals plot, other cultural elements in the narrative are subsumed within the dominant Anglo context. Narratorial intrusions which ostensibly explain cultural discontinuities in the pre-text also foreground both the characteristic bricolage structure of Shakespeare's texts and the cultural hegemony implicit in Miles's reconstructive retellings.

Pratchett's *Lords and Ladies,* a comic fantasy widely read by adolescents and adults alike, is a loose reversion of *A Midsummer Night's Dream.* There are parallels between the plots and characters of the two texts: Verence, the king, and Magrat, a witch, who are to be married on midsummer's day, occupy the positions of Theseus and Hippolyta; the Queen of the fairies takes on Oberon's function; Casanunda, Ridcully, Nanny Ogg, and Granny Weatherwax take the positions of the four lovers; and the Lancre Morris men along with their female counterparts, Diamanda and Perdita, take on the role of Shakespeare's mechanicals. There are few direct correspondences between the texts, however, and Pratchett's novel is more a bricolage constructed from a range of other texts than a straight retelling or reversion. It also uses the Tam Lin story (p. 205) and other folktale motifs—for example, unicorns and their susceptibility to virgins and, in a particularly wicked inversion, "Herne the Hunted" (p. 50).[2] It is an interesting text to look at here, especially in comparison with Miles's retelling. Whereas both retellings foreground the bricolage structure of Shakespeare's text, Pratchett's, unlike Miles's, flaunts that structure, constantly drawing attention to its own constructedness and to the discontinuities in the parallels between the focused text and its pre-texts. One way in which it does this is through metafictive play with beginnings and endings, whereby the alternative ending—that is, Shakespeare's ending in which all the characters marry—happens elsewhere in a parallel universe. Likewise a description of the study of invisible writings and the General Theory of L-space, which "suggests that . . . the contents of books *as yet unwritten* can be deduced from books now in existence" (p. 41), also functions metafictively to foreground the way in which the novel is constructed out of other texts. The novel also flaunts its intertextual links and discontinuities by throwing off half-quotations, by including whimsical foot-notes, or by overt references—all of which are illustrated in, for example, the parodic evocation of Shakespeare's plays in the closing footnote (see the epigraph to this chapter). The effect of these metafictive and intertextual strategies is quite the opposite of Miles's reconstructive approach to Shakespeare's text. Whereas Miles's version attempts to construct a linear, continuous, and ideologically unambiguous narrative out of the interrelated plots which structure Shakespeare's play, Pratchett's draws attention to its own lack of ideological and narrative continuity, and the disparate interpretations of Shakespeare's text. It also articulates a thematic concern which reflects on the ideological agenda of retellings like those of Miles, in its concern with the uses and misuses to which fictions can be put. As we pointed out earlier, Pratchett's fairies derive power from people's belief in them, an idea which has implications for the power of fictions, and of retellings in particular.

Miles's use of the mechanicals sub-plot to frame his retelling affects the ways in which characters are represented and hence the ideologies that are inscribed in the retelling. Although the mechanicals are depicted as foolish and comic figures in Bottom's dream, within the frame narrative they are presented quite positively. Quince is "the finest carpenter in the whole country" and both he and Bottom have a high social standing in their village. Quince also has virtues which clearly indicate his exemplary function in relation to the audience subject position constructed by the text—he is polite, a good carpenter, a very good reader, and has clean personal habits (p. 36). He also transmits cultural knowledge from the upper class to "ordinary people" (the working class), reading stories in the libraries of the "big houses" where he works and later retelling them. These stories are also of an exemplary nature and, unsurprisingly, they are all examples of that canon of retellings for children which is the subject of our study. Quince reads adventure stories; stories about ancient heroes and the "olden times in far-away Greece"; the lives of noble Romans and legends of gods and heroes; and stories of the voyages of great seamen. Further affirmation of the cultural capital of classical and traditional story appears in the embedded retelling of "Pyramus and Thisbe." Instead of replicating Shakespeare's comic, mangled version, with its implicit mockery of the Elizabethan fad for Ovidian narratives, Miles presents a serious retelling based on Ovid's *Metamorphoses* (Book IV, lines 55–166). In other words, Shakespearean cultural capital is enhanced by classical mythology. By these means, Miles's retelling is shaped in ways which both enable its incorporation into the canon of classic children's literature and remind readers of Shakespeare's function as a marker of canonicity.

In nearly all retellings the action starts and finishes in the wood. Events which occur in acts one and five of Shakespeare's play are retold in summary form, with the exception of Birch's version which does reproduce the mechanicals' comic performance of "Pyramus and Thisbe" at the wedding feast. Thus in most retellings emphasis is shifted away from the social hierarchy which orders Shakespeare's narrative to the comic events in the wood. The ideologies underlying the representation of these events vary according to the narrative treatment of two features: the representation of characters and the construction of comic effect. As texts Shakespeare's plays are relatively open to interpretation, and in any dramatic performance specific interpretations will emerge as a consequence of how characters are played. Some interpretive positions will be privileged and others foreclosed, and each performance becomes an act of interpretation. Likewise, any prose retelling is also a specific interpretation of the play, but the strategies used to instantiate Shakespeare's texts as prose retellings as opposed to performance are quite different. As Bottoms has argued, the range of narrative strategies used in retellings often constructs quite limited interpretive positions. Character descriptors, for example, tend to schematize characters according to character types. The character of Helena, in particular, presents interpretive problems as she can clearly be played in various ways, ranging from a comic to a tragic figure. Thus, the retellings vary considerably in the semantic range of the qualifiers used to describe Helena. In McCaughrean's version she is primarily a comic figure, described as "big, buxom Helena" and as a "big neglected girl" (p. 33), and throughout the narrative she and the other three lovers are depicted as foolish, and hence comic. Likewise, Garfield's text stresses the foolishness of all the lovers, not just Helena—for example the entry of Demetrius and Helena into the glade is a "violent crashing and rending, and gasping and panting" (p. 256). The comic effect here is produced through Garfield's language: the sheer number of verbs used is over the top and has a parodic effect. In contrast, the comic effect in McCaughrean's text stems from the represented incidents, rather than from the language used to describe them. For example, when Helena stumbles upon Lysander and Hermia asleep in the wood she trips over Lysander in the dark, "pummels at him" until he wakes, and when he embraces her knees and "press[es] his face to her thigh," she "stamp[s] on his foot" and stalks off (pp. 36–37). This is reminiscent of slapstick comedy. Furthermore, Garfield's more evocative use of language also articulates both the comic and tragic implications of the lovers' situation, and of Helena's predicament in particular. Helena is "tall, fair and tearful" and the discourse plays on associative connotations of Helena's willowy stature, as in "wept like a willow over a stream of her own making" and "tottering like a stricken willow" (p. 264). The repeated use of descriptors such as "wailing, pleaded, sobbed, wept, doleful cry," and so on, has a comic cumulative effect, but the tragic implications of the plot are also articulated through shifts in narrative point of view, as in the summary of the quarrel between Hermia and Helena: "a scene of such frantic confusion, such anger, such reproach, such accusation . . . had there been mortal eyes to watch, they would have made a waterfall of tears, instead of glinting with merriment at love's calamity" (p. 264). This description offers first the viewpoint of the narrator, then that of Puck. Bottoms is critical of Garfield's "self-consciously heightened style" which results from his attempts to approximate the poetry of his pre-texts "if not in quality then at least in cadence and vocabulary" (1996, p. 76). But in using a heightened style which draws attention to itself in this way Garfield is also exploiting the genric possibilities of narrative prose in a way that other retellers like Miles and McCaughrean do not. Garfield also uses the subtleties of narrative point of view to approximate the semantic density of Shakespeare's dialogue in a way which neither diminishes nor parodies that poeticism. For example, Helena's desire for sleep which in the pre-text is expressed as dialogue—"and sleep, that sometimes shuts up sorrow's eye / Steal me a while from mine own company" (III, ii, 435–436)—is translated into narrated discourse—"Helena, straying upon the scene and seeing nothing but her own sadness" (p. 266).

These discursive differences amongst the retellings also account for the different treatments of the key comic scene in which Bottom is partially changed into an ass and seduced by Titania. In performance, this humor is communicated visually, and the use of visual farce obviously creates problems for retellings in narrative prose. The narrative strategies used to represent this scene vary from one retelling to another, and hence the audience is positioned in different ways. Miles, McCaughrean, and Birch all spell out the joke, explaining from Puck's point of view what happens to Bottom when he disappears behind the hawthorn bush, and hence the ironic significance of Bottom's comment, "this is to make an ass of me" (III, i, 115). The audience position that this constructs roughly replicates that of a dramatic audience insofar as all three versions use dramatic irony: because Bottom is not aware of the transformation he has undergone he is the object of the audience's laughter. In Garfield's version, however, the irony which replaces Shakespeare's visual farce is much more subtle and makes greater use of the ironic potential of narrated prose. The episode is narrated mostly from Bottom's point of view:

> Bottom, who had retired within a hawthorn brake, stepped forth with that mixture of modesty and expectation that marks the well-graced actor who knows that all eyes will be upon him, and the rest of the company ignored. His expectations were answered. All eyes were most certainly upon him—and to a bulging extent. (p. 261)

The ironic tone and the slips between narrator- and character-focalized description signal that Bottom is about to be the butt of a joke, but the audience is not given specific information as to what has happened to the unknowing Bottom and is thus in a similar position to Bottom. The explanation of what has happened to him is delayed until after his transformation has had its effect on his companions, and again the explanation itself is marked by subtle shifts in narrative point of view, more characteristic of prose fiction than of drama.

> Bottom frowned and looked down upon himself to see what cause there was for dismay. . . . All that he could see was as it should have been, and proper to Bottom. It was only what he saw with that was

not. From the neck down he was Bottom the weaver; from the neck up he was—a monster. (p. 262)

This is followed by a description from Puck's point of view of what he had done to Bottom, just in case the audience hasn't yet caught on, though even here the specific information that Bottom has the head of an ass is preempted by a series of clues. Potentially, this playful approach has a similar effect to more sophisticated uses of dramatic irony in a play, where those members of the audience quick to pick up the clues will be offered a position of greater knowledge. In prose, the strategy of offering the audience a position from which to work the joke out for themselves also, of course, offers its audience a more empowered position than does a retelling which patronizes its audience by spelling out the joke.

The representation of the fairies and the nature and extent of their power is central to the ideologies shaping the reversions. Again there are some significant differences in the ways that the fairies are represented and hence how they are interpreted in the various retellings and within the metanarratives structuring texts. Interpretations of Shakespeare's fairies hinge on the ethical and moral paradigms perceived to be operating in the text. Warren (1983, p. 17) sees Shakespeare's treatment of the fairies as a departure from Elizabethan literature and folklore in which fairies were sinister creatures. A more benign orientation is evident, for instance, in Titania's sympathy for mortals who are dependent on her (II, i), and in the implication that she did not steal the child. The fairies can, of course, be played in a variety of ways in any one performance, but, as with the characterization of Helena, the prose retellings are marked by the somewhat limited interpretations given to the fairies. In Miles's, Birch's, and McCaughrean's versions they are basically benign, though there is a marked difference in the discursive styles used to describe the fairies in these versions. McCaughrean's version treats the fairies similarly to the lovers, as actors in a comic farce in which the lovers and the mechanicals are the unknowing victims of the fairies' mischief. Birch's version in general is marked by an extremely heightened register, especially in its descriptions of the fairies and their relation to the natural world: for example, "And now these proud and passionate monarchs never met on hill or dale, in forest grove or meadow green, but that their bitter quarrel soured the air, poisoned the winds and turned the earth to misery" (p. 9). In contrast, Miles's fairies are depicted according to that tradition in children's books by which fairies and elves have become minuscule beings—"really tiny" (p. 45), quaint and cute. Accordingly, his version loses the motivation for the quarrel between Oberon and Titania, and resorts instead to the (masculinist) explanation that Oberon is angry because Titania had been "very rude" to him that morning (p. 51). With the exception of Puck's transformation of Bottom, which is depicted simply as a bit of mischief (well, boys will be boys), the fairies' actions are motivated by kindness and a desire to be helpful. As Bottoms has pointed out, Miles tends to construct all of his characters as mischievous children (p. 82), a strategy which represents the fairies as relatively ineffectual and powerless. Garfield's fairies, however, are represented according to the older folkloric tradition in which they are a source of danger, powerful and potentially malicious, as is evident in his use of terms like "flickered," "darted," and "shadowy, formidable" (p. 254). Oberon's eyes "glitter mysteriously" and he smiles "vengefully" (p. 257), and Puck is his "grinning, mocking henchman" (p. 254). Garfield's characterization schematizes the fairies according to conventional paradigms of wickedness or evil: they are associated with the darkness; the relations between Oberon, Puck, and Titania are hierarchical; and their actions seem mainly motivated by malice, with the exception of Oberon's sympathy for Helena.

Pratchett's treatment of the fairies is similar to Garfield's, in that the fairies seem more malicious than mischievous, though Pratchett stresses that their behavior is amoral rather than immoral. He emphasizes their otherness, their lack of human emotions and failure to act according to any human moral system. Rather than being immoral, in the sense of being wicked or evil, they are simply situated outside the human world, "over there." Conventional links between the fairies and the natural world are maintained in the crop circles which appear all over the countryside, but as we suggested earlier, such links are also parodied—the circles appear everywhere, even in the Bursar's bowl of porridge (p. 40). Because Pratchett's fairies derive their power from people's belief in them, their enchantment of the lovers and the mechanicals in the pre-text is translated into the illusion of glamor and fictions constructed around them. The parallel universe which they come from is also a parasitic universe, feeding off beliefs held in the Disc World universe for its very existence (and see the confused conversation about parallel and parasitic universes on p. 84). Thus Pratchett plays on the metadramatic potential in the pre-text: just as the events depicted in the play might only be a dream, a fiction, so the fairies and elves in Pratchett's novel are merely fictional, illusory, as in turn are the play and the novel. However, for Pratchett, the parasitic nature of the fairies, and, by implication, of fictions in general, constitutes their danger. Thus the endings of Shakespeare's play and Pratchett's novel are radically different. Pratchett's close evokes its pre-text: "Where does it end? On a summer night, with couples going their own ways, and silky purple twilight growing between the trees. From the castle, long after the celebrations had ended, faint laughter and the ringing of little silver bells" (pp. 274–275). But, whereas Shakespeare's text closes with the fairies blessing the bridal chambers and palace, Pratchett's fairies are silent—"And from the empty hillside, only the silence of the elves" (p. 275).

Thus, Pratchett's use of the canonical texts of the past is ambivalent. It recognizes the cultural constructedness of their value, and the potential to confuse the metaethic of the canon with its attributed status as cultural capital. At the same time, Pratchett acknowledges that it *is* cultural wealth, and an enormously rich resource for a writer to draw on for making meaning and for establishing particular relationships between text and audience. But like Shakespeare before him, Pratchett refuses to treat the texts of the past with blind reverence. They can be sported with as well as drawn on for their riches, and, most importantly, they are not automatically to be endowed with any more status than contemporary literary forms or, for that matter, contemporary cultural formations. As a result, readers are invited to enjoy jokes about Shakespeare in the same way as jokes about the modern world. Thus, for example, when Granny Weatherwax (a senior witch who had appeared in Pratchett's earlier Disc World novels, including his reversion of *Macbeth*, *Wyrd Sisters*) complains about the loss of a sense of tradition amongst "the girls that want to be witches these days," Pratchett typically blends conventions of representation with allusions to teenage "Gothic" fashions of the 1980s and 1990s: "Velvet hats and black lipstick and lacy gloves with no fingers to 'em. Cheeky, too." (p. 162). This is a textuality which demolishes the museum walls, breaking down the distinctions between high culture and popular culture texts, and reminding readers that they inhabit a culture of great complexity, capable of making meanings in many different ways. One of its great comic messages is that culture must be read interrogatively, and hence its agenda coincides with the agenda of modern retellings of classic novels.

## CONTESTING IDEOLOGIES: REVERSIONS OF MODERN FICTION CLASSICS

Reversions of eighteenth- and nineteenth-century pre-texts are sites on which the metanarratives of high culture and traditional literature are frequently challenged. Their authors look at canonical texts of the past and identify there an imperialist metanarrative which entails assumptions about race, gender (especially masculinity), class, religion, and human nature. Imperialist metanarratives comprise "an ideological cluster, in which empire, crown, 'race,' armed forces and nation became synonymous" (Richards, 1989, p. 2).

The expansion of the British empire in the nineteenth century was simultaneous with the spread of Christianity, capitalism, and commercialism. Also linked to imperialism was "a definition of masculinity which combined sportsmanship, chivalry and patriotism" (Richards, 1989, p. 2). Boys' adventure novels of the nineteenth century by writers such as Ballantyne and Stevenson reflect, and to some extent inculcated, this cluster of ideological values. The instructive and socializing functions of Ballantyne's novels in particular have been stressed by commentators—they were adventure-romances aimed at "young males being readied to run an empire" (Green, 1989, p. 46).

Story motifs in adventure novels—especially motifs such as shipwreck on exotic and remote islands, native "savages," and pirates—are frequently structured around binary oppositions between concepts of civilized and natural, good and evil, Christian and non-Christian, innocence and experience, childhood and adulthood, and so on. This oppositional schema can be seen quite clearly in Ballantyne's *The Coral Island* or Barrie's *Peter Pan*, where the state of being civilized, good, Christian, innocent, and childlike is valorized over the corresponding oppositions, though Barrie's vision of childhood innocence is perhaps more problematic than Ballantyne's. Barrie's children are described as heartless and selfish, and to remain a child like Peter is to remain utterly solipsistic. The other side of childhood is also portrayed in the cruelty and malice of characters like Hook, an adult still living in a child's world. Variations on this oppositional schema also underlie other novels genrically linked with *The Coral Island,* such as Defoe's *Robinson Crusoe* (a pre-text for *The Coral Island*), Stevenson's *Treasure Island,* or Golding's *The Lord of the Flies,* but are instantiated in more complex and ambivalent ways.

The various reversions that we discuss in this section reflect and engage with imperialist metanarratives at different levels and from varying angles. They are boys' adventure novels, so the protagonists are predominantly adolescent males, and the primary audience for both the reversions and their pre-texts is also male. The boys' adventure genre is underwritten by a dialogic tension between two ideologies. Its story motifs involve boys in adult and heroic exploits, frequently in the service of the state, but at the same time the genre is informed by an ideology of masculinity and childhood that celebrates freedom, especially freedom from adult responsibility. A useful contrast is offered here by Farmer's *The Summer Birds,* a reversion of *Peter Pan,* which interrogates the ramifications for constructions of femininity implicit in the representation of boyhood masculinity as at once heroic and childlike. Golding, Barrie, and Grahame each extrapolates from the notions of childhood and innocence which are implicit in Ballantyne's oppositional schema, and which are an aspect of the humanist ideologies which ground literature for children in general. Oppositions between nature and society in children's texts frequently imply a construction of childhood as innocent and entail a maturational schema structured around the progression from childhood innocence to adult responsibility. Writers such as Barrie and Grahame replicate this schema, while Golding explores and questions its implications.

A key element that links many adventure novels is the thematic and ideological function of the setting. Settings in narrative are constructed schematically and are hence a primary way in which metanarratives shape stories. The setting of an adventure novel is structured intertextually through its literary, religious, and cultural pre-texts. It is usually an enclosed and isolated space, such as the remote island in Robinsonade narratives, or the river bank and the wild wood in *The Wind in the Willows* and Needle's *Wild Wood*. Thematically, as a figure for paradise and/or an idyllic pastoral retreat from the social world, such spaces can function as microcosms for human society. Different forms of social organization, and concepts of human nature and of good and evil can be hypothetically tested out. This feature constitutes a generic link between Robinsonade stories and the postdisaster genre we discussed in chapter 5. Indeed, Rubinstein's postdisaster narrative, *Galax-Arena* (1992), continues a chain of reversions, since it is, in part, a reversion of *Lord of the Flies*. The idea of survival in a strange and enclosed world presents analogies for the development, progress, or regression of the species and the structuring of social relationships and power relations. As an enclosed space, the setting (especially an island) is also analogous with the Garden of Eden, where, as we saw in chapter 2, Christian concepts of good and evil, original sin, the Fall, and redemption are played out. As an idyllic pastoral world the enclosed space of Ballantyne's coral island, Barrie's Neverland, and Grahame's world of the River Bank is both a figure for paradise and the world of childhood—a world separate from adult society and, in Barrie's and Grahame's versions, free of the restraints and responsibilities that characterize adult society.

Like *Lords and Ladies* and contemporary reversions in general, reversions such as *Lord of the Flies, Silver's Revenge,* and *Wild Wood* are bricolage texts—texts constructed out of a range of intertexts, discourses, and genres. Each of these novels engages with imperialist metanarratives associated with the Robinsonade narrative, but they also enter into dialogue with these metanarratives through their peculiar combinations of discourses which shape and structure the common story motifs. Golding's very literary novel is semantically dense. The discourse is highly symbolic, utilizing a range of literary and religious intertexts, and the novel has generated a range of readings; it has been read as a moral fable, a social fable, and a religious fable (Tiger, 1974, p. 42). In contrast, religious discourse in *The Coral Island*, Golding's pre-text, carries a primary ideological and exemplary function. In *Silver's Revenge*, Leeson combines his intertexts with parodic discoursal genres. The social setting of the novel is constructed polyphonically through a parody of nineteenth-century narrative voice and through the incorporation of a variety of social speech genres represented via the cast of extra characters that Leeson introduces.

Historically, British imperialism, Christianity, and the expansion of commercialism were inextricably linked. This historical context is reflected in the adventure novels of Defoe, Ballantyne, and Stevenson and it grounds the moral ideologies of those texts. While Defoe's and Stevenson's novels are more complex and at times quite ambivalent both thematically and morally, Hannabuss's disclaimer for Ballantyne's work is generalizable to the ideological positioning of many writers of imperialist adventure novels: "If there are paradoxes in [their] work, they draw upon the pervasive contradiction of [the] age between materialism and faith, power and justice, war and peace" (1989, p. 70). These paradoxes and contradictions provide points of entry or loopholes through which reversions such as those by Golding, Leeson, and Needle enter into dialogue with ideological assumptions underlying imperialist metanarratives. *Lord of the Flies* engages with the religious and moral ideologies of its pre-texts, inverting oppositions between civilized and uncivilized, innocent and sinful, which ground the imperialist metanarrative, especially as it is instantiated in Ballantyne's novel. Leeson's *Silver's Revenge*, a reversion of and sequel to *Treasure Island*, focuses on the moral implications of connections between class, commercialism, and imperialism which underlie Stevenson's novel. Needle's *Wild Wood* is a reversion of *The Wind in the Willows*. A pastoral version of the boys' adventure story, Grahame's novel is grounded in the same kinds of assumptions about class and power and oppositions between the natural and the civilized, childhood and adulthood, that inform earlier imperialist narratives, such as Ballantyne's, though for Grahame childhood is correlated with nature. Like Leeson, Needle is concerned with issues of class and power arising from the socio-cultural construction of meaning, and both writers dismantle oppositions between natural and civilized by drawing attention to assumptions about class and the basis of power in their pre-texts.

## ROBINSONADES AND THE INTERROGATION OF SOCIAL STRUCTURE

Defoe's *Robinson Crusoe* is a primary pre-text for nineteenth-century boys' adventure novels aimed at adolescent males, such as those of Ballantyne and

Stevenson, and for contemporary Robinsonade narratives. The focus of our discussion here is on Golding's reshaping of Ballantyne's reversion of the Robinsonade narrative for boys and Leeson's reversion of *Treasure Island,* but Defoe's novel (and the numerous retellings and reversions of it) lies behind and provides a context for Ballantyne, Stevenson, Golding, and Leeson. As Green (1989) has pointed out there are also indirect links between *The Coral Island* and *Robinson Crusoe, Treasure Island,* and *Peter Pan.* These links lie partly in story motifs common to the boys' adventure genre—shipwreck, the desert island, pirates, "native savages," and so on—but the novels are also linked through the underlying themes and the metanarratives that structure them.

In his discussion of reversions and retellings of *Robinson Crusoe,* Green has identified the following key story and theme motifs which comprise the Robinsonade narrative (p. 36):

1. The desert island setting.
2. The idea of starting a "new life."
3. Encounters with natives, representing concepts of otherness.
4. Human progress through technology.
5. Reconstruction and analysis of existing social structures.
6. A narrative structured around a rising curve of achievement and accumulation, representing human progress.
7. Economic triumph—the Robinsonade is the success story of the entrepreneur private citizen.

These motifs form a metanarrative which links Christianity, imperialism, nineteenth-century capitalism, and Enlightenment concepts of human progress, and they provide a frame for looking at how the material has been reshaped by Ballantyne and Golding, and Stevenson and Leeson. The various reversions engage ideologically with this metanarrative by selectively incorporating some motifs from this cluster and by altering or inverting others. In Defoe's paradigmatic version, a lone protagonist constructs a new life for himself on a desert island. As Green, Hannabuss (1989), and Michel-Michot (1991) all argue, Ballantyne reshapes Defoe's story so as to articulate the British Empire ethos which sees Christianity in the service of imperialism. Ballantyne's three boys are Christian imperialists, and their encounters with pirates and native islanders indicate a clear correlation of Christianity, good, and the British Empire, as opposed to non-Christian (pirates and natives), evil, and the uncivilized colonies. In Golding's reversion, a group of mid-twentieth century schoolboys are also isolated on a coral island, but many of the key motifs listed above are now inverted. Golding's schoolboys regress from a democratic mode of social organization to an authoritarian and tribal model, from "civilized" codes of behavior to a more primitive and savage lifestyle which involves ritualistic hunting of animals and human beings and finally murder. Unlike Crusoe and Ballantyne's three boys, Golding's schoolboys do not encounter any native inhabitants on their island. Instead the evil that Ballantyne's characters encounter in the native cannibals is found by Golding's boys to lie within themselves.

Differences between these three versions reflect in part their different historical contexts. As Michel-Michot has argued, Defoe's Crusoe is "the pioneer of the new age which eventually gave birth to the self-satisfied heroes of *The Coral Island*—the main difference being that Crusoe is the representative of the rising power and new energy that contributed to *build* the British Empire, whereas Ralph, Jack and Peterkin enjoy a position they have inherited, and simply *belong* to the empire" (p. 41). Golding's novel, written just after World War II, represents the "end of the cycle initiated by *Robinson Crusoe*" (p. 41) and the end of British imperialism and the ideologies upon which it was founded and which it sustained. By situating the story within a mid-twentieth century historical and ideological context Golding underscores the postwar loss of faith in progress and the perfectibility of the human race which had grounded and legitimated colonialist expansion. Although Stevenson's *Treasure Island* is not strictly speaking a reversion of the Robinsonade narrative, Leeson's reversion and sequel to *Treasure Island, Silver's Revenge,* which leaves the characters stranded on the island, incorporates genric motifs associated with this story. This, combined with Leeson's analysis of the social relations and the impact of industrialism and capitalism in the nineteenth century, foregrounds the imperialist assumptions that link the "Treasure Island" story with the Robinsonade story.

The desert island setting has an important metaphoric and analogic function in Robinsonade narratives. Typically, the (male) protagonist(s) are shipwrecked on a desert island where they are isolated from the outside world. The island setting is often conceived of as analogous with the Garden of Eden, where Christian concepts of good and evil, original sin and redemption are played out. In nineteenth-century literature and art the Pacific islands were represented ambivalently as paradisiacal, as settings for Christian martyrdom, and for licentious and erotic fantasies (Green, 1989, p. 45). The coral island settings of novels by Ballantyne, Golding, and Leeson bring together these religious and cultural associations. The setting is, however, frequently described in terms which construct it as both Paradise and as Eden after the Fall. Associations of the island with a Christian paradise are explicit in Ballantyne's version, in descriptions of the setting and of the conflict between Christians, natives, and pirates. The island is described by Peterkin as "the ancient Paradise" (p. 28), but Ralph, the narrator, continues, "We afterwards found, however, that these lovely islands were very unlike Paradise in many things" (p. 28). It is a fallen Eden, but the perpetrators of this fall are not the boys but the "savage" and "cannibalistic" native inhabitants. Erotic associations of the island setting are latent in the novel, in the subplot in which the three boys rescue Avatea, a young native convert to Christianity, from her non-Christian father. As Green has also suggested, there are links between the paradisiacal coral island setting of Ballantyne's novel and Barrie's Neverland island of lost boys, and between Ballantyne's very childlike Peterkin and Barrie's Peter Pan (p. 48).

These religious associations of the island are also present in Stevenson's *Treasure Island* and Leeson's *Silver's Revenge.* In Stevenson's novel, Jim's anticipatory imaginings of the island are full of stock clichés: he imagines a "strange" and "wonderful" island "thick with savages" and "dangerous animals" (p. 53). Descriptions of the actual island are characterized by an ambivalence: the woods are "melancholy" (p. 98), the foliage has "a poisonous brightness" (p. 99), and, significantly, the island is inhabited by snakes (p. 104). This ambivalence is partly a convention of the genre—like Ballantyne's coral island, Stevenson's island is a fallen Eden—but it also comes about as a result of Jim Hawkins's retrospective narration. As Nodelman (1983, p. 58) has pointed out, an older, more experienced Jim Hawkins is telling the story of his youthful adventures and the gap between the narrated (younger) Jim and the narrating (older) Jim results in an often ambivalent narrative point of view. The island is thus both an object of wonder and desire in all its strangeness for the young Jim and an "accursed" place, the site of a "dark and bloody sojourn" (p. 271) for the older Jim. Associations with Paradise are stronger in *Silver's Revenge,* where the link is made explicit, though rather ironically, in Tom's description of Alice and Somerscale's notions of "an island paradise" (p. 191). At the same time, Leeson is also playing with generic links between the Robinsonade narrative and social utopias. This aspect is treated playfully in references to the multiplicity of votes taken on whether to build a boat or a hut and the explicit allusion to conventional images of Noah's Ark—they had so many votes on this that they "invented a boat with a hut on top" (p. 195). The erotic associations of the island setting are also latent in the close of Leeson's novel, with various characters pairing up and in the scene where Tom Carter, the narrator, rolls in the surf with Silver's sensual Jamaican daughter, Betsy (pp. 193–194).

That the island setting of *Lord of the Flies* is not a paradise is clear in the emphasis on the heat, the impenetrable jungle, and the effects of too much fruit, sun, and isolation on the boys. Whereas Ballantyne's boys are always clean and well-fed on a varied and balanced diet, Golding's boys are filthy, partially clothed, and suffer from diarrhea. Associations of the island setting accrue through the novel's pre-texts and intertexts, and Christian elements are present more on a symbolic level. Simon, who in a combination of ritual and accident is murdered as he attempts to reveal to the other boys the identity and nature of "the beast" which they have invented and imagined on the island, is a Christ-figure. Through his name and analogous connection with Ballantyne's Peterkin, he is also, according to Golding (Gindin, 1988, p. 23), the New Testament "Simon who was called Peter"—the Disciple Simon Peter, named Peter by Christ, who was to deny Christ three times and, like Golding's Simon, a visionary martyred for his faith. Golding's reversal of the name change highlights a curious analogy between Simon and his biblical counterpart: Simon Peter's faith in Christ is strengthened through the intuition that comes as a result of his denial of Christ; Golding's Simon undergoes a kind of spiritual experience in his encounter with "the beast" or the Lord of the Flies in the forest, where he recognizes and acknowledges the existence of the beast as a part of himself, as a part of human nature (thereby denying its independent existence). The Lord of the Flies is, literally, the pig's head which the boys have impaled on a stick as a sacrifice to the beast. It is also a translation of the Hebrew *Ba'alzevuv* or the Greek *Beelzebub* (Woodward, 1983, p. 201). Thus "Lord of the Flies" represents the "devil" or propensity for evil within human beings, which the boys attempt to externalize through the creation of "the beast" and which Christian tradition has externalized through the creation of Satan. So while the biblical Simon Peter's denial serves to strengthen his faith in Christ, Simon's moment of epiphany highlights Golding's vision of a world in which there is no Christ and no redemption from that propensity to evil.

The idea of starting a "new life" in *Robinson Crusoe* and *The Coral Island* is clearly linked with Christian concepts of Paradise, the Fall, and redemption, and it highlights the inextricable link between Christianity and imperialism in the nineteenth century. Many twentieth-century commentators have noted how the colonies in the eighteenth and nineteenth centuries were imagined and represented in literature and art as "the new world" and as having biblical associations with a return to Eden, the new Canaan, or "the promised land." By being isolated from the outside world and in a sense freed of their past lives, characters are able to construct their own world on the island, to start afresh. This feature highlights some key differences between the moral and ideological positions of Defoe, Ballantyne, and Golding, as each writer differs in his conception of original sin and the nature of humanity, and as the focus in the novels shifts from religion, to Empire, to human nature.

In these novels, the conception of human nature, behavior, and action, and thus the idea of a new life, is shaped by particular ideologies of good and evil. As Michel-Michot has suggested, Crusoe's experiences in *Robinson Crusoe* allow him to realize his own sinful nature. He comes to accept his fate as God's punishment and sees his situation as providing the opportunity to create and invent a new life through repentance and reliance on God (pp. 42–43). The metanarrative reflected in this is evoked ironically in *Silver's Revenge,* when Tom Carter arrives on Treasure Island and meets the insane castaway Dick Johnson, who has replicated Crusoe's practical achievements, but is afflicted by bizarre religious obsessions and observances. Another response to this element of the Robinsonade pre-text appears in Paulsen's *Hatchet* (1989), a contemporary Robinsonade in which the Christian ideologies shaping the construction of a "new life" in *Robinson Crusoe* are secularized. Implicit in the idea of starting a new life is the baptismal notion of being "born again," but in Paulsen's novel this process of self-renewal is conceived of within a humanist metanarrative of self-development. Brian Robeson, an adolescent Crusoe figure (his name is a rough anagram of "Robinson"), can only begin anew once he starts to move out of solipsism and accordingly see himself differently in relation to the world.

Ballantyne had made a crucial departure from Defoe by following Rousseau, and Locke's conceptions of the child as inherently good and hence representing his three boys as innocent, that is, as free of original sin. The distinction between good and evil in *The Coral Island* is clearly demarcated: the Christian boys are good and evil is always externalized, located in the other (non-Christian natives and pirates). In *Lord of the Flies* the distinction between good and evil is not clear-cut at all, and, like Defoe, Golding internalizes evil—human beings are inherently sinful, and the creation of "the beast" represents the boys' attempts to externalize their fear of something which lies within themselves. However, like Paulsen, Golding repositions Defoe's Protestant conception of human nature within a secular humanist paradigm. For Golding, children, and human beings in general, have an inherent propensity for evil simply by virtue of being human beings, not because of any notions of original sin, goodness, or the possibility of redemption. There is a "darkness of man's heart" (p. 192) which Ralph weeps for at the close of the novel, because God and goodness do not exist. Golding further undermines the ideologies informing Ballantyne's novel by depicting evil not as some abstract notion of original sin, but as the desire for power over others. Character actions in the novel which we conventionally think of as wrong, such as murder, the deliberate infliction of pain on others, or arbitrary authority, are all motivated by this desire for power. In other words, it is the same impulse that motivates the imperialist enterprise in *The Coral Island* and which is masked and legitimated by the alliance between Christianity and imperialism in that novel.

A particular function of island settings as social microcosms is that they potentially enable the examination and reconstruction of existing social structures. The possibility of a "new life" carries with it the possibility of a new social order. This is a feature that clearly links Robinsonade narratives with utopian fiction and recent postdisaster fiction wherein society is hypothetically offered the chance to start again, but as with those fictions few Robinsonades in children's fiction have achieved such a utopian vision. In *The Coral Island* existing social and political structures are simply imposed upon the new world. Ballantyne's three principal characters come from different classes and it is the educated Jack who is the natural leader. A clear statement of Ballantyne's imperialist political and social ideology occurs in the words of Peterkin: "We've got an island to ourselves. We'll take possession in the name of the king; we'll go and enter the service of its black inhabitants. Of course we'll rise, naturally, to the top of affairs. White men always do in savage countries. You shall be king, Jack; Ralph, prime minister . . ." (p. 18).

The class distinctions in Ballantyne are replicated in Golding's Jack (the leader of the choir), Ralph (son of a British naval officer), and Piggy (a lower-class scholarship boy). As many readings of the novel have suggested, Piggy represents the intellect, Ralph embodies old-fashioned values of common sense and decency, and Jack embodies arbitrary and despotic authority. Thus Ralph and Jack also represent two conflicting types of social organization: democracy and fascism. In the opening chapters, the boys demonstrate a desire for rules and social structures, which is initially manifested in a democratic social order. They elect Ralph as their leader, hold assemblies, and make decisions by voting. Golding's conception of human nature, and the imperfectibility of the human race, has implications for his representation of the social structures and processes on the island—the "new social order" of the new life. Order quickly breaks down; communal decision-making gives way to despotism; rules are arbitrary; and conventionally "anti-social" behaviors, such as murder, are sanctioned through the creation of pseudo-religious rituals. In representing social structures as regressive, Golding suggests that the socializing and "civilizing" influences of British imperialism, Christianity, and "civilization," so valued by writers like Ballantyne, are in the long run too feeble to control and curb the desire for power over the other. An implication of this position is that social rules and structures can control and repress actions and behavior conventionally seen as evil or sinful, but society cannot ever entirely curb that innate impulse toward evil. Golding himself suggested the novel might be read with the Second World War as a moral and intellectual context, remarking of that war that, "The basic point my generation discovered about man was that there was more evil in him than could be accounted for simply by social pressures" (Gindin, 1988, p. 15). The novel thus becomes a political allegory, wherein Golding's subversive impulse, in relation to his pre-texts, has a conservative social function: behind the juxtaposition of fascism and democracy is a sense of longing for those old-fashioned decent values embodied by Ralph.

Inasmuch as the island setting functions as a microcosm for human society, survival on the island presents an analogy for the development, progress, or regression of individuals and of the species. The Robinsonade narrative typically articulates and celebrates human progress through technology and the protagonist(s) turn disadvantage to advantage through inventing or recreating the technology of the period (Green, p. 36). Defoe's Crusoe and Ballantyne's three boys are quite adept at inventing and using their knowledge of technology and the natural world acquired through observation and book-learning to their own advantage. *The Coral Island* in fact reads at times like a survival manual for shipwrecked boys. Paulsen's *Hatchett* plots Brian's technological progress alongside his personal development. In *Lord of the Flies,* however, Golding has reversed this process: the boys lack the skills and book-learning of Ballantyne's Jack, and so regress technologically and socially. While they recognize the genric similarities between their own situation and the adventure novels they have read, such as *Treasure Island, Swallows and Amazons,* or *The Coral Island* (p. 34), their book-learning has no practical basis. Their primary technological achievements are making fire (by using Piggy's spectacles), building crude shelters, and making hunting spears. Fire is important in the novel because of its symbolism and its ambivalence. In its primary purpose as a rescue beacon it provides a link with civilization, but this link is also symbolic. As we noted in chapter 3 when discussing the Prometheus myth, fire has accrued symbolic associations with knowledge, education, and culture. It is, however, also quite ambivalent in its use as a means of survival and rescue and its potential for destruction.

Green proposed that the Robinsonade narrative is typically structured around a "rising curve of achievement and accumulation" (1989, p. 36), representing human progress through the proper management and maintenance of natural resources. But whereas Defoe's Crusoe progresses through the different stages of civilization—from hunting and gathering, to agriculture and animal husbandry, and so on—Golding's boys reverse this trajectory. And although Ballantyne's boys progress technologically, their agricultural and resource management skills remain fairly static. They are depicted as occupying a "natural" position within the stable ecosystem of the island. Thus they do not need to manage their resources because the island simply supplies their basic needs and they are able to luxuriate "on the fat of the land" (p. 57). Another way of saying this might be that they plundered the island of its natural resources as if there were a never-ending supply, and the novel might be read from a postcolonial perspective as a narrative of exploitation. As Green has also suggested, the Robinsonade is a story of "economic triumph"; it is "the success story of the entrepreneur private citizen who becomes the island's official governor and the island itself becomes a part of the British empire" (p. 37).

That the process of colonization is natural is taken for granted in *The Coral Island*, where the link between Christianity, trade, and colonial rule has a legitimating function. It is an implicit assumption in the descriptions of the pirates in Ballantyne's novel that trade in the form of piracy is exploitation, but trade accompanied by Christian missionary work is a valid enterprise. Christianity, civilization, and capitalism were brought to the Pacific islands as gifts in return for the natural resources of the islands. There is, however, an underlying link here between imperialism, commercialism, and exploitation which causes some discomfort for Ballantyne's modern readers and which is taken up by Leeson in *Silver's Revenge* through the analogy between piracy, commercial exploitation, and the treasure hunt, and through the foregrounded, ubiquitous presence of slave labor as a mainstay of empire. As Gannon (1985) has pointed out, the pirate treasure in *Treasure Island* is blood money, and Stevenson "conveys in symbolic terms . . . the human cost of growing up in a world where it can be very hard to tell the respectable citizens from the pirates" (1985, p. 243). It is this central ambivalence about human nature and about the distinction between piracy and respectability in Stevenson's novel that provides the focus for Leeson's critique of class and capitalism in early modern children's literature.

## DISMANTLING BOUNDARIES IN *SILVER'S REVENGE*

*Silver's Revenge* is both a sequel to and a reversion of *Treasure Island*. It picks up Stevenson's story fifteen years later and tells the story of a second expedition to Treasure Island to retrieve the bar silver left behind. The story and the discourse also closely parallel and replicate *Treasure Island*. Leeson's novel has a similar structure to Stevenson's, uses several chapter titles which are the same or similar (as well as some outrageously different, in "Some Like it Hot" and "Red Shift"), and also incorporates two narrators, Tom Carter and Dr. Livesey. Many of the same episodes, such as the apple barrel scene, are repeated, but with variations and different consequences. In this sense, *Silver's Revenge* is a reversion, insofar as it is a repetition of similar events told from another point of view. The novel is framed as a "historical" record, mostly narrated (and so "written") by Tom Carter, an orphan and runaway apprentice, who is picked up by the roadside by Dr. Livesey and sent to stay with Jim Hawkins and his mother at the Admiral Benbow Inn. Having written his as yet unpublished account of his adventures on Treasure Island—that is Stevenson's novel *Treasure Island*—Jim Hawkins has taken to writing plays and epic romances in verse in an attempt to impress Lady Alice, Squire Trelawney's charge.

By heavily thematizing the processes of writing and narration, Leeson flags to his readers the intertextual instabilities of perspective and ideology that lie in the relationships between a pre-text and its reversions. The opening of *Silver's Revenge* parodies both the discourse of Stevenson's narrator and his assumption that facts are unproblematic. It begins with direct imitation—"Dr. Livesey, Master Hawkins, Captain Gray and the others asked me to set down the particulars of our coming here"—but then adds motivation in the form of a familiar cliché: "They say it will entertain and instruct folks . . ." (p. 8). The rest of the introduction then problematizes human motives, trust, and truth. Leeson also undermines his pre-text by incorporating successive retellings of Jim Hawkins's account of the previous voyage to Treasure Island (the story that Stevenson's novel tells). Silver/Argent and his companions, Wilton and Somerscale, steal Hawkins's account of this voyage, and Wilton gives a summary account of it at the assembly of the Merchant Venturers. This summary consists of the same events as Jim's version in *Treasure Island* but the perspective and register of the narration reinterpret them so as to criminally implicate Hawkins, Trelawney, Dr. Livesey and their companions. In his summary version of events, for example, the precautions taken to avoid a mutiny in moving the powder are described as "making a fortress" and creating "a private army" (p. 69). Dr. Livesey describes Wilton's account as "mangled and distorted . . . summarized and adorned," comparing it with "a review" of a book, as opposed to "the book itself" (pp. 94–95). The opposition of "book" and "review" assumes the "truthfulness" of the book, and this reflects dialogically and metafictively back on the relation between Leeson's text and its pre-text. Like Wilton's summary account, Leeson's reversion is a version of *Treasure Island,* but unlike Wilton's account, Leeson also acknowledges how events are shaped by discourse. Thus Wilton's narrative is countered by "Jim's" version of events (the text of *Treasure Island,* which he knows by heart, signaled by quoting the opening sentence: "Squire Trelawney, Dr. Livesey, and the rest of the gentlemen having asked me to write down the whole particulars of Treasure Island . . ."). In fact, though, the novel is reduced to a one-paragraph summary and what is described is the impact of the narration on the narratees, who universally confuse literary quality with truth (in much the same way as happens in retellings of Shakespeare). So what status has Leeson's own reversion in all this? One implication of this complexity is that none of the three versions constitute the "truth"; they are all different versions of the one story, and their variations come about as a result of the different contexts in which they are told, the different narrative voices through which they are told, and the different purposes for which they are told.

Leeson's shift in point of view comes about through the modifications he has made to the social and physical setting and the characters, the incorporation of a wider range of social discourses, and through the fact that events in *Silver's Revenge* are a close but different repetition of previous events. There is a significant time lapse between the events narrated in the two novels and they use a different narrator. However, there are many similarities between Jim Hawkins (Stevenson's narrator) and Tom Carter (Leeson's narrator)—their age, role as narrators, and social position. Thus, while the use of a different narrator means that events are narrated from a different character's point of view, the dominant narrator viewpoint in the two novels is very similar. Through his modifications to setting, character, and discourse, Leeson discloses the class assumptions underlying *Treasure Island* and foregrounds latent ambiguities in the oppositional schema that Stevenson used to locate characters morally. The shift in point of view is then the product of Leeson's different ideological positioning and structuring of the text.

The historical, physical, and social setting of *Treasure Island* is relatively vague. Descriptions tend toward clichéd romanticism, and there is a lack of social variation in the characterization. In contrast, Leeson's treatment of the social setting in particular is much more specific. *Silver's Revenge* is set against the context of social change and unrest caused by the growth of industrialism and capitalism in the late eighteenth century, and includes an account of a coalminers' dispute and riot, and detailed descriptions of the physical setting, which focus on the effects of industrialism on the landscape. Leeson's modifications to the discourse of the setting have a double function: they undermine the romantic overtones of Stevenson's novel, and foreground problems associated with class, industrialism, and capitalism. The contrast between the two novels is particularly acute in the descriptions of the seaport and industrial city of Bristol. The discourse of *Treasure Island* is romanticized and clichéd as Jim Hawkins describes the multitude of ships, the singing sailors with rings in their ears, whiskers curled in ringlets, tarry pigtails, and the smell of tar and salt (p. 58). This is in direct contrast with Leeson's grittier descriptions of the city: "the ships all jammed together in the river"; "the rubbish in the runnels" (p. 61); the dust, fumes, and haze produced by the glasshouses, foundries, workshops and tanneries; the gaping holes, hollows, and gullies cut into the earth by the mining machinery (p. 74); and so on.

A second way in which Leeson constructs an alternative point of view on the events narrated in *Treasure Island* and elaborates on the social setting is through his modifications to character and character discourse. He introduces many extra characters, including Tom Carter (orphan and runaway apprentice); the colliers and Ned Barker (a collier and trade unionist); Jamaican slaves and servants, including Betsy (Silver's daughter); Wilton (a lawyer); and Somerscale (a scientist and inventor). All of these characters are typecast through their speech—for example, Wilton speaks the discourse of law: "I would deny your right to seize this person without positive proof that an offence has been committed" (p. 48), and Somerscale, the discourse of reason: "Reason dictates that labor must be free. Such forms of bondage hold the nation's industry in chains" (p. 48). Thus the social setting of the novel is constructed polyphonically through the various discourses that characters speak.

A significant character modification in Leeson's novel is that of Silver, who has changed his name to Argent (a poetic term for silver). The adoption of a French name implies that Silver has appropriated a social position, having climbed the social ladder through his wealth. As Dr. Livesey suggests, it is a "fake" (p. 99) or assumed name. There is an implicit connection here between social class and birth, and the Doctor's response suggests traditional English contempt for both acquired wealth and the French. Silver/Argent is a prominent member of the Merchant Venturers company (a company of sea merchants) and chief shareholder of a coal mine. In *Treasure Island,* Silver, unlike his pirate comrades who spent their loot on "rum and a good fling" (p. 80), is a "man of substance" (p. 56)—he has a bank account, saves his earnings, and intends to set himself up as a gentleman when he returns from the voyage (pp. 80–83). Thus, Leeson has made more explicit what is hinted at in Stevenson's novel. However, by turning Silver the pirate into

Argent the capitalist, Leeson implies, much more overtly than was possible for Stevenson, who lacked the benefit of hindsight which informs Leeson's late–twentieth-century text, that capitalism is a form of piracy. Even Silver's parrot, Flint, has undergone a transformation in *Silver's Revenge,* now saying "ten percent, take it or leave it!" (p. 111) instead of "pieces of eight." The term "argent" also has associations with money lending (an argenter)— as it emerges when the *Hispaniola* is about to set sail for Treasure Island for the second time that it is Argent/Silver who owns and has put up the boat. As with other characters in the novel, Silver/Argent is also typecast through his speech. He speaks the discourse of capitalism or argentocracy (the rule or paramount influence of money), as in, "My proposition, friends, is that money overrides both law and custom and even natural justice and is a law and reason unto itself" (p. 48). Silver/Argent's skill, however, lies in his ability to code-switch between a range of discursive genres: the discourses of piracy, respectability, and capitalism. Thematically, this code-switching foregrounds the similarity between piracy and industrialism, grounded in the common denominator of "treasure seeking."

Leeson also uses repetition of similar but different story events and discourse elements to disclose class assumptions in *Treasure Island* and undermine its romantic aura. He closely replicates the plot of *Treasure Island* by incorporating episodes which are at once the same but different, and repeating snatches of dialogue, but in the mouths of different characters. He follows his pre-text so closely that the plots of the two novels might almost be mapped onto each other isomorphically, but the significance that events have is modified through changes to the discourse, setting, and the characterization. A very revealing example is when in *Silver's Revenge* a sentence spoken by Stevenson's Squire Trelawney is transferred to Silver/Argent: "No hang it all, it's not the treasure, it's the glory of the sea" (Stevenson, p. 55; Leeson, p. 111). Tom explicitly points out to Silver/Argent that he "sounds powerful like Squire Trelawney," and the function of this explicitness is to expose a narrative tendency to dress up greed and ambition as romantic heroism. Leeson refuses to do this, and in his retelling Silver and Trelawney become more and more closely linked. In the apple barrel scene it is these two who conspire against the rest of the company and, in an ironic reversal of class structures, the novel closes with them shifting rocks from Black Crag to uncover the bar silver, while Ned Barker—the trade unionist leader of the colliers—oversees their labor. There are implicit parallels between Silver and Trelawney in *Treasure Island,* but by turning them into rivals linked by their similarities, and eventually into co-conspirators, Leeson discloses the collusion and interconnectedness of capitalism and the British class system.

These perceptions gain more emphasis from Leeson's development of the doubling of characters implicit in *Treasure Island*. In chapter 4 we discussed the functions of monstrous doubles in heroic legend and fantasy, but the other self or *doppelgänger* occurs quite frequently in nineteenth-century fiction for adolescents, and in fictions such as Shelley's *Frankenstein* or Stevenson's *Dr. Jekyll and Mr. Hyde* which have been appropriated by adolescents. As a narrative and thematic strategy it is widely used in contemporary children's fiction (see McCallum, 1996). Parallels between Jim Hawkins and Silver in *Treasure Island* constitute Silver as Jim's *doppelgänger*, especially through Jim's discovery in himself of "a frightening capacity for . . . violent and ruthless action" (Gannon, 1985, p. 250). Frey and Griffith describe Silver as "a comic version of Jekyll and Hyde" (1987, p. 148), and they also draw an analogy between the Jekyll and Hyde schema and the oppositional construction of character groups in *Treasure Island*—the pirates as opposed to Squire Trelawney and company (p. 152). Silver, Jim, and Dr. Livesey are the only characters able to negotiate both groups (Jim and Silver by virtue of their duplicity, and Dr. Livesey out of his sense of moral duty).

In *Silver's Revenge* the doubling of characters moves toward a more complex social significance through Leeson's incorporation of a larger variety of character types. In Stevenson's novel there are really only two groups of characters: Silver and rest of the ship's crew, many of them ex-pirates; and those who have authority and the map (Squire Trelawney, Dr. Livesey, Jim Hawkins, and Captain Smollet). Although parallels between Jim and Silver create a moral ambiguity in the story, the morality of these two groups is otherwise fairly clear-cut, and the pirates are formally expelled from sociality by being marooned on the island at the end of the novel. Leeson, however, highlights this ambiguity by delineating the grouping of characters and the morality of each group differently. By the close of the novel, and after much movement of characters between groups, four groups have emerged. The first comprises Argent/Silver (pirate, merchant, mine-owner, and emerging capitalist), Wilton (lawyer), Somerscale (inventor, man of reason), Squire Trelawney (gentry and opportunist), and Lady Alice (opportunist). The second comprises the heroes of the story: Dr. Livesey (doctor, botanist, and "man of learning"), Jim Hawkins, and Tom Carter. The third comprises Ned Barker (the coal miner and trade unionist), the coal miners, and rioters. The fourth group comprises the Jamaican servants and slaves, Betsy, Nanny, and Daniel. Morally these four groups fall into two main categories, and by the end of the novel Argent/Silver and his associates have banded together against the rest of the crew and company and the slaves. The close, however, leaves all of the characters on the island together to reconstruct a new social order in which boundaries of class, socioeconomic background, and race might be amiably dissolved: Somerscale and Lady Alice become a couple, inventing things and dismantling the reason/passion dichotomy; the coal miners have dismissed the buried treasure and devote themselves to fishing and gardening; Ned Barker oversees Squire Trelawney and Silver/Argent as they "mine" for the bar silver; and Tom and Betsy are enjoying an interracial union within which all differences are resolved by "the best of three throws" (p. 195). Is this utopia?

## ACROSS THE DIVIDES OF CLASS AND CULTURE:
### SOCIAL PERSPECTIVES IN *THE WIND IN THE WILLOWS* AND *WILD WOOD*

We have mentioned genric and ideological links between classic texts such as *The Wind in the Willows* or *Peter Pan* and the Robinsonade and adventure novels we have been discussing. Needle's reversion of *The Wind in the Willows*, *Wild Wood*, has an ideological scope comparable to that of *Silver's Revenge* and uses similar narrative and discoursal techniques. Like Leeson, Needle has reshaped the story so as to disclose class assumptions underlying the pre-text by constructing another point of view on this story. Whereas Leeson proceeds by writing a sequel, Needle retells what is ostensibly the same series of events but from the viewpoint of a character given neither name nor voice in the pre-text, Toad's chauffeur who is summarily dismissed by Badger, Rat, and Mole in chapter 6 of *The Wind in the Willows*. In *Wild Wood* this character becomes Baxter Ferret, a Wild Wooder who retells the events surrounding the invasion of Toad Hall from the viewpoint of the Wild Wooders. In *The Wind in the Willows* the ferrets, stoats, and weasels take over Toad Hall while Toad is in prison. Their actions, in Grahame's novel, lack motivation, largely because the text does not represent their point of view or give them a voice. By telling the story from the viewpoint of the Wild Wooders, Needle ascribes motivation to their actions and makes the class conflict implicit in Grahame's novel more explicit.

The setting of *The Wind in the Willows* and *Wild Wood* has important thematic and ideological significance, analogous with the function of the island setting of the novels we have been discussing. Like the island, the setting of *The Wind in the Willows* has a double function. The world of the river bank is largely an idyllic rural retreat synonymous with the innocent world of childhood—a pastoral world separate from the society of adults and free from the restraints and responsibilities of adult society.

Zanderer has compared Grahame's romanticized and idyllic construction of childhood with Golding's contrasting vision in *Lord of the Flies*: "In their very different locales, which set the characters apart from their familiar worlds, we may begin to distinguish our unfettered moral natures. But Grahame stands squarely in opposition to Golding: the state of nature is sanguine; it brings out our best, our humanity; Golding's tale implies that civilization has only muzzled our fangs; when we return to nature we become bestially competitive" (1987, p. 17). In contrast to both these positions, Needle's revisioning of Grahame's world implies that it is not possible to return to nature and that life is always fundamentally social. Needle's revision is not, however, entirely in opposition to that of Grahame. There is an implicit political subtext in Grahame's novel, as many commentators have noted, which Needle foregrounds and makes more explicit. The romanticized vision of nature which Zanderer identifies is associated with the leisurely activities of the River Bankers. However, as many commentators have pointed out, the world of the River Bankers and the Wild Wooders is a microcosm for a society which is internally divided between the rich (the affluent middle-class River Bankers) and the working class (the Wild Wooders) (Green, 1983; Philip, 1985; Hunt, 1988). As Green has suggested, Grahame's attitude toward the Wild Wooders—the weasels, stoats, and ferrets—"betrays . . . his social anxieties, his irrational (but widely shared) terror of revolution and mob violence, the supposed dangers latent in an anarchic, industrialized, no longer ruralized subservient proletariat" (p. xviii). While this political element is only one subtext in *The Wind in the Willows*—and, as Philip suggests, to interpret the novel only on this level is to "read it perversely" (p. 104)— it is a subtext which, as Hunt points out, is obvious for Grahame's British readers (p. 159). Hunt's argument is given additional substance in Horwood's sequel to *The Wind in the Willows, The Willows in Winter* (1994), in which the class distinctions between the River Bankers and the Wild Wooders are accentuated by the use of conventionalized markers of "otherness" to designate those of "inferior" class.[3] The political element in Grahame's novel is also the focus of much of the criticism and commentary surrounding the novel, and it becomes the focus of Needle's Marxist reversion. Needle dismantles the opposition between nature and society underlying Grahame's novel by foregrounding those social structures underpinning the world of the river bank which remain implicit in it. Like reversions in general, Needle's retelling is selective and key episodes are reshaped so as to make more explicit as well as subvert the metanarrative about class conflict underlying his pre-text.

The setting of Needle's reversion has a double function, as it does in the pre-text, but Needle restructures the oppositions between childhood and adult society so as to elaborate more succinctly through the discourse of the novel the class relationships underlying Grahame's story. In Grahame's novel the river bank setting is representative of an idyllic version of childhood. The world of adult responsibility lies outside its scope, though, as Hunt has argued, "class and age are closely associated" and Rat's address to the field mice and hedgehogs is marked by a patronizing (adult-to-child) register and tone (p. 163). In *Wild Wood* Needle stresses this opposition between the worlds of childhood and adulthood so that the relations between the Wild Wooders and the River Bankers are more overtly depicted according to a hierarchical schema typically associated with relations between children and adults. In Needle's version, a primary grievance that the Wild Wooders have against the River Bankers is that they are patronizing, treating them as children and as a lesser species, and this idea is articulated through the discursive strategies that Needle uses to construct dialogue between characters. Needle also engages his pre-text in debate about social formations by retelling the same episodes, but narrating them from a different perspective: notable examples are Badger's dismissal of Baxter (p. 106); Mole's journey into the Wild Wood (which is interpreted by the Wild Wooders as a plot against them); and the carol singing episode (where Rat and Mole's treatment of the hedgehogs is quite overtly interpreted as patronizing).

Grahame's novel has two main (interlaced) strands: the story of Mole, and the story of Toad. Mole's story is a kind of *Bildungsroman,* a story of personal and social development. In Needle's version, Baxter Ferret is analogous with Mole, though his development is conceived more in terms of his emerging consciousness of class structures. Whereas Mole is socially naive in the opening of *The Wind in the Willows,* Baxter is politically naive and like Mole has little idea of what is going on around him or of how to behave toward other people. Both characters leave the safety of their homes, form friendships with characters who are more experienced and worldly (Rat and Badger in *The Wind in the Willows,* and O.B. Weasel in *Wild Wood*), and come to learn a little more about the world. In Toad's story Grahame's latent concerns with class codes and structures emerge. However, Needle does not replicate Grahame's double narrative; instead Toad's story is told from Baxter's point of view, through his involvement with Toad.

Grahame's and Needle's texts also employ contrasting discoursal modes. *Wild Wood* is narrated by Baxter Ferret in first person demotic discourse—using idiomatic and dialect phrases and terms—in direct contrast to Grahame's "high" literary style in "Dulce Domum" (chapter 5) and "The Piper at the Gates of Dawn" (chapter 7). Needle largely omits Grahame's literary allusions and quotations, replacing them by more everyday cultural intertexts—for example, he gives the Wild Wooders names of small independent breweries that produce "real ale" (Hunt, p. 161). Schemata for class distinctions are instantiated in both novels through the narrative discourse and dialogue. As Hunt has pointed out, just as in *The Wind in the Willows* the speech of Wild Wooders and other working-class characters is rarely represented directly, in *Wild Wood* the speech of the River Bankers is rarely represented directly (p. 162). Both texts use strategies of exclusion whereby the voice of the other is silenced and the position of the other is thereby effaced. Thus there is a direct relationship between the narrative techniques used to represent speech and the construction of subject positions for characters.

Hunt has argued that Grahame allows the discourse "to evade the confrontations latent in a book which deals obliquely with so many societal issues" by using character discourse which "vacillate[s] between parody, normal and 'authentic' speech" (p. 160). Thus, by representing the speech of lower-class characters, such as the engine driver, through literary artifice, and silencing other characters, such as Toad's chauffeur, Grahame omits linguistic markers of class. In contrast, Needle foregrounds class distinctions and conflicts by using demotic register for the narration and by accentuating linguistic markers of class in the discourse of both Wild Wood and River Bank characters. He includes a key episode where a conversational exchange between a Wild Wood character and a River Bank character is represented directly and the narration of the episode is used to reflect on the social and political function of language which underpins its representation in Grahame's novel. This episode has been discussed succinctly by Hunt (1988), but it is worth elaborating on its ideological implications here. The exchange occurs after an episode in which Toad collides with the lorry driven by Baxter Ferret, causing him to be sacked for the first time. There are marked contrasts between the register and dialect used to represent the speech of Baxter and Toad. Baxter's language is marked as a working-class demotic by idiom and grammar, for example, "It's me what's got the boot and am in a fair way to starve" (p. 63); Toad speaks a public-school discourse, and his tone and mode of address is patronizing: "Spit it out, my boy. . . . No need to be shy" (p. 63). More tellingly, the episode includes explicit comment on the role of language in constructing class distinctions and barriers. Thus when Toad asks Baxter to give him his employer's name so that he can "settle the account with him" (p. 63), Baxter attempts to ask Toad if this is an admission of guilt: "Would you be saying . . . ? I mean, does that allow that you . . . ? How can I put it, I mean. . . ." Baxter, the narrator, goes on to reflect on his own powerlessness in the exchange: "It was no use. I was in a new world, a different world. I didn't even know how to speak the same language" (p. 63). The episode demonstrates how characters such as Baxter are denied power through being denied a position from which to speak within hierarchical social relationships, and indirectly comments on the process whereby such characters are silenced or made comic figures in Grahame's text. Baxter's powerlessness is further emphasized when Toad offers him a job to "[k]eep [him] off the streets, what, and put a bit of bread back in the breadbin" (p. 65).

The narrative discourse of *Wild Wood* is also characterized by attention to the detail of the social setting. Descriptions of the daily life of the Wild Wooders (brewing, baking, housekeeping, working, and so on), contrast with the detailed descriptions of the "good life" led by the River Bankers in *The Wind in the Willows*. Thus Needle, like Leeson in *Silver's Revenge*, uses setting to recontextualize the pre-text. He puts the adventures of Toad, Rat, Mole, and Badger within a more fully articulated social context, wherein their pleasures are pursued at the expense of the Wild Wood characters who work for them. These discursive features also instantiate schemata for social class: the attention to everyday activities pursued for pleasure (messing about in boats, and so on) typify a schema associated with the affluent middle class; and the attention to more menial everyday activities activates a working-class schema. The abundance of food in *The Wind in the Willows* contrasts with the lack of food in *Wild Wood*. Grahame's lack of differentiation of the Wild Wooders, his depiction of them as a large generalized mass, contrasts with Needle's individuation of the stoat, weasel, and ferret characters. Baxter comments overtly on this feature early in his narration: "We might all look alike to the generality, but we're as different as chalk and cheese. And it's the differences that matter in this story" (p. 8).

These discursive and narrative strategies change the significance of the story of attempted, grand-scale property theft told in *The Wind in the Willows*. Needle's narrative techniques foreground the class conflict and injustices in the social system depicted in Grahame's novel. However, the ending of Grahame's novel, in which the rebellion is quashed and Toad remains at Toad Hall, an "altered Toad," instead of returning to prison, imposes limitations on Needle's reversion. The question arises as to whether these limitations on the closure of the text also constitute limitations on its ideological significance. In Grahame's novel, the unsuccessful rebellion and reestablishment of Toad and the River Bankers in Toad Hall implies an assertion of the rightful "natural" order of things. Does Needle's text also reassert the same metanarratives implicit in Grahame's text through the limitations imposed by the tyranny of closure, or do the narrative strategies used in *Wild Wood* change the significance of the underlying metanarrative, and if so, does it merely offer an alternative, but equally ideologically driven metanarrative?

Needle's reversion interrogates the metanarrative underpinning Grahame's novel by focusing on the ambiguities, absences, and silences in that novel. The social context which Needle constructs for the rebellion, to which the Wild Wooders are prompted by extreme poverty and unemployment, ascribes the Wild Wooders with motivations which are not admitted into *The Wind in the Willows* and instantiates a metanarrative of class struggle. The unexplained moral ambiguity in the close of Grahame's novel, in which the reformed Toad is simply allowed to remain at Toad Hall and does not have to return to prison, is explained (and hence foregrounded) in Needle's novel—once he is free, he is able to bring his wealth and influence to bear on the police and local justices (p. 181). In this way, Needle's reversion dismantles notions of "natural order" implicit in the closure of Grahame's novel. Both texts condemn Toad's behavior, but they do so for different reasons. As Hunt has suggested, Toad represents the nouveau riche, and he is criticized in Grahame's novel not "for breaking the law, only for breaking ranks"—that is, he breaches social codes (p. 166). Condemnation in Needle's novel is focused more on the class structures which enable a different set of laws to operate for Toad and for the Wild Wooders. In other words, he addresses the basis, rather than the maintenance, of social order. In *The Wind in the Willows* the Wild Wooders' rebellion is simply overthrown by the force and heroism of the "four Friends" (p. 242). Needle, in contrast, offers other explanations for the failure of the rebellion, in particular collusion and treachery from within the Wild Wood class, especially the suspicion that their leader "had more or less join[ed] forces with the 'class enemy'" (p. 184). An implication of Needle's reversion is that although there are four classes in the Willows world—the River Bankers, the Weasels, the Ferrets, and the Stoats—and the social relationship between these four classes is a descending hierarchy, class barriers are not insurmountable. After the rebellion O.B. Weasel, for example, gradually gets closer to Toad and his friends, and even buys himself a summer house by the river (p. 181). The implication, voiced by the narrator, that O.B. has "sold out his friends" (p. 184) activates other intertexts for the novel (for example *Animal Farm* as well as historical events since 1908). These intertexts, combined with the metanarrative of class struggle which is instantiated via the attribution of motivation to the Wild Wooders, suggest the imposition of modern cultural paradigms upon Grahame's text.

Another way in which Needle's reversion interrogates the ideologies underpinning *The Wind in the Willows* is through the narrative structure and framing of the story. Most of the novel is narrated by Baxter Ferret, but his story is framed by a prologue and epilogue narrated by an unnamed friend of Cedric Willoughby, to whom in turn Baxter has told his story. The epilogue is crucial, as it is here that the narrator raises questions about the possibility of collusion and treachery from within the Wild Wood class and hence activates an alternative schema to that informing Grahame's metanarrative of social order. One effect of the epilogue is that it destabilizes the sense of social order which both versions of the story close with. Baxter's narration closes with a summary of the events after the rebellion: he got his job back at Toad Hall as chauffeur and mechanic; Toad "was a reformed character" (p. 181); "things got better after the Toad Hall episode. . . . Some of the Wild Wooders got even more humble and kowtowish . . . while others, like the Chief Weasel say, become almost as posh as they were" (p. 182); and so on. The sense of a reestablished order is roughly similar to that of the close of *The Wind in the Willows*. The narrator of the epilogue, however, directly raises questions about O.B. Weasel's involvement in events and hence makes explicit what is only implied by Baxter's narration.

The double narrative frame, in which Baxter's story is told to Cedric Willoughby, who writes it down and then passes the manuscript on to the narrator, has an important function in the construction of a dialogue about the possibility of ascribing social or political significance to historical, and by implication fictive, events. Willoughby is the silent, absent figure in the narrative—he dies six months after meeting Baxter, having first extracted a promise from the narrator to finish his investigation of the story and "tidy the manuscript" (p. 6). The narrator describes Willoughby as obsessive, eccentric, and suffering from depression in the prologue, implicitly undermining the validity and authenticity of the story and his interpretations of it. On the one hand, the narrator's references to Willoughby's investigations and to other historical events, for example, the Peasant's Revolt, imply an assumption that historical events have significance; they don't just happen. By implication, fictional texts, like Grahame's, also have larger social, political, and historical significances. On the other hand, however, the narrator seems to be implicitly disclaiming these interpretations partly by crediting them to an "eccentric" and obsessed Willoughby and partly by implying that a researcher or historian infers meanings from events and hence constructs historical metanarratives. In this way, the epilogue constructs a dialogue between two positions: one which seeks to find a pattern and meaning (or metanarrative) in history and one which reports and comments on these theories but also disclaims them by accrediting them to someone else. This is a perspective which also neatly sums up the contradictory impulses to create reversions of classic texts which have been the subject of this chapter.

1. *Lord of the Flies* was not, of course, written as a book for adolescent readers, but has subsequently been appropriated as such, especially as a book read in schools.

2. Pratchett's Herne—"the god of the chased and the hunted and all small animals whose ultimate destiny is to be an abrupt damp squeak"—mocks a tired convention in general, but it is tempting to think a particular target is the guardian spirit in Carpenter's *Robin of Sherwood* (see chapter 6, above), especially since forest bandits armed with bows enter the text two pages later. Bricolage fantasies still contest metanarratives, after all.

3. For an extended discussion of relations between *The Wind in the Willows* and *The Willows in Winter,* see Stevenson (1996).

# REFERENCES

PRIMARY SOURCES

Adams, Douglas. *The Hitch Hiker's Guide to the Galaxy*. London: Guild Publishing, 1986 (1979–84).

Aiken, Joan. *The Stolen Lake*. Harmondsworth: Puffin, 1981.

*Aladdin*. London and Sydney: Twin Books, 1994.

*Aladdin*. The Walt Disney Company, 1992.

*Aladdin and His Wonderful Lamp*. Faerie Tale Theater: video, written by Mark Curtis and Rod Ash, directed by Tim Burton. Platypus Productions/ Lion's Gate Films, 1984.

Alderson, Brian, and Foreman, Michael (illus.). *The Arabian Nights*. London: Victor Gollancz Ltd., 1992.

Asbjornsen, Peter Christen, and Moe, Jorgen. *Popular Tales from the Norse*. Trans. George Webbe Dasent. 3rd ed. London: Bodley Head, 1969.

Asimov, Isaac. *The Story of Ruth*. New York: Doubleday, 1972.

Atterton, Julian. *Robin Hood and Little John*. London: Julia MacRae Books, 1987.

Bach, Alice, and Exum, J. Cheryl. *Moses' Ark: Stories from the Bible*. New York: Delacorte Press, 1989.

———. *Miriam's Well: Stories about Women in the Bible*. New York: Delacorte Press, 1991.

Bailey, John, McLeish, Kenneth, and Spearman, David. *Gods and Men: Myths and Legends from the World's Religions*. Oxford: Oxford University Press, 1981.

Baldwin, James. *Old Stories of the East*. New York: American Book Company, 1895.

Ballantyne, R.M. *The Coral Island*. Ware: Wordsworth Classic, 1995 (1857).

Barchers, Suzanne I. *Wise Women: Folk and Fairy Tales from Around the World*. Englewood, CO: Libraries Unlimited, Inc., 1990.

Barrie, J.M. *Peter Pan*. Ware: Wordsworth Classic, 1993 (1911).

Barth, John. *Chimera*. New York: Random House, 1972.

Bates, Martine. *The Dragon's Tapestry*. Red Deer, Alberta: Red Deer College Press, 1992.

Beers, Gilbert V. *Under the Tagalong Tree*. Chicago: Moody Press, 1976.

———. *With Sails to the Wind*. Chicago: Moody Press, 1977.

*Beowulf*. Trans. Kevin Crossley-Holland. London: Macmillan, 1968.

*Beowulf and the Fight at Finnsburg*. Ed. Fr. Klaeber. Lexington, MA: D.C. Heath, 1950.

Bevan, Clare. *Mightier than the Sword*. Harmondsworth: Puffin, 1989.

Birch, Beverley. *Shakespeare's Stories: The Comedies*. New York: Wings Books, 1993 (1988).

Briggs, Katharine M. *A Dictionary of British Folk-Tales in the English Language*. London: Routledge, 1970.

Bryan, W.F., and Dempster, Germaine. *Sources and Analogues of Chaucer's Canterbury Tales*. New York: Humanities Press, 1941.

Bullfinch, Thomas. *The Age of Fable*. London: J.M. Dent & Sons, 1920 (1855).

Burnford, Sheila. *Mr. Noah and the Second Flood*. New York: Washington Square Books, 1973.

Burningham, John. *Oi! Get Off Our Train*. London: Jonathan Cape, 1989.

Burton, Richard. *Tales from the Arabian Nights: Selected from the Book of the Thousand Nights and a Night*. Ed. David Shumaker. New York: Avenel Books, 1978.

Bushnaq, Inea. *Arab Folktales*. Harmondsworth: Penguin, 1987 (1986).

Carpenter, Richard. *Robin of Sherwood*. Harmondsworth: Penguin, 1984.

———. *Robin of Sherwood: The Time of the Wolf*. Harmondsworth: Penguin, 1988.

Carpenter, Richard and May, Robin. *Robin of Sherwood and the Hounds of Lucifer*. Harmondsworth: Penguin, 1984.

Carrick, Carol and Donald. *Aladdin and the Wonderful Lamp*. New York: Scholastic, 1989.

Carter, Angela. *The Virago Book of Fairy Tales*. London: Virago Press, 1991.

———. *The Second Virago Book of Fairy Tales*. London: Virago Press, 1992.

Child, Francis James (ed.). *The English and Scottish Popular Ballads*. 5 vols. Boston: Houghton, Mifflin & Co., 1882–98.

Christopher, John. *The Prince in Waiting Trilogy*. Harmondsworth: Penguin, 1983 (1970, 1971, 1972).

———. *Wild Jack*. London: Hamish Hamilton, 1974.

Cole, Joanna. *Best-Loved Folktales of the World*. New York: Doubleday & Co., Ltd., 1982.

Collins, Joan, and Hook, Richard (illus.). *Robin Hood*. Loughborough: Ladybird Books, 1985.

Colum, Padraic. *The Girl Who Sat by the Ashes*. New York: Macmillan, 1968 (1919).

Cooper, Susan, and Hutton, Warwick (illus.). *Tam Lin*. New York: Margaret K. McElderry Books, 1991.

Crossley-Holland, Kevin. *British Folk Tales*. London and New York: Orchard Books, 1987.

*The Dancing Princesses*. Faerie Tale Theater: video, written by Maryedith Burrell, directed by Petar Medak. Platypus Productions/Lion's Gate Films, 1984.

Dean, Pamela. *Tam Lin*. New York: Tor Books, 1991.

Defoe, Daniel. *Robinson Crusoe*. London: Penguin Classics, 1985 (1719).

de la Mare, Walter. *Stories from the Bible*. London: Faber and Faber, 1961 (1921).

Del Rey, Lester, and Kessler, Risa (eds). *Once Upon a Time: A Treasury of Fantasies and Fairy Tales*. London: Random Century, 1991.

Dickinson, Peter. *The Weathermonger*. London: Victor Gollancz Ltd., 1984 (1968).

———. *City of Gold and Other Stories from the Old Testament*. London: Victor Gollancz, 1980.

———. *Merlin Dreams*. London: Victor Gollancz Ltd., 1988a.

———. *Eva*. London: Victor Gollancz Ltd., 1988b.

Dixon, Rex. *A Book of Highwaymen*. Edinburgh: Thomas Nelson & Sons, 1963.

Dobson, R.B., and Taylor, J. (eds.). *Rymes of Robyn Hood*. London: William Heinemann, 1976.

Dulac, Edmund (illus). *Sinbad the Sailor and Other Stories from the Arabian Nights*. London: Hodder and Stoughton, 1914 (reprinted, New York: Weathervane Books, 1986).

Ebbutt, M.I. *Hero-Myths and Legends of the British Race*. London: George G. Harrap & Co., 1910; a selection reissued as *Heroic Myths and Legends of Britain and Ireland*. Ed. John Matthews. London: Blandford, 1995.

Edwards, John Emlyn. *The Adventures of Arthur Dragon-King*. London: Methuen, 1984.

Farmer, Penelope. *The Summer Birds*. London: Chatto and Windus, 1962 (revised version, The Bodley Head, 1985).

Fine, Anne. *The Genie Trilogy*. London: Mammoth, 1991.

Finkel, George. *Watch Fires to the North*. New York: Viking, 1967 (as *Twilight Province,* 1966).

Fisher, Catherine. *Fintan's Tower*. London: Bodley Head, 1991.

French, Fiona. *Rise and Shine*. London: Methuen, 1989.

Gardner, John. *Grendel*. London: Robin Clark Ltd., 1991 (1971).

———. *In the Suicide Mountains*. New York: Alfred A. Knopf, 1977.

Garfield, Leon. *The Pleasure Garden*. London: Lion Tracks, 1991 (1976).

Garfield, Leon, and Foreman, Michael. *Shakespeare Stories*. London: Linx, 1988 (1985).

Garfield, Leon, and Makarov, Igor. *Shakespeare, the Animated Tales: Romeo and Juliet*. London: Heinemann Young Books, 1992.

Garfield, Leon, Blishen, Edward, and Keeping, Charles. *The God Beneath the Sea*. Harmondsworth: Kestrel Books, 1970.

Garfield, Leon, Blishen, Edward, and Keeping, Charles. *The Golden Shadow*. London: Gollancz Children's Paperbacks, 1992 (1973).

Garner, Alan. *The Weirdstone of Brisingamen*. London: Collins, 1960.

———, (ed.). *The Hamish Hamilton Book of Goblins*. London: Hamish Hamilton, 1969.

Gilson, Charles. *The Adventures of Robin Hood* (originally pub. in 1940 as *Robin of Sherwood*). London: Collins, n.d. [1957]. Reset and reprinted in 1960 and again in 1965.

Golding, William. *Lord of the Flies*. Harmondsworth: Penguin, 1965 (1954).

Grabianski, Janusz (illus.). *Tales from the Arabian Nights*. Ed. Hedwig Smola, Trans. Charlotte Dixon. New York: Duell, Sloan and Pearce, 1964.

Grahame, Kenneth. *The Wind in the Willows*. London: Methuen, 1968 (1908).

Green, Roger Lancelyn. *King Arthur and His Knights of the Round Table*. Harmondsworth: Puffin, 1953.

———. *The Adventures of Robin Hood*. Harmondsworth: Penguin, 1956.

———. *Tales of the Greek Heroes*. Harmondsworth: Penguin, 1958.

———. *The Tale of Ancient Israel*. London: J.M. Dent and Sons; New York: E.P. Dutton, 1969.

Greenway, Shirley. *Aladdin and the Wonderful Lamp*. London: Pan Books, 1986.

Grimm. *The Complete Fairy Tales of the Brothers Grimm*. Trans. Jack Zipes. New York: Bantam Books, 1987.

Groom, Arthur, and Pollack, Anthony (illus.). *Robin Hood*. London: Dean & Son, n.d. [early 1970s?].

Guterman, Norbert. *Russian Fairy Tales*. London: Sheldon Press, 1945.

Haddawy, Husain. *The Arabian Nights II*. New York: W.W. Norton and Co., 1995.

Harding, Lee. *Waiting for the End of the World*. Melbourne: Hyland House, 1983.

Harris, Rosemary. *The Moon in the Cloud*. London and Boston: Faber and Faber, 1968.

Harrison, Michael, and Stuart-Clark, Christopher. *Noah's Ark*. London: Oxford University Press, 1983.

Hastings, Selina, and Wijngaard, Juan (illus.). *Sir Gawain and the Loathly Lady*. London: Walker Books, 1985.

Hawthorne, Nathaniel. *A Wonder-Book for Girls and Boys*. London: Ward, Lock & Co., 1903 (1851).

Hayes, Sarah, and Benson, Patrick (illus.). *Robin Hood*. London: Walker Books, 1989.

Henderson, Hamish. *The Muckle Songs: Classic Scots Ballads*. Tangent Records and School of Scottish Studies, Edinburgh, 1975.

Hesiod. *The Works and Days. Theogony. Etc.* Trans. Richmond Lattimore. Ann Arbor: University of Michigan Press, 1968.

Horowitz, Anthony. *The Kingfisher Book of Myths and Legends.* London: Kingfisher Books, 1985.

Horwood, William. *The Willows in Winter.* New York: St. Martin's, 1994.

Hughes, Ted. *Tales of the Early World.* London: Faber and Faber, 1988.

Hutton, Warwick. *Adam and Eve, the Bible Story.* London: Macmillan Children's Books, 1987.

Ipcar, Dahlov. *A Dark Horn Blowing.* London: Fontana Lions, 1981 (1978).

Jacobs, Joseph. *More English Fairy Tales.* London: David Nutt, 1894.

Jarvie, Gordon. *Scottish Folk and Fairy Tales.* Harmondsworth: Penguin, 1992.

Jones, Diana Wynne. *Castle in the Air.* London: Methuen, 1990.

———. *Eight Days of Luke.* London: Macmillan, 1975.

———. *Fire and Hemlock.* New York: Greenwillow Books, 1985.

———. *A Sudden Wild Magic.* New York: Avon Books, 1994 (1992).

Kaplan, Irma. *Heroes of Kalevala.* London: Frederick Muller, 1973.

Keeping, Charles, and Crossley-Holland, Kevin. *Beowulf.* Oxford: Oxford University Press, 1982.

Kemp, Gene. *The Turbulent Term of Tyke Tiler.* London: Collins, 1984 (1977).

Kingsley, Charles. *The Heroes or Greek Fairy Tales.* London: Collins, 1855.

Klein, Robin. "Zarab-Hasaka," in *Against the Odds.* Ringwood: Viking Kestrel, 1989.

Kreider, Karen, and Baker, Darrell (illus.). *Disney's Aladdin.* New York: Western Publishing Company, Inc., 1992.

Kyles, David. *Classic Bible Stories for Children.* London: The Warwick Press, 1987.

Lang, Andrew. *Orange Fairy Book.* London: Longmans, Green and Co., 1950.

Lattimore, Deborah Nourse. *Arabian Nights: Three Tales.* New York: HarperCollins, 1995.

Lawrence, Louise. *The Warriors of Taan.* London: Lions, 1988 (1986).

Lee, Tanith. *Black Unicorn.* London: Orbit, 1991.

Leeson, Robert. *The Third Class Genie.* Glasgow: William Collins, 1975.

———. *Silver's Revenge.* London: Lions, Collins, 1978.

———. *Genie on the Loose.* London: Fontana Lions, 1984.

———. *Smart Girls.* London: Walker Books, 1993a.

———. *The Last Genie.* London: HarperCollins, 1993b.

———. *The Story of Robin Hood.* London: Kingfisher, 1994.

Lindvall, Ella K., and Turbaugh, Paul. *The Bible Illustrated for Little Children.* Chicago: Moody, 1991.

*The Lion King.* The Walt Disney Company, 1994.

Lister, Robin. *The Story of King Arthur.* London: Kingfisher Books, 1992 (1988).

Lively, Penelope. *The Voyage of QV66.* London: Heinemann, 1978.

Lurie, Alison. *Clever Gretchen and Other Forgotten Folktales.* London: Heinemann; New York: Crowell, 1980.

MacDonald, George. *Phantastes.* London: Everyman, 1983.

Maclean, Katherine. *Old Testament Bible Stories.* Manchester: Clivedon Press, 1990.

*Maid Marian and Her Merry Men.* BBC 1988–89.

Malory, Thomas. *The Works of Sir Thomas Malory.* Ed. Eugene Vinaver. 2nd ed. Oxford: Clarendon Press, 1967.

Manning-Sanders, Ruth. *A Bundle of Ballads.* London: Oxford University Press, 1959.

———. *Stories from the English and Scottish Ballads.* New York: E.P. Dutton & Co. 1968.

Matthews, John. *The Unknown Arthur: Forgotten Tales of the Round Table.* London: Blandford, 1995.

Matthews, John, and Stewart, Bob. *Legends of King Arthur and His Warriors.* London: Blandford Press, 1987; introductions and retold stories reprinted as *Tales of Arthur.* London: Javelin, 1988.

Mayne, William. *The Farm That Ran Out of Names*. London: Jonathan Cape, 1990.

McCaffrey, Anne. *Black Horses for the King*. London: Doubleday, 1996.

McCaughrean, Geraldine. *One Thousand and One Arabian Nights*. Oxford: Oxford University Press, 1982.

————. *Stories from Shakespeare*. London: Orion, 1994.

McGovern, Ann. *Robin Hood of Sherwood Forest*. New York: Scholastic Inc., 1968.

McGowen, Tom. *The Magician's Apprentice*. New York: Lodestar Books, 1987.

————. *The Magician's Company*. New York: Lodestar Books, 1988.

McKinley, Robin. *Beauty*. New York: Harper and Row, 1978.

————. *The Door in the Hedge*. London: Julia MacRae Books, 1981.

————. *The Outlaws of Sherwood*. London: Macdonald & Co., 1988.

————. *A Knot in the Grain*. New York: Greenwillow Books, 1994.

McLean, Katherine, and Hodges, Edgar (illus.). *Old Testament Bible Stories*. Manchester: Cliveden Press, 1990.

McLeish, Kenneth, "Prometheus," in Bailey, et al. *Gods and Men*, 1981: 74–84.

McSpadden, J. Walker, and Hildebrandt, Greg (illus.). *Robin Hood*. Morris Plains, NJ: Unicorn Publishing House, 1990. Unpaginated.

Miles, Bernard. *Favourite Tales From Shakespeare*. London: Hamlyn, 1983 (1976).

Miles, Bernard, and Ambrus, Victor G. (illus.). *Robin Hood. His Life and Legend*. London: Hodder and Stoughton, 1985 (1979).

Milton, John. *The Poems of John Milton*. Eds. John Carey and Alastair Fowler. London: Longman, 1968.

Minard, Rosemary. *Womenfolk and Fairy Tales*. Boston: Houghton Mifflin Company, 1975.

Moray, Ann. *A Fair Stream of Silver: Love Tales from Celtic Lore*. London: Longman, Green and Co., 1965.

Morpurgo, Michael. *Arthur, High King of Britain*. London: Mammoth, 1996 (1994).

Morris, Jean. *The Troy Game*. London: The Bodley Head, 1987.

Nye, Robert. *Beowulf*. London: Orion, 1994 (1968).

Needle, Jan. *Wild Wood*. London: Andre Deutsch, 1981.

Oakley, Grahame. *Henry's Quest*. London: Macmillan, 1986.

Oldfield, Pamela, and Harris, Nick (illus.). *Stories from Ancient Greece*. London: Kingfisher Books, 1988.

Oman, Carola. *Robin Hood*. London & Melbourne: J.M. Dent & Sons Ltd., 1939.

Ovid. *Metamorphoses*. The Loeb Classical Library. Ed. E.H. Warmington. Nos. 42–43. Cambridge, MA: Harvard University Press, 1921.

Paterson, Katherine. *Park's Quest*. Harmondsworth: Penguin, 1990 (1988).

Peacock, Thomas Love. *Maid Marian and Crotchet Castle*. London: Macmillan, 1927.

Percy, Thomas. *Reliques of Auncient English Poetry*. 3 vols. London: Dodsley, 1765.

Pewtress, Vera. *Bible Stories Retold for Children*. London: The National Sunday School Union, 1943.

Phelps, Ethel Johnston. *Tatterhood and Other Tales*. New York: The Feminist Press, 1978.

————. *The Maid of the North: Feminist Folktales from Around the World*. New York: Holt, Rinehart and Winston, 1981.

Philip, Neil. *The Tale of Sir Gawain*. Cambridge: Lutterworth Press, 1987.

————. *The Penguin Book of English Folktales*. Harmondsworth: Penguin, 1992.

Philip, Neil, and Mistry, Nilesh (illus.). *The Illustrated Book of Myths: Tales and Legends of the World*. London: Dorling Kindersley, 1995.

Pierce, Tamora. *Alanna: The First Adventure (The Song of the Lioness, Book 1)*. London: Red Fox, 1992 (1983).

————. *The Girl Who Rides Like a Man (The Song of the Lioness, Book 3)*. London: Red Fox, 1992 (1986).

Pilling, Ann, and Denton, Kady MacDonald (illus.). *Realms of Gold: Myths and Legends from Around the World*. London: Kingfisher Books, 1993.

Pratchett, Terry. *Wyrd Sisters*. London: Victor Gollancz, 1988.

————. *Lords and Ladies*. London: Victor Gollancz, 1992.

Price, Susan. *Ghosts at Large*. Harmondsworth: Penguin, 1986 (1984).

————. *Crack a Story*. London: Faber and Faber, 1990.

————. *Head and Tales*. London: Faber and Faber, 1993.

————. *Foiling the Dragon*. London: Scholastic, 1994.

Pyle, Howard. *The Merry Adventures of Robin Hood*. New York: Junior Deluxe Editions, n.d. (1883).

————. *The Story of King Arthur and His Knights*. New York: Dover, 1965 (1903).

Quiller-Couch, Arthur. *The Oxford Book of Ballads*. Oxford: The Clarendon Press, 1910.

Riordan, James, and Ambrus, Victor G. (illus.). *Tales from the Arabian Nights*. Sydney: Hodder and Stoughton, 1983.

Ritson, Joseph. *Robin Hood: A Collection of All the Ancient Poems, Songs, and Ballads*. London, 1795.

Rosen, Winifred. *Three Romances: Love Stories from Camelot Retold*. Tadworth: World's Work Ltd., 1984 (1980).

Rubinstein, Gillian. *Galax Arena*. Melbourne: Hyland House, 1992.

Scott, Bill. *Many Kinds of Magic*. Ringwood: Viking, 1990.

Selden, George. *The Genie of Sutton Place*. New York: Farrar, Straus and Giroux, 1973.

Shakespeare, William. *A Midsummer Night's Dream*. The Arden Shakespeare. Ed. Harold F. Brooks. London: Methuen, 1979.

Singer, Marilyn, and Howell, Troy (illus.). *The Maiden on the Moor*. New York: Morrow Junior Books, 1995.

Snelling, John, and Theakston, Margaret (illus.). *Greek Myths and Legends*. Hove: Wayland, 1987.

Southall, Ivan. *The Curse of Cain*. Sydney: Angus and Robertson, 1968.

Spearman, David. "Beowulf," in Bailey, et al. *Gods and Men*, 1981: 104–111.

Spretnak, Charlene. *Lost Goddesses of Early Greece*. Boston: Beacon Press, 1984 (1978).

Stanton, Elizabeth Cady, et al. *The Woman's Bible*. 2 vols. New York: European Publishing Co., 1895–98.

Stevenson, Robert Louis. *Treasure Island*. London: Lamboll House, 1986 (1883).

Stinnet, Norman R., and Kimberly, Marion. *Robin Hood*. Classic Comics series. New York: Gallery Books, 1990.

Storr, Catherine, and Collingwood, Chris (illus.). *Robin Hood*. London: Methuen, 1984.

Suddaby, Donald. *New Tales of Robin Hood*. London: Blackie, 1950.

Sussex, Lucy. *Deersnake*. Rydalmere, NSW: Hodder and Stoughton, 1994.

Sutcliff, Rosemary. *The Chronicles of Robin Hood*. London: Oxford University Press, 1950.

————. *The Lantern Bearers*. Harmondsworth: Penguin, 1981 (1959).

————. *Beowulf: Dragon Slayer*. London: The Bodley Head, 1961.

————. *Sword at Sunset*. London: Hodder and Stoughton, 1965a.

————. *Heroes and History*. London: B.T. Batsford, 1965b.

————. *The Light Beyond the Forest*. London: The Bodley Head, 1979.

————. *The Sword and the Circle*. London: The Bodley Head, 1981a.

————. *The Road to Camlann*. London: The Bodley Head, 1981b.

Sutton, Rosalind, and Rowe, Eric F. (illus.). *Robin Hood*. Illustrated Classics series. Newmarket: Brimax Books, 1991.

Trease, Geoffrey. *Bows Against the Barons*. London: Hodder and Stoughton. Rev. ed. 1966.

Treece, Henry. *The Eagles Have Flown*. London: The Bodley Head, 1954.

Troughton, Joanna. *Sir Gawain and the Loathly Damsel*. London: Macmillan, 1972.

Turner, Brad. *Beowulf's Downfall*. Sydney: Harcourt Brace Jovanovich, 1992.

Untermeyer, Louis. *The World's Great Stories. Fifty-Five Legends That Live Forever.* New York: M. Evans and Company, Inc., 1964.

Unwin, Pippa, and Petty, Kate. *Wake Up, Mr Noah!* London: Macmillan, 1990.

Van Allsburg, Chris. *The Wreck of the Zephyr*. London: Andersen Press, 1984 (1983).

Vinge, Joan D. "Tam Lin," in Robin McKinley (ed.). *Imaginary Lands*. New York: Greenwillow Books, 1986: 183–212.

Virgil. *The Aeneid*. Trans. Robert Fitzgerald. Harmondsworth: Penguin, 1985.

Walker, Barbara G. *Feminist Fairy Tales*. Sydney: Bantam Books, 1996.

Wells, Rosemary. *Max and Ruby's First Greek Myth: Pandora's Box*. New York: Dial Books, 1993.

Wildsmith, Brian. *Professor Noah's Spaceship*. Oxford: Oxford University Press, 1980.

Williams, Marcia. *Sinbad the Sailor*. London: Walker Books, 1994.

Yeatman, Linda. *King Arthur and the Knights of the Round Table*. London: Guild Publishing, 1991.

Yolen, Jane, and Nolan, Dennis (illus.). *Wings*. San Diego: Harcourt Brace Jovanovich, 1991.

Zelazny, Roger, and Sheckley, Robert. *Bring Me the Head of Prince Charming*. New York: Bantam Books, 1991.

Zindel, Paul. *Harry and Hortense and Hormone High*. London: The Bodley Head, 1985 (1984).

## Secondary Sources

Abbs, Peter. "Penelope Lively, Children's Fiction and the Failure of Adult Culture," *Children's Literature in Education* 18 (1975): 118–124.

Addison, Erin. "Saving Other Women from Other Men: Disney's *Aladdin*," *camera obscura* 31 (1993): 5–25.

Ahmed, Leila. *Women and Gender in Islam*. New Haven: Yale University Press, 1992.

Ashe, Geoffrey (ed.). *The Quest for Arthur's Britain*. London: Paladin, 1971 (1968).

Auerbach, Erich. "Figura," in *Scenes from the Drama of European Literature*. New York: Meridian Books, 1959.

Aylwin, Tony. "Using Myths and Legends in School," *Children's Literature in Education* 12, 2 (1981): 82–89.

Babbitt, Natalie. "Fantasy and the Classic Hero," in Barbara Harrison and Gregory Maguire (eds.). *Innocence and Experience: Essays and Conversations on Children's Literature*. New York: Lothrop, Lee & Shepard, 1987: 148–155.

Barber, Richard. *King Arthur in Legend and History*. London: Sphere Books Ltd., 1973 (1961).

Barton, Yancy. "Padraic Colum's *The Children's Homer*: The Myth Reborn," in Perry Nodelman (ed.). *Touchstones*. Vol. 2. 1987: 55–63.

Behdad, Ali. "Orientalist Desire, Desire of the Orient," *French Forum* 15, 1 (1990): 37–51.

Bennett, David. "Plugging Classical Gaps: Myths and Legends Used in the Secondary Classroom," *Books for Keeps* 78 (1993): 20–21.

Bennett, J.A.W. (ed.). *Essays on Malory*. Oxford: Clarendon Press, 1963.

Berger, Harry, Jr., and Leicester, H. Marshall, Jr. "Social Structure as Doom: The Limits of Heroism in *Beowulf*," in Robert B. Burlin and Edward B. Irving, Jr. (eds.). *Old English Studies*. 1974: 37–79.

Bessinger, J.B. "Robin Hood: Folklore and Historiography, 1377–1500," *Tennessee Studies in Literature* 11 (1966): 61–69.

———. "*The Gest of Robin Hood* Revisited," in Larry D. Benson (ed.). *The Learned and the Lewed*. Cambridge, MA: Harvard University Press, 1974: 355–69.

Bettelheim, Bruno. *The Uses of Enchantment*. Harmondsworth: Penguin, 1978 (1975).

Bloom, Harold. Afterword to Mary Shelley, *Frankenstein*. London: Pan Books, 1994 (1963).

Booth, Wayne C. "Individualism and the Mystery of the Social Self," in Barbara Johnston (ed.). *Freedom and Interpretation*. 1992: 69–102.

Bottigheimer, Ruth B. "God and the Bourgeoisie: Class, the Two-Tier Tradition, Work, and Proletarianization in Children's Bibles," *The Lion and the Unicorn* 17, 2 (1993): 124–134.

———. *The Bible for Children: From Gutenberg to the Present*. New Haven: Yale University Press, 1996.

Botting, Fred. "Power in the Darkness: Heterotopias, Literature and Gothic Labyrinths," *Genre* 26 (1993): 253–282.

Bottoms, Janet. "Of *Tales* and *Tempests*," *Children's Literature in Education* 27, 2 (1996): 73–86.

Bourdieu, Pierre. *Distinction: A Social Critique of the Judgement of Taste*. Trans. Richard Nice. London and New York: Routledge and Kegan Paul, 1986.

———. *In Other Words: Essays Towards a Reflexive Sociology*. Trans. Matthew Adamson. Cambridge: Polity Press, 1990.

Bové, Paul A. *Intellectuals in Power. A Genealogy of Critical Humanism*. New York: Columbia University Press, 1986.

Brenner, Athalya. "The Hebrew God and his Female Complements," in Carolyne Larrington (ed.). *The Feminist Companion to Mythology*. 1992.

Brockman, Bennett A. "Robin Hood and the Invention of Children's Literature," *Children's Literature* 10 (1982): 1–17.

Brockman, B.A. "Children and the Audiences of Robin Hood," *South Atlantic Review* 48 (1983): 67–83.

Browne, Nick. "Orientalism as an Ideological Form: American Film in the Silent Period," *Wide Angle* 11 (1989): 23–31.

Bullock, Alan. *The Humanist Tradition in the West*. New York: W.W. Norton & Company, 1985.

Bunson, Matthew. *Vampire: The Encyclopaedia*. London: Thames and Hudson, 1993.

Burlin, Robert B, and Irving, Edward B. Jr. (eds.). *Old English Studies in Honour of John C. Pope*. Toronto: University of Toronto Press, 1974.

Burne, Glenn S. "Andrew Lang's *The Blue Fairy Book:* Changing the Course of History," in Perry Nodelman (ed.). *Touchstones*. Vol. 2. 1987: 140–50.

Campbell, Joseph. *The Hero with a Thousand Faces*. 2nd ed. Princeton: Princeton University Press, 1968.

Campbell, Joseph (with Bill Moyers). *The Power of Myth*. New York: Doubleday, 1988.

Carpenter, Humphrey, and Prichard, Mari. *The Oxford Companion to Children's Literature*. Oxford: Oxford University Press, 1984.

Carter, Angela. "In Pantoland," in Carter, *American Ghosts and Old World Wonders*. London: Vintage, 1994 (1993): 98–109.

Cech, John. "Pyle's *Robin Hood:* Still Merry after All These Years," *Children's Literature Association Quarterly* 8, 2 (1983): 11–14, 34.

———. "Shadows in the Classroom: Teaching Children's Literature from a Jungian Perspective," in Glenn Edward Sadler (ed.). *Teaching Children's Literature*, 1992: 80–88.

Chambers, Aidan. "Letter from England: Cracking the Code," *The Horn Book Magazine* 8 April, 1984: 242–247.

Chambers, E.K. *Arthur of Britain*. London: Sidgwick and Jackson, 1927.

Chambers, R.W. *Beowulf, An Introduction to the Study of the Poem*. 3rd ed. Cambridge: Cambridge University Press, 1959.

Chandler, Alice. *A Dream of Order*. London: Routledge and Kegan Paul, 1971.

Christian-Smith, Linda K. *Becoming a Woman Through Romance*. New York: Routledge, 1990.

Coggeshall, John M. "Champion of the Poor: The Outlaw as a Formalized Expression of Peasant Alienation," *Southern Folklore Quarterly* 44 (1980): 23–58.

Collingwood, R.G, and Myres, J.N.L. *Roman Britain and the English Settlements.* 2nd ed. London: Oxford University Press, 1937.

Coss, P. R. "Aspects of Cultural Diffusion in Medieval England: the Early Romances, Local Society and Robin Hood," *Past and Present* 108 (1985): 35–79.

Cranny-Francis, Anne. *Feminist Fiction.* Cambridge: Polity Press, 1990.

Dickinson, Peter. "Fantasy: the Need for Realism," *Children's Literature in Education* 17, 1 (1986): 39–51.

———. "The Oral Voices of *City of Gold,*" in Charlotte Otten and Gary Schmidt (eds.). *The Voice of the Narrator in Children's Literature: Insights from Writers and Critics.* New York: Greenwood Press, 1989: 78–80.

Dragland, S.L. "Monster-Man in *Beowulf,*" *Neophilologus* 61 (1977): 606–618.

Eagleton, Terry. "Deconstruction and Human Rights," in Barbara Johnston (ed.). *Freedom and Interpretation.* 1992: 121–146.

Egan, Kieran. "Layers of Historical Understanding," *Theory and Research in Social Education* 17, 4 (1989): 280–294.

Exum, Cheryl J. *Fragmented Women: Feminist (Sub)versions of Biblical Narratives.* Valley Forge, PA: Trinity Press International, 1993.

Fairclough, Norman. *Language and Power.* London: Longman, 1989.

Farmer, Penelope. "On the Effects of Collating Myths for Children and Others," *Children's Literature in Education* 8 (1977): 176–185.

Featherstone, Mike. "Heroic Life and Everyday Life," in Mike Featherstone (ed.) *Cultural Theory and Cultural Change.* London: Sage Publications, 1992: 159–182.

Frey, Charles, and Griffith, John. *The Literary Heritage of Childhood: an Appraisal of Children's Classics in the Western Tradition.* New York: Greenwood Press, 1987.

Frye, Northrop. *The Anatomy of Criticism: Four Essays.* Princeton: Princeton University Press, 1957.

———. *The Educated Imagination.* Bloomington: Indiana University Press, 1964.

———. *The Great Code. The Bible and Literature.* London: Routledge and Kegan Paul, 1982 (Ark edition, 1983).

Frymer-Kensky, Tikva. *In the Wake of Goddesses: Women, Culture and the Biblical Transformation of Pagan Myth.* New York: Macmillan, 1992.

Gannon, Susan. "Robert Louis Stevenson's *Treasure Island:* The Ideal Fable," in Perry Nodelman (ed.). *Touchstones.* Vol. 1. 1985: 242–52.

Gardner, John. *On Moral Fiction.* New York: Basic Books, 1978.

Genette, Gérard. "Introduction to the Paratext," *New Literary History* 22 (1991): 261–72.

Gerhart, Mary. *Genre Choices, Gender Questions.* Norman: University of Oklahoma Press, 1992.

Gindin, James. *William Golding.* London: Macmillan Publishers, 1988.

Girouard, Mark. *The Return to Camelot: Chivalry and the English Gentleman.* New Haven: Yale University Press, 1981.

Gombrich, E.H. "'They Were All Human Beings—So Much Is Plain': Reflections on Cultural Relativism in the Humanities," *Critical Inquiry* 13 (1987): 686–99.

Gorak, Jan. *The Making of the Modern Canon.* London: Athlone, 1991.

Gough, John. "An Interview with John Christopher," *Children's Literature in Education* 15 (1984): 93–102.

Grant, Michael. *Myths of the Greeks and Romans.* London: Weidenfeld and Nicholson, 1962.

Graves, Robert. *The Greek Myths.* 2 vols. Harmondsworth: Penguin, 1960 (1955).

Green, Martin. "The Robinson Crusoe Story," in Jeffrey Richards (ed.). *Imperialism and Juvenile Literature.* 1989: 34–52.

Green, Peter. Introduction to *The Wind in the Willows*. Oxford: Oxford University Press, 1983.

Greenfield, Stanley B. "A Touch of the Monstrous in the Hero, or Beowulf Re-Marvellized," *English Studies* 63 (1982): 294–300.

Grieve, Ann, and Sullivan, Shirley. "Myths and Legends: The Hero; a Bibliography," *Review Bulletin* 2 (1987): 24–31.

Grigson, Geoffrey. *The Englishman's Flora*. Frogmore: Paladin, 1975.

Hamon, Philippe. "Text and Ideology: For a Poetics of the Norm," *Style* 17, 2 (1983): 95–119.

Hannabuss, Stuart. "Ballantyne's Message of Empire," in Jeffrey Richards (ed.). *Imperialism and Juvenile Literature*. 1989: 53–71.

Hannabuss, Stuart, Litherland, Barry, and Morland, Stephanie. "Fiction for Children, 1970–1980: Myth and Fantasy," *Children's Literature in Education* 12 (1981): 119–150.

Harms, Jeanne McLain, and Lettow, Lucille J. "The Beginning: Children's Literature and the Origin of the World," *Children's Literature in Education* 14, 2 (1983): 113–123.

Harrison, Jane Ellen. *Prolegomena to the Study of Greek Religion*. Cambridge: Cambridge University Press, 1922 (1903).

Hawkins, Harriett. *Classics and Trash: Traditions and Taboos in High Literature and Popular Modern Genres*. New York: Harvester Wheatsheaf, 1990.

Heller, Agnes. "Death of the Subject?" in George Levine (ed.). *Constructions of the Self*. New Brunswick, NJ: Rutgers University Press, 1992: 269–284.

Holt, J.C. *Robin Hood*. Rev. ed. London: Thames and Hudson, 1989.

Howes, Craig. "Hawaii through Western Eyes: Orientalism and Historical Fiction for Children," *The Lion and the Unicorn* 11, 1 (1987): 68–87.

Hume, Kathryn. *Fantasy and Mimesis: Responses to Reality in Western Literature*. New York: Methuen, 1984.

Hunt, Peter. "The Good, the Bad and the Indifferent: Quality and Value in Three Contemporary Children's Books," in Nancy Chambers (ed.). *The Signal Approach to Children's Books*. Harmondsworth: Kestrel Books, 1980: 225–246.

———. "Dialogue and Dialectic: Language and Class in *The Wind in the Willows*," *Children's Literature* 16 (1988): 159–68.

Huse, Nancy. "Padraic Colum's *The Golden Fleece*: The Lost Goddesses," in Perry Nodelman (ed.). *Touchstones*. Vol. 2. 1987: 64–76.

Huyssen, Andreas. *After the Great Divide: Modernism, Mass Culture and Postmodernism*. London: Macmillan, 1986.

Ingraham, Janet Ann. "Bible Stories for Children: Israelites, Miracles, and Us," *Catholic Library World* 62, 1–3 (1990): 300–303.

Irwin, Robert. *The Arabian Nights: A Companion*. Harmondsworth: Penguin, 1995 (1994).

James, E.O. *The Ancient Gods*. London: Weidenfeld and Nicolson, 1960.

Jefferson, Ann. "Intertextuality and the Poetics of Fiction," *Comparative Criticism* 2 (1980): 235–250.

Jezewski, Mary Ann. "Traits of the Female Hero: The Application of Raglan's Concept of Hero Trait Patterning," *New York Folklore* 10, 1–2 (1984): 55–73.

Johnston, Barbara (ed.). *Freedom and Interpretation: The Oxford Amnesty Lectures 1992*. New York: Basic Books, 1992.

Jones, Diana Wynne. "The Heroic Ideal—A Personal Odyssey," *The Lion and the Unicorn* 13, 1 (1989): 129–140.

Jones, Edgar. "Ancient Myths and Modern Children," *Use of English* 37, 1 (1985): 25–34.

Keen, Maurice. *The Outlaws of Medieval England*. New York: Dorset Press, 1989 (1961; 1977).

Ker, W. P. *Epic and Romance: Essays on Medieval Literature*. Repr. New York: Dover Publications, 1957 (1896).

Kirk, G.S. *Myth: Its Meaning and Functions in Ancient and Other Cultures.* London: Cambridge University Press, 1973 (1970).

Knight, Stephen. "Bold Robin Hood. The Structures of a Tradition," *Southern Review* 20 (1987): 152–167.

———. *Robin Hood: A Complete Study of the English Outlaw.* Oxford: Blackwell, 1994.

Kroll, Norma. "*Beowulf:* The Hero as Keeper of Human Polity," *Modern Philology* 84 (1986): 117–129.

Larrington, Carolyne (ed.). *The Feminist Companion to Mythology.* London: The Pandora Press, 1992.

Lasser, Michael. "Weaving the Web of Story: Archetype and Image as the Bearers of the Tale," *Children's Literature in Education* 10 (1979): 4–10.

Lesnik-Oberstein, Karin. *Children's Literature: Criticism and the Fictional Child.* Oxford: Clarendon Press, 1994.

Lieberman, Marcia. "'Some Day My Prince Will Come': Female Acculturation Through the Fairy Tale," *College English* 34 (1972): 383–95.

Lively, Penelope. "The Wrath of God: An Opinion of the 'Narnia' Books," *Use of English* 20 (1968): 126–29.

Lowe, Lisa. *Critical Terrains: French and British Orientalisms.* Ithaca: Cornell University Press, 1991.

Lumiansky, R. M. (ed.). *Malory's Originality.* Baltimore: Johns Hopkins University Press, 1964.

MacCulloch, J.A. *The Religion of the Ancient Celts.* Edinburgh: T. & T. Clark, 1911.

MacDonald, Ruth. "The Tale Retold: Feminist Fairy Tales," *Children's Literature Association Quarterly* 7, 4 (1982): 18–20.

MacIntyre, A. *After Virtue.* London: Duckworth, 1981.

Martin, Douglas. *Charles Keeping: An Illustrator's Life.* London: Julia MacRae, 1993.

Matthews, John. *Gawain: Knight of the Goddess.* London: The Aquarian Press, 1990.

May, Jill P. "The Hero's Woods: Pyle's *Robin Hood* and the Female Reader," *Children's Literature Association Quarterly* 11, 4 (1986–1987): 197–200.

Mayerson, Philip. *Classical Mythology in Literature, Art, and Music.* Lexington: Xerox College Publishing, 1971.

McCallum, Robyn. "Other Selves: Subjectivity and the *Doppelgänger* in Australian Adolescent Fiction," in Clare Bradford (ed.). *Writing the Australian Child.* Nedlands: University of Western Australia Press, 1996: 17–36.

McGillis, Roderick. "The Community of the Centre: Structure and Theme in *Phantastes,*" in Roderick McGillis (ed.). *For the Childlike: George Macdonald's Fantasies for Children.* Metuchen, NJ: Children's Literature Association and The Scarecrow Press, 1992: 56–65.

Merrill, Robert. "John Gardner's *Grendel* and the Interpretation of Modern Fables," *American Literature* 56 (1984): 162–180.

Michel-Michot, Paulette. "The Myth of Innocence: *Robinson Crusoe, The Coral Island* and *Lord of the Flies,*" in Jeanne Delbaere (ed.). *William Golding: The Sound of Silence.* Liege: University of Liege Press, 1991: 35–44.

Millett, Kate. *Sexual Politics.* London: Virago, 1977.

Mills, Alice. "Two Versions of *Beowulf,*" *Children's Literature in Education* 17, 2 (1986): 75–87.

Monk, Patricia. "Dragonsaver: The Female Hero in Barbara Hambly's *Dragonsbane,*" *Journal of the Fantastic in the Arts* 4, 4 (1991): 60–82.

Montgomery, Catherine J. "The Dialectical Approach of Writers of Children's Arthurian Retellings," *Arthurian Interpretations* 3, 1 (1988): 79–88.

Moody, Nickianne. "Maeve and Guinever: Woman's Fantasy Writing in the Science Fiction Market Place," in Lucie Armitt (ed.). *Where No Man Has Gone Before: Women and Science Fiction.* London: Routledge, 1991: 186–204.

Moore, Robert. "From Rags to Witches: Stereotypes, Distortions and Anti-Humanism in Fairy Tales," *Interracial Books for Children Bulletin* 6, 7 (1975): 1–3.

Moorman, Charles. *The Book of Kyng Arthur: The Unity of Malory's Morte Darthur.* Lexington: University of Kentucky Press, 1965.

Morris, Pam. *Literature and Feminism.* Oxford: Blackwell, 1993.

Nagy, Joseph Falaky. "The Paradoxes of Robin Hood," *Folklore* 91 (1980): 198–210.

Newsinger, John. "Rebellion and Power in the Juvenile Science Fiction of John Christopher," *Foundation: The Review of Science Fiction* 47 (1989–90): 46–54.

Nodelman, Perry. "Searching for *Treasure Island*," in Douglas Street (ed.). *Children's Novels and the Movies.* New York: Frederick Ungar Publishing Co., 1983, pp. 58–68.

———. "Introduction: Matthew Arnold, a Teddy Bear and a List of Touchstones" in *Touchstones.* Vol. 2. 1985: 1–12.

———. *The Pleasures of Children's Literature.* 2nd ed. New York: Longman, 1996.

——— (ed.). *Touchstones: Reflections on the Best in Children's Literature.* Vol. 1. West Lafayette, IN: Children's Literature Association Publishers, 1985.

——— (ed.). *Touchstones: Reflections on the Best in Children's Literature.* Vol. 2. Fairy Tales, Fables, Myths, Legends, and Poetry. West Lafayette, IN: Children's Literature Association Publishers, 1987.

Oring, Elliott. *Folk Groups and Folklore Genres.* Logan, UT: Utah State University Press, 1986.

Ostriker, Alicia. "The Thieves of Language: Women Poets and Revisionist Myth Making," in Elaine Showalter (ed.). *The New Feminist Criticism.* New York: Pantheon Books, 1985: 314–38 (1981).

Parker, Judith. "Reading Against the Grain (*Children of the Dust*)," in Emrys Evans (ed.). *Young Readers, New Readings.* Hull: Hull University Press, 1992: 42–54.

Parks, Ward. "Prey Tell: How Heroes Perceive Monsters in *Beowulf*," *Journal of English and Germanic Philology* 92 (1993): 1–16.

Payne, F. Anne. "Three Aspects of Wyrd in *Beowulf*," in Robert B. Burlin and Edward B. Irving, Jr. (eds.). *Old English Studies.* 1974: 15–35.

Petry, Michael John. *Herne the Hunter. A Berkshire Legend.* Reading: William Smith, 1972.

Philip, Neil. *A Fine Anger: A Critical Introduction to the Work of Alan Garner.* London: Collins, 1981.

———. "Kenneth Grahame's *The Wind in the Willows*: A Companionable Vitality," in Perry Nodelman (ed.). *Touchstones.* Vol. 1, 1985: 96–105.

Phillips, Jerry, and Wojcik-Andrews, Ian. "Telling Tales to Children: The Pedagogy of Empire in MGM's *Kim* and Disney's *Aladdin*," *The Lion and the Unicorn* 20, 1 (1996): 66–89.

Phy, Allene Stuart. "The Bible as Literature for American Children," in Allene Stuart Phy (ed.). *The Bible and Popular Culture in America.* Philadelphia: Fortress Press, 1985: 165–191.

Piehl, Kathy. "Noah as Survivor: A Study of Picture Books," *Children's Literature in Education* 13, 2 (1982): 80–86.

———. "'By Faith Noah': Obedient Servant as Religious Hero," *The Lion and the Unicorn* 13, 1 (1989): 41–52.

Potter, Joyce Elizabeth. "Eternal Relic: A Study of Setting in Rosemary Sutcliff's *Dragon Slayer*," *Children's Literature Association Quarterly* 10, 3 (1985): 108–12.

———. "'Beautiful for Situation' Bible Literature and Art in Modern Books for Children," *Children's Literature Association Quarterly* 11, 4 (1986/7): 186–92.

Propp, Vladimir. *Morphology of the Folktale.* 2nd ed. revised and edited by Louis A Wagner. Austin: University of Texas Press, 1986.

Purkiss, Diane. "Women's Rewriting of Myth," in Carolyne Larrington (ed.). *The Feminist Companion to Mythology.* 1992: 441–457.

Raglan, Lord. "The Hero: A Study in Tradition, Myth, and Drama, Part II," reprinted in *In Quest of the Hero.* Princeton: Princeton University Press, 1990: 87–175.

Rahn, Suzanne. "'It Would Be Awful Not to Know Greek': Rediscovering Geoffrey Trease," *The Lion and the Unicorn* 14, 1 (1990): 23–52.

———. "An Evolving Past: The Story of Historical Fiction and Nonfiction for Children," *The Lion and the Unicorn* 15 (1991): 1–26.

Rank, Otto. "The Myth of the Birth of the Hero," reprinted in *In Quest of the Hero.* Princeton: Princeton University Press, 1990: 1–86.

Richards, Jeffrey (ed.). *Imperialism and Juvenile Literature.* Manchester: Manchester University Press, 1983.

Rimmon-Kenan, Shlomith. *Narrative Fiction: Contemporary Poetics.* London: Methuen, 1983.

Robinson, Fred C. "Elements of the Marvellous in the Characterization of Beowulf," in Robert B. Burlin and Edward B. Irving, Jr. (eds.). *Old English Studies.* 1974: 119–37.

Rose, Ellen Cronan. "Through the Looking Glass: When Women Tell Fairy Tales," in Elizabeth Abel, Marianne Hirsch, and Elizabeth Langland (eds.). *The Voyage In: Fictions of Female Development.* Hanover: University Press of New England, 1983: 209–27.

Rowe, Karen E. "Feminism and Fairy Tales," in Martin Hallett and Barbara Karasek (eds.). *Folk and Fairy Tales.* Peterborough, Ontario: Broadview Press, 1991: 346–367.

Rumbold, Margaret. *Playing with Fantasy: How Diana Wynne Jones Pushes Back the Boundaries of the Genre.* Unpublished MA Thesis, Macquarie University, Sydney, 1995.

Rushing, Janice Hocker. "*E.T.* as Rhetorical Transcendence," *Quarterly Journal of Speech* 71 (1985): 188–203.

Sadler, Glenn Edward (ed.). *Teaching Children's Literature: Issues, Pedagogy, Resources.* New York: The Modern Language Association of America, 1992.

Said, Edward. *Orientalism.* London: Routledge and Kegan Paul, 1978.

———. "Orientalism Reconsidered," in Francis Barker et al. (eds.). *Literature, Politics and Theory.* London: Methuen, 1986: 210–29.

Scheffel, David. "European Ethnology and the Question of Social Banditry," *Ethnologia Europaea* 12 (1981): 88–97.

Sidwell, Robert T. "Rhea Was a Broad: Pre-Hellenic Greek Myths for Post-Hellenic Children," *Children's Literature in Education* 12 (1981): 171–176.

Smith, Paul. *Discerning the Subject.* Minneapolis: University of Minnesota Press, 1988.

Smol, Anna. "Heroic Ideology and the Childrens' *Beowulf,*" *Children's Literature* 22 (1994): 90–100.

Sprinker, Michael. "The Current Conjuncture in Theory," *College English* 51, 8 (1989): 825–31.

Stallybrass, Peter. "'Drunk with the Cup of Liberty': Robin Hood, the Carnivalesque, and the Rhetoric of Violence in Early Modern England," in Nancy Armstrong and Leonard Tennenhouse (eds.). *The Violence of Representation.* London: Routledge, 1989.

Stephens, John. *Language and Ideology in Children's Fiction.* London and New York: Longman, 1992a.

———. "Postdisaster Fiction: The Problematics of a Genre," *Papers: Explorations into Children's Literature* 3, 3 (1992b): 126–130.

———. "Stories Across Cultures Through Time, Place and Space," in *Ways of Seeing: Story from Different Angles.* The Children's Book Council of Australia Second National Conference, May 5–8 1994; Port Melbourne: Thorpe, 1994: 17–25.

Stephens, John, and Ryan, Marcella. "Metafictional Strategies and the Theme of Sexual Power in the Wife of Bath's and Franklin's Tales," *Nottingham Medieval Studies* 33 (1989): 56–75.

Stevenson, Deborah. "The River Bank Redux? Kenneth Grahame's *The Wind in the*

*Willows* and William Horwood's *The Willows in Winter*." *Children's Literature Association Quarterly* 21, 3 (1996): 126–32.

Stone, Kaye F. "The Misuses of Enchantment: Controversies on the Significance of Fairy Tales," in Rosan A. Jordan and Susan J. Kalcik (eds.). *Women's Folklore, Women's Culture*. Philadelphia: University of Pennsylvania Press, 1985: 125–145.

———. "Feminist Approaches to the Interpretation of Fairy Tales," in Ruth B. Bottigheimer (ed.). *Fairy Tales and Society: Illusion, Allusion, and Paradigm*. Philadelphia: University of Pennsylvania Press, 1986: 229–236.

Stott, Jon C. "Native American Narratives in the Children's Literature Curriculum," in Glenn Edward Sadler (ed.). *Teaching Children's Literature*. 1992: 41–40.

Sutherland, Robert D. "Hidden Persuaders: Political Ideologies in Literature for Children," *Children's Literature in Education* 16, 3 (1985): 143–157.

Tatar, Maria. *Off with their Heads: Fairy Tales and the Culture of Childhood*. Princeton: Princeton University Press, 1992.

Taylor, Beverly, and Brewer, Elisabeth. *The Return of King Arthur: British and American Arthurian Literature since 1900*. Cambridge: D.S. Brewer, and Totowa, NJ: Barnes & Noble, 1983.

Thompson, Raymond. *The Return from Avalon: A Study of Arthurian Legend in Modern Fiction*. Westport, CT: Greenwood Press, 1985.

Tiger, Lionel. *Men in Groups*. London: Panther, 1971.

Tiger, Virginia. *William Golding: The Dark Fields of Discovery*. London: Calder and Boyars, 1974.

Turner, David. *Robin of the Movies*. Kingswinford: Yeoman Publishing, 1989.

Turville-Petre, E.O.G. *Myth and Religion of the North*. London: Weidenfeld and Nicolson, 1964.

Varnado, S.L. *Haunted Presence: The Numinous in Gothic Fiction*. Tuscaloosa: The University of Alabama Press, 1987.

Vickery, Gill. "The Arthurian Antecedents of Gene Kemp's *The Turbulent Term of Tyke Tyler*," *Children's Literature in Education* 24, 3 (1993): 185–193.

Vinaver, Eugene (ed.). *The Works of Sir Thomas Malory*. Oxford: Clarendon Press, 1947.

Virgil. *The Aeneid*. Trans. Robert Fitzgerald. Harmondsworth: Penguin, 1985.

Vogler, Christopher. *Writer's Journey: Mythic Structure for Storytellers and Screen Writers*. New York: Michael Wiese Productions, 1992.

Vytkovskaya, Julia. "Slav Mythology," in Carolyne Larrington (ed.). *The Feminist Companion to Mythology*. 1992: 102–17.

Walker, Barbara G. *The Woman's Encyclopedia of Myths and Secrets*. Cambridge: Harper & Row, 1983.

Warner, Marina. *Alone of All Her Sex: The Myth and Cult of the Virgin Mary*. London: Weidenfeld and Nicolson, 1976.

Warren, Roger. *A Midsummer Night's Dream: Text and Performance*. London: Macmillan, 1983.

Waugh, Patricia. *Metafiction: The Theory and Practice of Self-Conscious Fiction*. New York: Methuen, 1984.

Whalley, Joyce Irene, and Chester, Tessa Rose. *A History of Children's Book Illustration*. London: John Murray, 1988.

Whitaker, Muriel. "Swords at Sunset and Bag-Puddings: Arthur in Modern Fiction," *Children's Literature in Education* 8, 4 (1977): 143–153.

Williams, Raymond. *Culture*. London: Fontana, 1981.

Woodward, Katherine, "On Aggression: William Golding's *Lord of the Flies*," in Eric S. Rabkin and Martin H Greenberg (eds.). *No Place Else: Explorations in Utopian and Dystopian Fiction*. Carbondale: Southern Illinois University Press, 1983: 199–224.

Young, Carol C. "Goodbye to Camelot," *English Journal* 75, February (1985): 54–58.

Zanderer, Leo. "Popular Culture, Childhood and the New American Forest of Postmodernism," *The Lion and the Unicorn* 11, 2 (1987): 7–33.

Zipes, Jack. *Fairy Tales and the Art of Subversion: The Classical Genre for Children and the Process of Civilization.* New York: Wildman; London: Heinemann, 1983.

———. "A Second Gaze at Little Red Riding Hood's Trials and Tribulations," in Jack Zipes (ed.). *Don't Bet on the Prince.* 1986: 227–260.

———. *Fairy Tale as Myth/Myth as Fairy Tale.* Lexington: The University Press of Kentucky, 1994.

———. (ed.). *Don't Bet on the Prince: Contemporary Feminist Fairy Tales in North America and England.* Aldershot: Gower, 1986.

# INDEX